RUGBY LEAGUE

In Its Own Words

RUGBY LEAGUE

In Its Own Words

**TIM WILKINSON
RAY GENT**

First published in Great Britain in 2004 by
IMPRESS SPORT LIMITED
Fountain Chambers
Fountain Street
Halifax
HX1 1LW

ISBN 0-9547884-1-9

Designed and produced by Impress Sport
Printed in Great Britain

Including material contributed by

David Beales
Dave Dooley
John Drake
Trevor Foster
Sam Grundy
John Huxley
Colin Hutton
Geoff Lee
Dave Pagett
Cliff Spracklen
Chris Westwood
Dr Jack Whittaker

Illustrations

The majority of the pictures have been kindly supplied by Robert Gate and Andrew Varley. Other sources include Cindy Russell, Denis Whittle, Dave Williams and Simon Foster.

Acknowledgements & Bibliography

Research backed up and filled in with thanks to
ABC of Rugby League - Malcolm Andrews
An Illustrated History of Rugby League - Robert Gate
A Short History of Carlisle RLFC - Tom Clarke
A People's Game - Geoffrey Moorhouse
International Grounds of Rugby League - Trevor Delaney
Central Park Memories - Philip Thomas (*Wigan Observer*)
The Central Park Years - Dave Swanton
The Road to Oppy Wood - AD Gerrard
Rugby's Great Split - Tony Collins
Rugby League Fact Book - Robert Gate
Rugby League Grounds Guide - Peter Lush & Dave Farrar
Salford Rugby League Club - Graham Morris
The Thrum Hall Story - Andrew Hardcastle
hunterlink.net.au *('The Vault')*
rfl.uk.com
rl1908.com
rlfans.com
totalrl.com
and others mentioned as we go along...

CONTENTS

Foreword			11
Introduction. Before 1895. Pre-History			13
1	1895 - 1900	Happy Birthday	35
2	1901 - 1910	The New Century	53
3	1911 - 1920	The Great War	79
4	1921 - 1930	The Roaring Twenties	109
5	1931 - 1938	Haves and Have Nots	139
6	1939 - 1950	World War Two	165
7	1951 - 1960	The Thrifty Fifties	197
8	1961 - 1970	The Swinging Sixties	239
9	1971 - 1980	Northern Soul or Lost Soul?	265
10	1981 - 1990	Greed is Good	311
11	1991 - 2000	The New Age	349
12	2001 - date	The Noughties	383
13	Postscript	A Look Through The Window	413
Appendix			417
Subscribers List			423

RUGBY LEAGUE. IN ITS OWN WORDS

FOREWORD

The books written on the subject of Rugby League over the years are many and various, and I trust that there is a space on the shelf for one more.

In telling my story here, with a little help from a few of my friends, it's bound to be the case that, in summing up nearly 110 years of history and events in about 140,000 words, it will seem that some subject areas get a bit skated over.

For example, whilst this story outlines such matters as the 1895 split, the persecution of the game in France and the class war against which the Greatest Game was played for so many decades, these issues have all been done in great and fascinating detail elsewhere.

If you feel a certain aspect of the game's history and development merits further reading, the chances are that someone has already written a book about it - and knowing the passion and wholeheartedness with which Rugby Leaguers write, it'll no doubt be a damn good read.

These books are well worth searching out, indeed some have

become synonymous with the subject they cover, but this book, my game's own life story, isn't necessarily the place to chew these issues over again in as much exacting detail.

Although I'm increasingly a world game and have pretty much always been played at both ends of the world, my story is told here from largely a 'hearth and home' British perspective.

Hopefully, most of my story is here, but as well as facts and figures the intention is that there is a good dose of social and historical context and a fair measure of human interest and warmth as well, so read on and enjoy the ride.

"Anyone who does not watch Rugby League is not a real person."
- John Singleton, Australian celebrity businessman.

INTRODUCTION

BEFORE 1895 -
PRE HISTORY

"A reporter is an observer, a bystander, a witness!" That is the popular theory, but in reality it's not so, writes Kate Adie, the journalist and broadcaster.

Most of Ms Adie's career has been spent at the sharp end of the news as a television war correspondent. Part and parcel of her daily job has been subject to personal risk from bullets, bombs and attack. These often unpleasant, dangerous surroundings and often adverse weather conditions, all in stark contrast to those back home, have provided her with a wealth of tales to tell.

In Kate's autobiography, *The Kindness of Strangers*, she portrays a much deeper picture looking behind the headlines, into background and circumstances and the not immediately apparent. Kate describes her job of reporting and documenting history as it unfolds as like being "a privileged gnat alighting on the face of history, part of events great and small...secrets are discovered, one being able to smell the atmosphere, feel the vibrations of emotions...and unfortunately every so often, someone tries to swat you."

Similar feelings, no doubt, to those writers of the countless other great autobiographies penned throughout the course of history, some by the famous, others by ordinary folk who wish to tell their own tale of personal achievement. Another person's life story can make fascinating reading for people who have a moment of their busy lives to spare, stepping into someone else's shoes to live their life, especially if the author is someone of whom they already know a little.

So why am I, the spirit of Rugby League, talking about autobiographies? Well, when I considered telling my story again, in early 2003, my sport had something of an optimistic feel about it. Prospects were good and, with an expanded league structure in place, a whole raft of new teams due to kick off a season of Rugby League in places never before dreamed of and with a refreshing new leadership at the helm, the sport seemed at something of a watershed. All this enthusiasm got me pondering over my time on this earth and having had a fortunate and interesting life, I felt that now might be a suitable moment to sit down and write my own autobiography, telling my life story in my own words.

Having gathered together a few scribbled notes and newspaper cuttings I called on a few of my younger friends to help, and between us I think we've captured a good deal of the story of my life and the circumstances surrounding it. From my momentous birth to that of a grand old man, the love affair with my fans during the years in between would rival *Romeo and Juliet.*

A good selection of outstanding books have already been penned about me, but I hope that this one will give my story a personal touch so that you can, in Ms Adie's words, "feel the atmosphere, take in historic events, enjoy a laugh" but, more than anything, feel that you are in my company for a moment in time.

Back home

It's a red letter day for me today. My busy diary includes a visit to my birthplace and top of the agenda is a meet up with Tim and Ray, co-authors of my autobiography, and Graham the publisher. Where better than the George Hotel in Huddersfield? The text you will be reading by now is nearly ready and the centre of discussion will be the next developments in readiness for the printers.

Like Rugby League fans throughout my lifetime I could travel to Huddersfield by road or train, so I'll have to decide.

Road transport seems to be the more popular these days, but in 1895 it was the preserve of the few, and basic motor cars and busses were not as reliable, rapid or as comfortable as trains, but without the smoke and sparks when you went through a tunnel!

For years, my supporters had no choice other than back-roads or trans-Pennine routes such as the A62, Snake Pass or over Saddleworth or Rishworth Moors. These days, the first choice is to follow the blue motorway signs.

Dubbed 'The M62 corridor' by Fleet Street, my most-travelled main road has picked up a title that some of my fans hate and others proudly wear like a badge of honour. The motorway, snaking and weaving its way across the backbone of England between Liverpool and Hull, claims to be the highest motorway in the land, although the summit point of Britain's motorway system is also in Rugby League country, on the M6 at Shap in Cumbria.

The first sod of the M62 was cut in 1966, opened by the Queen in 1970 with the last section completed in 1976. Today's incessant thundering traffic gives justification to the surrounding moor's indignance at this tarmac intrusion, disturbing centuries of natural tranquillity in *Last of the Summer Wine* and *Where the Heart Is* country (in which I'm proud to say I have a principle part!) Isolated farmhouses compliment the stark scenery, sending out a further message to modern-day developers. Progress has to be made, but be environmentally friendly.

Some say the M62 came into being after Oldham Council campaigned vigorously about traffic congestion through their town in pre-motorway days, as Oldham used to be the gateway to Halifax and the West Riding. Another theory suggests that it was constructed principally to transport Rugby League fans to and from away games, only later being made available to the general public. If you believe that, then you might believe that the carriageway near Huddersfield had to be split into two after a local farmer refused to move! More likely is that it makes best use of the natural contours and also stops snow accumulation. On a serious note, its original intentions were to link the expanding towns and suburbs of Lancashire and Yorkshire and provide a more convenient and faster route through some hazardous terrain, especially in winter. It has undoubtedly made travel easier, if a little more stressful.

I don't know how many times I've seen that big concrete spike on the moors above Huddersfield as I've travelled over the tops, and I've often wondered what it is. If you don't already know, Emley Moor is the tallest freestanding structure in Britain and it pumps out television pictures, radio and telephone signals to most of West Yorkshire and beyond. It's not the original though, that was a steel lattice mast about 1,200 feet tall, that fell down in 1969 chopping the local Methodist chapel in half (although, thankfully not the Minister), so the story goes.

Another pair of landmarks is the two huge reservoirs. On the Pennine side of the road with the carriageway running along its headwall, Scammonden Dam holds 1,730 million gallons and running alongside and below the motorway is Booth Wood Reservoir, built in 1966 to supply Wakefield. I recall that in the drought of 1995 you could almost see the bottom. With the Turnpike Inn and old road down below the old A672 makes a tranquil contrast beside its busy neighbour. A trip over Britain's highest motorway always has a talking point, especially with the scenery and colours changing with the seasons.

Although the road route always has something interesting to look at, given the choice it seemed somehow appropriate to make the journey by train, replicating the arrival of my founding fathers in 1895. No Puffing Billy to transport me though, the last steam train in England, the *Oliver Cromwell*, left service in 1968, so it's a dirty old diesel now. A train journey used to have a certain magnificence and excitement but rather than a treat, a modern rail journey is more of an ordeal.

Sitting comfortably in the carriage the first thing I notice is the cosmopolitan feel, very different from the more soberly and conservative 19th century. Everyone around me is wearing casual clothes rather than having dressed smartly to travel in public and the chatter I overhear takes in several different languages.

Compared to when I travelled around here first, the landscape has changed out of recognition. For a start there's that odd-looking building you can see from the train, the modern replacement for Fartown, the McAlpine Stadium.

At last I reach my destination, the imposing railway station of Huddersfield, with its fine Italian façade designed by William Walker, and its adjoining Head of Steam public house, so popular on match days.

Being a few minutes early there is time for a moment to look around, soak up some atmosphere and do a little reminiscing. Stepping out into the light and down onto St George's Square and the splendid stone buildings surrounding it, the first things to strike me were the bronze statue of Harold Wilson, the last Yorkshire-born Prime Minister, and the hustle and bustle of the town centre.

Proudly standing above its peers as one of the largest towns in the country, I couldn't help but get a little dewy-eyed over the contrast between the town now and how it appeared in 1895.

In Victorian times, Huddersfield could claim to be one of the best producers of worsted cloth in the world. The Jubilee Tower, built on the site of a Neolithic fort to celebrate Queen Victoria's Diamond Jubilee, overlooks the town. The early development of Huddersfield was credited to one family, the Ramsdens, who were responsible for gaining Royal Assent to hold a market and then building the Cloth Hall, Ramsden's Canal and railway. A few years prior to my birth, construction work commenced on the Town Hall, followed by confirmation of County Borough status in 1888. In 1920 Huddersfield Corporation purchased the Ramsden Estate including almost the entire town centre and, as a result, Huddersfield became affectionately known as 'the town that bought itself.'

Many new and modern structures have sprouted up altering the townscape considerably, yet nestling comfortably amongst the tarmac, plastic fascia boards and pedestrian walkways are some of the elegant, Victorian and Georgian architecture of my childhood. Standing the test of time and the worst excesses of the demolition ball, these period-crafted designs whisper a quiet message of comfort, serenity and calmness. The solid stone buildings have a feeling of permanence and, looking up, it's reassuring to see the stone lion and statue of Britannia guarding over the town from her perch above the Yorkshire Building Society. I'm sure this place will be here forever.

A few things have changed though. When did electric streetlights appear in Huddersfield? The only illumination to guide us through the smogs and pea soupers used to be by gas lamp.

Where have all these cars come from? I suppose it's progress that the trams and workmen's horse and carts I grew up with are a thing of the past. It's not now a matter of dodging dung on the cobbled streets and flagged pavements as you walk along, they're now relatively clean, but covered in disgusting gobs of chewing gum. The motor vehicles of today have brought a plague of pollution, noise, congestion and parking meters with them, and they seem to make everyone so angry.

Looking around, I can't even see in the shops for parked cars and traffic. Colourful shop signs, some I recognise (Marks & Spencer, Halifax and many privately-owned businesses) but some I've never heard of and can't even conceive of what they do. What sort of oriental torture is a Tie Rack? Who is the Burger King and do they really sell corpses in the Body Shop? Where are the ironmonger, milliner and haberdasher?

I don't miss the smoke-blackened buildings or the belching mill chimneys but are there any big factories left in Huddersfield? The mills all seem to have been cleaned up for art galleries, posh flats and university buildings.

I remember pubs and CIU working men's clubs on every street corner serving a wide variety of mild, stout, pale ale and bitter beers. What you got depended on where you lived, Higsons beer in Liverpool, Taylor Walker and Greenall Whitley in Warrington, Samuel Websters ales in Halifax, Wilsons in Manchester, Hartleys around Ulverston and James J. Hunt in York. All I can find now is this curious foreign fizzy lager stuff. That would have been no use in slaking the thirst of miners, mill workers, dockers and shipbuilders in my earlier days. Those fine northern breweries have all gone now, sucked into ever-bigger corporate black holes for the value of their property.

Talking of black holes, the last deep mine in Yorkshire closed recently, the Prince of Wales pit near Pontefract, and where are all the slagheaps that blighted the countryside? They've all gone green and got sheep on them now. That's an improvement, I suppose.

There's not much cotton woven in Lancashire nor wool or shoddy in West Yorkshire these days, do we all really prefer polyester from the Far East? Even the mill at Wigan Pier is some sort of visitor centre these days. It seems the Humber trawler fleet has gone the same way - what does everyone do for a living these days?

Now ready for the meeting it's time to step inside the George. At least one reliable thing about today's world is the Victorian grandeur of the George Hotel and, as in my past, it still takes the breath away with its sheer unabashed panache.

Built in 1851, it's now Grade ll Listed to stop anyone mucking around with it. Set on the wall near the main entrance is a plaque of significant interest. It commemorates the 1895 International, a meeting of like-minds set up to help raise the profile of international Rugby League, especially in countries new to the game. Entering the building, I must admit time has eclipsed the memory in trying to remember the décor and layout since I was but a small lad. Yet even after over 100 years, I still get goose-pimples given the venues significance in terms of my life. It is awe-inspiring stuff.

Crossing the hallowed threshold into the respectful hush of the hotel lobby, the reception desk is on the left and the grand St George's ballroom ahead. Also to the left is the Charter suite where the meeting to bring me into this world is said to have been held. Look right and you'll see the Founders Bar. It's a modestly-sized room, but so full of character. Here amongst the chink of tea cups and the gushing sound of the first lunchtime pint being pumped, today's meeting took place to progress the writing of my life story. You'll be pleased to know that the discussion went as well as the 1895 one that gave rise to my birth and you're now holding the result in your hand.

Now that I'm here, and seeing as there is no better place to recount my life, pull up a chair and I'll tell you my story. It's a tale of intrigue, passion, struggle and humour that from time to time has resembled one of the war-torn landscapes in Ms Adie's story.

I hope that by the end you don't want to swat me!

A job for the boys

How best would you describe me? Well, in the past, when folk had 'real' jobs and made things that you could actually see and touch, their appearance would give you many clues about them. During my youth, the usual sort of occupations were ones like factory labourer, navvy, collier, bargeman, bottle hand and carpenter. You could add to the list train driver, signalman, railway clerk, electric man and turner.

Today we seem to be swamped with 'professionals' like technical consultant, careers officer, financial advisor, computer programmer or that robot woman who always answers the phone. As for me, my well worn passport states 'sports entertainer' and those of you who know me will confirm that I am pretty darned good at it.

My performances have evoked many emotions throughout my lifetime with plenty to smile and laugh about but, there again, a tear or two has been shed in anguish and disappointment. I'm sure the good times have outweighed the bad though.

I used to only entertain during the ferocious winters of yesteryear on such romantic stages as Odsal, Watersheddings and Thrum Hall. Nowadays I sing my song and do my dance in the milder months of spring, summer and autumn, which I must say is more comfortable for all concerned, although with the amateur game still sticking to winter one can certainly say that I am now an 'all-rounder!'

A touch of the Irish and much more

My birth certificate states that I was born on 29th August 1895 in the splendour of the George Hotel, right in the middle of that northern English industrial town of Huddersfield. The family christened me the Northern Rugby Football Union, which I must admit I changed by deed poll a few years later.

Being born in Huddersfield you might think that I must be a Tyke but actually there is more to it than that. I've got Lancastrian ancestry and Cheshire and Cumbrian blood as well. In later years, you could add in genes from other parts of the country and then a touch of Welsh, Irish, Scottish and stock from France, Australiasia and the Pacific and many others.

On that momentous day, as the local textile mills tried their best to eliminate the skyline with thick, belching smoke from their tall, blackened chimneys there was more to my birth than might meet the eye of anyone casually passing by the George. My roots go back further in time, so it's worth ten minutes to settle down and take a peek into events that led up to my birth.

My family tree goes way back to the days of folk football well before the industrial revolution started when folk then lived and worked in the countryside. I suppose with no television, cinema or Tigers or Wildcats to watch life had to have its entertainment. So, apart from things like hopscotch, marbles and skittles, there was folk football for those who wanted a rough, tough pastime.

Rough, Tough and Tumble!

"It's a funny old game," as Jimmy Greaves used to say. Everywhere seemed to have its own rules regarding folk football, or in some cases there were no rules at all. Sometimes all the men in the village joined in, at other places each side had a maximum of 100 players. I'm not sure how many referees there were, probably none. Mind you, the whistle may not have even been invented then.

Depending on where you lived, you could carry or kick the ball, give it a throw and maybe even hide it until the coast was clear. Of course, the ball was just a pig's bladder and there could be more than one ball on the pitch, which might stretch from one village to the next or right across the town. At Ashbourne in Derbyshire one game involved over 1,000 men. Pitch sizes varied depending on locality and in this case the goals were three miles apart. The pitch at Whitehaven, up in blustery, cold Cumberland, had one goal post at the docks with the other at a wall at the far side of the town.

Shrove Tuesday always seemed like a good day for a game as did Christmas Day, New Years Day and over Easter. Not surprisingly, players and spectators alike usually consumed plenty of ale and drunkenness could lead to violence and all too often the bloodshed would result in serious injury and even the death of the odd player or two. No doubt the enterprising local undertaker would be on hand.

Now, there are those amongst us who get carried away with memories of the good old days, but I have to say some of those folk football matches seemed pretty boring. Much of the time they were just like one big scrum, with pushing, shoving and kicking and the odd sly punch thrown now and again, but then everyone seemed to enjoy themselves, except of course for those who died.

With the advent of steam power, commercial coal mining and improving technology came the Industrial Revolution and the impetus for the nation to advance with confidence, but also with it came social change and upheaval never seen before.

New machinery, such as the steam traction engine, was very versatile and could do the job of several men. While new technology improved efficiency in farming it had an adverse effect on rural workers and over the space of a few years the heavy shire horses that pulled the ploughs became obsolete. Since many houses were tied to jobs, mechanisation caused people to lose both livelihood and home, forcing them to seek employment in the rapidly growing towns in the mines, mills and factories. For quite a while after that folk football declined.

Villages lost their markets as produce was increasingly taken to the towns to feed the burgeoning urban population. Although most rural folk lived in primitive, one-roomed cottages, conditions and sanitation were much better than in the towns and life-expectancy increased, even though country people were less well off.

At the beginning of Victoria's reign in 1837 only about one-fifth of the population lived in towns, but in her last year in 1901 the figure had risen to threequarters. During this period the population of Britain had doubled from around 20 to 40 million people. Rows of terraced slums sprung up around the factories to accommodate the vast influx of country folk. Alas, poverty became a social disease and the crime-rate spiralled. Few houses had running water or drains and townsfolk had to cope as best they could with a new problem, that of homelessness.

Drunkenness became another blight on society, even among children. Alcohol was cheap, with beer at less than a penny a pint, and easier to acquire than clean drinking water.

Working in service for the wealthy allowed an escape from the bleak hardships. During 1851 over one million people out of a population of just 20 million had taken on a servants role.

The measure of wealth turned upside down with a change in emphasis from land ownership to material possession and monetary accumulation as businessmen made vast fortunes from manufacturing.

The new factory owners didn't take too kindly to folk football as missing bodies could disrupt production, particularly when some of the workers couldn't clock on because of their injuries or death.

Whilst various labour-saving devices and machinery came into being during Queen Vic's reign - for example Wheeler and Wilson invented the sewing machine and another innovation was the first typewriter - workers were forced to work long hours under appalling conditions for low wages. Many emigrated to the 'new worlds' of Australia, Canada and America, seeking new opportunity.

As the 19th century wore on and Victoria's reign continued, the British Empire grew and the economy thrived. Living standards and social conditions began to get a little better, providing the bulk of the population with not only the time but also the means to enjoy life a little more. The 1847 Factory Act limited women and young people in textile mills to ten hours work a day, or ten and a half if Saturday afternoon was taken off, becoming known as the 'Ten Hours Act.'

In 1850, that year's Factory Act legalised a ten and a half-hour working day for all in the textile and most other industries, but in exchange they were granted a two o'clock end to work on a Saturday. Leisure time was on its way.

The public schools had also started playing their own varieties of football and soon the likes of Eton, Harrow, Rugby and Winchester were putting in their two penn'orth. Things didn't move quite as quickly as in today's mad world and so it was not until the 1860s that the two games of association football and rugby football became distinct. The latter was by far, the more popular helped, in no small way, by the publication of the highly popular book, *Tom Brown's Schooldays.*

To bring order and a common set of rules to the respective codes, in 1863 the Football Association came into being and eight years later the representatives of 21 clubs formed a national governing body for rugby football.

Rather significantly, they were all based in the south of England with the majority in London. You won't be surprised to learn that most of the rugby clubs of the day had been formed and were run by men from the upper classes.

Interestingly enough, both games were still called football and handling the ball was also permitted, until a little later into the century when it was banned in soccer, except of course by the goalkeeper and Diego Maradona from Argentina.

A further reduction to working hours came in 1874 when another Factory Act passed through Parliament, introducing various other reforms. Employment of children under the age of nine in mills was at last prohibited and work on a weekday restricted to 10 hours and six and a half on a weekend, allowing everyone to finish work at one o' clock on a Saturday afternoon.

The loosening of the shackles and constraints of Saturday working for ordinary people allowed a taste of freedom, giving factory workers a chance to play sport, usually either association football (the dribbling game) or rugby football (the scrummaging game, there wasn't that much handling in it then.)

With a booming economy and a degree of enlightened philanthropy from a few industrialists, a number of cultural changes evolved throughout England. An improvement in working class living conditions, rising literacy standards spreading with the advent of the 1870 Education Act and with it the appearance of new magazines and newspapers (The *Daily Mail,* Britain's first national newspaper, was launched in 1896) to replace the regional and dialect press. Dr. Barnardo's children's charity started the same year.

Institutions such as the Co-Operative movement, Boots the Chemist and Lipton's grocery stores all started during the move towards the centralisation of English society, with their aim to be nationally-represented instead of operating only regionally.

After 1891 schooling became free for all, although women still had few rights and it was the husband who dominated domestic affairs. Women were forced to take their children to prison with them on being sentenced.

Tough times for tough people.

'A game just for gentlemen'

Now, the upper and middle classes liked to keep a bit of distance between themselves and the less fortunate towards the bottom of the social ladder and, rather unsportingly, wanted to keep rugby amateur, effectively reserving its participation to a sport for 'gentlemen' only. The Corinthian ideal decreed that sport should be enjoyed for its own sake, unsullied by the excesses and overly competitive attitude that comes with the pursuit of victory and playing for money.

Nevertheless, my ancestors spread the game from the late 1870s onwards, and increasing numbers of men employed in the mills, mines and the factories participated around working class areas such as Lancashire, West Yorkshire, Humberside and South Wales.

The gentry and self-employed had the luxury of having Saturday afternoon free to take time out to play sport, whilst the working classes only clocked off work at one o'clock. No doubt the miners arrived later still having to head back from the coal seam to a welcome wash and brush up.

In some places these new players joined existing clubs, many of which had been set up by public school educated people.

Elsewhere, they got together to set up their own teams. Local chuches also formed clubs, two examples being Leeds Parish Church (a team with a fearsome reputation for 'dirty' play) and Wakefield Trinity, formed in 1873 as part of the Holy Trinity Church Young Men's Society.

In an early form of sponsorship, many churches helped promote rugby which they viewed as a healthy, outdoor pursuit that would keep young men on the straight and narrow and away from other diversions such as the demon drink. A brief look down the amateur leagues soon turns up a list of clubs with church affiliations and, even today, Saints Mary, Jude, Patrick, Cuthbert and Anne, amongst others, play Rugby League!

Factory life also spawned works teams but, in most cases, others were based at a pub, or alehouse as it was known then. This influx of working class players didn't go down very well with the Rugby Football Union's public school educated leaders and their amateur stance of wanting to keep rugby a gentleman's recreation, as distinct from paid work.

A rough game and little compensation

The *St Helens Reporter* Saturday 5th April 1890 brought bad news.

> "On Saturday, during the progress of a rugby football match between St Helens 'A' and West Leigh, a serious accident happened to Edward Smith aged 19, of Waterloo Street, St Helens. Smith was a new player and had no bars on his shoes, and the result was that he slipped and fell on his head, which was crushed down upon his chest. Paralysis quickly set in, and Dr Jones was called in and ordered his removal to the Workhouse Hospital, where he lives in a dying condition. He was the only support of his widowed mother."

Between January and March 1889 there were nine rugby deaths and it was reported that, in the three seasons from 1890 to 1893, games in the British Isles produced 437 significant casualties including 71 deaths and 121 broken legs. Deep concern centred on the behaviour of a growing number of roughneck spectators who were giving the administrators no end of trouble, barracking the referee and booing the away team. These early 'fans' no doubt saw themselves as participants in the match rather than mere observers and viewed the match as a spectacle and so demanded value for their admission money. Any player who strayed too close to the crowd was fair game for a surreptitious trip or a punch. Travel outside one's own community was still rare and visiting supporters were often seen as hostile invaders to be distrusted and, if necessary, repelled.

With several clubs 'moving the goalposts' to modern stadia these days, I think it's of interest to remember what grounds were like back in the days of the Northern Union. When St Helens moved to Knowsley Road in 1890, five years before the start of it all, the 'ground' was just an unfenced field. An entrance fee of 3d gained access to the one small stand in an otherwise open arena with free entrance to other spectators.

The committee altered all that by buying fencing at a cost of £101 and six shillings. Spectators then had to pay at pigeonholes at the town end, with just four turnstiles making their appearance in 1893. Trust St Helens to make the fans pay up!

What's in a name?

Those not liking the modern marketing nicknames of Tigers, Wolves, Eagles and so on, might be surprised to learn that the name 'Rochdale Hornets' was the original!

'Hornetto', one of my young friends from the totalrl.com message board, gave this interesting account reference one famous old name. "There has been a 'Rochdale Football Club' playing rugby in the town since 1866 - but Rochdale Hornets Rugby Football Club was founded 20th April 1871 at a meeting at the Roebuck Hotel in Rochdale. Over 50 'football' sides had been playing in the town - most notably St Clements, Rochdale Juniors and Rochdale United - and the members of each club decided that a 'town' team would benefit the development of 'Rugby Football' in the town. Names on the table that night were Rochdale Wasps, Rochdale Grasshoppers, Rochdale Butterflies (true!) and Rochdale Hornets.

"Thank goodness Rochdale Hornets got the nod; can you imagine having to sing "come on you Butterflies" on a Sunday afternoon? Interestingly, as the only team at the time with an enclosed ground, Rochdale Hornets was the first team in rugby to charge at the gate! Collectors usually went round the ground to take money, just like many amateur grounds still do today.

"In fact, at one point, Rochdale charged one shilling for horses but nothing for ladies. No doubt the horses were not in the seated area though."

The spectre of professionalism

Bubbling under the surface was the whole issue of professionalism. Even in the early days of folk football, monetary rewards were not uncommon.

In 1773 a match took place at Walton near Wetherby for the great sum of 20 guineas. A century later, payments of various kinds were regularly being made, sometimes to compensate players for having to take time off work both for playing and training sessions. At other times, they encouraged a player to move from one club to another.

Now, a one o'clock finish was fine if your team had a home match but pretty discouraging if you were playing away. As a result those who had to take time off on a Saturday morning felt it only right that they or their family didn't suffer financially. In other words, they wanted what became known as 'broken time' payment as compensation for lost wages. Not an undue expectation, you would think?

This issue was pretty acute in the industrial regions of the north of England and particularly among the 12 clubs that comprised the Yorkshire Senior Competition. Hull FC's Reports and Accounts for the season 1883/84 listed £18 as being spent on "players loss of time through accident and attendance at matches." On another occasion when they reached a cup final, members of the Hull team received a request not to work on the morning of the game and were paid compensation for not doing so.

In Leeds, on Whit Monday 1883, the ruling body offered a prize of £15 to the winning team and £1 to each team winning their first-round match. In 1886, rumour at the time claimed that Batley had given half the gate money from their match against Barrow to their players. (I presume some of the other half went to the Barrow lads?) Leeds paid out more in broken time compensation in what proved to be their last season as members of the RFU than they did in their first season in the Northern Union, saving £294 by being honest about payments.

'Pay for play' was not strictly a northern phenomenon. In the south west of England, for example, Gloucester and clubs in Torquay were investigated in the 1890s and found guilty of violations of the game's amateur regulations. Down in the midlands, the Leicester and Coventry clubs came under scrutiny when I was around seven years old and, of course, Welsh Rugby Union had been plagued with accusations of professionalism for as long as Lancashire and Yorkshire were.

However, the situation in the north of England differed greatly from the rest of the country because of the sheer scale of working class involvement. For the RFU, the game's middle class leaders increasingly saw the absolute impossibility of controlling payments for play in Lancashire, Cheshire and Yorkshire as a direct threat to their authority.

Of course, several of the 'old guard' controlled the northern clubs before I appeared on the scene. Proof of this are the backgrounds of three Presidents of the RFU, all determined opponents of professionalism in Harry Garnett, a paper manufacturer from Bradford, William Cail of Northumberland, the manager of a large chemical works and JWH Thorp a textile manufacturer from Cheshire.

While each man may have been quite proud of his northern roots they all shared with their RFU colleagues in the south a generalised disquiet about the growth of working class participation and domination of a game that they primarily wanted to keep as a gentleman's form of recreation. This was certainly true in Lancashire, where the Liverpool and Manchester clubs saw themselves as a cut above the rest of the Red Rose clubs. Not surprisingly, most of their leaders had been educated at public schools and particularly at Rugby and Cheltenham.

By professionalism, what the holders of the public school amateur ethos really objected to was payment to those from the lower end of the social ladder. As the *Yorkshire Post* wrote on 11th October 1886:

> *"They (artisans, mechanics and labourers) must not forget that the rules now governing the game have attained a definite form. The chief object - we might say the only object - for which the game is fostered by those who, combining ability with responsibility, control its destinies is a recreation - a pleasure in fact - that shall produce in a most acceptable form, relaxation for both mind and body."*

That said, it seemed that 'gentlemen' could accept expenses. In 1888, 20 players undertook a commercial rugby tour to Australia, all but one of whom were from the north of England. All were paid, including the captain, Andrew Stoddart, who received over £200, although on their return a veil was drawn over the matter in exchange for an oath that no RFU rules had been infringed.

Amongst rugby players sauce for the goose wasn't necessarily sauce for the gander.

Cash payments were not always the most common form of remuneration for players, being an obvious drain on club finances. In 1881, Dewsbury had begun the practice of rewarding players with a leg of mutton for each game won in the cup. (Maybe this explains why their ground is called the Ram Stadium!) This quickly became standard practice and better performances merited even greater incentives.

Two tries scored by a Batley player in 1885 earned him "one leg of mutton, two bottles of port and two shilling's worth of eggs." Mutton took on the importance of a vital aid to training for cup matches, with Leeds giving their players a leg of mutton every week when preparing for a cup run. I suppose a good sponsor in those days would have been the local butcher or the egg man. Meaty stuff for the northerners!

These payments, made mainly to the increasing number of working class players, caused great concern among the leaders of the RFU, spreading fear that this rapidly growing 'player-power' would mean that the 'gentlemen's' whip hand in the running of the game would weaken. If disorder in the ranks continued, payment for playing would soon allow the working classes to dominate the game as had happened in association football. In other words, it was time to put the working class in their place and put an end to their mutton!

Football and cricket too

Association football had its own equivalent of the broken payments argument when Preston North End accused Blackburn Rovers of making compensatory payments to their players, contrary to the sport's rules at the time. This led directly to the setting up of the Football Association to administrate the game, leaving the Football League relegated to organising fixture lists.

Cash payments for playing in cricket were also out of the question, but it seemed lucrative expenses for 'gentlemen' were quite acceptable. WG Grace has a famously prodigious level of expenses and the Surrey and England cricketer WW Read received recompense of £1,137 on the 1887/88 tour of Australia. He must have had a jolly good time, methinks.

Whilst frowned on by some for playing the game a little too seriously, by 1889 both Yorkshire and Lancashire had thriving, lucrative knock-out cup competitions and had established inter-county matches which had proved northern England as the powerbase of rugby football. The rest of the country was either satisfied (or being made to be satisfied) with a more Corinthian fixture list of 'friendlies.'

The 12 top Yorkshire clubs now planned the next step of organising a league amongst themselves to maximise revenue, a plan which the Yorkshire RFU forbade. The West Lancashire clubs jumped at the idea too and organised their own structure. By March 1892, 10 of the Yorkshire clubs went ahead anyway and founded their own competition under the snappy title of the 'Senior Competition of the Yorkshire Rugby Union.' Nine Lancashire clubs immediately did the same. Those down south weren't so keen. Not only were these northern lads the best players, organised into the best teams, they were running their own competitions now. Not on, old boy!

The palpable unfairness of the different treatments for players from differing backgrounds created a sharp contrast, especially in Yorkshire from whom most of the England team was drawn. In June 1893, the England team had played an international in Dublin requiring the England players to miss three days work. Complaints arising from this caused the Yorkshire Union to meet, the upshot being that the president, James Miller had the task of pushing through his committee's recommendations of the Yorkshire clubs' proposal for broken time payments.

A meeting with the wider RFU was called on the subject, although the Yorkshire men had made a tactical error, in effect forewarning the RFU of their intentions and thus buying the amateur lobby the chance to take defensive measures in terms of canvassing other clubs and organising proxy votes.

On 20th September 1893 the adversaries came face to face at the Westminster Palace Hotel, London. The serious implications ensured that it was the largest gathering in the history of the RFU's administration at the time, as 431 people packed into the room for the debate. Mark Newsome, Chairman of the Dewsbury club, had seconded James Miller's proposal in favour of broken time, the amateur cause being defended by the Northumbrian chemical industrialist, William Cail.

The debate between the two factions was heated with the final vote going overwhelmingly in favour of the anti-payment lobby by 282 votes to 136. Disappointingly, there wasn't much solidarity between the Yorkshire factions or even between Yorkshire and Lancashire clubs, and the broken time cause wasn't helped as some of the northern delegates missed the vote getting lost *en route* in the big city.

Unhappy to take no for an answer and with the arguments for professionalism (or more correctly, semi-professionalism) polarising rugby, battle lines were drawn between those who viewed rugby football with an amateur ethos and the northern teams who were forging ahead, both on the field and off it. The tail could no longer be allowed to wag the dog.

To try and keep the family together the Yorkshire RU, who still administrated the rest of the game in the county, decreed that the bottom team from the division of the headstrong Senior clubs should have to play off for relegation against the top two of the league below them. Disregarding this, Hull and Wakefield Trinity were re-elected anyway, denying Morley and Castleford a crack at 'em. The Senior clubs didn't care for this challenge from those who would meddle with their competition and who would see lesser clubs invited to their elite table and resigned *en bloc* from the YRU. The Lancashire Senior clubs were engaged in a similar power struggle and duly followed suit, quitting their county union.

By the summer of 1895, the great rugby split gathered momentum. To further isolate the dissident clubs on 13th August, the RFU boss Rowland Hill decreed fresh, stringent anti-professional regulations, forbidding even playing on a ground where gate money had been taken. These were due to come into force at the RFU annual meeting on 19th September 1895.

It now looked inevitable - the commercially successful northern clubs couldn't live within the rules that the RFU required and faced eviction. They didn't want a gentlemanly pastime, they wanted progress. Where's the door?

The Yorkshire Football Crisis

The 24th August 1895 issue of the *Bradford Observer* warned of the gravity of the situation under the banner: "The Yorkshire Football Crisis." (I notice that 'football' still didn't seem to involve a round ball then!)

"Further inquiries into the present attitude of the contending parties in Yorkshire Rugby Football do not

afford much hope of a reconciliation. The crash has yet to come but it gets increasingly difficult to throw off the feeling that a startling development is at hand. When two parties are striving for the mastery and each is resolved not to give way to the other, strong measures are inevitable. It is useless to attempt to disguise the fact that a desperate plunge is contemplated by the bulk of the clubs, which formed the Yorkshire Senior Competition. As we said yesterday, there is particular good reason to believe that negotiations are actively going on for the formation of a Northern League, like that which was formed some time ago but was promptly tabooed by the Rugby Union."

With the Yorkshire clubs and the RFU at an impasse a hastily-organised meeting was convened at the Mitre in Leeds on 27th August 1895 where the 12 Yorkshire Senior Competition clubs passed a resolution "to push forward as expeditiously as possible the formation of a Northern Rugby Football Union."

In the knowledge that various Lancashire clubs had similar aspirations of self-governance and broken time payments, and nine clubs had concluded the same thing at a meeting at the Spread Eagle in Manchester the same evening, it looked like the point of no return.

As a matter of utmost urgency the dissidents from the respective sides of the Pennines agreed to convene two days later and the George Hotel, Huddersfield was selected as the venue.

The rugby world stood by for an eruption to rival that in Krakatoa 12 years earlier.

1

1895-1900
HAPPY BIRTHDAY

My birth certificate gives 29th August 1895 as the day I was officially born. For the family historians among us, it's interesting to find out what your ancestors did before you came along, like doing your family tree and linking the names of relatives long since dead and buried to stories of the things they will be remembered for. In my case I suppose you could say that my mum was Rugby Union and my dad was workers rights. As with any inquisitive young 'un, a few questions spring to mind. Why, why, why?

Why did it happen then, on that day and why in Huddersfield? Why not Hull, Halifax or Hunslet? Simply enough, being the mid-point on the trans-Pennine railway, Huddersfield was relatively easy to reach by the train both from Hull, the farthest club in the east, and St Helens, the farthest to the west.

Why at the George Hotel? Well, if you fell down the steps coming out of Huddersfield railway station, thirty yards or so away, you could fall into the George. And many people have done.

Why on a Thursday evening and why couldn't all those committeemen wait until the weekend? Well, time was of the essence since if the fixture lists for the coming season could be got out by the weekend then the Northern Union season could start a fortnight before the RFU clubs they were breaking away from.

At the George

Mine was a difficult birth. On that fateful day at the George the meeting convened at 6.30pm sharp, behind firmly-closed doors. Labour lasted three hours and after plenty of gas and air, 21 club representatives from Lancashire, Yorkshire and Cheshire voted to bring me into the world.

The resolution was to form a breakaway Northern Rugby Football Union there and then and push forward without delay, its establishment based on the principle of payment for *bona-fide* broken time.

All the delegates voted for my birth with the exception of one, a Mr Holdsworth of Dewsbury, who stated that he had not yet had the time to consult the Dewsbury Football and Cricket Club Committee. He did, however, nervously add that no doubt they would agree but he could not vote 'yes' on their behalf. Mr Holdsworth's anxiety turned out to be well-founded as Dewsbury's Chairman, Mark Newsome, later decided to withdraw his club's application to the Northern Union and seek reinstatement to the Yorkshire Rugby Football Union. Mr Newsome was the mill owner who had originally seconded the broken time motion at the RFU meeting at the Westminster Palace Hotel - he later became Chairman of the RFU.

Dewsbury's hesitation proved their undoing. One of their players queried their decision with the question, "What wages are you paying up here?" On receiving the reply, "none," he responded, "It's no use me stopping here then." Eventually the club folded to be replaced by a different Dewsbury side that joined my family in later years.

The Heavy Woollen club having declined its place in history, Stockport took the initiative and confirmed their intentions to the meeting by telegraph. Runcorn subsequently joined the fun to make up the 22 founder members.

Thanks, lads. I think that the world is a better place for what you decided to do on that day. Strange, though, that no women were present at my birth, though I am pleased to say there are plenty amongst us now, and rightly so.

The roll of honour of brave and fine men representing the 21 clubs that night was as follows:

> *J. Goodall (Batley), F. Lister (Bradford), H. H. Waller (Brighouse Rangers), E. Gresty (Broughton Rangers), C. Holdsworth (Dewsbury), J. Nicholl (Halifax), J. Clifford (Huddersfield), C. A. Brewer (Hull), J. L. Whittaker (Hunslet), H. Sewell (Leeds), J. Quirk (Leigh), J. Hampshire (Liversedge), A. Fattorini (Manningham), J. Platt (Oldham), W. Brierley (Rochdale Hornets), F. Dennett (St. Helens), G. Taylor (Tyldesley), J. H. Fallas (Wakefield Trinity), J. E. Warren (Warrington), F. Wright (Widnes) and E. Wardle (Wigan.)*

The meeting closed, the delegates then stepped out into St George's Square and headed off into the night towards destiny and challenges as yet unknown...

There were no headlines on the front page of the following day's *Yorkshire Post* (as this was usually classified advertising) to announce my arrival but, tucked away on the back page, was a small column headed: "The Football Split." The glad tidings cost one penny, but mentioned very little detail other than a list of the clubs involved and that the dispute was with Rowland Hill, secretary of the RFU.

We later learned that the rules of the new competition were to remain the same for the time being, although the suggested reduction in numbers from 15 to 13 men per team had been under discussion for a while in any case.

Broken time payments of six shillings were agreed as the permitted standard sum, which would render anyone who took them illegal in the 'amateur' circles. The six shillings would be available as a match fee, but it wasn't the intention that playing rugby should be the sole occupation of any player. The *Wigan Observer's* comment was that: "Freedom from the thraldom of the southern gentry was the best thing that could happen." A *Hull Daily Mail* correspondent wrote: "The clubs who have stuck a blow for freedom are to be commended for throwing off the cloak of hypocrisy, conceit and subterfuge, and standing out for those essentially English characteristics - honesty and straightforwardness."

A point to note was that any 'rugby' club started before my birth had RFC after its name and was allowed to keep this by the English governing body. However, after my birth they had to have RUFC to distinguish it from my clubs in the Northern Union. I suppose my birth did cause some rumpus.

Kick off!

Well, that's the bit you probably already know something about, but what happened next?

The new administration had to move post haste in reorganising and arranging my first Northern Union fixtures, including cancelling and rescheduling matches already committed to under the previous regime. The hurried decision to kick off just prior to the scheduled RFU fixtures in an attempt to steal their thunder only compounded the confusion.

One such case involved that of a team of glassworkers employed by Pilkington Brothers and called St Helens Recreationals. Now St Helens Recs planned to stay put and had forthcoming games with seven of the breakaway clubs, which could not now be fulfilled.

The match officials, who were possibly also known as the 'untouchables' by the RFU, and in fact George Harrop, a referee who volunteered to officiate at one of my first Northern Union matches, "expressed his delight that thus he would the first member of the Huddersfield club to fall under the ban of the English Rugby Union."

As for the results for 7th September 1895, the inaugural week of the Northern Union, they were as follows:

Batley 7	Hull 3
Bradford 11	Wakefield Trinity 0
Broughton Rangers 0	Wigan 9
Leigh 3	Leeds 6
Liversedge 0	Halifax 5
Runcorn 15	Widnes 4
St. Helens 8	Rochdale Hornets 3
Stockport 0	Brighouse Rangers 5
Tyldesley 6	Manningham 0
Warrington 5	Hunslet 4

(Huddersfield and Oldham did not manage to get their game organised.)

Is your favourite team in there, I wonder?

Onlookers mentioned large crowds turning out although, generally, play was poor with players being out of condition, early season, as well as some well-known players being absent. Don't forget the long journeys that had to be undertaken for the away side with no fast transport in those days. In fact, the Leeds team set off on the return journey from Leigh at 7.50pm, only arriving back at Leeds at 12.15am. Something to send a shiver down the spine of the Hull executive as they contemplated the long, arduous journeys over to the Lancashire clubs.

At the end of the debut NU season, Manningham were crowned the first Championship winners in 1896, having pipped Halifax to the title. Rochdale Hornets finished bottom of the pile wining only four games and drawing eight over the season. St Helens, as in 2003, had two points deducted but this time for fielding an ineligible player.

For posterity, the final table from my debut season is over the page.

But that was that, with no league competition again until 1901-02. The cost, time and logistics of the travel involved and the large number of games played in the eight-month season caused a rethink of the NU fixture list and the Championship's original format abandoned. Perhaps the breakaway had been unduly rushed?

The first season showed good returns for most of my 'rebel' clubs with Oldham being most successful returning a profit of

NORTHERN UNION INAUGURAL SEASON 1895
FINAL TABLE

		P	W	D	L	F	A	Pts
1	Manningham	42	33	0	9	367	158	66
2	Halifax	42	30	5	7	312	139	65
3	Runcorn	42	24	8	10	314	143	56
4	Oldham	42	27	2	13	374	194	56
5	Brighouse R	42	22	9	11	247	129	53
6	Tyldesley	42	21	8	13	260	164	50
7	Hunslet	42	24	2	16	279	207	50
8	Hull	42	23	3	16	259	158	49
9	Leigh	42	21	4	17	214	269	46
10	Wigan	42	19	7	16	245	147	45
11	Bradford	42	18	9	15	254	175	45
12	Leeds	42	20	3	19	258	247	43
13	Warrington	42	17	5	20	198	240	39
14	St Helens	42	15	8	19	195	230	36
15	Liversedge	42	15	4	23	261	355	34
16	Widnes	42	14	4	24	177	323	32
17	Stockport	42	12	8	22	171	315	32
18	Batley	42	12	7	23	137	298	31
19	Wakefield T	42	13	4	25	156	318	30
20	Huddersfield	42	10	4	28	194	274	24
21	Broughton R	42	8	8	26	165	244	24
22	Rochdale H	42	4	8	30	78	388	16

£1,148. Hull also increased their takings thanks to an increase of 50,000 spectators. Halifax increased their gate receipts by 50 per cent, and even bottom-club Rochdale with a poor playing season cleared a modest £96. This was indeed a vindication of my birth.

The sketchy evidence available suggests that just prior to my birth the senior Northern clubs had seen a decline in profitability. The expense of ground refurbishment and covert player payments had taken a heavy toll. In terms of extremes Bradford and Leeds, with large capital investments in their grounds faced the treadmill of constantly seeking success, while small town clubs, such as Brighouse Rangers and Tyldsley found income too difficult to generate to warrant their continued existence amongst the elite. Even though both clubs won their respective county leagues in 1895, it still resulted in a financial loss.

This success certainly held sway and was crucial in attracting a second wave of 'defectors' from the RFU. As in Salford's case, being a working class club and losing money they held an extraordinary general meeting at the request of members to discuss joining the NU, pointing out that the club had lost £713 over the preceding four years. It would certainly be down, down, down if the club didn't expand from their 'amateur' status. Only three out of 400 members opposed the switch.

Close neighbours Swinton, having announced a loss of £450 in the previous season made similar overtures towards joining the NU at their general meeting, which was greeted with endorsement. The decision certainly proved the antidote to the concern that over the previous four seasons the annual gate money had slumped from £1,016 to £383 coupled with season ticket holders having halved. The decisions were to prove right when, over the next two years in my NU, they made profits of £450 and £529.

There is much more detail that I could tell you about the birth and expansion of my Northern Union but this book is not the place to do so, as some previous good books about my early self already have done. In fact, whilst penning this piece, I gleaned some information from Tony Collins' great book, *Rugby's Great Split*, which is a mine of information. I also recommend Geoffrey Moorhouse's *A People's Game* and *Rugby League Fact Book* by Robert Gate. Indeed, it is an honour to have such literary talent write about me, as well as all the other game's many scribes.

The Senior Competitions

Given the ambitious logistics of the first season and the need for so many games to be rearranged, itself causing a degree of instability, in season 1896/97 and for the remainder of the century the Northern Union expanded but split into two county-based divisions, the Senior County Competitions.

Whilst membership of the Northern Union doubled it was open to question whether all the clubs were up to standard for the highest level of rugby. So what did happen to some clubs in the early pioneering years?

Expanding from the original 22 to 30 clubs, Yorkshire gained Bramley, Castleford, Heckmondwike, Holbeck and Leeds Parish Church whilst over in Lancashire, Morecambe, Salford and Swinton joined the fold. Before the turn of the century, Lancashire also acquired the Cumbrian club Millom and, over in Yorkshire, the changes continued with Hull Kingston Rovers added.

Broughton Rangers won the first Lancashire Senior Competition in 1896/97 completing a 26-match programme with 43 points, one ahead of Oldham. Morecambe finished bottom with just three wins and soon after folded.

Brighouse Rangers finished the equivalent Senior Yorkshire Competition with 48 points from 30 games, taking the title by two points from Manningham. Heckmondwike took the wooden spoon with only three wins and four draws.

Relegation to junior football for Morecambe and Heckmondwike after a poor first season in the Seniors eventually led to both clubs calling it a day a few years later, although Morecambe did make a brief return to the Seniors later.

In 1897/98, Oldham triumphed in the Red Rose county ahead of Swinton. A play-off had to be arranged in Yorkshire the same season as Hunslet and Bradford both finished on 48 points with Hunslet taking the title 5-2 in the deciding tie.

For season 1898/99, Broughton Rangers pipped Oldham whilst Batley triumphed over Hull in the final Yorkshire Senior League table by one point.

Following their glory of winning the first NU championship, Manningham only lasted the pace until 1903 when the club 'switched codes' again, this time converting to soccer to become Bradford City FC.

One would imagine that all this early change and disruption would have an effect on my well-being but I was born out of sterner pedigree and even with many more changes to follow only strengthened my resolve to continue.

All change

Some of the first rule changes happened in 1897, marking the departure of the respective governing bodies into two genuinely separate codes. The method of scoring in the Northern Union altered with the value of field-goals and penalty-goals being reduced to two points, whilst tries became worth three.

Following on from Manningham's championship win, the

following year I inaugurated a new knock-out competition and 52 clubs entered the first round in pursuit of 'The Northern Rugby Football Union Challenge Cup,' as I originally called it.

Batley beat St Helens 10-3 in the final of the first Challenge Cup, as I shall henceforth refer to it. A crowd of 13,492 watched the game at Headingley and saw the gleaming trophy, made at Fattorini's jewellers of Bradford at a cost of £60, raised for the first time.

In season 1897/98, Batley doubled up by winning the cup at Headingley again, this time against Bradford, 7-0, with the turnout doubled to 27,941. The last Challenge Cup final of the decade was played at Fallowfield, Manchester, where 15,762 fans witnessed a 19-9 win for Oldham over Hunslet.

Cup Final Roses skulduggery

Speaking recently to John Huxley, media manager of the RFL, he recounted this interesting piece about the first Challenge Cup final and the skulduggery of those in Yorkshire. No wonder there was a 'Battle of the Roses'!

One of Rugby League's great days out has been the final of the Challenge Cup competition. The roots of this prestigious knock-out event were firmly-rooted in the success of the former Yorkshire Rugby Union Cup competition, which was known throughout the region as 'T'owd Tin Pot' and had attracted big crowds even before the 1895 split. 'T'owd' it might have been but it was certainly a money-spinner. Once the Northern Rugby Union had got through its first season in 1895/96, the first thing they did was to introduce their own version of the Yorkshire Cup, called the Challenge Cup.

The first ever final was contested at Headingley in Leeds on 24th April 1897. It was already a well-appointed venue and the Northern Union knew it was a suitable stage on which to allow their new competition to come to a conclusion.

The first two finalists set the preferred Trans-Pennine mould for the rest of time, one team from Yorkshire in the shape of the 'Gallant Youths' of Batley against St Helens from Lancashire. (Good old Cumberland might have something to say about this, or should it be Cheshire!) At that stage in Northern Union history, Batley were the equivalent of the modern Bradford Bulls or Leeds Rhinos, a top-dog outfit. Their team contained such stars as the all-Welsh wing-centre partnership of Wattie Davies and Dai Fitzgerald.

Dai had originally come up from Wales to join Leigh but subsequently moved across the Pennines to sign for Batley. He was a driving force in the Gallant Youths' side and such was his influence that two years later, when he was suspended for not having a proper job, Batley's fortunes slumped. The suspension came about after a private detective hired by my governing body found out that his job as a coal agent didn't actually involve any work. When he returned from suspension in 1900 the Heavy Woollen area club, twice cup finalists in 1897 and 1898, went back to the 1900/1901 final.

His wing partner, Davies, was the Victorian equivalent of David Beckham. Besides being a fine rugby player he was also a notable athlete and one of his party tricks was to jump over a horse from a standing start. It must have been a fairly small animal!

St Helens arrived at the final after a poor season of league form but once cup fever had gripped the town and the club it was a different matter. When cup final day dawned the contrast was stark. For a start there were far more Batley and Yorkshire-based fans in the ground than Lancastrians.

There were suspicions that the balance had been unfairly tipped by a patriotic Yorkshire railway worker in Huddersfield. More than 2,000 St Helens fans had taken the train to Leeds to follow their team to the final. The journey, however, took three hours most of which was spent waiting in the tunnels around Huddersfield because, it was alleged, the signalman who controlled the path through to Leeds kept giving priority to other trains. Eventually, the Saints fans made it to Headingley but, unfortunately, by the time they reached Headingley their team were trailing Batley, 7-0.

The Gallant Youths had also struck a psychological blow against their opponents even before a ball had been kicked in anger because they had taken the field wearing a brand new strip featuring a snowy white shirt. St Helens, on the other hand, had to make do and mend with a rag-bag of unmatched shirts. The *Athletic News*, one of the sporting newspapers of the time, recorded the St Helens strip - most of which had seen service during the cup run - as: "faded and washed out blue and white jerseys." Mind you, as Saints had just endured a period of financial worries it is the opinion of many historians that they couldn't have afforded a new strip for the game in any case.

Footnote:

Over 100 years later, I didn't need 'dodgy' railway workers to slow things down. Virgin trains offered a service to Cardiff for the 2003 Challenge Cup final, aimed at travellers cautious of the infamous road traffic congestion in South Wales that a big event at Millennium Stadium attracts.

With an inevitable irony, Virgin advised: "those who have bought tickets for the journey but have been unable to secure reservations are advised that they may be directed to other trains. We are unable to guarantee arrival in Cardiff in time for the kick-off."

Unequivocal success, but…

Despite the confident assertion that my birth and early life would falter it was far from the case. A great family of support witnessed immense growth and the first years saw wholesale change to the betterment of my life. By 1899 all but 25 of the 240 former Rugby Union clubs in Yorkshire and Lancashire had gone over to my Northern Union. It was indeed a tribute to the pioneers who made it possible that in such a short time, the NU was now a larger organisation in the Roses counties than the original Rugby Unions were.

However, the original six shillings per day limit did have its drawbacks with many questioning whether this would be enough, especially for the likes of South Wales, when covert payments in Rugby Union were known to be higher. My six shillings lacked the appeal needed to attract converts from the Principality.

With no real modern day type 'salary cap' policing in place, some clubs made larger cash inducements than were allowed. (Talking of the police, they were another sore point in those days, having a ban on their staff playing my sport as well.) Stockport was rumoured not only to be paying £2 a week during the playing season but also with a job at 30 shillings a week in the summer, and this only three weeks after my birth.

These 'irregularities' were cause for concern amongst some club members. By 1897 it was clear that misuse of club funds was widespread with the comment in the London-based *Mascot:* "it does not seem likely that the Northern Union officials will long be able to shut their eyes to the existing state of things in their own clubs. Either they must constitute a searching enquiry and punish clubs that have practised professionalism or openly embrace the paying of players."

A seven-man committee was formed in the November of that year to clarify the whole issue of professionalism. It had been the NU's intention that whilst broken time compensation were only fair, players should not be full-time sportsmen, rather their sport being additional to their main employment.

Indeed, any unemployed man was refused the right to play as his rugby payment would become his sole occupation. No professional player could be employed as a billiard marker, a waiter in a licensed house, or employed in connection with a club.

Many leading NU officials were also publicans and could easily skirt round the regulations by employing their players in 'ghost' jobs, these also being offered as signing-on inducements. Coincidentally, many leading players in the modern game end up as publicans anyway.

The main upshot, however, was that on 19th July 1898 professionalism became legal and open. In fact, some players had attained celebrity status, even appearing on cigarette cards and the like. For many, a moustache was *de rigeur.*

Warrington's Jackie Fish, a Victorian hero

As darkness envelops the night skies, the mystery of the stars beckons all. Some radiate a vibrant display of sparkling light, whilst others are cloaked in the shadows of darkness, too remote in space and time to be seen by the naked eye. My sporting firmament has borne stars of such magnitude that are instantly recognisable to the public long beyond their sporting careers are over. Then there are those who briefly twinkle before fading into anonymity. Rugby League's own constellation contains stars of contrasting magnitudes, one of whom will forever be known as Jackie Fish.

If I were a gambling man it would be a safe bet that most of you haven't heard of Jackie. It isn't a name that conjures up too many thoughts. That's not to say he wasn't a shining star in his heyday. It seems appropriate that he should have a moment of glory once more with his own biography. Life isn't always about the brightest stars.

Christened John Fish he came into the world born in Runcorn in 1880, before moving on with his family to the small village of Lostock Gralam as a small boy. Initially he imposed his rugby talents on the open playing fields in the village, turning out for the local team. Quicksilver speed and a sharp eye for the try line soon had the local Warrington scouts praising his virtues. The club committee wasted little time in offering him a trial in their 'A' team against a Lostock XV with his initial performance meriting a further meeting with club officials. Ecstatic at their find, Jackie soon put pen to paper for the princely sum of £50, paid in silver.

His rise to hero status of the period happened sooner rather than later after scoring a sensational try against Barrow on his debut on 15th October 1898. Fame spread like lightning with Wigan becoming aware of his outstanding pace. They too had a high-flyer by the name of Buckie Green and suggested they pit both players together in a £100 a-side sprint challenge. Jackie won the prize on offer at Springfield Park, Wigan convincingly, leaving Buckie in his shadow. In a game against Bradford, their very own speedster Fred Cooper, who incidentally was himself an AAA sprint champion and 10-second man over 100 yards, couldn't catch Jackie, who scorched his way to two long-distance tries.

For loyal and dedicated service, Warrington granted Jackie a testimonial in 1910 which raised £268 15s 11d. Worth every penny.

With war imminent Jackie enlisted into the army to serve King and Country where more success followed, winning the Aldershot Command Sprint Championship at the tender age of 35. Suffering from a weak chest he was eventually invalided out of the forces.

Jackie passed away 23rd October 1940. Not for him eternal, posthumous stardom but, nonetheless, a shining light in his time.

The 'Greatest Game' was built around men like Jackie Fish. I am proud to have been associated with him.

Life on a bigger picture

It's always an interesting comparison to read about other events of the day, so here are a few interesting snippets from around the time of my birth.

In 1895 the FA Cup trophy was stolen from a shop window in Birmingham where it had been on display courtesy of holders Aston Villa. After a replica trophy had been presented to Lord Kinnaird for services to the FA, a new one was made by Bradford jewellers Fattorini & Sons and was won, appropriately in it's first year, by Bradford City.

Initially, it was intended that Paris would host the first modern Olympics in 1900, but Athens offered to stage an earlier Olympiad in 1896 and their proposal was accepted. With problems similar to those of a 108 years later, Greece ran into financial difficulties before the games could begin and Hungary, preparing for its millennium celebrations, repeatedly offered to step in as a replacement.

Crown Prince Constantine of Greece set up an organising committee and public donations saved the day. Just over 200 men, representing 14 countries competed in some 43 events. The majority of the participants were from the host nation with tennis, track and field, fencing, weightlifting, cycling, wrestling, shooting, swimming and gymnastics all contested. Cricket and soccer tournaments were cancelled due to a lack of participating teams while rowing and sailing competitions fell victim to poor weather. No rugby though! Event winners received a silver medal, a certificate and a crown of olive leaves. Runners-up were given bronze medals and a crown of laurel while third-placed participants went home empty-handed.

Progress in science during the year of my birth as Wilhelm Rontgen discovered X-rays. There is no 'shadow' of a doubt that it has helped my players over the years in assisting them to get back to fitness.

Another innovation was the National Trust being born and with it some of the country's treasured castles, homes and beauty spots being preserved for future generations to admire. In fact, yours truly has managed to visit some of the outstanding Trust countryside that can be found all around my place of birth, where many of my players have been put to task during training over the years.

A little bit of affordable luxury as King Camp Gillette invented the safety razor in 1895, consigning the cut-throat, and countless sticking plasters, to the bin.

Interestingly enough, in 1895 the British collieries produced 190 million tons of coal to fuel the nations mills and factories, where many of my supporters earned their daily corn, a stark contrast to my seventies chapter, a time beset by the miners strike.

The first Promenade concert took place on 10th August 1895, the brainchild of the impresario Robert Newman, manager of the newly built Queen's Hall, London. His aim was to reach a wider audience by offering more popular programmes, adopting a less formal promenade arrangement and keeping ticket prices low. "I am going to run nightly concerts to train the public in easy stages," he explained, "popular at first, gradually raising the standard until I have created a public for classical and modern music."

I wonder what he'd make of my pre-match entertainment these days?

Millennium

The 2000 Millennium celebrations were indeed a joyous occasion worldwide. Modern technology brought television pictures of different culture's events from round the world into every living room. Starting with the Pacific island of Kiribati, hour by hour spectacular firework displays illuminated the night skies as each time zone rang in the new age.

There had been global warnings of potentially disastrous computer malfunctions due to the unrecognisable date and even predictions of a worldwide shortage of champagne, none of which, of course, happened.

Over in Britain, the *Yorkshire Post* (price 40p) welcomed the New Year with a headline: "Happy New Millennium - global party as world heads into the new era and Queen opens Dome as spectacular show seen by billions of TV viewers," followed by three pages of coverage.

For many, the party was spoiled by profiteering as many public venues charged for entrance, sadly representing an opportunity to make a financial killing rather than to celebrate the world's birthday. Served them right when they struggled to get staff to work.

What then of the celebrations at the turn of the century at the end of December 1899? How did the good folk mark the occasion and what media response did the event receive?

Well, to be honest, it was something of a non-event as far as the press was concerned. Containing little in the way of good cheer, or news of it elsewhere, the *Times* of Monday 1st January 1900 (price 3d) made reference to the new millennium only in the debate on the letters page as to the correct date it should be considered to have started. This year or next?

The paper largely took the form of a 'report and accounts' with the state of the Empire, agriculture, exchequer issues and a weather report for the year. The Boer War dominated the news of the day with updates on the movement of troops, casualties and "embarkation of horses."

If you wanted some fun, you'd have to wait until the new Hippodrome Theatre, Drury Lane, was opened on 6th January with *Jack and the Beanstalk*. Up north, the next day's *Leeds Mercury* (10 pages, one penny) didn't see the need to make much fuss either, although it did report some interesting flavour of the time and a couple of events.

House coal in Leeds "was advanced by one shilling per ton for all classes of coal, nuts, slack and smudge." In a small article on page three, between "A Todmorden Mystery," announcing the discovery of a dead farmer - "his head being frightfully cut" - and news that "two small motor cars are to be run for hire in Leeds next month," came news of the new epoch.

"The New Year commenced with a clear sheet at both Halifax police courts."

"Inmates at Whitby workhouse had their annual tea and entertainment yesterday," and also, "Mr W Morgan, managing director of the Peoples Palace and Acquarium gave a New Year dinner and entertainment yesterday to over 200 old people and Harrogate Methodist Free Church held their annual New Year gathering." Momentous stuff!

However, a letter from W Leicester drew concern to a "matter of serious public import" being that "180 music and dancing licences had been applied for, three fourths of which were by hotel and public house keepers. Music and dancing may be harmless enough but when they are sought in drinking saloons the result can scarcely fail to be disastrous to our young people." Be warned!

Having played a full programme on Saturday 30th December 1899 Bradford were top of the Yorkshire Seniors with 30 points from 18 games whilst Leeds and Liversedge were equal bottom with seven points from three wins and a draw. Leeds Parish Church and Holbeck were not far above them.

"It was a pity that the conspicuous improvement shown by the Leeds 15 in their game with Manningham at Headingley should have been witnessed by so small a crowd, only some 1,400 or 1,500 people being present."

In a contrast to the introspection of the *Times*, the *Leeds Mercury* printed results from as far afield as the Cumbrian Senior Competition, Rugby Union and Association football from England and Scotland.

The *Yorkshire Evening Post* 'Late Buff Edition' (price, one halfpenny) was a little less po-faced. Having reported that Queen Victoria had sent a message to the troops in South Africa, it went on to advertise that William Whittaker & Co (the Bradford Old Brewery) offered Silent Dew Scotch Whisky at 21 shillings per gallon. It was left to Brooke Bond's tea to make the most fuss claiming that: "Brooke Bond's tea is the tea for the New Century ("supplying no less than 100 out of every 1,000 lbs. of tea consumed in the United Kingdom every 38 minutes of the day").

In short, the new millennium didn't seem particularly important to the papers, if indeed it had happened at all! For me though, if I did but know it, I had a hundred years of battle ahead.

2

1900-1910
THE NEW CENTURY

Off to a bit of a stumbling start. At the age of five - and still a bit unsteady on my pins - I was quickly finding my feet in the big, bad world, full of curiosity for the strange people and places I was keen to explore. Would I survive the century in front of me? In fact, would I survive at all given the opposition I was still encountering?

As it turned out my early teens were a real boom age for the game, so much happened around this time and with countless personalities, it's difficult to tell the stories without them getting tangled together, but I'll try.

As a popular advert of the day told us: "*Cadbury's Cocoa Makes Strong Men Stronger*". I'll have a cup and then tell you what was happening in the world around me.

State of the nation

The year 1900 saw the birth of Elizabeth Bowes-Lyon, later to become the Queen Mother. The venerable lady shared nearly my whole lifetime. God bless you, Ma'am.

Considerable doubt surrounded 1st January 1900, over whether the country was beginning a new century or if there was still another year to go. The first leader in the *Times* began with the words: "The New Year, the last of the 19th century..." and readers' opinions in the correspondence columns were divided, while the Queen herself didn't note the change of century in her journal or letters either in 1900 or in 1901.

The *Yorkshire Evening Post* of 1st January 1901 offered: "a few looks ahead by dipping into the new century."

Mr Crowther, curator of the Philosophical Hall suggested that: "the utilisation of the energy of the tides and methods for more accurately predicting the weather will be two important events."

Councillor Henry of Holbeck predicted: "tremendous alterations and additions to the water supply of the city (£3 million.) The better housing of the working classes will also be a feature of the century," adding, "we need not fear flying machines."

Mr Walt Wood forecast two periods of recession during the next 10 years (building society interest rates had dropped to three and a half per cent but just increased again to four per cent) and a proportionate number of working men in the House of Commons.

The masses were coming around to rejecting the notion held for so long that inherited privilege wasn't necessarily a prerequisite to a reasonable life. With this thinking came the birth of the Labour Party. Launched at a meeting of like-minded organisations at the Memorial Hall, London, on 27th February 1900, it returned two MPs including one, James Kier Hardie, at that year's General Election.

The swing towards less authoritarian government was evidenced in 1906 as the Liberal Party won a landslide General Election. Later in the decade, in 1908, Asquith became Prime Minister with one Winston Churchill in his cabinet. Old Age Pensions arrived in Britain at between one and five shillings for those over 70 years of age, whose income was below 12 shillings a week.

Another institution, the *Daily Express* came into the world in 1900 and reported on the colonial activities that continued around the Empire. In South Africa the second Boer War stretched the 'thin red line' with the siege of Mafeking its most celebrated incident. Colonel Robert Baden-Powell (later the founder of the Scout Movement) and a detachment of British troops were besieged by the Boers from October 1899 until May 1900. The news of their relief aroused public hysteria in Britain, the celebrations becoming known as 'mafficking'. At the end of another siege, Ladysmith, the *Daily Express* reported that: "Students of art at the Royal Academy, on hearing the news instantly searched for a Union Jack, and not finding one painted one on the spot." Talking of students, Britain wasn't top of the class as there were only 20,000 university scholars in total at the beginning of the century, the same as the University of Sheffield alone today.

The richest man in the world at the turn of the century, Andrew Carnegie, had left his native Dunfermline some years earlier to found the Carnegie Steel Company in Pittsburgh. With over $100 million to his name he gave 90 per cent of his brass away again, establishing over 2,500 libraries, museums and concert halls for the public good. You've probably got one in your town.

Where else to start 1901 but with the death of Queen Victoria? Aged 82 and during her 64th year on the throne, "The Victorian age is over" the *Daily Telegraph* wrote, then, "the supreme woman in the world is gone...never, never was there loss like this." The Annual Register, looking for precedents, had to go back to King Alfred.

Victoria's successor, Edward VII, lent his name to the next era, that of 'Edwardian'. The very word conjures up an image of an elegant lady, promenading with her parasol; at least it does to me, although I was still very young.

Amongst the well-to-do, the craze for Parisian fashion attached an alternative title for the era, that of 'La Belle Époque'. A smart man would wear a three-buttoned frock coat, high collar, bow tie and a bowler hat and would more than likely carry a silver topped cane and fob watch on a gold chain.

Small feet were regarded as elegant and both males and females often wore shoes a size too small. Children tended to dress as small replicas of their parents.

Travelling suits were available for the new motoring classes, women having veils to protect from oil, fumes and dust from unmade roads, and in 1903 it became necessary to impose a 20mph speed limit on Britain's roads.

Still thought of as 'horseless carriages' the Queens highways were used by around 10,000 cars in 1900, most of them made abroad, although 1906 delivered us the first Rolls Royce. Traffic outside towns and cities was light. Roads were poor, often unsuitable for road traffic and petrol 'stockists' rare.

Almost 22,000 miles of railway had been laid by 1900, with towns and villages not on the track isolated and considered remote.

In London, horse trams, horse buses, licensed hansom cabs and clarences posed serious problems of equine traffic congestion and a bit of a whiff from their 'exhaust.'

A new electric underground, the 'twopenny tube' Central London Railway, opened in June 1900 by the Prince of Wales, linking Shepherd's Bush and the Bank of England with eleven stops between.

Not a life of progress and gentility for everyone though. Seebohm Rowntree completed his landmark survey of social conditions in York, Poverty, a Study of Town Life in 1901. Whilst about a third of London's population lived in poverty on about £1 a week or less, according to Rowntree, the York figure approached 28 per cent. Rowntree also interested himself in the rural poor, the poorest of whom, one clergyman had written, "did not live in the proper sense of the word, they merely didn't die." I know what he meant.

Cereal growing agriculture was on the wane, villages again became depopulated, towns increasingly overcrowded and five-sixths of Britain's food supplies arrived from overseas as the country found itself dependent on foreign imports.

A smallpox epidemic swept Britain in 1902, with hospital ships *Geneva Cross, Castalia, Alber Victor, Maltese Cross, HMS Atlas* and *HMS Endymion* all moored on the Thames to treat patients. Only revealed officially in 1903, statistics showed how many would-be recruits for the Boer War had to be turned down on health grounds, physical unfitness and malnutrition.

Picasso painted in his blue period of sad and cold images,

whilst developing an experimental style of 'Cubism' whereby the subject was represented as if seen simultaneously from every angle at once.

On the 17th December 1903, Wilbur and Orville Wright made the first human flight, all of 12 seconds, at Kittyhawk, North Carolina. By 1909, Monsieur Bleriot had flown the English Channel in 43 minutes. *Bravo!*

Two earth-shattering events occured in 1905. Firstly, Einstein's Theory of Relativity was published, putting physics into order. Then, more literally, San Fransisco was laid waste by a powerful earthquake, causing a 21ft-wide rift and killing 2,500 people as 497 urban buildings were destroyed.

1907 heralded the birth of Gene Autry. Now, I didn't have that much in common with the 'Singing Cowboy' but he is fondly remembered on large parts of Humberside, or at least his horse 'Ole Faithful' (that's 'Ole' not 'Old', by the way) is. For some reason, it's an animal that supporters of Hull FC have always had a soft spot for.

So, that's my recollection of Britain at the turn of the Millennium, with Rugby League barely out of nappies.

Growing pains

To this point, I suppose I pretty much amounted to Rugby Union with a semi-professional administration and playing staff.

The game bore little resemblance to that of today, with numerous scrums, frequent kicking, either during open play or from a mark, dribbling in a 'kick and rush' tactic and plenty of drop-goals. The forwards did not usually play in a set position.

I reckoned a few rule changes could easily enhance my entertainment value and establish my individual identity.

Given that, as properly employed working men, my players had to be in a fit state to go to work after the weekend's game, in 1906 a rule change introduced a sort of 'mini-scrum', to restart the game after every tackle. This became known as the 'play-the-ball' and was a welcome alternative to the dangerous practice of 'rucking' with the foot at a pile of bodies for the ball on the ground or 'mauling' players with the ball in hand. Dropping the two flankers from the scrum reduced the number of players on a team from the original 15 to a much more appropriate 13. Hey presto, Rugby League!

I guess these two rules were the watershed between the old game under a new regime and the totally separate sport I was to grow into, but a few other changes also happened earlier during the decade.

In season 1901/2 the charge at goal kicks was outlawed (shame, that was rather good fun) and, in 1902, the punt-in from the sideline to restart play went the same way, replaced by the 10-yard scrum.

By 1905, open professionalism prevailed and the shady dealings of the illicit extra payments were consigned to the dustbin - in the Northern Union code at least!

Another distinguishing feature to put a little more daylight between the different codes came in 1906 as the 'ball back' rule was introduced, meaning that a kick for touch had to bounce in the field of play first.

With the rules sorted out a little better how would the competitions fare?

Championship chopping and changing

In my first few years, clubs continued to come and go and the format of the Championship changed, literally, every season.

One of my founders, Tyldesley, left the Lancashire Senior Competition before the 1900-01 season to be replaced by Barrow. Clubs were in two geographically-divided divisions, one Lancashire and one Yorkshire each playing its fellow county clubs home and away. Oldham headed the Lancashire pile with 45 points from their 26 games. The Yorkshire Seniors played 30 games, Bradford coming out on top despite they, Hull and Holbeck and St Helens in the Lancashire competition all being deducted two points for a breach of the professional payment rules.

Like the *Tyrannosaurus Rex* skeleton discovered in 1902, I felt as if I was about to turn into a monster as the leading seven clubs from each county league resigned to form, I suppose, an early 'Super League.' Broughton Rangers won the first season, but again problems as Salford, Runcorn, Bradford and Warrington all had two points deducted for breaching the professional rules, and Swinton and Hunslet, worse still, four points. These rules, as I've just mentioned, changed in 1905.

The league expanded in 1902/3 with the addition of Hull KR, St Helens, Widnes and Wigan and the remainder of the Senior competitions merged to form a second division, which included such luminaries as Birkenhead Wanderers, Lancaster, Morcambe, Normanton and South Shields. Sadly, Leeds Parish Church and Liversedge disappeared. At season's end, Halifax were kings, playing with more fizz than the new imported drink, Pepsi Cola, although Brighouse and St Helens suffered relegation in favour of Keighley and Leeds.

More tinkering in 1903/4 as the first division introduced a Championship play-off with the first winners being Bradford who beat second-placed Salford 5-0. See, having a play-off isn't a new Australian idea, they hadn't even started playing my game in Australia yet! The second division lost Manningham to the round ball and Stockport, after a brief life, dropped out, replaced by Pontefract.

Writing in 1949, J M Jones tells how in about 1903 at the age of 17 he played one of his first games for Bramley at the Barley Mow ground, the opponents being the Lancaster team. Playing scrum-half, Jones could not understand why the backs outside him were having such an ordinary game. The centres either knocked on or threw the ball forward, the fullback kept kicking direct into touch and their powerful winger was repeatedly tackled into touch. "Well", thought the young scrum-half, "I'll have a go myself, I can't do any worse than they are doing." At the next scrum his forwards gave him quick possession and he went clean through for a try under the posts.

Instead of compliments from the rest of his teammates he felt a chilly silence. One of the forwards rounded on the innocent lad calling him a "bloody young fool." It seems the forward, and one or two of the other players had joined a threepenny sweepstake at their works from which the winner would have won 30 or 40 shillings, a princely sum in those days, but it all depended on Lancaster scoring first. The forward had the assistance of all the likely scorers but hadn't thought the 17-year-old scrum-half likely to be one of them.

Still unable to stay on an even keel, 1904/5 saw Oldham win the title, no play-off, but the second division lost Holbeck and South Shields, reducing the structure to 14 teams.

The fairly stable fixture format again fell into confusion the very next year, 1905/06, as the two divisions were lumped together. Lancaster had dropped out, leaving 31 clubs, who played their county colleagues home and away and such inter-county games as they could manage. Accordingly, some teams played many more games than others, (e.g. Morcambe played 26, Oldham 40) with the Championship decided on percentages. Leigh won with 80 per cent, although Oldham, who came fourth with 72.5 per cent, had won five games more!

Sorry to labour the point, but 1906/07 the 31 clubs reduced to 26 as Liverpool City joined, but Brighouse, Castleford, Millom, Morcambe and Normanton all left and Pontefract resigned after eight games. Play-offs reappeared, back in fashion for the top four, Halifax beating Oldham, having finished top with 82 per cent. Poor Liverpool City ended up bottom unable to muster even one win from their 30 matches, conceding 1,398 points and scoring only 76.

Deep breath. Not surprisingly, after their performance the year before, Liverpool City decided that Northern Union wasn't for them and disappeared in 1907/08, but new contenders Merthyr Tydfil and Ebbw Vale joined the throng, boosting the table back up to 27 clubs.

The play-off final went to form with Oldham (and their dizzying 90 per cent record) meeting Hunslet twice, the first a 7-7 draw then a win for Hunslet 12-2. This was a significant effort from Hunslet, as I'll go on to tell you in a minute.

In season 1908/09, the Welsh contingent strengthened to six out of the 31 teams as Aberdare, Barry, Mid-Rhondda and Treherbert joined. Merthyr did the best of the Red Dragon challengers, finishing eighth with 63 per cent but only managed 18 games. Bradford disbanded but soon reappeared with a new surname, one that would serve them well until the end of the century - Northern.

Domestically speaking

If the Championship had been a movable feast at least my Challenge Cup showed a bit more stability.

Headingley staged the final five times, with steady turnouts of between 15,834 in 1906 for Bradford's 5-0 victory over Salford and 32,507 for Halifax's first of two successive cups, this time against Salford again in 1903. Photographs in my album show 29,569 inside Headingley for the 1901 cup final with many perched on the North Stand roof.

If Halifax and Warrington were the cup final specialists of the age, then Salford were the 'nearly men'. In fact, Salford finished beaten finalists four times during the decade. Hull's luck was out as well, suffering defeats by Hunslet, Wakefield and a replayed final against Leeds. Four chances to win the cup in three years, all blown. A losing finalist is never a good thing to be, and seven times during the decade the loser was nilled.

Warrington beat Hull KR 6-0 to lift the 1905 Challenge Cup, the only two tries scored by our friend Jackie Fish. My eye was caught earlier in the competition by Hull KR winger George 'Tich' West who amassed a remarkable record of 11 tries in his 53 points against Brookland Rovers, perhaps a little out of their depth.

Hunslet's All Four Cups 1908

Broughton Rangers entered the history books during an epic campaign of 1901/02 in achieving the first league and cup double, but some lads from south Leeds soon put this feat into the shade.

By the start of the 1907/08 season Hunslet had built up a squad of tremendous talent that not only put fear into the opposition but also gained the respect of their adversaries, a mix of youthful energy, experience, speed, strength and skill. The foundation of the team centred on the forwards, nicknamed the 'Terrible Six', supported by a lightning back division, including Billy Batten, the famous Goldthorpe brothers, Walter and Albert and ably coached by Billy Hannah.

When the season's battle commenced on 7th September with a comfortable home win against Dewsbury few could have foreseen the glory to follow.

The Parksiders travelled north of the River Aire to Headingley on Saturday 21st December 1907 where a crowd of 15,000, giving gate receipts of nearly £400, attended the Yorkshire Cup final game against an injury-ravaged Halifax. An Albert Goldthorpe penalty opened the scoring followed by a drop from Eagers just before the break were the only scores in a tight first half. 'Arh Albert' set one half of the crowd alight in dribbling through to score a try early in the second period but failed to convert, however he made up for this later with a drop-goal. Smith kept the scoreboard ticking over with an unconverted try, Ward nipped in with a drop and, towards the end, a good move saw Batten cross the whitewash to seal a Hunslet 17-0 victory over Halifax and put the Yorkshire Cup on the sideboard.

No cup involved, but the notorious New Zealand All Blacks (or All Golds, depending on whether you got the joke) played a tour match on Boxing Day 1907 and a Parkside crowd of around 20,000 turned out for the spectacle. This proved an exciting game with plenty of good kicking from Albert Goldthorpe and the famous Australian, Dally Messenger, who was guesting for the visitors. The game came to a controversial and dramatic end with a Wilson try levelling the scores. Albert's conversion hit the upright and bounced out, and the final whistle was blown at a draw, Hunslet 11 New Zealand 11. Now, you don't see that every day.

Hunslet arrived for the Challenge Cup final at Fartown, Saturday 25th April 1908 against Hull, having accounted for Leeds, Oldham, Barrow and Broughton Rangers in the earlier rounds. The team fully realised that with the Championship play-off the following week a historic achievement was possible.

They had been fined the substantial sum of £10 for fielding a weakened team, which were beaten 36-0 by Wigan in the previous league game at Central Park. Hunslet had the Indian Sign having won 26 of the 40 meetings between the two teams. Not a great match for the purists but the inclement weather did have a bearing on the playing conditions. Snow had fallen most of the morning and although it had abated by kick-off a further snowstorm arrived in time to welcome the players for the second period.

In spite of this, a crowd of 18,000 braved the weather, contributing over £900 in gate receipts. Eagers gave Hunslet the lead with a drop-goal, an Albert Goldthorpe burst set up Fred Smith who touched down, Albert converted and Hunslet led 7-0 at half-time. In the second half, following a 'mark' by Smith, Albert kicked his second goal to increase the lead. Farrar scored the second Hunslet try following a cross-field kick by Eagers, Albert Goldthorpe converted to take the lead to 14 points and that's how the Challenge Cup final ended, Hunslet 14 Hull 0 and another pot for the trophy room with not a point against in two finals.

Although having gone through a rocky patch losing four away games, including one at Merthyr Tydfil, Hunslet had progressed through the league season very well including a 23-game unbeaten run. By the last game of the season, in which they beat Dewsbury at Crown Flatt, they already had the Yorkshire League trophy in the bag having won 21 games and lost only three (the Yorkshire teams having played each other home and away results produced a 'league within a league'). The final standings in that table gave them a nine-point margin over second-placed Halifax who, in turn, were four clear of Wakefield Trinity. Cup number three.

After the snowstorms of the previous week the weather improved dramatically, as it is inclined to do in God's own county, for the League Championship final showdown against Oldham at Salford on Saturday 2nd May 1908. Oldham had finished top of the Championship table with 28 wins from 32 games, whilst Hunslet had won 25 from 32. Some 14,000 spectators were able to cast off their winter warmers to watch an exciting, although not an open contest, in some glorious early summer sunshine. Albert Goldthorpe scored all the Parksiders points with a try and two goals but it ended at 7-7. The replay followed the following week. If the Huns wanted the 'All Four Cups' title they would have to work darned hard again.

On a beautifully warm and sunny afternoon another crowd of around 14,000 each paid one shilling for the rematch, this time at Belle Vue, Wakefield. Albert Goldthorpe gave Hunslet the lead with a long-range penalty and later in the half he doubled the advantage. Just before the break Walter Goldthorpe scored an opportunist try next to the posts although his brother missed the easy conversion leaving the half-time score at 7-0. Oldham, having missed six kicks in the first half, opened the second-half scoring with a penalty to give them some hope. Hunslet withstood a period of pressure and scored next with a drop-goal from Place. They were never in danger after that and the win was sealed in the final minutes when Walter Goldthorpe went in for his second following a good move involving Batten, Eagers and Smith. Hunslet 12 Oldham 2, four out of four and a new tin of Brasso on the Hun's shopping list.

After this famous victory crowning a unique season the team returned by train to Leeds, where a great reception awaited them. They were driven in a four-in-hand carriage through the city as a brass band preceded them and a huge crowd followed *en route* back to Parkside. As the Hunslet club anthem goes: "We've swept the seas before boys, and so we shall again!"

Pass the Batten

A gifted member of the Hunslet 1908 'All Four Trophies' team, Billy Batten, certainly developed into an interesting character. His most famous party trick involved leaping over opponents like an athlete jumping hurdles, although a rule change eventually led to that tactic being banned for safety reasons.

Batten was a difficult man to bring down due to a 'knees up' style of running. Equally fearsome in defence, he mastered the art of smother tackling the opposition with one fellow player saying it was like "being hit by a ton of coal."

Billy had toured Australia in 1910 whilst at Hunslet, but the Parksiders' pockets weren't deep enough to meet the terms requested by one of the game's early superstars and Billy left Parkside for pastures new, signing for rivals Hull in 1913. A record fee of £600 lured him away, twice the highest previous record, confirming his status as the highest-paid player in the game at a rumoured £14 per match.

Leaving Hull for Wakefield Trinity in May 1924 for £350, still a considerable sum, within two years he had helped Wakefield to two Yorkshire Cup final victories, the last coming 19 years after receiving his first winner's medal with Hunslet.

The door closed on his career with just eight appearances for Castleford before retiring in 1927 at the age of 38.

Despite being an outstanding player, Batten only contributed 10 appearances to Great Britain's cause (only one of these whilst at Hull), mainly due to the intervention of the First World War. Standing his corner didn't help his cause, refusing to play in trial matches to test his fitness after injury, thus ruling him out of the 1914 and 1920 tours to Australia. He reckoned the selectors had ample time to decide if he was good enough. Batten turned out four times for England as well as notching up four appearances for Yorkshire, plus of course taking the honour of captaining both.

Billy's family had Rugby League running though their veins. His nephew, Stanley Smith of Wakefield and Leeds turned out to be a great winger in following Billy's footsteps at Test level, twice touring Australasia. Stanley achieved the rare feat of scoring a hat-trick of tries in an Ashes Test at Sydney in 1932. His sons Eric, Bob and Billy Batten Jr. all played top class football. Eric, in particular, starred for the great Bradford Northern team of the post-war years, scoring 435 tries.

Billy Jr's own son, Ray Batten, continued to keep the family tradition alive well into the 1970s with Leeds, continuing the Batten sporting heritage for both club and country.

First of many

Look as I might, there's no such place as 'Other Nations' on my atlas - although I suspect it's largely in Wales. Nevertheless, the first international Northern Union match was arranged for Tuesday 5th April 1904 between England and Other Nationalities at Wigan. Unfortunately, attention was a little distracted as

Bradford and Broughton were playing in the Northern Union Cup third-round replay (after a second 0-0 draw, a record crowd of 24,233 and receipts of £726 9s 6d), so their players were not available.

After a late start, England took the field with 11 men until Lomas arrived, forgiven when he scored a try, for a 3-3 half-time score. The 12-a-side game (I hadn't quite settled on 13 and was quite happy to experiment) finished 9-3, three tries to the 'Others' and one for my old pal Jackie Fish, the experiment entertaining the 6,000 payers.

Apart from two Scots, the 'Others' were indeed all Welsh, drawn from the Huddersfield, Leeds, Oldham, Salford and Wigan clubs.

The *Yorkshire Post* next day reported: "the game was remarkably open. Taking the hostilities as a whole the Other Nationalities deserved to achieve victory. The fact of only 10 forwards constituting the pack appeared to lessen both the number and duration of the scrummages and tended to provide the players in the rear with an abundance of work." Wise words!

The *Times*, however, found space in it's 'Sporting Intelligence' column for horse racing from Manchester, RU rules football with a fairly hopeless Barbarians side losing again, this time at Devonport Albion and Association Rules football (including Corinthians versus Magyar Athletikai, 9-0, in Hungary.) Also, a long list of foursome scores from such as Felixtowe, Hayling Island and Bromley & Bickley golf clubs, a £75 prize for a 14,000-up billiards match from Leicester Square and a win for England over Scotland at curling...but, guess what, no mention of me!

All Gold

My fame and fortune spread to the other side of the world during these early years of the century and it started like this.

In 1905, the NZRU sent the original All Black team to England. In a hopelessly one-sided tour, they stormed their way through the RFU's depleted teams not yet recovered from the devastating loss of players and clubs to the Northern Union caused by my birth in

1895. Incidentally, I heard that these 'amateur' All Blacks collected a king's ransom of £1,963 as 'expenses'.

The tourists lost only one game out of 32 and scored 830 points for with only 39 against. The former pride of the RFU, their Yorkshire team, was soundly defeated by the All Blacks 0-40, while the neighbouring Lancashire county couldn't raise a team worthy of the name. The north of England had clearly become the Northern Union's domain.

Some of the New Zealand players saw the NU game in the flesh and were impressed by the play and the money it generated for the clubs and star players. One of the party, an Aucklander called George W. Smith, was so taken with what he saw that when the party passed through Sydney on their voyage home in early 1906, he met up with a Sydney entrepreneur, James J. Giltinan, to discuss the opportunities the new game offered.

In the meantime, a young Wellington Post Office worker and rugby player, Albert Henry Baskerville, became aware from a newspaper report of the huge crowds the games in the north of England were attracting and sent an offer to the NU to bring a New Zealand touring party over.

Baskerville's lone interest in the faraway game of Northern Union was attributed to an incident in the Wellington Post Office in 1906. Apparently a fellow employee, known simply as 'Old Harry', suffered a coughing fit and slumped to the floor. After Harry had been treated, Baskerville picked up a copy of the *Manchester Athletic News* that the old boy had been reading and his eye was caught by an article which heralded that 40,000 enthusiasts had paid more than £1,000 to watch a Northern Union game at Bradford.

With memories of the rampant 1905 All Blacks still vivid in England, the NU management were willing to be tempted by the income an international tour might offer to their clubs, although they felt they needed a guarantee as to the calibre of the proposed touring team.

The tour went ahead on the basis that some of the original All Blacks would be included in the touring party. George Smith duly arrived back in New Zealand and after learning of Baskerville's plans, the two teamed up and set about recruiting players. Having become aware of the impending tour, the NZRU promptly applied pressure to any All Black or New Zealand representative player it suspected of involvement. It also banned Baskerville from entry into any of its grounds as the animosity and hysteria increased.

The NZRU even managed to have the New Zealand Government's Agent General in London deliver the following statement to Fleet Street in an effort to undermine the tour's credibility: "Everything is being done to hoodwink the public in England...we may be pursuing a phantom team. There is no news of its sailing from New Zealand. This secrecy may be part of a plan to act as a make-believe to Northern Union supporters."

This, of course, was a sign of what was to come for another 100 years. Not to worry, I've got thick skin and plenty of self-belief, but it was a dirty trick all the same.

By the time this misinformation hit the news stands the 29-man touring party, including Baskerville and Smith, had indeed set sail across the Tasman Sea bound for Sydney. The first stage of their adventure awaited, a three-game series against a rebel New South Wales side organised by Smith's contact, James J. Giltinan.

In Australia, the famous name tagged to the team, 'All Golds', appeared in print for the first time, intended to be a derogatory play on the 'All Blacks', the gold being a reference to their 'mercenary' receipt of money. Their playing strip was no different to any other All Blacks team and later when they toured England the team was known as The Colonials or as the Professional All Blacks, but 'All Golds' had a certain resonance to it.

The Sydney matches, played using Rugby Union rules, were very successful and sowed the seeds for development of the NSWRL Rugby League competition the next year. One of the NSW players was so impressive that he was invited to join the All Golds' party for their onward tour bound for England, Dally Messenger, of whom more in a few moments...

The All Golds arrived via Folkestone at Leeds station accompanied by Northern Union officials and delighted the crowd with an impromptu Haka. Having pitched camp, their tour began at Bramley as 6,000 gathered to see the curious attraction of the leading rugby players from the other side of the globe.

The 6-25 win started a sequence of successes, including that Boxing Day draw at Hunslet, until the wheels came off at Wigan where 30,000 had assembled to see James Leytham score a hat-trick in the 12-8 win.

Despite the faltering performances the All Golds still clinched the series. After a poor display in their 14-6 defeat by England at Leeds (8,182), they had two wins. Firstly, at the second-biggest ground in England, Stamford Bridge, Chelsea, 6-18 (14,000) and then at the Athletic Ground, Cheltenham, by 5-8 (4,013.) One notable point of the Cheltenham game came with the sending off of the New Zealand forward Cross, thought to be the first ever dismissal in an international. Like so many grounds in my history, it's covered in houses now.

All in all, a mixed bag of a tour. The profit stood in the order of £5,500, a worthwhile pot of gold from which the players were paid £150 per man, with the exception of Messenger who received £350.

Whilst not wholly successful on the pitch, having played 35, won 14, lost 19 and drawn two, the 1907/8 New Zealand All Golds did make their mark by being recognised as the team that unleashed the Northern Union game from its English origins.

The arrival of the All Golds in Sydney would trigger Australia's own 'Great Split' and see the birth of Rugby League there. Equally, in New Zealand the All Golds would leave a lasting legacy to the game in that country and in the north of England the tour caused a boom in the membership numbers in many clubs. More importantly, of course, they also gave rise to international competition between Rugby League nations.

I might just have a drink on the strength of that, as I recall that's just what I did at the time!

Aussie Rules!

After the seismic effects of the All Golds' tour to New South Wales, unrest within the Aussie Rugby Union grew as a leading forward, Alec Burdon, broke his shoulder whilst playing. He received no compensation for his loss of earnings or medical bills. The poor bloke had endured pain and financial disadvantage by playing for the ARU yet had to suffer the consequences in silence. That was no way to carry on, so fortified with the knowledge that players in Britain had made the same stand for appropriate payment, 1908 saw an Aussie split of their own.

A new governing body, the New South Wales Northern Union was founded on 8th August 1908 on George Street (now there's a coincidence!), Sydney, with Harry Hoyle, a New South Wales politician, the first president, erstwhile cricketer Victor Trumper the treasurer and James Giltinan the secretary of the new administration.

The eight founder teams were Balmain, Eastern Suburbs, Glebe, Newcastle, Newtown, North Sydney, South Sydney and Western Suburbs.

The 20th April 1908 saw the opening day of the first season of the Sydney Premiership as the first round of league games under Northern Union rules in Australia kicked off in a couple of 'two for the price of one' opening offers. Birchgrove Oval hosted Balmain's beating of Western Suburbs 24-0 and South Sydney's defeat of North Sydney 11-7. Wentworth Park saw Newtown beat Easts 32-16 and Glebe defeat Newcastle 8-5. As if that wasn't enough excitement, a ninth club, Cumberland, from the Parramatta area, formed later that day and joined the competition in time for the second round although at the end of the season they merged with Western Suburbs.

Only 10 rounds were played, followed by semi-finals and a final won by Souths 14-12 in front of a 4,000 crowd.

The play-off system used in the first few years was a little odd. At the end of the normal rounds of fixtures, the top four teams played another round, then the top two teams on the ladder played a final to determine the Premiership. In 1910 it was decided that semi-finals would only be played if they could affect the final result, and in 1912 the system was abolished in favour of a first past the post system, although it was still used in lower grades.

I have to admit, my first season in Aussie was a financial disaster. While still finding its feet, and under enormous media pressure to produce a competition worth the ructions it had caused, the fledgling league had to deal with a shortage of star players, refereeing problems, a lack of exposure in the conservative press and the cost of ground rental. The five captains who had switched codes were publicly ostracised, and many players were faced with the sack at work and barred from entering the Sydney Cricket Ground, then the home of Rugby Union in Australia.

South Sydney finished the first season top of the pile and defeated Eastern Suburbs in the play-off final 14-12...and thus the premier sporting division in the world, some would say, was born.

The first tour 'Up Over!'

At the end of the 1908 season and keen to follow in the footsteps of the All Golds, the Australian team boarded the *RMS Macedonia* and set sail for the arduous two-month journey to Great Britain. An epic 46-game tour awaited them skippered by Dinny Lutge and his vice-captain Dally Messenger, taking their bow on a somewhat unlikely stage at Mid-Rhonda in October for a 6-20 win.

Seeking the widest possible audience, the tourists clocked up some fair mileage, playing at such exotic venues as Aberdare, Birmingham, Ebbw Vale, Everton (twice), Glasgow, Merthyr Tydfil (twice), Newcastle, QPR, Southport, Tonypandy and Treherbert.

Of the five matches played against England, three were accorded Test status. The first of them, on 12th December 1908, staged at QPR's ground at Park Royal in west London, attracted a crowd of only 2,014, with receipts barely reaching £70 in what should have amounted to something more than a side show curiosity.

The *Times* that day had contained the briefest of previews in that: "Northern Union Rules - a match between the Northern Union and the Australian team will be played at Park Royal this afternoon. The game begins at 2.30." Nothing else. As a contest, the match ended a 22-22 draw, with two goals and six tries to the NU, five goals and four tries to the Australians, three of which, the first Test hat-trick, were by Jim Devereux.

As I would learn to live with as my life progressed, my game would be subject to a consistent media treatment in Britain - very little herald and plenty of post mortem. The Monday edition did, however, carry a match report:

> "In arranging to play the first of their Test matches with the professional Australian team on the ground of the QPR club the NU authorities were avowedly activated more by financial considerations than by any expectations of establishing this form of Rugby football in the London district. They anticipated that the match would yield a substantial sum in gate money. In this they were disappointed, for the event did not attract more than 2000 people.
>
> "In a sense this was to be regretted for the quality of football seen deserved a much larger patronage. The play was at times exceedingly fast and the result lay in the balance until almost the last moment of play. The NU had a fine set of forwards, who broke up the scrummage quickly, and by their smart heeling-out tactics provided many opportunities for passing and running by the backs.
>
> "The one deficiency which the forwards exhibited was in staying power, and this nearly cost their side the game after they appeared to have victory easily in their grasp."

Does anything change? Some recognition from the *Times* then, well worth the 3d cover price, and containing a useful advert for the latest novelty, a nickel plated 'Thermos' table jug at 31s 6d (essential for the rugby terraces!) At least the draw at QPR served to keep the powder dry for the next game at Newcastle where England drew first international blood 15-5 in front of 22,000, the biggest crowd of the tour by some 10,000.

Continuing the use of outlying grounds, Birmingham staged the third Test where 9,000 people watched the series clinched by England 6-5 at Villa Park, strangely played on a Monday afternoon. The two other games against England finished with a 14-9 home win at Huddersfield (5,549) and the first Northern Union game to be played in Scotland, a 17-17 Wednesday afternoon draw at Celtic Park, Glasgow. Whilst an exciting game, the Glasgow public only knew one language, soccer, and only 3,000 gave the Northern Union game a chance.

The tour concluded on 8th March 1909 with a 9-14 defeat of a Lancashire select, six months after leaving Australian dry land, with a tour record of won 18, drawn 6 and lost 22. Whilst modestly-attended at some pretty experimental venues, the first Kangaroos were watched by an aggregate of over a quarter of a million spectators. This didn't raise much brass though and the return fares had to be paid by the Northern Union. The tour had been underwritten by James Giltinan who was left ruined and then given the order of the boot by the NSWNU. Victor Trumper also departed.

Whilst it all looked like it was going wrong in Aussie, I'm never far from a change in fortune. The Kangaroos had coincided with a Wallabies tour of Blighty and, back in Sydney, a businessman called James Joynton Smith saw the appeal in a series of games between the two. After some clandestine negotiations and a wedge of cash rumoured to have been about £1,800, the Wallabies were persuaded to switch code *en masse* for payments of between £50 and £200 depending on the star quality of the player. With an average salary of about £2 a day, you can see the appeal.

Four games were played in September 1909 finishing two-all. The aggregate attendance of 41,000 turned a nice profit and with the NSWNU back in pocket and loaded with the best players around, it had the momentum to build the strongest competition in the Rugby League world. The future of the game in Australia was secured.

Don't shoot the Messenger!

Born 1883, died 1959 and, in his pomp in the first decade of the century, amongst my games all-time notables is one Dally Messenger.

Playing for both Australia and New Zealand and both Queesnsland and NSW takes a fairly remarkable chap. Dally was just that.

A top performer in both rugby codes from 1907 to 1913, his part in ensuring Rugby League's popularity with the New South Wales public at the time of their breakaway was profound as his defection virtually assured the Rugby League code kept public popularity there in the early years.

In 1905 and at the age of 22 Messenger joined Eastern Suburbs Rugby Union club. He captained the second-grade team to victory and after a 10-minute rest played in the first-grade final, another victory for Eastern Suburbs.

Dally Messenger's name was made by the time the 1906 'unbeatable' New Zealand All Blacks team arrived in Sydney on their way home from the floggings they had handed out on their tour of Great Britain. At the time of Eastern Suburbs' switch to Rugby League in August 1907, Messenger had played three Rugby Union Tests, all against New Zealand in the 1907 series.

On turning to the professional game, he played three matches for New South Wales against Baskerville's All Golds and then toured England as their guest.

In the first local season of Rugby League in 1908, Dally played three Tests against New Zealand, 2-1 to New Zealand, and toward the end of the year toured with the first Kangaroo team to Great Britain. In all, Messenger played seven Tests, three against New Zealand and four against Great Britain, scoring four tries and kicking 16 goals.

Dally was adept at any sport involving reflexes and a ball, including Australian Rules. English soccer clubs Manchester United and Tottenham Hotspur were reported to have offered him contracts during the All Golds tour in 1907. He was also an accomplished sculler and sailor. Not all unpredictable dazzle and skill, his teammates considered him to be the toughest and fittest man they knew. He could kick equally well with either foot and a story goes that he once took off his boots and kicked a goal from over halfway, barefooted.

An innovator, always prepared to try the unorthodox, on rainy match days he would take to the field and immediately roll on the ground to make himself slippery and more difficult to tackle. Legend has it that one of his tries came after he ran to the opposition fullback, suddenly stopped, calmly handed him the ball and after a moments confusion by all but Dally himself, grabbed the ball back and raced away for a try.

Messenger had the remarkable distinction of having played for Sydney, New South Wales, Queensland, Australia, Newcastle and New Zealand's representative sides in his amazing career.

With Dally at the helm, Eastern Suburbs became the champion side of the Sydney premiership in 1911, 1912 and 1913. Further, Dally's ninth and last season was in 1913 and a knock-out competition towards the end of the season was held to mark his retirement although he made a return in 1917 in a fund-raising match for the war effort.

Dally Messenger's name was considered of such national importance that a stand at Sydney Cricket Ground now bears his name.

A prestigious award in the Aussie domestic game is to this day named after him, the 'Dally M' medal is awarded to the player of the season. Most apt, I think.

Hot toddy!

One of my famous ex-players gets a starring role in every Challenge Cup final...

Long after his departure and final journey beyond this world, the name Lance Todd would remain synonymous with the Challenge Cup final. The Lance Todd Trophy would become a revered and highly-acclaimed prestigious individual award for a man of the match performance. Voted for by the gentlemen of the press corps in the dying embers of the game, Wakefield centre Billy Stott took centre stage in 1946 laying claim as the first recipient.

But what of the man himself? With Todd at centre, the All Golds completed their British tour in February 1908 at Cheltenham and without further delay he put pen to paper in signing for Wigan from New Zealand's Parnell Rugby Union club. Ironically Wigan achieved the distinction of being the first club side to lower the Kiwi colours set before a tightly-packed Central Park crowd. In one incident the bulging weight of the fans caused a retaining fence to collapse, although fortunately no serious injuries occurred.

Wigan paraded Todd to a faithful, midweek support of 20,000, eager for some instant heroics against Oldham on 19th February 1908. Although Lance made an immediate impact by scoring a debut try it wasn't enough to secure a winning bonus. Silverware didn't take long to materialise when, in the following season, he helped Wigan to the Lancashire Cup and League title success over Oldham.

In a personal capacity, he topped the try-scoring charts in 1911/12, crossing the whitewash 21 times. In a Wigan career of 185 appearances his record stood at 126 tries and seven goals. The final curtain-call at Wigan created much furore with the club announcement that Dewsbury had taken over his services on 23rd January 1914. A heated public meeting resulted in a vote of no confidence in the Wigan directors.

During his first outing for Dewsbury a serious injury curtailed any further part on the playing front and, with retirement the only viable option, the seaside beckoned with Blackpool Golf Club offering the job of secretary.

The lure of Rugby League couldn't be resisted, Lance returning to the fold as Salford manager. A great thinker of the sport, he presented a paper in the 1930s to the RFL titled *New Playing Period For Rugby League* in which he advocated a new season that would start on the first weekend in March and run until November. He argued: "Of course we shall hear immediately that summer is the cricket season, but by what divine right was it allocated to cricketers, and why should football be the only sport that gives way to them?"

He also commented: "that terrible period in the depths of winter when the mud is ankle deep and kills all possibility of decent, attractive football being played." Lance pointed out that it cost clubs around £150 per season in straw to protect the pitch in winter thus destroying the grass and incurring more repair costs. Another feather in Lance's cap was his role as the first expert summariser on BBC radio.

The story of Lance Todd at Salford became legendary.

Infamously nicknamed 'the three thousand mugs' at the time, the 1920s were best forgotten by Salford fans. It was a period of survival, on and off the field, the team opened the decade with their worst ever league placing, finishing last in 1920/21. An indication of Salford's struggles came with the reappearance of Jimmy Lomas for eight matches in 1923 whilst approaching his mid-forties. A dramatic change of fortune occurred during the summer of 1928 with Lance Todd taking over the helm as team manager after reading a 'coach/manager wanted' newspaper article. In his first season in charge (1928/29) Lance guided the club from 26th place in the table up to the dizzy height of fourth using virtually the same set of players.

Todd had a remarkable eye for talent and over the next 11 years up to the Second World War, he discovered and nurtured some of what would become of the greatest names in the history of the sport.

His most glittering prize was future Rugby League 'Hall of Fame' inductee Augustus 'Gus' Risman, who signed in the summer of 1929 from the Cardiff Scottish Rugby Union club after trials with Salford reserves. Gus proved the perfect lieutenant for Todd, an inspirational captain who would lead the team by example as they dominated the Rugby League world of the 1930s, the most successful period in the history of the club.

They won the Championship three times (defeated finalists once), Lancashire League Championship five times (second on three occasions), Lancashire Cup four times (runners-up twice) and, when everyone thought it was never meant to happen, the Challenge Cup at Wembley in 1938, returning in 1939. The era was encapsulated through a successful 1934 club tour of France when their hosts proclaimed them *'Les Diables Rouges'* - the Red Devils!

Todd's side seemed capable of going on for many more seasons and bringing further honour to the city when, on 3rd September 1939, the Second World War began resulting in the 1939/40 season being aborted. A wartime Emergency League was organised but, at the beginning of January 1941, Salford decided to cease play, due to poor gate returns, until peace resumed. With no rugby to play Lance became a captain in the Salford Home Guard. In November

1942, the tragic death of Lance Todd occurred when the car in which he was travelling hit an electric tram standard in Oldham.

I'm running ahead with the story here, but such was Lance's influence on the game well into the century. Hats off to Lance.

Empire building

On 6th April 1909, Commander RE Peary of the American Navy conquered the North Pole. Talking of striking out into the unknown, I did some myself. There is no doubt about it, to go from virtually nothing to a professional game with an international presence before I was barely in my teens must say something about my progress.

I started the decade as a Roses county sport in a fairly fragile condition, but by the end I had put down roots with leagues established and clubs throughout areas of England, Wales, Australia and the makings of something in New Zealand. I had even ventured into ambitious international tours and had a few already under my belt. Things were looking up and I had prospects.

I started the decade needing to make myself more distinct and exciting and now I'd got my own rules and a clear identity.

My own man at last, but could I build myself a future?

3

1910-1920
THE GREAT WAR

After a turbulent start, by 1920 I had settled down to what I hoped would be a steady job of an established domestic season with the perk of regular visits overseas.

I had friends abroad, who I could invite home from time to time, and my own star players were celebrities in their own communities. The public was getting used to me now and I was establishing records and astonishing performances that would become legendary in years to come.

Could I stretch out, put on a few pounds and cut the apron strings in earnest?

Whilst the 1910/20 decade was filled to the brim with drama in the sporting arena, I'm sorry to say it was also a time of much conflict at home and worldwide.

A 'tug of war' developed on the industrial front in Britain with working people forced to tighten their purse strings in attempting to accommodate basic daily living. The early decade's civil unrest became just a forerunner to more tragic events as the world erupted into the Great War, a bloody conflict on a scale never seen before. Let me first tell you about the industrial and social climate in Britain at the beginning of the decade.

Strike it hot

Social unrest in the pre-war years of 1914/18 caused deep concern for those in power. In fact, a near-constant state of rebellion bubbled menacingly under the surface of the workforce as events unfolded and many people suffered severe hardship in their quest for a better quality of life.

Women fought tooth and nail for the vote, the Irish took to the streets for independence and, above all, the labour force demanded change, the same pressure for social justice and change that forced the Russian revolution and overthrow of the Tsars in favour of communism in 1917.

Many British workers wanted to go beyond the Labour party's inadequate offerings and indeed their own Trade Union's stance. Strike action seemed the only route to achieve an improved lifestyle and some 1.2 million people struck in 1912 alone, three times the number of people downing tools from the year of my birth to 1909.

Since the last big upturn in worker's struggles from 1888 to 1892 the common man had suffered defeat in a series of conflicts and by 1910 deep-rooted bitterness had taken a firm grip on ordinary people, making that year a watershed. Crippling rent and price rises, coupled with a real fall in wages of 10 per cent between 1910 and 1912 stoked the fires within. The more radical, eager for a bloody-nosed fight, wanted extreme action and with it mobilisation of mass strikes, whilst the leaders of the newly-formed Labour party sought to temper their actions to try and influence the Liberal government.

In 1910, the coal mining industry in Britain suffered two fatal tragedies when 344 pitmen died at Hulton, Lancashire and 136 others at Wellington pit, Whitehaven. The importance of this could not be underestimated.

The mining community of South Wales knew it and set about lighting the blue touch paper of industrial unrest. Over 300,000 miners walked out in protest of conditions and pay, bringing confrontation with the police. Sabotage to the collieries and one miner's death in the square of Tonypandy created headlines. Although the men were forced into retreat by going back to work in August that year the marker had been put down for others to follow.

With the powder keg lit and ready to explode the National Seamen's Union proposed strike action for June 1911 to force their bosses into recognising them. However, the restless seamen of Southampton could not wait and struck six days early. Gaining momentum, the Hull dockers followed suit with 15,000 walking out. An olive branch of an early settlement didn't wear with the angry dockworkers threatening to 'fire' the dockyards.

Like a domino effect it inspired the railway workers in the Mersey area to take action and the solidarity of battle overcame the local sectarian divide as Catholics and Protestants marched in unison. Gunboats sailed up the River Mersey as 3,000 troops and a large police presence moved into Liverpool to quell the uprising. A peaceful demonstration by 80,000 people turned to tragedy on 13th August when two demonstrators paid the ultimate sacrifice of losing their lives.

I could go on to tell you about the student strike, women worker's action and even a strike by cricket ball makers in Kent who, together with a wide cross section of society's hard done by 'took their bats home'. Suffice it to say that the prevailing industrial confrontation was overtaken by events as the Great War broke out, and emphasis moved to northern France.

Other events of my teenage years

Launched with great pomp and ceremony in 1911, *HMS Titanic* met her watery end at 2.20am on 15th April 1912, with an appalling loss of life that stunned the world at large.

Thought 'unsinkable' by a Victorian public prepossessed by the fear of death at sea, *Titanic* hit an iceberg and went down off Halifax, Nova Scotia, on the eastern coast of Canada. Three Halifax ships had the grim task of recovering victims, many of whom were laid to rest in three of the city's cemeteries. The stark reminder is rows of black granite gravestones, each with the fateful date of the disaster inscripted. Whilst an SOS message picked up by the liner *Carpathia* helped save 706 souls, some 1,513 passengers and crew drowned.

Another human tragedy at the racecourse during the 1913 Derby as Miss Emily Davison threw herself under the King's horse as part of the 'Votes for Women' campaign. A protest march the next year resulted in 57 women arrested.

'Discovered' in 1912 by Charles Dawson, a mandible and a small piece of a skull comprising *Eanthropus dawsoni* or 'Piltdown Man' hoaxed the scientific world until 1953 when the jaw-bone was confirmed to be that of an ape with filed down teeth. The 500-year-old skull had been aged to look 500,000 years old. Makes me feel quite young again!

Good old, or not so good old, British summertime first saw the light of day in 1916, whilst in 1917 the one and only cowboy, Buffalo Bill Cody died.

Spanish 'flu swept through Britain and France killing more than 2,000 per week with figures suggesting casualties were claimed at a faster rate by the 'flu than by bullets in the trenches during the Great War.

The atom was split by Rutherford on 3rd January 1919, whilst Alcock and Brown were first to cross the Atlantic non-stop by air. But without doubt the decade was defined by one terrible event brought about on 28th June 1914, the day Archduke Franz Ferdinand, heir to Austro-Hungarian Empire, was assassinated in Sarajevo, the catalyst for the start of the Great War

The Great War 1914-18

War causes suffering, pain, grief and hardship, all of which were encountered on a mass scale during this decade of my story.

Without wishing to glorify events, it is appropriate that this chapter details the Great War years in tribute to those who gave their all for freedom. My life, and indeed sport in general, had to take second billing.

Previously, most wars had been fought by professional soldiers, regular recruits that had signed up for army life, to whom war came as part and parcel of the job. The Great War was different in that ordinary folk received call up papers from their government compelling them to join in a mismanaged, corrupt bloodbath whether they were suited to army life or not.

After the last bullet had been fired and final drop of blood spilt communities felt their fallen war heroes who, subjected to terror, suffering and sheer tragedy had ultimately sacrificed their lives for peace, deserved a lasting tribute. In many pretty rural village greens, industrial town squares and bustling city centres war memorials were built in dedication, lest we forget.

Speaking of dedication and bravery both on the sporting scene and in the front line of battle, I'll tell you a story of one such hero in a moment.

Many good folk connected with my life will have no doubt endured the consequences of the conflict and sometimes followers of my great game are a little slow to recognise our own heroes.

Please let Dave Beales, a Hull supporter, tell the story of one man and his exploits, one man whose name we should all know as a fitting example of the bravery shown by many.

A game fit for heroes

We've all heard tales of the many heroes of The Greatest Game on the field of play but there's certainly been no shortage of Rugby League players that have distinguished themselves in their off-field activities too. The one that springs readily to my mind is 2nd Lt. John Harrison VC MC.

Born the fourth of seven children, to John and Charlotte Harrison on 12th November 1891, the first son to this boilermaker/plater and his wife was also given the name John but was soon called Jack to distinguish him from his father. Life in East Hull in the late 19th century was difficult at best and young Jack soon learned to look after himself, growing up strong, courageous and well able to fight his corner. In 1901, Jack became a pupil at Craven Street School, where he remained until he reached the age of 18, leaving with a Preliminary Certificate in mathematics. It was the usual practice for male children of manual working families to leave school at 12, but John and Charlotte had decided to set aside whatever the family could afford to help develop the talents of their children.

Their sacrifice was rewarded when Jack gained entry on a teacher training course at St John's College, York. Jack's departure coincided with a lock-out in the shipbuilding trade, bringing yet more hardship to the Harrison family. Strife such as this coupled with the death earlier in the year of King Edward VII brought to an end the golden era of Edwardian England.

The principal of St John's College, Revd. Henry Walker, was a strict disciplinarian, believing in regular attendance in chapel as well as hard work in the classroom and on the playing field. Jack thrived in this environment, excelling at football, cricket, tennis, swimming and athletics but it was his prowess on the rugby field that first brought him to the attention of York Northern Union Rugby Football Club. It was during this period that Jack's leadership qualities first surfaced when the college made him captain of rugby football.

In 1912, Jack returned to his native city as a certificated teacher at Lime Street Senior Boys School, at an annual salary of £80. Jack's exploits with York preceded his return and an invitation to join Hull NURFC was accepted, making his debut in the black & white irregular hoops on 5th September 1912.

Between that date and 1916, he played 116 matches, scoring 106 tries and two goals and was selected for the 1914 tour of Australia and New Zealand. In the 1913/14 Challenge Cup final he scored one of Hull's two tries that ensured a 6-0 victory over Wakefield Trinity and in the following season clocked up 52 tries, a club record that stands to this day.

There was another side to Jack Harrison, away from the rugby field, he was a more than competent violinist and pianist and was once described by a female friend as being "a handsome chap who was attractive to women, he knew it and took full advantage of it." On 1st September 1914 Jack married Lillian Ellis at Hull Registry Office. The Great War had already been in progress for one month at this time, although it had little impact on this new family in Hull.

By September 1914 the introduction of 'Pals Battalions' saw men enlisting at the rate of 33,000 per day, although at this time with a new wife and a child on the way, Jack saw no reason to join them. On 15th June 1915, a son, John, was born to Jack and Lillian, although he was known to the family as Jackie to avoid confusion.

The battles across the Channel were taking their toll on officers and men and it was felt necessary to offer immediate entry for officer training to men whose qualifications were deemed appropriate. It goes without saying that Jack's qualifications were more than appropriate and on 4th November 1915 Jack reported for nine months training at Berkhamsted. It was during this training period that two of the bloodiest battles of the campaign were started which, before their end, would see the deaths of over a million men.

On 5th August 1916, Jack Harrison was commissioned as Temporary 2nd Lieutenant and posted to the 11th Battalion of the East Yorkshire Regiment and was posted to active service on September 19th. It is interesting to note that during October 1916, when the Hull Brigade was sent back from the front for rest and recuperation, the 11th Battalion won the Brigade Rugby Tournament.

Life in the trenches was as bad for junior officers as it was for enlisted men. Extremes of heat and cold, bluebottle-infested corpses, putrefying in no-mans-land, where rats and feral cats also fed and infested the trenches, accompanied inadequate rations. Disease was rife, pneumonia, meningitis, dysentery and typhoid took their toll, as did trench foot which was caused through standing in freezing water and could cause toes or even feet to fall off.

Constant barrages from heavy artillery, shrapnel shells, machine guns, trench mortars and flame throwers all combined to ensure a death rate, even in 'quiet' periods of 300 Allied men per day. By the war's end, one man would be killed for every minute it lasted. This is where Jack Harrison learned the trade of a front-line officer.

The 11th and 12th East Yorks re-entered the front line at Arras on 20th February 1917 and at 2.30 am on the 25th, they were ordered to stand to. The attack started at 6.00am and by 7.50 Jack had sent word back that the battalion had taken the German front line. By 9.00 am they were in the German third line, by 9.40 they were ordered to withdraw and for his courage that day, the following appeared in the *London Gazette* on 17th April 1917, under the heading 'Military Cross': "T/2nd Lt John Harrison, East Yorks Regiment. For conspicuous gallantry and devotion to duty. He handled his platoon with great courage and skill, reached his objective under the most trying conditions and captured a prisoner. He set a splendid example throughout."

Preparations for the Spring Offensive were soon underway. On 20th April, the Hull Brigade were moved to Ecurie, north of Arras, to await orders. By this time, the 1,000 or so officers and men of the original Pals Battalions had been reduced to half that amount, their replacements literally came from anywhere. Casualties meant that the original Pals had virtually disappeared.

The area around the village of Oppy was well fortified, the Germans had laid a blanket of barbed wire in front of their lines, machine guns and trench mortars complemented the defences. The line itself was guarded by crack troops from the 1st and 2nd Guards Divisions. The men of the Hull Brigade set out on the night of 2nd May under a clear sky with a full moon, they had to surmount a ridge that left them clearly silhouetted against the night sky. This led to an immediate bombardment of the holding areas behind the British line, no-man's-land and the Brigade's assembly area.

When the British barrage opened up at 3.45am, the Germans responded. The dry weather meant that the area was soon enveloped in thick choking dust. The British barrage was timed to advance 100 yards every four minutes and soon outran the attacking battalions, leaving them exposed to heavy machine gun fire, which decimated the Yorkshire men. Two attacks by 'B' Company were repulsed with heavy losses. Jack Harrison, leading 'B' Company, made another attempt to penetrate the barbed wire defences, only to be pinned down by a machine gun firing from the Southern end of Oppy Wood. Exploding shells rained steel splinters and shrapnel balls to the rear of the Company, while machine guns poured 600 rounds per minute to their front. Desperate measures were required and Jack showed no hesitation in taking them.

Telling his men to keep the machine gun under constant fire, he left the line. Armed only with a pistol and a Mills Bomb, he ran towards the source of the enemy fire. It was now that he needed all his speed and ability to side-step from the rugby field, he dodged and weaved his way from shell-hole to shell-hole until he was close enough to hurl his grenade. Silhouetted by flares, Jack's men saw him fall forward as soon as he had thrown the bomb, the machine gun was silenced.

On 14th June 1917, the *London Gazette* announced that King George V had approved the award of the Victoria Cross to with the following words:

> *"T/2nd Lieutenant John Harrison, MC, 11th (S) Bn. East Yorkshire Regt. Oppy, France, 3rd May 1917 for most conspicuous bravery and self-sacrifice in attack.*
>
> *"Owing to darkness and to smoke from the enemy barrage and from our own and to the fact that our objective was in a dark wood, it was impossible to see when our barrage lifted off the enemy front line. Nevertheless, 2nd Lieut. Harrison led his company against the enemy trench under heavy rifle and machine gun fire but was repulsed. Re-organising his command as best he could in no-man's-land, he again attacked in darkness but with no success. Then turning round, this gallant officer single-handedly made a dash at the enemy machine gun, hoping to knock out the gun and so save the lives of many of his company. His self-sacrifice and absolute disregard of danger was an inspiring example to all. (He is reported missing, believed killed.)"*

By the time the citation appeared, Charlotte was already aware that her husband would not be returning from France.

The story does not end there. The pupils of Lime Street School raised the money to erect a plaque in memory of their former teacher. It remained in place on the school wall until the Luftwaffe bombed the school in 1941. The plaque was rescued from the ruins and is now situated in Hull's Guildhall.

In the early 1920s a fund was established to ensure a suitable education for the young Jackie Harrison. At the age of eight, he attended Hymers College, which led to his attendance at Nottingham Public School, Trent College. Jackie (or John as he was now known) followed his father onto the playing field gaining honours in Rugby Union and cricket. He was selected to play for England against the All-Blacks in 1936 but injury forced him to step down, his position in the team taken up by Prince Alexander Obolensky. John also followed his father into the army, becoming an officer cadet at Sandhurst, gaining a commission in the Duke of Wellington's (West Riding) Regiment.

As war broke out once more in 1939, John was one of the British Expeditionary Force in France. Unfortunately on 1st June 1940, he too was killed in action during the evacuation at Dunkirk. The Harrison line had come to an end and Charlotte had lost both of her men in conflict. Although a block of pensioner's flats, Jack Harrison Court, had been named in Jack's honour in 1986, during 2002, a discussion on the Hull FC internet message board led to the formation of a committee to provide a lasting tribute at the club's new home, the KC Stadium. An appeal was launched not only for a memorial but also a trust to provide an annual award to an individual or group of children that, through The Greatest Game, had shown courage in overcoming adversity.

Donations were received from far and wide, including fans of other clubs, veterans associations and even other sports. The memorial was commissioned in mid-2003 and was unveiled on 15th November 2003, prior to the second Great Britain v Australia Test. Jack Harrison, husband, father, citizen soldier, sportsman, hero. "Greater love hath no man than that a man lay down his life for his friends." (*St John, Chapter 15, V 13.*)

Footnote: •
Although the military top brass doubted the reasoning behind

the Victoria Cross as a way of honouring the 'common' soldier for gallantry of the highest order, thinking it might undermine the team effort in times of conflict, Queen Victoria and Prince Albert introduced the concept in 1854.

The medal itself has been made by Hancock's jewellers since inception and is struck from a Chinese bronze cannon captured during the Crimean War. In fact the jewellers keep several medals in a safe, ready for award, and although worth very little blank, when inscribed one can fetch £30,000 to £200,000 at auction.

Over threequarters of the 1,351 medals awarded to date have been done so by a person who as a sibling had to make sacrifices to bring up their family in difficult circumstances. Although possibly coincidental, duty, dedication and responsibility to others are essential characteristics in achieving the VC.

Chocks away

As well as ground troops, aeroplanes played a large part in the Great War, but not without some humour.

One naval captain had the misfortune to break up five training planes in four days. Not content with this magnificent effort, three judges sought refuge in a hangar and watched through an open door during his test. Unable to take any more stress they quickly gave him a pass and requested he park his machine on the far side of the airfield. In taking on this 'challenge' he broke the underside of the carriage causing havoc probably never seen again. I couldn't visualise the enemy quaking in their flying kits!

Curiously, the top brass banned parachutes during the conflict. The powers that be didn't fancy the idea of pilots abandoning their expensive flying machines, although some airmen had the novel idea of using car inner tubes as makeshift life belts when crossing the Channel.

Unlike their soldier counterparts, pilots were often quite a friendly bunch. Whilst not exactly sending a sympathy card, on a plane being shot down a message would often be dropped to explain what had happened.

After a German submarine sank the ship *Lusitania* off the Irish coast on 7th May 1915 with the loss of 1,201 people including 128 Americans the USA entered the war. Zeppelins began bombing Britain in 1915 and a naval pilot, Reginald Warneford, won a VC for being the first British pilot to shoot one down.

With much changing technology during the campaign, first one side, then the other took advantage. With the advent of aircraft being fitted with machine guns it led to many dogfights and hundreds of planes being downed. Nine British 'aces' alone were responsible for crippling 570 enemy aircraft between them.

For identification, planes were painted in vivid colours of one's country, and maybe their own personal flag. Von Richthofen's Fokker was a vivid scarlet red, making it easy for troops below to identify the 'Red Baron's' large fighter group as it swept overhead.

All this eventually led up to the formation of the RAF, on would you believe it, 1st April 1918. Yet it wasn't all 'plane sailing' afterwards. For many years the services had a ban on personnel participating in Rugby League. 'Sport for all' had not yet arrived.

Time to adjust!

Now in my mid-teens the time came to progress from my earlier unsettled life that had seen much chopping and changing of rules and competitions, and get some more stability on which to build.

In 1911 legislation passed by my games guv'nors decreed that all games should last for 80 minutes and not the lottery of clubs deciding to choose 70 or 80. Another vote winner was the compulsory numbering of shirts, one to thirteen, please note!

To put the icing on the cake, in 1911 King George V accepted an invitation to become my patron, whilst simultaneously the 17th of Earl of Derby, whose home was in St Helens, became my Life President. This indeed was recognition beyond my wildest dreams.

One important issue for the welfare of the players was the dispensing with the services of the Essex and Suffolk Insurance Company, replaced by my very own Northern Rugby Union Mutual Insurance Society.

At the first NU annual general meeting it was announced that season 1910/11 only produced £46 in claims and so meant no serious injuries, a far cry from the previous century when many players suffered broken bones, as well as more tragic events.

Don't pull the wool over our eyes!

Historical events often get clouded by the mists of time, creating doubt in those trying to unravel fact from fiction as the years go by.

Great sports rivalry builds up over the decades both between players and their respective passionate supporters and with it comes controversy. None more so than on the biggest stage in my game, the Ashes, with the debate starting right from the off, as Jim Lomas led my British team over for the first time to play our Australian cousins in 1910.

With the Ashes in Pommy hands after the 1908/9 inaugural series, who actually did win the first-ever series in Australia?

The record books vary, although Great Britain's representatives were having none of this misty business; it amounted to only a two-Test series, but only after a good old wrangle and an attempt to have the Aussie wool pulled over their eyes.

So what was the story? First up, a 42,000 crowd gathered at the Royal Agricultural Society Showground, Sydney, to witness a win for the Brits over Australia 20-27.

In a close-fought game the second match also went the Pom's way 17-22, in front of 18,000 fans at the Brisbane Exhibition Ground.

Here's where the bother starts. Aussie later claimed that that the Brisbane game didn't deserve Test status, and in fact was merely a tour game. This theory was supported to a degree by the facts that the team included seven Queenslanders, players who wouldn't necessarily make the full Test team, and local lad Bill Heidke led the team rather than the usual captain, Dally Messenger.

Three further representative status games were played, firstly against a Combined New South Wales and Queensland team - accepted as a tour 'filler' rather than a Test - and two against 'Australasia', a side that included two New Zealanders in winger

Albert 'Opai' Asher and fullback Riki Papakura.

In the first of the two 'internationals', played at the RAS Showground, the teams fought out a 13-13 draw whilst the second 'international' went Australia's way 32-15 at Wentworth Park, Sydney. There were 50,000 fans at each, so they seemed important at the time!

What actually constituted Test status? Britain insisted that only the first two games against Australian-only players counted as the genuine articles and the series therefore ended 2-0. Australia claimed that the first clash with Australia and the two 'internationals' with Australasia were the Test matches and the series was a tie, one-all plus a draw. Who actually did win the series?

To add some fuel to the fire, Rugby League historian Robert Gate's fine *Rugby League Fact Book* only acknowledges the two Australia games, stating that Great Britain won the series 0-2.

Alternatively, another fine informative tome - originating from down under - *ABC of Rugby League* by Malcolm Andrews gives the results of four games, including the two matches featuring the Kiwi players, designating them as the first and second 'internationals' rather than Tests. Malcolm also notes that Great Britain played under the more correct title of England, as they then did.

Furthermore, the respected British reference book, *Sport International*, took the Australian point of view as late as 1960.

Eventually consensus was reached as Australia fell in line with Britain enabling the match scheduled for the Sydney Football Stadium in 1988 to be promoted as the 100th Ashes Test.

One record that isn't in doubt is the most tries in a Test with Jim Leytham's four against Australia in the second Test, an achievement that still stands to this day.

Dish of the day

With international tours now on the menu, I thought I'd test the public's appetite.

Now I have always been one to speculate to accumulate but the Aussie Tour over here in 1911/12 was a bit of a disaster as we attempted to spread the gospel of Rugby League.

The industrial, coal mining and shipbuilding area of Newcastle upon Tyne seemed to suit my working man's style and St James's Park hosted the first Test, but it wasn't quite to the Geordies' taste, attracting 6,500 as Britain lost 10-19.

Not much cheer in the fair city of Edinburgh for the second encounter at the Heart of Midlothian ground and with it a close-fought match that finished 11-11 before just 6,000 fans. Downhearted, it was down to the West Midlands as Birmingham witnessed the Aussie's taking the spoils 8-33 at Villa Park, again little hunger for Rugby League as, only 4,000 turned out.

Maybe I'm being a little unfair on the British crowds as travel from my heartlands was no doubt difficult and expensive for the less fortunate in those days. For the locals, the Newcastle game was played on a Wednesday and the Villa Park Test on a Monday, New Years Day, so I didn't exactly make it easy for myself. There is also plenty of dispute as regards the popularity of early matches. Malcolm gives the crowd figure for the Edinburgh clash as being 8,000 against Robert's 6,000, which goes to show that compiling a book isn't easy when either a printing, typing or research source error adds to the mist of time. Foggy work indeed!

With trouble brewing on the European mainland, what turned out to be the last Test series before the Great War interrupted events took place in 1914 as Britain went overseas again. With all Test matches played in Sydney good crowds of 40,000, 55,000 and 34,420 witnessed Great Britain winning the series 1-2 with scores of 5-23 to Britain, a reversal of 12-7 and lastly 6-14. The first game was played at the RAS Showground with the second and third fought out at the Sydney Cricket Ground, and therein lays a story...

Rorke's Drift

The third and final Test of 1914 entered Rugby League folklore creating heroes with a backs to the wall performance by Great Britain, forever remembered as the 'Rorke's Drift Test.'

With the first Test played on the last Saturday in June and the second only two days later, the Ashes decider had been scheduled to take place as the Lions passed back through on their return from the New Zealand leg of the tour. Controversially, the Aussie authorities hastily rearranged the game for the following Saturday to capitalise on public interest. Three Tests in eight days! British officials complained bitterly that they had only seven fit players and the schedule amounted to little short of sharp practice, but this fell on deaf ears.

Britain's team manager, Mr J Clifford, was so upset at the way the date of the final game had been advanced without his agreement that he called an impromptu players meeting to explain the reason for the rescheduling and tell them that he expected everyone to play as never before.

His rousing speech makes for stirring stuff. "You are playing a game of football this afternoon, but more than that you are playing for England and more, even, you are playing for right versus wrong. You will win because you have to win. Don't forget that message from home, England expects every man to do his duty." Mr. Clifford was moved by the response, as players clenched their fists in readiness.

To the tune of *Boys of the Bulldog Breed*, Wagstaff proudly marched his troops onto the soft and heavy playing arena but circumstances were to conspire against the British from the off.

With barely a couple of minutes gone Frank Williams twisted his leg resulting in him virtually becoming a passenger on the wing. In a nip and tuck first half the British led 0-9 at the interval but at a cost. The courage that would be needed in a second half of disaster and drama had doubtless not been seen before in Rugby League.

Other British players continued to play on though injury, and did so until the pain took its toll on mind, body and soul. Playing on valiantly having already broken his thumb in the first half but continuing with it tightly-bandaged, immediately the second half started Douglas Clarke smashed his collarbone, following a fall on his shoulder. Twice he continued courageously, strapped ever tighter but unable to take any more he eventually had to be led from the field in tears.

Having injured his leg in the first half, Frank Williams became the next casualty, leaving the field after suffering further damage to the same limb. Britain down to 11 men.

Seemingly now an impossible situation, Billy Hall had to retire with concussion, the Poms now down to 10 against 13 with 30 minutes remaining. Could true British grit hold out in the face of such adversity?

The legendary Huddersfield centre, Harold Wagstaff, magnificently rallied his remaining troops and led a great tackling stint by the 10, including a wonderful try for Britain. Although Australia did score the final try of the match, the British held on and, to cap it all, Billy Hall managed to come back on for the last 10 rearguard minutes and seal an implausible victory.

Years later, whilst reminiscing with Colin Hutton, a Lions coach of a later vintage, our conversation turned to the 'Rorke's Drift' Test match. Lo and behold, Colin let slip that he is a distant relative of Albert 'Chick' Johnson who scored that amazing last try for the Brits. Now, Chick was an expert at dribbling a ball and, boy, was it to come in useful. With 20 minutes to go, Chick received the ball from Harold Wagstaff, put the ball to ground and started to dribble half the length of the field beating the Australian full back Hallet and bearing down on the Aussie line for a virtuoso score. The ball never left Albert's toes, as if tied with a piece of string to his foot.

Coincidentally, Colin and Chick both played for Widnes, with Colin playing 131 games and achieving 17 tries and 167 goals, going on to represent Lancashire. Chick played between 1909 and 1923 and registered three goals and 35 tries in 239 appearances. Also Chick and his dad, Jimmy, also known as Chick, both played in the same Lancashire match.

Footnote:

The original battle and siege of Rorke's Drift as immortalised in the 1964 film Zulu, starring Michael Caine, was enacted on the afternoon of 22nd January 1879 where the British Army suffered one of its most bloody and humiliating defeats. The scene had been set at another British Army camp at Isandhlwana, 100 miles north of Durban in what was then known as Zululand, an independent

Kingdom ruled defiantly by Chief Cetewayo. Zulu warriors had slaughtered 1,700 troops with the battle then moving menacingly towards the camp at Rorke's Drift. British soldiers, splendid in their scarlet tunics, were a glowing target for the less-equipped warriors.

At 3.30pm Private Fred Hitch saw the whites of the enemy eyes. He had been making tea outside Rorke's Drift, a small Swedish village in Natal. Fred hurried to the fort that B Company, 2nd Battalion, the 22nd Regiment had been left to guard. His company commander, Lieutenant Gonville Bromhead asked how many there were and got the reply, "From 4,000 to 6,000, Sir." "Is that all?" he replied in a laconic voice, "we can manage that lot very well." History shows the joker wasn't far wrong. Eighty four soldiers and 36 patients in the hospital were left to face the Zulu troops.

That day bravery of outstanding quality earned 11 Victoria Crosses, the most in any one conflict. Fred Hitch was the only London cabbie to earn the award. A defeat made to look like a victory was an early example of spin-doctoring that even Queen Victoria herself joined in with.

The domestic season

The Championship continued to be a top-four league play-off to determine who met whom in the final and made for some mouthwatering semi-final clashes to whet the appetites of my fans.

One of my favourite sayings in life is, "if at first you don't succeed, then try, try again!" Having lost three consecutive Championship finals Oldham weren't about to call it a day and a new decade gave the club renewed impetus to strive once again for the winner's rostrum. Continuing the chase they achieved the distinction of the first back to back championship winners in the sport. Not to be outdone on the other side of the Pennines, Huddersfield repeated the feat the following two years. Sadly Wigan contested all four finals with no rainbow at the end.

Leeds had mixed fortunes, losing their solitary final appearance to Huddersfield in 1914/15 but clocked up a record score in their 102-0 drubbing of the hapless Coventry in the last league fixture of the 1912/13 campaign, the only game at the

The George Hotel, Huddersfield, pictured in 1895. The Northern Rugby Football Union was born here on 29th August that year, when 21 leading Lancashire and Yorkshire clubs broke away from the Rugby Football Union. (see page 36)

Manningham (Bradford) were crowned the first Northern Union Champions in 1896. (pp39)

The first Challenge Cup Final was played at Headingley, Leeds, on 24th April 1897 between Batley (in white) and St Helens, who looked anything but championship material in shirts of differing style and colour. A crowd of 13,492 watched Batley win the game 10-3. (pp42)

Batley also won the 1901 Challenge Cup Final, again staged at Headingley, on 27th April against Warrington. The game's rules were still evolving - the picture shows a Warrington player about to re-start play with a 'punt-out'. (pp61)

Opposite, Albert Goldthorpe led Hunslet to 'All Four Cups' in 1907/08. (pp61)

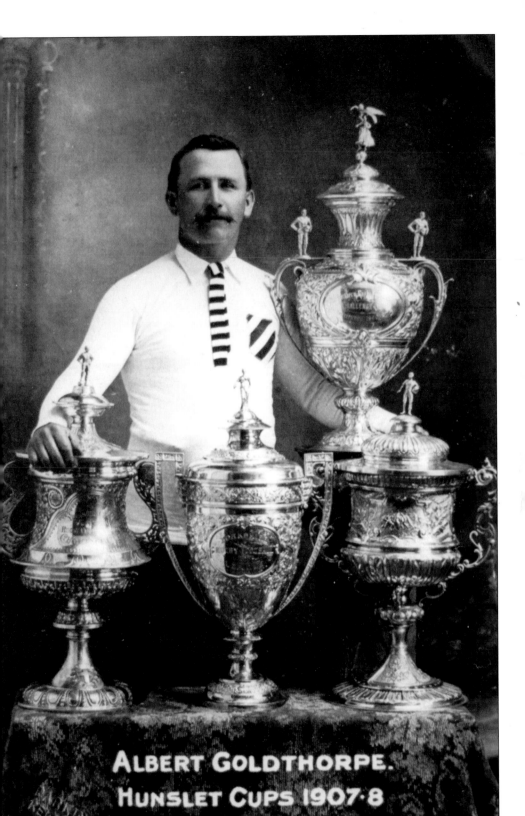

ALBERT GOLDTHORPE.
HUNSLET CUPS 1907·8

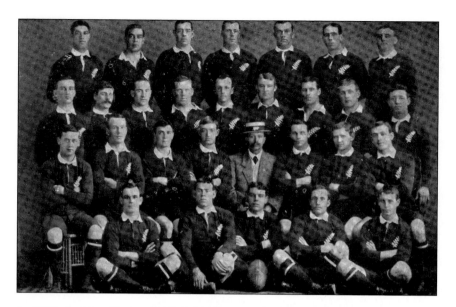

In 1907, the New Zealand 'All Golds' became the first team to tour overseas. Organised by 24 year-old postal worker Albert Henry Baskerville, the team had to prepare and travel in secret to avoid action from the NZRFU. They began their tour in Australia, playing three games before heading to Britain. Baskerville is seated third from left on the front row. (pp66)

Albert Rosenfeld, the son of a Jewish tailor, played for Eastern Suburbs in Sydney. He came to Britain with the 1908 Australian Kangaroos, and never went home. In a remarkable nine-season career with Huddersfield, Rosenfeld scored 388 tries and played in 14 cup finals, winning all but three. In the 1913/14 season, he crossed for 80 tries, a feat never since matched. He finished his career with stints at Wakefield and Bradford Northern. (pp102)

On 8th August 1907, the New South Wales Rugby League was formed by James Joseph Giltinan. In 1908 he took the first Australian touring side on a 46-match visit to Britain. He is pictured here, the suited manager surrounded by his players. On his immediate right is Herbert Henry 'Dally' Messenger, Australia's greatest player of the era. By persuading 'Dally M' to join the new code, Giltinan secured the future of the NSWRL. But the tour was a personal disaster and bankrupted him. Showing no appreciation for the founding father of the game in Australia, he was dumped as NSWRL president on his return. (pp71)

In 1910, the Northern Union sent its first touring team overseas. Captained by Salford's James Lomas, the tour was a huge success with 14 wins from 18 games and a healthy profit of £1,445 (pp91)

Billy Batten played on the wing for Albert Goldthorpe's all-conquering Hunslet team of 1907/08. But it was at Hull where he made his name, joining them in 1912 for a record fee of £600. The highest-paid player of his generation, Batten scored 90 tries in 225 games for Hull before moving to Wakefield (1924) and Castleford (1927). (pp64)

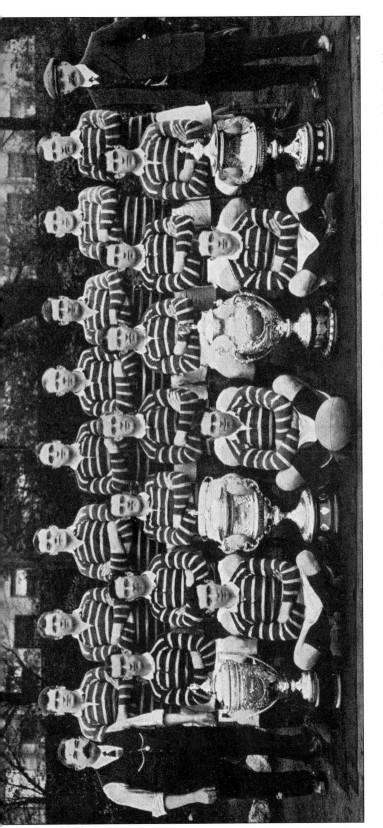

Huddersfield emulated Hunslet's 'All Four Cups' when, in 1914/15, their 'Team of All the Talents' swept all before them. Captained by Harold Wagstaff (middle rows, fifth from left) the cosmopolitan team included three Australians, three New Zealanders and five Welshmen. Albert Rosenfeld is seated in the middle of the front row. (pp103)

Harold Wagstaff became known as the 'Prince of Centres'. He was only 15 when he made his Huddersfield debut in 1906, and by the age of 20 was a seasoned international and captain of his home-town club. In total, he made 494 appearances for Huddersfield, and led them in their clean-sweep season of 1914/15. On the international stage, his greatest moment came when leading Great Britain to victory in the legendary 'Rorke's Drift' Test in Sydney in July 1914. (pp93)

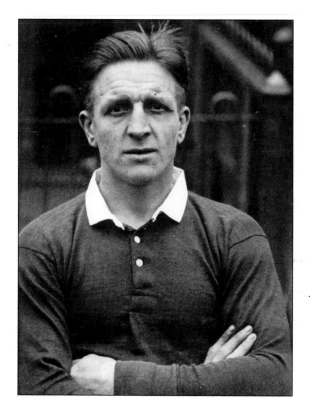

Jonty Parkin signed for Wakefield Trinity in 1913, aged 17. He was the first player to go on three tours down under. twice as captain in 1924 and 1928. One of the most astute scrum-halves in the game's history, he played 342 games for Trinity before paying his own transfer fee to Hull KR in 1930. (pp136)

sport's professional level where every player on a team scored. No less than 24 tries, eight for Fred Webster, proved the end for Coventry and a loose-change collection amongst the sparse 3,000 end of season crowd couldn't save the Midlanders, who gave up the ghost shortly afterwards.

As befits their reputation, Leeds registered four more runners-up spots before finally shaking off the 'bridesmaid' tag in 1961 to claim the prestigious Championship for the first time.

Going to the wire, nothing separated Leeds and Hull in the 1910 Challenge Cup final finishing 7-7. Leeds, however, sprinted away in the replay at Fartown 26-12. A swansong for Broughton the following year with their second, but sadly the club's last, Challenge Cup tie with Wigan once again ending up in the loser's dressing room 4-0, Harris taking the glory with two goals.

In 1912 it was Dewsbury's turn and the next year the biggest turn out of the decade, 22,754, witnessed Huddersfield turning over Warrington in a close-fought affair.

On their fifth attempt, Hull at last claimed the silverware in a 6-0 defeat of Wakefield Trinity in 1914. Perhaps more remarkably, earlier in the competition, the wheels fell off for Swinton Park against Huddersfield who rattled up a 119-2 win. More on the Huddersfield v Saints final of 1915 (the last Challenge Cup final before suspension for the war, in fact the last of the decade) shortly.

During the war years only friendly matches were played, although, with no real league structure in place, there was something resembling a competition as newspapers began compiling merit tables. The extraordinary times also led to an experiment in 1917. Due to a player shortage, with many able-bodied men in the forces, I experimented with 12-a-side.

In October 1914 came a decision that would ruffle a few players' feathers: a decree that clubs would have to cut wages by at least a quarter. This in turn led to the captains of Halifax, Huddersfield, Oldham, Rochdale Hornets and Wigan threatening a strike. After two games were postponed the decision was reversed and, in the end, the clubs were left to negotiate their own wage cuts with players.

However, by the summer of 1916 all players would be unpaid

until the conclusion of the war apart from travelling expenses and tea money.

This temporary resumption of amateur status by Northern Union players led to a number of them turning out alongside RFU players, although, even then the RFU issued a statement that they could only play together in *bona fide* Naval and Military teams.

The rules regarding this war amnesty were stretched to the limit as many challenge matches took place, played to raise valuable money for charities. In fact, 10,000 paying spectators turned out to see an Australian and New Zealand Army Corps side losing narrowly 13-11 to a North of England Military XV at Leeds, which contained Harold Wagstaff and three of his companions at Rorke's Drift.

Unfortunately the 'fair weather' came to an abrupt halt as the RFU gave instructions for matches to be cancelled immediately after Armistice as, quite frankly, they'd had enough of rugby ceasefires. Oh well, good old Rugby League out of one war and back into another!

With hostilities both suspended and resumed Rugby League returned to its routine.

Oldham, Rochdale and Wigan registered two Lancashire Cups each before the war, whilst in 1918/19 Rochdale beat Oldham 22-0 before 18,617 at Salford. East of the Pennines, the mighty Huddersfield took five Yorkshire Cups with one each for Wakefield and Batley.

Three cheers for Huddersfield's Ben Gronow who became the first player to register 300 points in season 1919/20. More on him later.

On with the Kiwis

There is no doubt that the New Zealand Kiwis have added flavour and excitement to my international calendar over the years, although even with the added spectacle of their Haka, they often take second billing behind the Australians.

First, let's set the scene and see what life was like in general, then move on to the early developments of my sport in those beautiful yet volatile islands during the 1910s.

New Zealand had been granted Dominion status in 1907, and had set about building an enlightened society, becoming the first country in the world to grant women the vote, which it did in 1893. From there they went on to support the British suffragette movement and by 1919 Kiwi women could stand for Parliament, just a year after British women were granted the vote.

The New Zealand Army came into being in its modern form by The Defence Act of 1909. British instructors arrived to create the new Territorial Force, raised by compulsory military training and set at 30,000 men. By the outbreak of war on 4th August 1914, New Zealand was able to offer an expeditionary force to the 'mother country' and, until final demobilisation in 1919, New Zealanders served King and Country in Samoa, Egypt, Turkey, Palestine, France, Belgium and Germany. A total of 110,386 men and women from New Zealand saw action in the Great War of which 100,444 of these served overseas, 18,166 paying the ultimate price.

During the period 1910 to 1920, I think the major influences that held sway in New Zealand were firstly the Great War, and secondly the influenza plague of 1918 which killed thousands of New Zealanders. Then began the Great Depression.

Although a predominantly agricultural economy, industrial unrest reigned in New Zealand. The 12th November 1912 became known as 'Black Tuesday' as strike action by the militant Waihi Trade Union at the Waihi Goldmining Company turned to tragedy with the killing of a striker, Fred Evans. Once broken, the following days witnessed many strikers being hunted down by armed mobs with hundreds fleeing the stricken town in what was one of New Zealand's most vicious civil conflicts. Many more years of industrial action followed with Evans becoming a martyr of the labour movement. Each year a commemorative service is held at his grave in Auckland's Waikaraka cemetery.

What of Rugby League in New Zealand? Well, with the game established in Australia and the All Golds having broken the ground for professional rugby, my Kiwi cousins got under way, forming the NZRL on 25th April 1910. In 1911 a four-club competition began in Hawkes Bay. Prior to the Great War, Rugby League spread throughout the entire country from North Island to South Island and attracted players and administrators of the highest calibre, with the game even spreading to minor population centres such as Nelson, Dunedin and Southland.

The game remained predominantly amongst urban Maori and Polynesian peoples, whilst 'traditional' Union remained a largely 'European' man's game. Whilst local competitions existed for club players, those seeking a professional career inevitably headed for Sydney or the north of England.

The domestic seasons 'down under'

The Aussie game continued to thrive and Newtown took the 1910 Premiership, followed by three seasons when Eastern Suburbs ruled the roost.

The Great War did not disrupt the Australian game too badly as Balmain dominated what was then the Sydney club Championship in 1915 to 1917, whilst Souths took the last title in the first year of hostilities, as well as the last.

Leaguies were predominantly working class and one theory published in the French Rugby Union paper *Le Monde du Rugby* suggested that a good number of my players were Catholics of Irish extraction who held no brief for either the Royals or Britain at war. In fact, many NSW based players did sign up to do their duty and with many others being civil servants, having less chance of being called up, or in essential civilian jobs they could also keep my game alive.

A little different across the Tasman, as the Wellington club Championship ground to a halt from 1916 to 1918. However, the equivalent competition in Auckland continued and just a pause in Christchurch.

New Zealand did cancel a tour to Australia because too many of her best players were in Flanders or along the Dardanelles, but trust my Aussie cousins to come up with the idea of a tour to Britain during 1915/16. The gist of the message from NSWRL asked if it was 'convenient.' As I wasn't party to the reply I can only guess that it wasn't very complimentary! I suppose you, the reader, could come up with your own suggestions!

The Anzac Test

Some of you will no doubt have heard of the Anzac Test match that Australia and New Zealand play, but how did it arrive at its name?

On 25th April each year, Australians and Kiwis commemorate Anzac Day, the Australian and New Zealand Army Corps (the ANZACs) and especially their involvement at Gallipoli.

Australia had become an independent nation in 1901 but retained a bond of loyalty to the British motherland. Out of a population of only five million, the Australian government committed 300,000 brave Australian young men to battles looming in western Europe, Turkey and the Middle East. During the Great War the grim toll amounted to over 60,000 dead and 156,000 wounded or taken prisoner.

The infamous Gallipoli campaign took place between 25th April 1915 and 9th January 1916 with the objective to push through the Dardanelles straights with the prized capture of the Turkish capital of Constantinople being the ultimate aim. If the mission had been a success then the Turks, who were allied with the axis powers of Germany and Austria-Hungary, would have been unable to hamstring Britain and France in their war efforts.

With the British and French naval fleets having failed to take the Gallipoli peninsular, the allies decided there was no option but to attack by an amphibious landing of 35,000 men under Lieutenant General Hunter Weston at Cape Helles. A smaller support force consisting of 17,000 Anzacs under General Sir William Birdwood were to land at what became known as the Anzac Cove, a mile north of their intended destination and surrounded by high cliffs. Come nightfall the Anzacs had suffered 2,000 casualties as the enemy repelled them and the force at Cape Helles also struggled under the Turkish attack, losing a third of its men. For two weeks the allies were stuck on the beach under heavy attack. Much of the failure was attributed to poor co-ordination and leadership from the British General Sir Ian Hamilton, who chose to command from on board a ship. Around 25,000 more troops were to follow in August but to no avail. Although more offensives were attempted the campaign finally admitted defeat.

Dysentery and frostbite had taken its toll on the 90,000 allies who were pinned down for 10 months by the Turks. Thousands of young men, including 1,816 Lancashire Fusiliers, one lad aged only 15 years and 10 months, lost their lives or were wounded. The Sandringham Company mysteriously disappeared in action in Gallipoli, dramatised in a moving television documentary, *All The King's Men*, in which David Jason played the lead part of a First World War Commander.

The political aftermath saw Asquith replaced as Prime Minister by David Lloyd George in December 1916.

A sobering thought is that for such a small country in terms of population, a total of 102,000 Australian servicemen died in the defence of freedom in the wars of the 20th century. So now for any readers who didn't know the reason behind the Anzac Test, I hope this has enlightened you.

A talent supreme...

Handsome, try-scorer extraordinaire, hero! All superlatives required to describe Albert Rosenfield.

An Eastern Suburbs threequarter, the Australian selection committee picked him to tour in 1908/09. He wasn't by any means an instant star on these shores, appearing in no more than 15 games out of 45, including one Test match. His five tries didn't exactly set the tour alight but Albert did have the fortune to play against Huddersfield! Impressing the Fartown board as the club had beaten Australia 5-3 they saw enough to offer him a contract the very same evening. To put the icing on the cake he captured the heart of a local lass and settled down to a life amongst the warm, friendly folk of Yorkshire.

Small in stature, at 5ft 5 inches, his height didn't hinder him in becoming a giant of the sport. The local Rugby League folk would warm to his immense sporting talents in becoming a jewel for the club as Albert progressed to become one of the finest wingers my sport has had the privilege to watch.

During a glittering career, he thrice topped the try-scoring charts. Chipping the opposing fullback became a favourite tactic for his army of fans to savour. In nine spellbinding years, his total try tally was an impressive 388. During the 1911/12 campaign he scorched in for 78 touchdowns surpassing this for an all-time record of 80 in 1913/14. Only Warrington's Brian Bevan had a sniff of beating the record in 1952/53 with 72 tries to his credit.

The following season Rosenfield again topped the charts with 56 and in doing so helped his teammates to win 'All Four Cups'. Luckless Wakefield Trinity had wished they had never turned up for one match on Boxing Day 1911, as Rosenfield delivered a knock-out blow, helping himself to eight tries.

A Claret and Gold legend, he graced 14 finals, only suffering setbacks three times, his career also taking him to Wakefield and Bradford.

Albert passed away in his adopted Huddersfield in 1970 at the ripe age of 85, the last survivor of the first Kangaroos.

I take my hat off to one outstanding player.

...in a talented bunch

The Huddersfield team were known as the 'Team of All Talents' and during their 1915 'All Four Cups' season lost only two matches, as crowds flocked to see them play.

But there were other stirrings in my home town...

As early as 1882 the FA had tried to wean the Hudderfield public away from the oval ball by staging an FA Cup semi-final at Fartown. Despite an encouraging crowd of 6,000 the inroads to establishing a professional soccer club in the town of my birth took a little while longer to gain positive momentum.

Playing at Fartown had been the preferred option of the soccer club's founding directors until hitting a sticky wicket in that the Northern Union specifically discouraged ground sharing with football, a shame as a different attitude could have seen more quality stadiums being built in the north of England.

If not Fartown, then the Leeds Road Recreation Fields were an obvious alternative so, in 1907, the Huddersfield Association Football Ground Co. formed with capital of £500 and purchased the site. A pitch was laid and Huddersfield Town AFC launched. No busy clicking turnstiles though, or shelter from the elements with changing facilities at the mercy of a local publican and the remnants of a disused tramcar. Ambitious directors sought to emulate neighbours Bradford Park Avenue and sports ground specialist Archibald Leitch drew up plans for a new ground, submitted in June 1910 in an application to the Football League for full membership. Good sales talk secured the objective and quick building work saw the ground ready for use in September that year.

Unfortunately the pitch, having been re-laid in 1911, deteriorated into a quagmire and crowds of fewer than 7,000 compounded matters to the extent that the Terriers sank, like the pitch, into liquidation in May 1912. Nowadays, the Leeds Road ground is a retail park.

The rugby lads, on the other hand, enjoyed better fortune in assembling a quality side to take all before them. Top signings included All Golds Edgar Wrigley, Bill Trevarthen and Con Byrne complimented by Australians Albert Rosenfield, Pat Walsh and Tommy Gleeson. From down in the Valleys, the club acquired the services of Welshmen Johnny Rogers, Tommy Grey, Jim Davies, Jack Chilcott and top goal-kicker Ben Gronow from Bridgend. Top Cumbrian wrestler Douglas Clark joined the fold having previously twice won the Grasmere Cup in spite of being gassed at Ypres and wounded at Passchendaele. Hunslet's 'Terrible Six' forward Willie Higson came on board, as well as Jack Longstaff from Halifax. Stanley Moorhouse was discovered in a Huddersfield school team to be joined by his great partner Harold Wagstaff from just over the hill at Holmfirth. Although not all playing together in any one side before the Great War, these players formed a solid foundation for plenty of success.

Amongst the silverware to follow pride of place has to go to the team that followed in the footsteps of the great Hunslet side and won the 'All Four Cups'.

The first trophy of the campaign was secured on 28th November 1914 with an emphatic thumping of Hull 31-0 in the

Yorkshire Cup final, which incidentally was the last before the Great War. Every Huddersfield threequarter scored a try, with Wagstaff claiming a brace.

Prior to the Challenge Cup, Huddersfield took both the Yorkshire League and Championship final against Leeds 35-2.

The Talents had only one tight game during the competition, at Leigh in the first round, with a Moorhouse try settling the issue. The cup run afterwards became plain sailing with three convincing wins. The challenges of Widnes, Salford and Wigan melted away like a spring thaw and in overcoming them the Talents registered a total of 89 points with a very mean defence conceding a miserly five points.

A contrast in playing personnel at the final on 1st May 1915. Saints were very much a homespun team, having nine men who were born in the town and two others coming from the outskirts. In contrast, Huddersfield were more cosmopolitan having only one local boy, Stanley Moorhouse, in the Claret and Gold. Controversially, the Saints were in dire financial circumstances and just before the kick-off the players were told no bonus win or lose. Did it have a bearing on the game? The Saints lads may well have been demoralised.

Either way, a score of 37-3 took the cup in style, securing the final piece of the jigsaw of all the available trophies in one season. In doing so John Willie Higson achieved a unique record as the only man to be in two teams to do the clean sweep, having played in the Hunslet side that cleaned up before them. All four trophies were put on display in Rosenfeld's tobacconist shop next to the Empire cinema in John William Street.

The final tally for Huddersfield in an era disrupted by the Great War read three Championships, three Challenge Cups, six Yorkshire Cups and six Yorkshire League titles, stretching into season 1921/22. Indeed, a Team of All Talents.

One of the Talents was the prolific Welsh goal-kicker Ben Gronow. A stone mason by trade, Ben had been the first man to kick-off at the famous Twickenham ground whilst playing Union for Wales. Having switched codes and turned out against the 1911 touring Australians he missed the 1914 tour to Australia through a broken collarbone. Ben went on to gain selection for the 1920 and 1924 tours but soon after this period Ben's career took a mysterious turn.

Ever since the first Kangaroo tour to England there has been a steady exodus of Australian Rugby League players to England, although in the following first 50 years only one player of note left an English club to take up a playing career in Australia - Ben.

In an unprecedented move the rural town of Grenfell, New South Wales announced that they had secured Ben's services as captain-coach. Why on earth would a Rugby League superstar of Test match calibre, indeed one with his own fan club, sign for a modest rural club in the Aussie outback?

Huge financial inducements were offered to coaches at the time, so it appears that upon forming their club around 1924 Grenfell did likewise. Ben's first game for Grenfell was on 30th May 1926 against Caragabal, a long way from Huddersfield or the Valleys.

Another of the Talents, Harold Wagstaff, died very young at the age of 48 and is buried in Holmfirth, where he was born.

What a waste

The conflict of war represents the worst of man's inhumanity to man and the ultimate failing of politicians.

The Great War was a new low-point for civilisation, being fought in terrible, inhumane conditions by young men who were never to experience the good times in life. Remembering those who gave their all is but a small ask of us. The end came in 1918 on the 11th hour, of the 11th day, of the 11th month, the poppy fields of Belgium and northern France providing us with a symbol of remembrance.

Not only did the war create many new boundaries in Europe and beyond, but the boundaries on the home front were gradually changing. From a previous century when certain sections of society had no voice in their own future we had moved on with the advent of women winning the right to vote.

It was a period of political seeds being sown, which was

eventually to lead to more working class participation in government, thus mapping out improvements in basic living standards.

Although fit as a fiddle, in my mid-twenties, my growth had been stunted a bit by the intervention of The Great War. I'd been robbed of many young men and my competitions had been disrupted by the country's greater need as sport generally was put on ice.

Life for me had been a stop-start affair but there were, nevertheless, sporting heroics on the field of play. The Rorke's Drift Test match would go down in sporting folklore, remembered for that 'backs to the wall' effort and Huddersfield's Talents set a new precedent in how to play the game. There was to be a temporary truce between the oval ball sports of the Northern Union and RFU, but not a lasting marriage.

Royal patronage came my way, flattering I suppose, but my roots mean more to me than anything.

All character building, but I feel that I'm ready for big things in my next decade.

My situation, although often mangled by mis-translation, was summed up nicely by the German philosopher Friedrich Nietzche, who stated: "Out of life's school of war, what does not destroy me makes me stronger."

4

1920-1930
THE ROARING TWENTIES

By the age of 25 I offered part-time employment to young men in the north of England, the Queensland and New South Wales states of Australia and both north and south islands of New Zealand.

For my players it was hard work rushing straight from the day job to the ground after a week's slog for another 80 minutes physical punishment, but plenty of people seemed willing to do it and thousands more were happy to pay to watch. A bit of spare brass always came in useful.

Players of great renown were tempted to 'go north' (or sometimes south!) and play for me from all over the British Isles and even from overseas, especially backs. I'm not quite sure why, but backs usually got paid more than forwards did. Maybe they needed a bit extra to purchase their designer footwear, many backs having their boots made specially from soft kangaroo leather, although I suppose they were classed as the 'glamour boys' of the game and expected to score most of the tries.

One or two momentous decisions for the game came during the twenties, not least of which was in 1929 with the massive and radical decision for me to appear at the national stadium of Wembley to play the final of the Challenge Cup.

Bringing the blue riband event to the capital, a new audience and home of the national media was a major leap forward in terms of the profile and dignity of the occasion, according it the national status it has enjoyed since. I believe I carried it off with astounding success, if I say so myself.

As a sport I was in my mid-twenties and fit as a fiddle, but what about those that surrounded me? Let me set the scene of post-war Britain and the view of the world during the 1920s. It's a while back but I think I can pretty much remember.

Cold climate

The post-war recession deepened by 1921 and unemployment reached two million which accounted for some 18 per cent of the workforce, nearly one in five. The working men not long returned from the living hell of trench warfare in Belgium and France hadn't expected this. It wasn't what they had been promised, and it wasn't what they deserved. Women too had served at the front as medics and at home filling in for the jobs left by men who had forsaken hearth and home to fight. The Great War had left a generation prematurely aged, weary and psychologically-scarred.

Elsewhere in Europe, defeated Germany didn't fare too well either and the economic damage the Great War had done, worsened by the heavy financial reparations demanded by their victors, started the hyper-inflation that soon led to the 1923 exchange rate of 7,000 marks to one dollar. Spiralling prices necessitated a wheelbarrow of money on occasions.

Rather than a nation of pen pushers and keyboard tappers like we have today, in 1926 a total of three million men (about one-fifth) of the adult male working population of the whole country) were employed in heavy industries. Dirty, hazardous and hard manual work was what made the country tick, such as mining, rail and transport, docking, printing, the building trades and iron & steel manufacture, and a lot of it happened round Rugby League land.

On 3rd May 1926, the Trades Union Congress called out 1,750,000 workers in a General Strike to force the government to prevent private pit owners cutting the wages and conditions of coal miners further, as they had done earlier in 1925. The Conservative government of the day had made up the shortfall since 1925, but it didn't look like this would happen again. A deal was struck between the head of the coal industry and the TUC behind the back of the miners' union, which included the reversion from a seven-hour to an eight-hour shift. The TUC declared the strike over after nine days, although the miners stayed out until October.

October 1929 felt the shiver of the Wall Street Crash. On the worst of a series of ever more panic stricken days some 13 million shares changed hands in one session, causing the value of the New York Stock Exchange to drop like a stone. Industrial and commercial investments quickly became worth hardly anything, casting a shadow over the economies of the entire developed world.

Fewer new houses got built during the 1920s than any other decade of the century as virtually all economic investment stalled. Better tighten our belts another notch, lads.

Although the early 1920s seemed like a never ending grind, the world kept turning and times were rapidly changing.

Society women who had the time and energy to contemplate such matters felt newly self-assured, having received the right to vote via an Act of Parliament in 1918 forced by the Suffragettes' direct action.

Emancipation of women continued with the 'Flapper'; not a grasscutting attempt at a goal-kick, but a new style of woman, complete with cigarette holder, rouged cheeks, Eton Crop hair do and shorter, more casual clothing, with hemlines closer to the knee than ankle. I say!

Progress in science and technology as well. By 1922 Britain boasted no less than 96 motor car manufacturers, although owning one was far beyond the reach of most. Rolls Royce, Bentley, Sunbeam and Daimler were the famous names then, and have become classics today with the most expensive British car of 1920 being the Leyland Eight, a technically-advanced machine that initially went on sale for £2,500, a king's ransom.

During 1923, the first transatlantic telephone call was made from New York to London - I wasn't at all sure that wireless technology would be of much interest, although people tell me that these mobile phones are now starting to catch on...

In 1926 a Scottish inventor name of John Logie Baird demonstrated his prototype mechanical television and this even more outlandish notion of moving pictures and the newly-formed BBC came together in 1929 with the first television transmission. It wasn't to be the flash in the pan that some thought it would be, many doubting that the quality of entertainment viewed through a thick glass screen in a small wooden box could ever rival the spectacle of live theatre or cinema. In fact the 'box' had a great effect on the development of the Greatest Game and, some would say, saved my bacon in the mid 1990s - or took my soul, depending on how you look at it.

Although 1928 was many years before free public health care had been thought of, some relief came to the sick as Alexander Fleming discovered penicillin that year.

Achievement and exploration saw some notable events. George Carnarvon and Howard Carter found King Tut's tomb in 1922 and opened it two years later to reveal amazing treasures. By 1929 no less than 11 people connected with the opening of the tomb had died. Public opinion was divided, maybe the deaths were a coincidence or, if the rumour was true, had a terrible curse been unleashed?

'Lucky' Charles Lindbergh flew the Atlantic to Paris solo on board his plane *Spirit of St Louis* in 1927. I'm always surprised he didn't run out of fuel. In politics, Gandhi was jailed for stirring up pacifist resistance to the continued British rule of India. Trotsky sought asylum from Russia into Britain on the run from Stalin's Soviet government having lost the power struggle after Lenin's death in 1924. His application was refused by the Labour government Home Secretary of the day, who you'd have thought would have been sympathetic. Maybe he didn't want to set off on the wrong foot with Stalin's new regime. Was it the right decision? Take your pick...

Britain still controlled Palestine and Iraq, quelling uprisings against British imperialism and 1922 saw the ratification of the Irish Free State, dividing the island, starting a civil war and no end of bother ahead.

With the economic problems at home, an uncertain post war panorama in Europe and a disintegrating overseas Empire, Stanley Baldwin had his plate full when elected Prime Minister in 1924.

The first unabridged performance of Gustav Holst's *The Planets* took place on 15th November 1920 in the Queen's Hall. Albert Coates conducted the London Symphony Orchestra and a huge ovation greeted Holst as he was summoned up onto the stage. Many a brass band has recited from that epic since. *I vow to thee my country.*

What else did the common man do to amuse himself when he wasn't at the rugby? Well, a favourite in Hull was the actress Lillian Gish (that's a joke, if you didn't get it - rhyming slang?) in her 1920 film *Way Down East.* Other popular celebrities of the day were Buster Keaton, Mae West and Al Jolson (his *The Jazz Singer* was the first 'talkie' film; one memorable quote of the era came in 1927 by Harry Warner of Warner Brothers who opined: "Who the hell wants to hear actors talk?")

Charlie Chaplin made a series of films including, perhaps the favourite, *Gold Rush.* Later in the decade, Laurel and Hardy rose to popularity and Micky Mouse made his debut in 1928 in a cartoon called *Steamboat Willie.* Now *that* was entertainment! All Americans you'll notice, the comedy and film scene was flooded with American talent at that time, somehow regarded as superior to anything produced in Britain.

At least the public had somewhere nice to watch these wondrous films from, as 'Oscar Deutsch entertains our nation', opening his first Odeon cinema in 1928. Warmth, a comfortable seat and even carpet was quite a luxurious experience, one which proved popular as Odeons quickly sprang up all over the country.

America, as seen in the films, was indeed another world and always a source of intrigue when you rarely got much change of scenery from the factory and a pint of mild at the working men's club. Talking of which, prohibition in the USA had led to some

32,000 illegal drinking den 'speakeasies' in New York alone. The kingpin of the illegal trade in Chicago, Al Capone, had seven of his competitor's men 'rubbed out' in the 1929 St Valentines Day Massacre gunfight. The north of England seemed a dour place in comparison.

Down Under

Compared to today, international tours were much more regular and extensive, ideal for raising public awareness and interest, earning revenue and improving the kudos of the Rugby League player who, it must be said, had been regarded by some with 'superior' morals as having dirty hands by playing for money. Sport should be for pleasure, thought those at Twickenham, and not to be considered work. Fine, unless the rent man is knocking.

Barely 150 years since Captain Cook made footfall at Botany Bay, the decade started with the 1920 tour to Australia and New Zealand led by Harold Wagstaff, which ended in tears for the Poms after a 2-1 series defeat. Two straight wins for the home side 8-4 at Brisbane Exhibition Ground and 21-8 at the Sydney Cricket Ground sealed the Ashes for Aussie.

Britain retrieved the third Test of the tour at the Sydney Royal Agricultural Showground. A further 11 out of 12 wins by the touring party against state and local sides followed (although one heavy 42-6 loss against New South Wales) but the Ashes would remain down under in the care of the Australians for a while.

On to New Zealand, where better fortunes lay ahead for the visitors starting at Domain Cricket Ground, Auckland which hosted a crowd of 34,000 (not bettered in New Zealand until the 1988 Rugby League World Cup final) for a Lions win of 7-31. Lancaster Park, Christchurch, saw a 3-19 Lions result in the only Test to be played at the closely-guarded fortress of Rugby Union as the owners, the Victory Park Board, subsequently denied Rugby League's further use of the ground.

Still, 10,000 or so saw the only Rugby League Test ever played on the ground. With the series decided, the third Test ended 10-11 at the barren, outlying Basin Reserve, Wellington tempting only

4,000 outdoors. A further seven straight wins against regional representative sides followed before the ship set sail for home.

The loss of the Ashes would never do and the British winter of 1921/2 saw an incoming tour by Australia to do battle for the sport's most prestigious title. All started well for the home side with a 6-5 win at Leeds, 31,303 paying a new British gate receipts record of £3,959.

When the Kangaroos squared the series at Hull, the Boulevard's stadium management had taken the opportunity to extend the capacity to accommodate the 21,505 turnout. The decider featured one of the sport's greatest stars, Harold Wagstaff, enjoying his swansong at a snowy Salford sealing a 6-0 result (21,000) and the return of the Ashes to Britain, as God intended.

Keen to help the cause the Aussies took part in a promotional exercise with a game against England at Arsenal FC's Highbury ground. Posts were borrowed from London Scottish RUFC although the soccer goals couldn't be removed as they were sunk in concrete. An Aussie tribal war dance didn't prove enough though as England won 5-4 in front of 12,000, the proceeds of which were donated to the Russian famine relief appeal. A kind heart and generous nature even then, if I might blow my own trumpet for a moment.

Again our intrepid lads set sail for Australia and New Zealand in 1924 for a 27-game 'double-header' tour led by Jonty Parkin who duly became the first player ever to go on three voyages down under and the only captain to have returned home with the Ashes twice. (Actually, that's more than Captain James Cook ever did, he only brought back plants!)

Starting with a bang, Jonty's men scored successive wins in Sydney, by 3-22 (50,005) and again 3-5, both at the Sydney Cricket Ground (33,842), with Aussie winning the dead rubber at the Brisbane Exhibition Ground.

Continuing on to New Zealand during August 1924, this time the Kiwis proved a tougher proposition on their home soil and defeated the Lions in the series two wins to one. The brand new Carlaw Park, Auckland, 16-8 (22,000) and Basin Reserve, Wellington, 13-11 (6,000) games went to the Kiwis. Britain took the only Test ever played at Tahuna Park, Dunedin 18-31, the ground being made available by the Otago RU just a few days beforehand. Some 14,000 locals turned up despite a hastily arranged Rugby Union counter-attraction being staged at nearby Carisbrook.

Now I don't want to dwell on this sort of behaviour or the many and various injustices and discrimination I suffered at the hands of another code. Let's just say that the anti - League climate in New Zealand was just as acrimonious and unpleasant as in England, Wales and, as I'll explain later, France.

Indeed, Selwyn Pearson, as I write, currently chairman of the New Zealand Rugby League, told the story in the *New Zealand Herald* of 4th October 2003 of how he was once offered some inspirational words by his headmaster. "Rugby League," he was told, was "a game played, followed and supported by low-life." To reinforce this message, a teenage Pearson had it caned into him - six of the best instead of the usual four strokes of the cane - for the terrible sin of wagging a school game of Rugby Union to play League.

Escapologist Harry Houdini died from a ruptured appendix on Halloween 1926 and, similarly, there could be no escape for the Kiwis who having made the epic journey from the southern hemisphere were welcomed to British shores in the winter of 1926/7.

A bit of a fraught experience all in all, an emphatic three-nil to Britain and results of 28-20 at Central Park, (Wigan's debut Test) 21-11 at Hull and 32-17 at Leeds in a game almost cancelled due to a threatened strike within the New Zealand party over expenses. The aftermath of the dispute saw seven Kiwis sent home and later given life suspensions. The Yorkshire public had seen enough by then and only 6,000 turned up to see the final game in the whitewash.

Kiwi rugby was evidently not the attraction that the Aussies were. Crowds started at 14,500 at Wigan, and dropped to a disappointing 7,000 at Hull. However, the miners' continuation of the General Strike was still ongoing at that time, having a direct effect on many household budgets around those parts.

Classed as one of the finest, some say the best, loose forward to play for New Zealand. The Auckland champion Bert Avery had been the captain and Kiwi's outstanding player on the troubled tour. He made his international debut in 1919 against the touring Australians and scored tries in two of his 13 Tests. Bert went on to amass 23 tries which stood as a New Zealand record for nearly 30 years.

As the 1928 summer Olympics took place in Amsterdam, the first to feature women competitors, Jonty Parkin's Lions, resplendent in their smart new shirt design of white with a blue and red 'V', set off on the now well-worn path to the Antipodes to defend the Ashes.

The Tests showed the same pattern as the previous expedition in 1924, with Welsh deadeye goalkicker Jim Sullivan's Lions edging the first Test in Brisbane at the Exhibition Ground 12-15 with Dally Messenger making a celebrity appearance at the kick off and a ground record of 39,300 spectators. This match saw the Green and Gold worn for the first time by the Aussie players. A second Test win at Sydney Cricket Ground by 0-8 (44,548) sealed the series but Aussie defended the whitewash by winning the third Test on the return to the Sydney Cricket Ground (37,380.)

On again to New Zealand during August 1928. This time the Kiwis posed a formidable challenge with a surprise win over the Lions at Carlaw Park, Auckland 17-13, popular with the 28,000 turnout. Fighting performances couldn't save the Kiwis going down to the Lions in losses at the Caledonian Cricket Ground, Dunedin 5-13 (12,000) and 5-6 at English Park, Christchurch's soccer ground, with a 21,000 lock-out on hand to watch. Yes indeed, Rugby League was big news in New Zealand at this time.

Aussie, New Zealand and Britain (who, strictly speaking, played under the name of England until the game resumed after the end of World War Two) were still the only three Test status teams. France had yet to join the fold, although teams such as 'Other Nationalities' had been assembled for exhibition matches and both England and Wales had played independently.

Great fun for all, the 1920s ended with Great Britain the dominant force in international Rugby League.

A Chinese market garden

Chicken fried rice, chop suey and Rugby League! I've never explored the Orient to any great extent although, apart from the handful of brave lads playing in Japan these days, I do have one connection. Carlaw Park in New Zealand became the premier ground for Rugby League entertainment in the 1920s having been carved from a piece of land once used as a Chinese market garden.

During the early years, the municipally-owned Victoria Park in the Freeman's Bay area of Auckland stood proud as the main venue for Rugby League in New Zealand, although when a decision by the council big-wigs gave the Auckland League instructions to erect fences to keep the crowds under control the time had come to look for a new home.

The committeemen inspected various locations before coming across the market garden surrounded by thick undergrowth. Once the Great War was over and Mr Ah Chee's lease expired negotiations were completed and the Auckland RL became the new tenant.

Under the stewardship of the Auckland League chairman, James Carlaw, and using mainly volunteer labour, the ground works got under way to reclaim the hillside from a wilderness and allow terraces to be built. The six-acre site allowed for two pitches and the project neared completion by the beginning of 1921. Headquarters were borne from an existing house being moved round the site to be near the turnstiles.

Albeit in a pretty basic state with just perimeter fencing around the pitch the ground opened for business on Saturday 25th June 1921 as City Rovers became the first winners there defeating Maritime 10-8.

Expenditure was £8,000 and a unique fund-raising scheme had been undertaken to raise capital for a new grandstand with subscribers being offered guaranteed rights to ground admission for 21 years.

Although various alterations have taken place as time has gone by, Carlaw Park remains much the same as it did with room for a 30,000 crowd but very little in home comfort. For as long as I can remember it was the only stadium in the country that was foremost a Rugby League venue.

I've got to mention Jonty Parkin's name again here as, on 2nd August 1924, Carlaw staged Jonty's Great Britain team playing their first Test against New Zealand in front of 22,000 spectators. The home country won an historic victory 16-8.

Only a couple of minutes walk from Auckland's main railway station, Carlaw Park proved a convenient location for supporters. Unfortunately, heavy winter rain running down from the surrounding hills often turned the pitch into a gluepot, and sadly the Auckland Warriors elected not to use the ground on gaining entry to the ARL competition in 1995.

Other newer stadia can offer more comfort these days, but don't forget us old 'uns!

Bed of Roses?

As for domestic representative matches, my first two Roses contests of the decade went to the Yorkists, then an 11-11 draw at Hull followed by six in a row for Lancashire. I visited a good variety of venues but crowds of 13,000 at St Helens in 1925 for a Lancashire 26-10 win and 12,000 at Warrington in 1927 were the only five-figure turnouts. Otherwise unspectacular, the other games varied between 4,000 at Rochdale in 1921 for a White Rose 2-5 and 9,000 at Wakefield for a Red Rose 13-18.

Whilst it was an interesting event in an era hungry for representative sport, the Roses matches can't really be said to have enthralled the public.

Results-wise, the House of Lancaster's dominance was no coincidence, as the powerbase of the British game seemed to be on the wet side of the Pennines in the 1920s.

After a five-year absence due to the Great War, I thought it high time for my Challenge Cup to resume in 1920, so I embarked on what turned out to be a bit of a peripatetic wander around the north, mainly Lancashire grounds and trophy rooms. Once Huddersfield had taken the first Challenge Cup of the decade, against Wigan at Leeds (the public, out of the swing of things, struggled to exceed 14,000 at Headingley) a period of Lancashire domination for the rest of the decade followed.

In 1921 Leigh beat Halifax 13-0 at Broughton, a Manchester ground called The Cliff, with which some of my younger readers might not be familiar. I understand a curious outfit called Manchester United later took it over as a training ground. Halifax players were offered a match fee of £10 to win, a far cry from the six shillings a match broken time in place in 1895.

The 1922 Challenge Cup winners were Rochdale Hornets who overcame Hull 10-9 at Leeds with the 34,827 turnout setting the new high water mark for a Rugby League crowd total in Britain.

Only one break in the Lancashire clubs' dominance came during the decade, by the Loiners in 1923 when they defeated Hull 28-3 at Wakefield, a Yorkshire crowd totalling a highly respectable 29,335 inside Belle Vue. Envious eyes must have been looking south though, as Wembley Stadium with its capacity of 127,000 was swamped by an estimated 200,000 Bolton and Spurs fans, King George V and a white horse at the inaugural Wembley FA Cup final.

In 1924 the cup came back west of the Pennines. Rugby League fans in Rochdale still talk about the strangest try ever scored on the Athletic Grounds, the former home of Rochdale Hornets, by A J Van Heerden, the famous South African playing on the wing for Wigan against Oldham. All that is fact, but stories can be exaggerated in the telling, so no one should be surprised to hear that in scoring the try Van Heerden dived between the legs of a horse on which a policeman was seated. Some even say that he jumped over the horse! The plain, unvarnished truth is that he gathered a cross kick from his centre, and in order to reach the try line he had to run around a mounted policeman.

The explanation for the presence of a horse on the pitch is that several mounted police were needed to keep control of the largest crowd ever seen at a game in Rochdale, indeed the biggest crowd at any game since the start of the Northern Union in 1895. There were so many spectators on the popular side that the police allowed many onto the cinder running track that surrounded the pitch, but once on the track the police were unable to control them without the use of six mounted policemen. Twice play had to be held up when spectators encroached onto the field of play, and it was following one of these stoppages that Van Heerden scored his try.

Official figures for the match were 41,831 spectators, receipts of £3,714 (both were records at the time). Oh, and the result. Wigan won easily 21-4.

Earlier in the competition, a Cumbrian junior side, Flimby & Fothergill, had the misfortune to meet Wigan in the first round and were on the wrong end of a then record 116-0 flogging.

For those not inclined towards Rugby League, other entertainment in 1924 included the first crossword being published in the *Times* and the Mah-jong craze.

In 1925, Oldham won themselves 16-3 against Hull KR at Leeds (28,335) and in 1926 Swinton beat Oldham 9-3, again at Rochdale.

On 23rd February 1920, a handful of radio enthusiasts listened hard to their 'cat's whisker' crystal radio sets to hear the first public radio broadcast made in Britain. A faint, ghostly voice drifting from within the Marconi Company's Chelmsford broadcasting station spoke the inaugural words: "The London, Brighton and South Coast Railway trains to Brighton leave London from Victoria Station." Whilst irrefutably true, this pronouncement hardly fired the public imagination and four months later Dame Nellie Melba, the toast of Australian sopranos, made a more appealing broadcast from Chelmsford and the country sat up and listened. The government-funded British Broadcasting Corporation was quick to provide competition and in 1922 the call sign: "This is 2LO calling" crackled out of crystal sets up and down the country as the BBC broadcast to the nation from Savoy Hill. Public broadcasting had arrived.

There was great excitement as the BBC chose the 1927 Challenge Cup final as its first to be broadcast on national radio. Oldham came good on such an auspicious occasion to the tune of 26-7 over Swinton at Wigan (33,448.) In 1928 Swinton got another turn, this time winning 5-3 against Warrington, again at Central Park.

Overall, through the 1920s, with all the Lancashire success, the Challenge Cup was pretty much a redwash. Poor old Humberside, two appearances by Hull and one by Hull KR, all defeats.

Wembley and the Wigan Walk

I've never been worried about trying something new and showing a bit of ambition, so as my Challenge Cup threatened to outgrow many of the traditional Rugby League grounds 'up north' 1929 saw the radical and risky move of taking my final to London. If the biggest stadium in the land was good enough for the Football Association Cup final, then it was good enough for my premier knock-out competition, even if the journey was a formidable one of some 200 miles from the heartlands.

Before the decision to take the game to Wembley no fewer than ten different venues had been used since the first final in 1897. Not everyone was sure about the idea of moving to Wembley, a proposal by Welsh delegate John L. Leake at my annual conference in Llandudno in 1928. The vote came out with 13-10 in favour. Wembley wasn't the only contender though, as Crystal Palace wanted consideration but the twin towers got the nod.

The semi-finals were both fraught affairs with such a unique goal to play for and on 6th April Dewsbury clashed with Castleford at Fartown, Huddersfield and became the first team to win through to a Wembley final with a 9-3 win. An attendance of 25,000 bore receipts of £1,562 to see the spectacle.

On the same afternoon across the Pennines, Wigan played St Helens Recs at Station Road, Swinton, that game attracting 31,000 supporters who paid some £2,209. A reserved stand ticket cost a pretty penny, in fact five shillings 9d.

The game ended as a 7-7 draw forcing a replay four days later, this time at Leigh's old ground, Mather Lane. London Midlands & Scottish railways laid on special trains leaving Wigan at 1.45pm to assist in getting another big crowd of 21,940 to Leigh. Receipts were £1,442 and the Wigan supporters saw their side emerge as the other Wembley finalist by 13-2.

Wigan's captain Jim Sullivan speaking following the semi-final warned: "We are determined to show London that something other than a good joke comes from Wigan. The team I shall take will be the fastest seen in the handling game. May the best team win on the day." Would his fighting talk come good?

Seven months before the game, plans were made for the printing of between 10,000 and 15,000 handbills for distribution to Rugby Union spectators outside Twickenham on the matchdays when England played Wales and Ireland. I wonder if the brave distributors got moved on!

The FA Cup final had been played at Wembley the weekend before and had been all-ticket. This caused confusion with many Rugby League fans thinking the Challenge Cup final would be all ticket as well. Notices in newspapers reassured supporters that they could pay on the day and advised that: "there are 120 turnstiles that can get 120,000 people in one hour and there are 20 acres of parking and congestion is unheard of at Wembley." A brave boast!

Seats were to be priced at 10s 6d, 7s 6d and 5s, whilst tickets for standing were three shillings. Standing tickets sold on the day were two shillings.

Challenge Cup final day, 4th May 1929, dawned with windy and overcast conditions. It's grim down south.

A message was received by Mr. J. Wilson, Secretary of the Rugby Football League, via Lord Stamfordsham on behalf of the King: "I am commanded to convey to the Rugby Football League an expression of the King's best thanks for the loyal message of greetings to its patrons on the occasion of the Cup final in London and wish all present at the match an enjoyable afternoon."

That morning's *Times* previewed the event, dedicating it just over half of one of its sports page's seven columns, thereby affording it comparable status to their review of a drawn friendly cricket match between Worcester and South Africa. I don't know who their sports editor was, but it seemed that after my 34 years of existence the *Times* readership were somewhat in the dark and needed an explanation of what Rugby League actually was - or rather what it wasn't: "The RU game, itself a proud descendent of six or so games evolved by English Public Schools, is widely accepted as the true rugby football. It is essentially a game fit for amateurs and as such its popularity has spread throughout the Empire in the most remarkable manner."

Next followed a *précis* of the "Historic Split" as they entitled it, and the conclusion that Rugby League: "has lived and still lives very considerably upon the rude but manly traditions in sport of Yorkshire and Lancashire themselves." Not exactly news, or indeed relevant to the day's proceedings. This lot established, there then followed a team list for both sides, but nothing else about the match itself. I wonder if the same journalist is still working on the *Times* sports desk today?

The big game was hot news in the north though, and 15 'excursions' from Yorkshire, plus one arranged by the *Leeds Mercury* newspaper, carrying 3,000 supporters favouring Dewsbury arrived at St Pancras. A further 25 "excursions and special trains from 4.00am" arrived at Euston, bearing some 5,000 Wigan supporters. One group emerged carrying a smoked haddock on a six-foot pole, which they paraded round all day, claiming it had been caught at Wigan Pier. Fish and supporters were bedecked in cherry and white.

The distance from home wasn't a problem for one Wigan supporter, a Mr WH Townsend an ex-collier who, rising to the occasion, took to Shank's pony and walked all the way to Wembley resplendent in Wigan's strip. History does not record if he got the bus back though, or whether he needed a new pair of boots! (I think he might have got the idea from Alan Price, a well known Lancashire athlete who as the result of a £25 side-wager, set off from Bolton to run to Wembley Stadium in 40 hours running time to see Bolton Wanderers versus Portsmouth in the FA Cup final. He was forced to give up eight hours from Wembley with a sprained ankle and instep.)

Supporters aligned themselves along county lines, wearing favours of their nearest club regardless of their own local team's colours.

The Dewsbury team was billeted at the Great Central Hotel and Wigan at the First Avenue Hotel. Both teams attended the Whitehall Cenotaph and a wreath prepared by Ernest Ballance, a passionate Dewsbury supporter, was laid.

At the ground, Dewsbury's Wembley team were led out by loose forward Joe Lyman who had been signed from Featherstone Rovers as a junior for 130 golden sovereigns (they only deal in bullion in Featherstone, y' know.) Wigan's captain, Sullivan, had cost the astronomical sum of £750 when transferred as a junior from the Cardiff Rugby Union Club and had quickly become a giant within the game.

Mindful of the national stage the Challenge Cup final was to be played on and the attention it would receive that day, moments before kick-off Fred Kennedy, Chairman of the RL Council, apparently went into the respective dressing rooms and implored both teams "to provide a sportsman-like spectacle."

Dewsbury player Jim Rudd became the first player to claim a try but his effort was disallowed as Wigan duly saw off the Dewsbury challenge by 13-2, Sullivan himself scoring the first points in a Rugby League match at Wembley Stadium, kicking a penalty after only three minutes.

Dewsbury later complained that the request for sporting, open play ran contrary to their usual uncompromising forward-dominated game and the instruction to tone down their physical tactics had cost them the match.

I'd had my grand day out and I think we'd all enjoyed it.

Wembley postscript - read all about it!

Apart from the score the *Yorkshire Evening Post* hadn't managed to get much of a match report back to the presses that evening, but an article enthusing about the carnival atmosphere summed proceedings up with the opinion that "the success of the League's venture is already assured and there seems no reason to doubt that in future years the final will be played at Wembley." How right they were!

Having featured in London for the first time, the national papers could hardly ignore me. To many sports journalists it represented their first contact with the game, some watched with an open mind, some viewed with suspicion.

The following are extracts from the following few days

newspaper reports, some good, some not so good.

The *Times* reported: "Obviously the Rugby League division of their sides into six forwards, two half-backs, four threequarter backs and one fullback represented a further move towards the speeding up of the game, whilst drastic changes to the rules regarding kicking to touch, tackling and scrummage half-back play all tended to work in the same direction. The bringing of a professional cup final to London has been viewed by some as a dark conspiracy against amateurism; actually, of course, the invasion came about because Wembley provided what none of the Rugby League grounds could offer, accommodation for 40,000 and over. Both the Wigan and Dewsbury teams showed one thing that is all too often lacking in Rugby Union play, though the old Welsh sides and the All Blacks were masters of it, this consisted of intensive backing up and an adroit use of the short reverse pass. This 13-a-side rugby indeed looks made for the Harlequins." Does it indeed!

The *Daily Express* kept an open mind. "Rugby Union supporters who had been to the game called it 'rotten', this was sheer prejudice. They conveniently forgot that the first-half play was the fastest seen this season. This professional game is more highly-specialised than the unpaid variety. Only the most definitely biased can apply the word 'rotten' - I thought it was excellent." Well, well, well, and media types today keep trying to tell me that Rah Rah is the 'technical' game!

The *Daily Mail* took a report from an unnamed Rugby Union player. "Many Rugby Union players were watching their first game of Rugby League. They saw what an improvement the absence of a line-out was. WE Crawford would probably have something to say about the touch-kicking rule. The Irish fullback would doubtless be full of admiration for the skill of his professional confreres in kicking as far down the line as possible before the ball bounces and rolls over the line. There is an art to this alone. The tackling was deadly as a rule. It is not a game for girls."

A mixed bag from the *Morning Post* though, from a reporter seemingly watching his first game. "From the Rugby Union point of view there was no flaws to be found with the kicking or tackling. It would not be fair to judge Rugby League on this one game played in unfavourable conditions, a hard and dusty ground and a wind that came in gusts and a light frolicsome ball. But it strikes me strongly as a game for the spectators as well as the players. The play-the-ball rule is farcical to the rugby spirit and I cannot see that anything has been gained with the abolition of the line-out. It will make no converts in the south and the west."

At variance to most of the other national hacks, not so positive from the *Daily Telegraph*. "It was certainly open but as no means fast. There was far too much aimless kicking and the handling except in few instances was clumsy."

In marked contrast to their usual treatment of the game these days, the *Manchester Guardian* seemed happy to stand up for the northern game. "Most Rugby Union players will be grateful to the authorities for showing them the Rugby League cup final, even though it made the average southern club game look rather weak and watery. It showed, however, the possibilities of intense training, hard running, and the closest possible marking. Though the cup final fervour could not quite fill the stadium, there was plenty of enthusiasm for a fast and interesting game...the most astonishing revelations which the game gave to the southerners were the terrific speed at which it was fought out, and the place-kicking of Sullivan for Wigan. Such kicking has rarely been seen in the south, and though Sullivan got the ball over only twice it was always close, and twice hit the post from seemingly impossible angles."

As ever, Rugby League was generally compared to Rugby Union and regarded as a derivative rather than as a sport in its own right. Still, mustn't grumble, at least I'd caught a few eyes and generally impressed Fleet Street.

Wembley Cup Final fallout

Plenty more fallout from the momentous occasion followed and the *Wigan Observer* of 11th May 1929 reported:

"Three enthusiastic followers of Wigan who travelled to

London on Saturday without paying their fare appeared at Willesden (London) Police Court on Monday. All three, Jack Meadows, William Eccleston and James Rigby of Hindley arrived by an L.M.S. football excursion train without tickets. They were wearing clogs. Meadows who pleaded he had a wife and three children said they had left Wigan on the spur of the moment. Eccleston said he had followed Wigan all season and had not missed a match and he didn't want to miss the final. Rigby declared he had never been on a train before and wanted to see what it was like. Each fined 20s or five days."

Some 30,000 Wigan supporters assembled at the L.M.S. railway station to greet Wigan with the cup. Wallgate, Market Place and Standishgate were packed solid and the club's cherry and white colours were liberally displayed.

As promised, the team took the cup to Central Park to display it at the Laing Cup final match between All Blacks and Bickershaw Hornets.

The Mayor, who had arrived back from London the day before, gave the team a civic reception and Harry Lowe the Wigan club chairman thanked all concerned.

When Wigan player Syd Abram arrived by tramcar from Wigan to Hindley he was met by a large crowd who had been waiting up to two hours. As he alighted from the tram he was loudly cheered and carried shoulder high to his home in Liverpool Road.

Further, the Wigan club received messages of congratulations from Thomas Crompton, chairman of Liverpool FC and the Earl of Derby.

On the part of the vanquished, railway fog signals announced the Dewsbury team's arrival. A civic reception was held in the station waiting room and some 10,000 people gathered in Dewsbury Market Place to welcome their men home.

As to the viability of the switch from the north to the capital, I needn't have worried. The *Yorkshire Evening Post* assessed that around 20,000 northerners had made the long journey, many of whom I suspect were unlikely to have ventured that far from home before, out of a total of 41,500. This was as good as the other biggest crowd of the decade, and better than most by some way, and suggests that the other half of the crowd were southerners.

In terms of profile and prestige the move of the final to Wembley was a major leap forward for the game and served to establish a tradition that would endure and grow to a pivotal occasion for families, workmates and teammates alike, the adventure to the Challenge Cup final.

Well done, everybody.

As a postscript to the first Wembley final and the boom years that seemed to lay ahead, over the same weekend a meeting of the RL Council at the Hotel Metropole, London, considered a letter from Brigadier General Critchley, head of the Greyhound Racing Association and President of the White City Stadium company. He proposed the expansion of Rugby League to include a dozen new clubs at centres such as Bristol, Plymouth, London and Cardiff (presumably all based at greyhound stadia.)

In true Rugby League style, a further meeting was arranged...

Champions and challengers

I must admit, my Championship competition lacked a little symmetry during the 1920s as the decade started with 25 clubs, expanded briefly to 29 then reverted back to 28.

The number of fixtures played also varied wildly, for example in 1927/8 Leeds played 42 matches, presumably hungry for revenue, whilst Widnes only played 32. Similarly in 1928/9 Hull KR played 40 fixtures, Broughton Rangers only 30. Although these were the extremes, in no season did every team play the same number of games. It all came out in the wash though, as the top four at the end of the season played off with first versus fourth and second versus third and the final at a neutral venue to find the champion.

The Championship wasn't quite as successful for the Lancashire clubs as the Challenge Cup and Roses matches had been. Hull won the 1920 final over Huddersfield 3-2 and the next year again over their greatest rivals, Hull KR, 16-14, the two having finished top and second of the regular table.

The professional code of rugby was no stranger to money changing hands for players. Harold Buck became the first player to command a £1,000 transfer fee as, in 1921, Hunslet wrung this unprecedented amount out of their old mates, Leeds. By comparison, the Crossley 20/70 sports car, described by *The Motor* as: "One of the best cars ever produced in England," a two-seater guaranteed to be good for 75mph, and the stuff of dreams for a manual worker, started at £845.

The Northern Union changed its name (or 'corporate identity' as we might now say) in 1922 and adopted the new title (or 'rebranded' itself) Rugby League. Just as well really, as Northern Union was a bit parochial and not really appropriate to my Kiwi or Aussie colleagues, who came up with the snappy new moniker. Another governing body had beaten the NU to the 'League' punch though, as in 1920 the League of Nations, the forerunner to today's United Nations Organisation, came into being in Paris.

1922 was also the centenary celebration year of Joshua Tetley's brewery in Leeds, a company that grew to be synonymous with the game. Where would Rugby League have been without years of sponsorship from that institution? A worthwhile association from all parties no doubt, the brewers support being fair exchange for the decades of 'a penny a pint' from the working man. As regards the title, it was Wigan's year in 1922 beating Oldham 13-2, again the top two.

In 1923, at last a trophy for Hull KR, winning the final against Huddersfield 15-5, something for the trophy cabinet at their new ground of Craven Park on Holderness Road. Rovers had moved there only the previous year (and departed from it in 1989 for New Craven Park at Greatfield, once known with no hint of irony as Poorhouse Lane.)

Something of a wild card in 1924, Batley came good from their usual mid-table position to finish second behind Wigan. Then in their one and only Championship title win before or since, the Gallant Youths overturned the cherry and whites in the final 13-7, scuppering Wigan's chance of a league and cup double.

Another top versus second final in 1925 as Hull KR kept their form of recent years to beat emerging giant Swinton, 9-5.

A new face joined the family that year as Castleford stepped up to join my professional ranks. Representing their town at a ground nicknamed the 'Sandy Desert' which is today used by Lock Lane ARLFC, their first game pitched Cas against one of the days premier clubs, St Helens Rec's. Cas found life hard in their debut season and finished bottom of the table with five wins and a draw from their 36 games. That year's title went to Swinton, who topped the Recs 13-8.

Pontypridd also took their bow in the 1926/7 season, winning seven and drawing one from their 32 games to finish 27th out of the 29 clubs involved that year. (Ponty resigned eight games into the next season after a win and seven losses, their records being expunged.) Wigan showed the new arrivals how to do it, finishing top then converting the League Leaders trophy into the Championship by 22-10 over Warrington who reached the final from second.

Breaking off for a moment, I must tell you this story whilst I remember.

Captain Malcolm Campbell was also a man in a hurry in South Wales in 1927, in his new car *Bluebird* which had taken took two years to build at enormous cost, using a 450hp 12-cylinder Napier Lion aero engine. Having recently lost his World Land Speed Record to an American, Campbell rushed to Pendine Sands, desperate to reclaim his title and without waiting for favourable weather or tide conditions set out on the soaking, soft beach. He managed a time through the flying kilometre at 179 mph and was running even faster on his return run when he hit a sharp bump in the sand which knocked his goggles off. Driving one handed at nearly three miles a minute on streaming wet sand, he managed to replace them and regained enough speed to regain the record at an average of 174mph. Wow! My kind of bloke.

An unusual name in the 1927 final, with St Helens Recreationals topping the table over Swinton but missing out on the trophy in the final, 13-8. St Helens Recs' other notable final during their two dozen years of top-flight Rugby League was in 1926 when the town was divided as the Recs met St Helens in the final of the Lancashire Cup. Saints won it 10-2.

By 1926 Featherstone Rovers were a mid-table club on the up, having turned professional earlier that decade joining the league in 1921/2, moving to more appropriate new premises at Post Office Road (the post office itself known locally as 'Klondike') By 1928 they had reached the Championship final. It would have to save for another day though as they lost 11-0 to Swinton, winners for the second year on the bounce and underlining their status as the game's top dogs by completing their Championship and cup double, in fact 'All Four Cups' that year.

My 1928/9 season saw some tentative steps into expansion into Cumbria, as we now know it, with Carlisle City fielding a team. Following a trial match in August 1928 between the 'Probables' and 'Possibles,' a team largely from West Cumberland was selected to represent the fair border English city with its crooked cathedral (well worth a visit). On Wednesday afternoon, 28th April 1928, a conference was held in the County Hotel, Carlisle, between the directors of the Carlisle and Cumberland Greyhound Racing and Sports Ltd and representatives of the Rugby League to discuss the formation of a first-class Rugby League team in the city.

At an extraordinary meeting of the Northern Rugby League which followed the annual meeting in Leeds on Wednesday 16th June, Carlisle were admitted to the membership of the league for 1928-29 season by 20 votes to two with Leeds and Featherstone voting against.

The first match on 25th August attracted 2,000 curious spectators to watch them go down 3-10 at home in Harraby to Wigan Highfield. Mr R Lowry of St Bees was to go into the record books in scoring Carlisle's first ever try. After three more defeats Carlisle had success against Keighley at home before an encouraging crowd of 3,000. Sadly, support for the club had dwindled to 400 for the final home fixture against Warrington and Carlisle's first excursion into Rugby League ended in resignation on Thursday, 8th November 1928 following their tenth and last match (against Rochdale) all but the Keighley fixture having been lost.

Huddersfield ended the season as champions by a single penalty kick over third-placed Leeds.

An unusual feat in 1929 as the mighty boot of Arthur Atkinson kicked an enormous 75-yard penalty for Castleford in beating the Saints 20-10 at Knowsley Rd.

Bradford Northern were either bottom or second-bottom seven times during the decade with Bramley and Keighley also struggling along.

In Australia, founder club Glebe were expelled from the Sydney premiership competition.

The Pride of Lions

If the 1900s belonged to Hunslet in winning 'All Four Cups' and the next decade went Huddersfield's way when they attained the same dizzy heights, so step forward the pride of Swinton in achieving the same record in season 1927/28. If you count the Salford Royal Hospital Cup in the pre-season charity win over Salford then the Lions actually went one better!

This monumental effort built on previous successes. Having just missed out on the Championship title in 1925 as runners-up to Hull KR, gaining the Lancashire League trophy as second prize, the Championship trophy duly arrived in the Swinton cabinet in season 1927, a first for the Lancashire outfit. The Challenge Cup had already landed at the club the previous year after the defeat of Oldham. Three goals by Morris claiming the prize after each side had touched down once.

Further success had come for Swinton in the Lancashire Cup final of 1926, defeating Wigan at Broughton and a runners-up spot in 1923-24 having gone down to St Helens Recs 17-0 (25,656).

Marching into the 1927-28 season expectations were high for the star-studded Swinton team with an all-Welsh half-back pairing of Bryn Evans working the scrum to supply Billo Rees, who had arrived from Glanamman, and quickly established himself as the best number six in Rugby League. To add more Welsh flavour, Bryn's brother, Jack played at centre while on the other flank stood Frank Evans who had forsaken Llanelli. The pack, whilst not quite on a par with Hunslet's 'Terrible Six', were nonetheless a formidable force to be reckoned with.

In an absorbing match against Wigan on 19th November 1927, Swinton advanced along the road to glory by lifting the Lancashire Cup. The Wigan team that day had a truly international feel in containing three New Zealanders and two South Africans as well as the mighty Jim Sullivan. The only scores in the first half were a try for Cracknell converted by Morris. A second-half penalty by Sullivan was not enough as the Swinton forwards earned their corn that day, sweet revenge for the 21-0 drubbing that Wigan had inflicted just three weeks before in the league at Central Park, only their second defeat all season. Although St Helens Recs took a win just a week after the final only three more games were lost during the rest of the season, one at home, to Oldham by 8-9.

As the season drew to a close Swinton pipped St Helens Recs to the Lancashire League by three points to bag trophy number two.

Completing the regular league season Swinton finished top of the Championship table with a 79.16 per cent winning record with Leeds runners-up with 76.19 per cent. Before the Championship could be concluded there was a little matter of a Challenge Cup semi-final against Hull at Huddersfield, with it just going to Swinton 5-3 setting up a battle royale against Warrington in the final showdown.

Nearly there on the 14th April at Central Park, Wigan, as the two teams were to clash in the last pre-Wembley Challenge Cup final. Swinton certainly believed in doing things the hard way as the only first-half score came from a try by their winger Chris Brockbank. Swinton's hearts fluttered in the second period when Warrington's Charlie Seeling scored a try after the Wire scrum-half, Billy Kirk had to leave the pitch accompanied by two priests. Thankfully no divine intervention was needed and cup number three was secured with a late Jack Evans drop-goal. The game attracted a crowd of 33,909, par for the course in the twenties.

Hunslet stood next in line as the Lions of Swinton secured a Championship semi-final win 12-2 in a difficult game, while Leeds suffered in the other semi at the hands of comparative new boys

Featherstone, 15-12, in a nail-biter. Oldham's windswept Watersheddings ground, high in the Pennines, set the stage for the Championship final and Swinton's grand slam aspirations. Swinton duly pulled rank over the newcomers and took the final trophy in the set by a score of 11-0.

With all this success and money flowing in, Swinton were able to abandon their rented ground at Chorley Road and move to larger premises at Station Road. Three players, Billo Rees, Bryn and Jack Evans, then went on the tour with Jonty Parkin in 1928.

I raise a toast to Swinton for their four, or should that be five, cup successes. Truly a golden age for the town.

Jim Sullivan, a true Welsh hero.

Wonder tries and fantastic goal-kicking feats will always catapult a player's name into the headlines. To achieve real star status means maintaining a level of consistency that others can only aspire to. The name of Jim Sullivan ranks as one of the brightest, immortalised as a goal-kicker extraordinaire and player supreme.

Born in Cardiff on 2nd December 1903, by the tender age of 16 Jim had risen to become first choice fullback for the Cardiff Rugby Union First XV. Just 26 days after his 17th birthday he gained representative honours by playing for the Barbarians at Newport. Jim's future as a Rugby Union star burned ever brighter being selected for a Welsh trialist's spot, but little did he realise that his Union career was to set just as quickly as it had risen.

What came next is what fairy tales are made of. On the 18th June 1921 the mighty Wigan RLFC raided South Wales to sign the starlet with a £750 cheque. Some questioned such a princely sum for a player so young, however, the Wigan scouts had no doubt done their homework and it turned out to be the bargain of the century.

Jim's first game for the cherry and whites took place on the 27th August 1921 with his final match against Batley on the 23rd February 1946. Jim's kicking game became legendary, finishing top of the goal charts on no less than 16 occasions, a feat which even by itself would place him as an all-time great.

Not content with place-kicking, he was also a dab hand at punting the ball with his trusty boot, his drop-kicks reaching prodigious distances. In a Wigan club record of 774 club appearances, Jim registered a massive total of 2,317 goals and 83 tries accumulating 4,883 points. In all his 928 first-class matches his totals read 2,687 goals and 96 tries amounting to 6,022 points. The amazing consistency of Jim Sullivan is demonstrated in the statistic of achieving 100 or more goals per season each year from 1921 to 1939 inclusive.

Flimby & Fothergill became goal-kicking cannon fodder as Sullivan set a record of 22 goals in that 116-0 Challenge Cup match, although no doubt the icing on Jim's cake would be as the inspirational captain of the Wigan team that took the first Wembley Challenge Cup final. He went on to play in 17 finals, including a guest appearance for Dewsbury in a Yorkshire Cup final in 1944.

A record 26 appearances for Wales, 25 games for Britain, three for England and six for Other Nationalities were to underline a truly great feat for a fine ambassador. Jim toured with the Lions in 1924, 1928 and 1932 and declined a fourth in 1936, which would have been a record.

Jim went on to become the Wigan coach leading them to success between 1946 and 1952 before travelling over Billinge Hill to take the Saints to their first Challenge Cup win in 1956 and two Championships in 1953 and 1959. A truly inspiring man whose Hall of Fame inclusion was to become a mere formality.

The village of fame

A stranger passing through the small pit village in West Yorkshire, once home to a thriving and close mining community in days gone by, would probably be oblivious to Sharlston's own 'Hall of Fame'!

Life used to be tough and uncompromising as the good folk focused their energies on hewing coal from the many seams winding their way under the surrounding countryside. Close-knit, the villagers would be proud of their efforts to help keep the economy ticking over. Honed on a hard life at work, villagers would offer no quarter on the rugby pitch with aspirations that one of their own could one day make it to the top. So if the passing stranger just happened to speak to any local Rugby League fan the chatter would no doubt come round to the fact that the village had borne not one, but two jewels in the Rugby League crown in Jonty Parkin 1913/32 and Neil Fox 1956/79.

The name 'Back o' t' Wall' would also possibly not register with the stranger but it is most certain that this famous pitch gave Parkin his early matchday experience with the possibility of representing North Featherstone. Yet it was Belle Vue, home to Wakefield Trinity, that witnessed these two greats keeping the Trinity faithful spellbound.

In 1913, as a 17-year-old, Jonty put pen to paper and set in motion an illustrious career, although unfortunately the Great War temporarily interrupted his progress. On resumption, just like a Yorkshire whippet, Jonty was out of the traps making up for lost time. Jonty graced the playing arenas down under on three tours, very few players matching that since. Alongside another famous player, Harold Wagstaff, he led from the front in captaining two British touring sides from start to finish, an achievement no other player has equalled. No one else has brought the Ashes home twice. Jonty played 17 times for Great Britain suffering just three defeats. Seventeen caps were won playing for Yorkshire, whilst representing England a dozen times. In a 342-game career with the Dreadnoughts Jonty clocked up 91 goals and 88 tries.

The little wiry half-back was no slouch when it came to exchanging opinions with the referee and in doing so no doubt turned a few results. A very loyal servant for his chosen club, testimony to that fact is his seeing out no fewer than 21 playing partners.

Although Jonty reached the very pinnacle at Test level, his 17-year club playing career only produced one piece of silverware, the Yorkshire Cup final 9-8 success against Batley in 1924 with 25,546 watching Parkin score the only Trinity try and kicking a goal.

At the age of 34 and nearing the end as a professional Rugby League player, in a transaction that led to a change in the by-laws forbidding players from doing the same again, Jonty extended his career by paying his own £100 transfer fee after Hull KR explained that they could not afford him.

In a long career of 828 games at centre threequarter for Wakefield, Bradford, Hull KR, York, Bramley and Huddersfield between 1956/79, 'Hall of Famer' Neil was part of the famous Fox dynasty, with brothers Don and Peter and father Tommy, all having top-notch playing and coaching pedigrees. Don hit the heights in the 1960s, and I'll save his story until then.

If our stranger were to pass by Sharlston and have a moment to stop and chat, just mention me and explain why Sharlston has it's own 'Hall of Fame.'

End of the era

Well, let's sum up the 1920s. Britain, in common with the rest of western Europe, hadn't got over the Great War so well and times were pretty hard for most. Although Britain, and especially northern England, was a grim industrial place for people who lived there, their introspective view of the world was changing fast. With entertainment technology being invented, no doubt soon to be in mass production, I wonder how this will effect live sport?

Having got to the end of my 35th year, an age at which most would think about retiring their weary bones from the rigours of Rugby League, for the game itself I considered myself pretty chipper and still felt I had a spring in my youthful step.

All told, although difficult times economically, I think the 1920s were times of growth for the game. We tried a few new faces, some more successful than others, but I've never been frightened to experiment a bit.

I thought that the move of the Challenge Cup final would stand the competition in good stead for a few years although I did think a bit of a reorganisation in my fixture list was due to neaten things up a bit.

I was ready for my next decade and the new challenges that that brought, so let's see what state we are all in then.

5

1930-1939
HAVES & HAVE NOTS

Still a bleak time for most, I recall that the 1930s were a decade when more people than not were skint and had other things than Rugby League on their mind.

Many areas of the country were still recovering from the hardships and loss of menfolk from the Great War and the sneeze of the 1929 Wall Street Crash that had crossed the Atlantic and caused Britain's economy to catch double pneumonia.

In my mid-thirties, I was in my prime and looking to spread my wings, but it seems that all around me wasn't prospering as well as I'd hoped. In fact, most of the country and its people were in a terrible state.

Social conditioning

Today pundits of the game reflect on the 'good old days' of bumper crowds and massive public awareness but I can tell you this rose-tinted perception wasn't necessarily borne out by the facts of the 1930s, and certainly not as I remember them. The phenomena of my having 80/90,000 cup final crowds only became the norm in the sports starved post-World War Two era. The reality at the beginning of the 1930s was different. Even with the novelty of a day out in London, the Wembley cup final could only attract a turnout of 36,544, a fraction of its capacity and a crowd that whilst encouraging to the expansionists would be considered a disaster today. The typical cup final figure hovered around the 40,000 level until the end of the decade. Only then did crowds swell to the order of 50,000, with the best being the last final before the war (55,453), still hardly a triumph in today's terms.

Although travel to the capital was just beyond reach for some, my early cup rounds did prove popular and ground records were set at a cup semi at Wakefield (37,676) and at Hull against Leeds (28,798), both in 1936 and at Salford against Warrington (26,470) in 1937.

A time of 'haves and have nots', the 1930s were a divisive decade. Without much in the way of a welfare state other than charitable organisations to lend a hand to those down on their luck, the rich and poor knew where they respectively stood. With little opportunity to aspire, where you were on the ladder of fortune was where you were stuck.

The Great Depression continued through the 1930s with unemployment peaking at three million in 1932. In Trafalgar Square, 100,000 demonstrators were forcibly dispersed by mounted police at one of the many hunger marches promoted by Wal Hannington in his role of leader of the National Unemployed Movement.

The decade progressed with no improvement, little governmental assistance and real deprivation, a state of affairs captured on canvas so eloquently during this decade by the Salford artist LS Lowry.

Born of desperation and with the closure of the local shipyard being the final straw, 200 men marched the 300-odd miles from Jarrow to London in an attempt to open the blind eye that was being turned to the poverty in the 'grim north'. The Jarrow Marchers as they became known arrived on 1st November 1936.

Whilst the working man was no stranger to the perils of

bronchitis, emphysema and pneumonia, a particularly severe influenza epidemic in the winter of 1932/33 claimed around a quarter of a million lives in Britain alone. That's about the whole population of the city of Kingston upon Hull today. No NHS then, of course.

Mass entertainment came at a matinee at the flicks with a few hours of escape courtesy of *Flash Gordon, King Kong* or a glimpse of the silver screen stars of the day such as Joan Crawford, Katherine Hepburn and Fred and Ginger. You'll never see 'em up our street, unless they're on at the Odeon.

But this was a decade of the starkest of contrasts. Whilst some children had no shoes for their feet, for those with a full wallet and a new set of spats the *art deco* style was *en vogue*. This applied aspirational themes such as stylised ocean liners, cars and skyscrapers in chrome, glass, mirrors and polished black finishes to architecture, furniture and design. Think Agatha Christie's *Poirot*.

High society aspired to the thrusting progress and glamour defined by the American way and transatlantic luxury travel abounded for those not worried about the cost. The keel for the White Star liner *Queen Mary* was laid in Clydebank in 1931 but work was halted due to a national shortage of finance and the general depression and work only recommenced in 1934. The nine storey floating palace came into service in 1936 to plough a luxurious furrow across the Atlantic alongside her French counterpart, *Normandie*.

For those who preferred the novelty and increased speed of air travel the flying boat or the airship was a stylish alternative. Complete with aluminium piano in its cocktail lounge the *Hindenburg* sedately and quietly purred across the Atlantic at between 1,500 and 4,000 feet, faster than any liner, until tragedy struck on 6th May 1936. As it came in to moor at Lakehurst, New York, the airship burst into flames leaving 35 souls to perish in the inferno.

Manchester Airport opened as Ringway in 1938 handling 7,600 passengers in its first 14 months. These days about 20 million travellers pass through each year, including one or two touring parties over the years.

The public had never had more opportunity to travel and passenger train speeds of around 90mph were not uncommon. As a show of strength by London North Eastern Railway on 3rd July 1938, the steam record was set with the steamlined A4 class Mallard pulling a six-car set and a dynamometer car totalling 240 tons managing 126 mph.

By now most towns had tarmac surfaced roads to accommodate the increase in motor cars. Motoring became popular in 1930s for middle and upper classes with a typical small family saloon car in 1935, such as the Austin 10 or Morris Minor costing £175 to £200.

The *Halifax Courier and Guardian* reported in 1935 that Louis Sutcliffe of Bradshaw, near Brighouse, achieved the dubious distinction of becoming the first person in the Halifax borough to be summoned under newly introduced driving regulations. A nationwide 30mph speed limit had come into force in built-up areas and police cars with gongs would halt the offenders.

Sutcliffe was seen driving his motorcycle combination towards King Cross at speeds of up to 40mph. It was discovered that his machine contained no speedometer and although he denied the charge, he was found guilty and fined £1. He told the magistrates he could not afford a speedometer as it would cost as much as the cycle was worth.

For the well-to-do outdoor types, a 17-day winter sports trip to Norway was available via the travel adverts in the *Times* for £17, and a selection of liners offered scheduled sailings to Cape Town, Freemantle, Pepeete, New York and other friendly destinations, as jumbo jets do today. In entertainment, the Charleston dance craze gave way to the jitterbug, Bing Crosby crooned for all he was worth, offering a taste of American cool for those lucky enough to have a Bakelite radio set with its valves glowing away in the corner of the room. By 1939 there were nine million radio licences in Britain. Radio licences? Well, the BBC needed to raise revenue and hardly anyone had a telly yet.

Most towns also had their own gas works providing a source of heat and lighting for many. Interestingly enough there was a floodlit RL match around this time that did indeed use gas-lit floodlights with the ball being whitewashed.

With the National Grid completed by 1933 and domestic electricity becoming more widespread, entertainment began to assume more glamorous proportions, especially for the well to do. Television sets started to become commercially available, but only one channel. The BBC started broadcasting in 1936, although the signal from Alexandra Palace petered out after Bedfordshire. Not to worry as the world, it seemed, stopped at the edge of the Home Counties.

The growing middle classes opted to live in the new suburbs that began to appear on the outskirts of towns. These new commuters in professional occupations could secure a mortgage and buy their own houses, often for less than the working classes paid in rent. Semi-detached houses with gardens became popular, distinct from the terraced working class homes with their back yards.

A typical three bedroomed house in the 1930s cost between £400 to £500 and could be secured with a £5 deposit and weekly payments of 60p to 70p. A well established five bedroomed mansion in Hampstead could be yours for £2,500 or thereabouts.

Sanitation improved dramatically in towns in the 1930s. By that time, all towns had a mains water supply and improved drainage systems. Life expectancy was up by 15 years compared to 1918 and the 54-hour working week was down to 48 hours by 1939.

Only around the 1930s tea ceased to be a luxury and became more easily available. What a change for the good old cuppa to be a staple rather than a treat. Many households of the past used to lock the tea up.

A little bit of luxury for womenfolk as a new synthetic material, nylon, was invented in 1935. Not so enlightened everywhere though as, even as late as the thirties and even forties, many women had to give up children born out of wedlock with many even going to institutions from where mothers had to fight years later for the right to be reunited.

"It was the best of times, it was the worst of times", as Charles Dickens once wrote. For most, it was mainly the worst.

International affairs

As Amy Johnson, a Hull lass, flew solo from England to Australia in 1933, coming the other way that year were the Kangaroos who met with an equally warm welcome but substantially less success, suffering a 3-0 series defeat.

During the thirties, the Ashes were draped in a Union Jack and the international aspect of the game provided an exotic highlight to the everyday grind that the game's traditionally working class fanbase craved.

Britain already held the Ashes following the 1929/30 home series. The first Test on a long tour was on 5th October 1929 at Hull KR, the only Test ever staged there. An 8-31 thrashing dispensed by Aussie was the precursor to three close games. The British pulled their bootstraps up at Leeds (9-3), the only ever Test 0-0 draw at Swinton before a then-record British Test crowd of 34,707 and an unprecedented fourth and deciding Test at a brimming Rochdale Athletic Grounds (3-0). Only 15 points in four hours play, crikey, those lads could defend! The tour finished with a game between Aussie and Wales at dear old Wembley, perhaps a strange choice being so far from the Valleys, but 16,000 thought it worth a look at the tourists, who saw the trip off with a 10-26 win on the 18th January.

A rough time for sportsmanship elsewhere as during the 1932 Aussie summer an international incident began to brew. Cricket was to be rocked by accusations of ungentlemanly conduct on the 'bodyline' tour. Douglas Jardine, the 'gentleman' England captain, preferred to refer to the dangerous bowling tactics of his 'player' teammates as 'leg theory', but the fact remained that bowling as if to injure the batsman's upper body and head was not in the spirit of sport.

Sporting and diplomatic relations were strained to the point that questions of sovereignty were raised in the respective parliaments.

Under Jim Sullivan's captaincy the Lions followed the cricketers out to Australia on their 1932 tour, intent on defending their version of the Ashes. The first Test on 6th June saw the first of two wins at the Sydney Cricket Ground, 6-8, in front of the biggest crowd yet at a Rugby League game of 70,204, a Test record to this day. Evidently times were better in the land of plenty than the mother country. Aussie got their revenge at the Gabba cricket ground in the 'Battle of Brisbane' (15-6.) A roughhouse game if ever there was one, Aussie were reduced to 10 men at one stage - don't forget there were no substitutes in those days. The Lions then finished on a 13-18 high note clinching the series, with another good showing of 50,053 Sydneysiders in.

On to New Zealand and two wins in Auckland at Carlaw Park (9-24 and 18-20) and one at Monica Park, Christchurch (14-25) - with estimates of 25,000 and 6,500 at the Auckland games and 5,000 at Christchurch - underlined the Lions' superiority throughout the game. Heady days!

A three-month winter tour by the Kangaroos in 1933 saw a British whitewash starting at a sell-out 34,000 Belle Vue speedway stadium in Manchester where two Jim Sullivan goals secured a 4-0 win. Another squeaker with a 7-5 win at Leeds and the British put the tin hat on it with a 19-16 victory at Swinton. Crowds were slightly down on the previous visit with only 10,990 for the 'dead rubber' on a foggy day at Swinton and a series aggregate of 74,608 whilst respectable was not much different from current levels.

The 1936 Lions again travelled to the southern hemisphere in defence of their Ashes and unblemished record in New Zealand. The tourists didn't disappoint those awaiting the telegraphed news reports and newsreel footage which arrived back in Blighty weeks later via one of those liners I was just telling you about.

Although they started with a 24-8 loss at the Sydney Cricket Ground with 63,920 on, the Poms retained their status as top dogs with two 7-12 wins, the first at Brisbane Cricket Ground (29,486) then another on their return to Sydney (53,564.) Aussie chances went the same way as the last thylacine, or Tasmanian Tiger, which died in Hobart Zoo that year. The trip then relayed on to Carlaw Park, Auckland with two wins for Britain 8-10 (25,000) then 11-23, the 17,000 locals seemingly anticipating the inevitable, with the other six regional games having gone to the tourists convincingly.

The decade closed with a third incoming tour by the Aussies in

1937. Britain edged home 5-4 at Headingley (31,949), winning more comfortably at Station Road, Swinton 13-3 (31,724) and ending with anti-climax at Fartown, Huddersfield 3-13, the 9,093 present having seen enough. Harry Sunderland then took his party across the Channel where, with his captain, Wally Prigg, they broke some new ground.

Great Britain had held the Ashes throughout the thirties and had been unbeaten in New Zealand. Matches were closer, although remember it was still only three points for a try.

There was no incoming tour from the Kiwis during the decade although a new nation, France, was only just beginning to emerge as a new member of the Rugby League playing family.

Bon Chance!

Whilst Rugby Union was well established in France, that game was conducted on a blatantly 'shamateur' basis and was fraught with player and spectator violence. Charges of illegal payments and the threat of expulsion from the international Rugby Union community saw some of the black sheep clubs and players of the French RU send a delegation to discuss their options with my British RFL administration.

Seizing the opportunity to generate interest in France, an exhibition game between the 1933 Kangaroos and England was organised by the Aussie tour manager and visionary, Harry Sunderland, and played at a frozen Stade Pershing in Paris on New Years Eve. A big turnout and a 63-13 win for Aussie showed there was scope for progress.

March 1934 saw the French make their first tour of England as an excluded Rugby Union international, Jean Galia, persuaded a group of 16 French Union players to convert to the 'rebel' code and organised a short pathfinding tour to Britain. Jean was an exceptional athlete, boxer and cyclist and centre with Toulouse and Villeneuve, and his rebel team played games at Wigan, Leeds, Hull, Warrington, Salford and at London's White City stadium.

Galia is regarded by many as the founding father of the French game and is honoured in Perpignan with a road, Rue Jean Galia, in his name. Jean's bravery and commitment in the face of opposition from those in France who would see him fail should not be underestimated, Jean is a real Rugby League legend.

Later that year, the *Federation Francaise de Jeu a Trieze* was formed and staged its first international against England in Paris with England winning 21-32.

On the strength of this progress, more new clubs joined my family as September 1934 saw the formal kick off of the French professional league, with its 10 founder clubs Albi, Sport Olympique de Beziers, Bordeaux, Xlll Catalan, Cote Basque Xlll, Lyons, Celtic de Paris, Pau, Roanne and Villeneuve.

The French game started to blossom at club level and although the 'Chanticleers' were not accorded Test status until 1957, there were a number of international matches against England and Wales forming an early European Championship centred at the magnificently appointed (and named) Stade Buffalo Velodrome.

Pressure exerted by, shall we say, 'others' caused many of my young clubs to struggle for somewhere to play as local authorities in such as Perpignan, Albi and even Paris were lent on to have *rugby a treize* excluded from municipal stadia, as they tend to be in France.

Despite these dirty tactics the game continued to thrive and make good ground. A statistic detailed in Trevor Delaney's comprehensive *International Grounds of Rugby League* reminds me that such was the pendulum's swing in French rugby power by 1939 the French Rugby Union had lost 313 of its 784 clubs and my *rugby a treize* organisation had already accumulated some 220 member clubs. Fabulous progress, but as we will later see, not for long as fate intervened.

The Vichy puppet government, established to administrate southern France after the Nazi invasion of Paris and the north, abolished Rugby League by decree, and confiscated its assets, which I might add still have not been returned. One of these days I'll get back what is rightfully ours and damn the politicians and vested interests that shelter the apologists and collaborators who robbed me.

I'll leave it to you to investigate the details of this sorry episode of man's inhumanity to man, a story which Mike Rylance's epic *The Forbidden Game* tells in all its bloodboiling detail.

Back in Blighty

While I prospered internationally, far from the glamour competition many recall it to have been, my Roses matches of the 1930s can't really claim to have sparked the public imagination.

Overall the decade saw five wins to Lancashire and three to Yorkshire, the only five-figure crowd of the decade (10,049) was drawn to Warrington in 1931 to see Lancashire beat Yorkshire 11-8. Low crowds of 2,000 at Oldham (1933), 4,300 and 3,652 both at Rochdale (1930 and 1938) typified the era, where hand to mouth survival was foremost in the working man's mind and live entertainment a luxury out of the reach of many. If people had to pick and choose their games, they didn't seem to favour the Roses match.

Sir Arthur Conan Doyle died in 1930, too early to have his creation, Sherlock Holmes, investigate the rum goings on in the Headingley Roses Mystery. Strangely, two matches were abandoned due to adverse weather, both as draws and both at Headingley. The 1935 contest was stopped at 5-5 due to fog, with only 1,500 inside, and the 1938 game was halted at 10-10 due to torrential rain, again with only 3,000 on hand. Just think of the pies left unsold!

The Roses didn't smell too sweet during the thirties, in fact no more so than they had done in the twenties.

Cups and comps

As a contrast to the Challenge Cup final domination of the nineties and more recent years by a handful of the same old teams, during the 1930s the Challenge Cup final saw a pageant of many and various clubs. The likes of York, Swinton, Hunslet, Keighley and Barrow all featured as 13 different clubs contested the 10 finals.

Widnes were Wembley regulars with two visits to the royal box, beating St Helens 10-3 in 1930 (36,544) and Keighley 18-5 in

1937 (47,699) but suffering a loss to Hunslet 11-5 in 1934 (41,280) on the Parksider's 50th anniversary.

The blue and white Halifax ribbons were tied on the cup twice. The Thrum Hallers rained on York's big day, their only ever Wembley appearance, 22-8 in 1931 (40,368) and thumped Salford 20-3 in 1939 (55,453) in a clash of two of the league's top four that year.

To put some flesh on the bones of the 1931 final, here's an extract from Halifax's club historian and timekeeper, Andrew Hardcastle's splendid *The Thrum Hall Story* (1986), which captures the flavour of the event and the feeling round the town nicely:

> *"Preparation for the big day included visits to West End Golf Course intermingled with country walks and occasional ball practice, and a theatre visit on the Thursday night. If somewhat unusual by modern standards, it cemented team spirit and left the players feeling fresh.*
>
> *They left for Wembley on the Friday morning by the 9.35 train, a great crowd of well-wishers thronging the station approach to see them off. All the players are reported to have been wearing favours in the club colours - some had blue and white rosettes as big as dinner plates, while (stand-off) Ivor Davies carried a cardboard replica of the Cup. Once in London they were stationed at the Kings Head Hotel in Harrow, some 20 minutes from Wembley. They visited the stadium in the afternoon and had a players meeting in the evening followed by an early night. The following morning there was a short walk and early lunch before departure for a hot and sunny Wembley at 11.45 a.m. It is estimated that around 7,000 people from Halifax made the trip by road and rail to see them there.*
>
> *Meanwhile back in Halifax, Cup Final fever was gripping the town. Hawkers of rosettes and blue and white dolls did a roaring trade in Southgate, whilst a shop in the Arcade Royale had a window display of blue*

and white ties, ambiguously called 'cup ties'. A large crowd gathered at Thrum Hall in the afternoon to listen to the broadcast commentary of the match, doubtless irritating the cricketers on the adjoining field in their enthusiasm. A 22-8 victory proved to be a splendid advert for the game.

After the match the party left for a 7.00pm celebration dinner at the Great Central Hotel, whilst the following day saw them at Brighton - where it never stopped raining. The return to Halifax came on Monday afternoon, with arrival at Halifax at 6.47pm to a tremendous reception. It began with 22 fog detonators (one for each point) exploding on the lines as the train passed over, followed by a coach journey through an estimated 100,000 crowd to a civic reception at the Town Hall, the King Cross brass band leading the way, just as it had done in 1903.

The celebrations did not end there. The following Thursday there was another dinner this time given by the club president at the Old Cock. The players received many presentations, including a tin of toffees each from Sir Harold Mackintosh, a pipe each from Fred Hartley of Commercial Street and a souvenir album in postcard form from the Halifax Courier."

The 1939 Wembley visit by Halifax was a similar story, although:

"Salford's preparations had not gone so well - a stay on a farm with accommodation in draughty cow sheds left two or three players laid up with colds. All but one recovered sufficiently to play, but they were perhaps not at their best.

Some 8,000 spectators travelled down from Halifax for the match. Pratt's engineers were one firm who gave their workers the morning off (broken time?) and paid the return fares of 200 men. Another party planned to have a midday meal in Halifax before motoring to Yeadon for a special plane to Croydon and a motor run to Wembley."

On returning home:

"The heroes were met by another 100,000 gathering and again there were fog detonators on the lines-20, then a pause, then 3 more to reflect the score. The crowd on the platform was supposed to be a select gathering of important people, but the more forward- thinking supporters got around this by purchasing tickets for Sowerby Bridge. After a noisy reception the players then left for Thrum Hall where a crowd of 7,000 had gathered to see the local Workshops Final between Hartley & Sugdens and Rawden & Weavers. Later in the week the cup was taken on a tour of the Calder Valley."

Marvellous stuff. Whatever your club, a copy of *The Thrum Hall Story* is well worth searching out, if you can find one.

After such tumultuous excitement of such an expedition and triumphant return, the 1932 Leeds versus Swinton players must have felt a bit short changed as their final was played away from Wembley at the more familiar and mundane Central Park, Wigan. The game had to be brought forward to enable the early departure of the Lions party down under. The earlier available date of 9th April coincided with an England versus Scotland soccer match and the next week was out of bounds as the FA would not permit rugby seven days before their FA Cup final scheduled for 23rd May.

The less glamorous although admittedly more convenient trip didn't help raise the crowd above the 29,000 mark who saw the Loiners scramble home 11-8. Poor old Swinton had reached each of the three finals before the move to Wembley, and now missed out again. The Lions never did get to Wembley.

They say that life begins at 40, and during the year of my 40th anniversary in 1935 it was Castleford's turn to bring the pot back with them for the first time, seeing off Huddersfield 11-8 (39,000.)

No luck for Warrington though, twice returning empty handed from defeats by Huddersfield 17-21 in 1933 (41,874 in the ground plus the first royal guest of honour, Edward, Prince of Wales) and Leeds 2-18 in 1936 of which the 51,250 paying punters contributed £7,200, both records.

On the pitch for Huddersfield was former Cross Keys Welsh RU scrum half Alex Givvons, who later became a loose forward with Oldham. Having turned professional in 1932, Givvons was the first black player in international Rugby League, capped by Wales six times between 1936 and 1939.

After giving 60 years service to Oldham and Huddersfield as player, coach and committeeman, he was honoured in Oldham by having a street, Givvons Fold, named after him when Watersheddings went.

Rugby League staged its own *War of the Worlds* to rival that of the Orson Welles radio play that caused so much panic across America in 1938, hoaxing an invasion by Martians.

The invaders that year were not from the red planet, rather the Red Devils from Salford who exterminated Barrow's hopes 7-4 (51,243). Surprisingly for such a famous name, the mighty Salford had their only Wembley moment of glory that day, never prevailing in the Challenge Cup final before or since.

Who got the pots?

A Rugby League match was cheap entertainment at this time, if you could afford entertainment at all. Typically, ground admission for a boy was three old pennies.

As regards my Championship, between 1930 and 1939, 28 northern clubs competed for the title, playing 38 league games each amongst each other to determine the top four who then continued to play-off to determine the champion. In eight out of ten Championship finals, the teams involved had finished top and second, so the system seemed to work fairly.

The Davids and Goliaths of the day weren't quite as they are today. Salford were the form team of the decade, topping the table no less than four times, and winning the Championship three.

Swinton too were vying with them for top dog, making their way to three Championship finals and winning two.

Variety was again the spice with seven different clubs winning the Championship during the decade.

Huddersfield needed a replay to beat Leeds 10-0 after a 2-2 draw to become 1930 champions.

The 1930/31 season was the first to feature a uniform fixture list for all clubs, each playing 38 games, although with 28 clubs competing in the table not all played home and away. Swinton were undoubtedly champions, topping the table by five points over Leeds then beating them 14-7 in the play-off final.

Next year had five points clear daylight between the top two and the rest as Huddersfield and St Helens came to the fore, with Saints upsetting the form book to take the title play-off from second.

Salford emerged into a force in 1932/33, topping the table by no less than five wins more than Swinton, then 10 points more than them in the play-off final.

Again, in 1934 Salford were fully nine points clear of Wigan by the seasons end, but, like the Hammer horror films that were founded that year, they must have had a nightmare as the Riversiders caused a shock, 15-3.

King George and Queen Mary celebrated their Silver Jubilee in 1935, as did Swinton winning the Championship final again, 14-3 over second-placed Warrington.

A new name on the trophy in 1936 as Hull had some overdue success and defeated Widnes convincingly 21-2 in a very black and white final.

Salford were back again for the title in 1937, captain and all-time great Gus Risman kicking five goals in a tense finish as the Red Devils edged past the runners-up Warrington by 13-11. It had been a long competition that year, but that was the way sport could be.

In those days an international cricket match lasted five slow days and when Joe Davis, during his 15-year reign as world champion, played the Aussie challenger Walter Lindrum for the World Championship of snooker at Leicester Square, the event taking place over a marathon 71 frames.

The 1938 Championship final showed that the decision making amongst the 'blazers' in Rugby League has at best been arbitrary and often improvised on the hoof, if not a little acrimoniously. Was it ever thus...?

Hunslet and Leeds qualified for the Championship final that year and between them agreed that the big game would be more appropriately played between the two Leeds-based clubs within the city at Leeds United's Elland Road ground. However, the League Management Committee rejected this proposal stating that the game should be played 'out of town' at Wakefield's considerably smaller Belle Vue, as scheduled.

Riding the crest of the public uproar, the two clubs appealed and a deputation to the committee, who met again but postponed their decision so two of its members, out of the country on French business, could arbitrate. At the again reconvened meeting Elland Road got the nod and a 54,000-plus crowd, Wakefield got some financial compensation and the city of Leeds got its 'derby'. Hunslet won 8-2. The whole episode was worthy of a mention in the *Beano*, which first went to print the same year.

Cole Porter's hit musical of the time was *Anything Goes*, and this was the case in something of a curiosity on Christmas Eve 1938, as Leeds were scheduled to play host to the big drawing Salford. The rugby pitch at Headingley was frozen, so anticipating a 12,000-plus holiday crowd, 'Plan B' was put into effect and the posts were moved onto the cricket field and a full-sized pitch marked out. The Aussie stand-off Vic Hey duly became the only player to score a try on the Headingley cricket ground as Santa came early for the Loiners with a 5-0 win.

Finally, the top two in 1939 were Salford and Castleford. Salford (for the third time that decade) took the Championship trophy home.

As was so often the case during the twenties, the strugglers at the beginning of the thirties were Bradford Northern, bottom in 1930, '31 and '32 before finding some form and escaping to mid table by 1936. Poor old Bramley bumped along the bottom in 1933 and 1938 with Featherstone Rovers at rock bottom in 1934, '35, '37 and pretty much down there the rest of the time.

Leeds' cliché of being perennial underachievers was appropriate even then, as despite finishing strongly in the table regularly without ever actually topping it they reached three Championship finals - and lost them all.

I mentioned earlier about spreading my wings. The game found a foothold in London during the 1930s. During 1933/1934 London Highfield played at White City Stadium and finished 14th on the final table with 20 wins, before returning north in 1934. On doing so they changed their identity to Liverpool Stanley and enjoyed two good years managing a creditable second-place finish in 1936, only losing twice all season and only three times the next, before returning to the pack and relative mid-table obscurity.

During their time at White City they were afforded the honour of receiving the touring Australians on 22nd November 1933 and being a fairly radical experiment I ought to elaborate on that early floodlit game a little. The next day's *Times* reported proceedings:

> *"Happily the weather and the visibility were fairly good and a crowd of over 12,000 was able to see the Australians at any rate to some advantage, for they won easily by four goals and four tries (20 points) to one goal and one try (5 points). It probably was not a great game as judged by any standards but it was clear that in every way the Australians were the better side. That they had already lost seven games in the north suggests that London Highfield, the sole representative of the south so far still have a long way to go in their aspirations.*
>
> *"The scrimmages lasted barely seconds. In the loose also the handling and agility of the Australian big fellows were quite remarkable. Much of the handling of the Australians was magnificent in the sense that a pass invariably was given and taken at top speed.*
>
> *"One can imagine that with a little more tactical skill in their heads the Australians would be a great side. London had the luck to snatch a try whilst most of the players were watching an injured Highfield player*

being attended to."

Glad you enjoyed it, Sir.

In the 1935 competition another London club, Acton & Willesden fielded a team finishing 21st out of a division expanded to 30, and also in 1935 Streatham & Mitcham joined the fun, finishing 24th.

Sadly my expansion to 'the smoke' was a short-lived adventure, Acton dropped out the next year to be replaced by Newcastle, who finished 29th out of the 30-team division and Streatham & Mitcham, although recording 14 wins, didn't last the season and forfeited their remaining 12 matches.

The Newcastle club persevered until 1938, again finishing second-last (out of 29) before the adventure into the exotic came to an end and the league reverted to 28 northern clubs.

In those days the town of St Helens fielded a second club in St Helens Recs as did Wigan with Wigan Highfield. Six 'Hot-Pot' derbies! Then again, there seem to be about that many today.

An innovation in the management of the team came in 1932 as Jim Sullivan was appointed as Wigan's first coach. Prior to that all they had was a trainer. Tommy McCarty, known simply as 'Carty', started as trainer in 1919 and retained his position as trainer when Sullivan was appointed player-coach until the end of the Second World War.

European Community

With the Rugby League experiment sweeping southern France like a brushwood fire, an early adventure was to match up the respective competition winners either side of the Channel.

As winners of the Challenge Cup, Castleford travelled to Stade Buffalo, Paris to meet Lyon-Villeurbanne, winners of the first French knock-out competition, the *Coupe de France*, recipients of the Lord Derby Cup. Cas won the game 21-24 with around 4,000 spectators on hand.

The following week the winners of the Rugby League Championship, Swinton, travelled to meet Villeneuve, the first winners of the *Ligue Francaise de Rugby a Treize* in Bordeaux. A close match ended 25-27 to Swinton, to the disappointment of the 15,000 *treizistes* there.

Standing room only

Bradford Northern had been based at Birch Lane since 1908, but by 1934 the time was right for a move, into the cavernous Odsal.

The site had been a quarry that had been built up by controlled tipping of domestic waste and ash, with the ground's present public bar, the Trevor Foster Lounge, starting life in 1935 as the newly-built club house and dressing rooms, high above pitch level. I'm led to believe that 'sal' is the Saxon or Norse for clearing, so Mr Od's clearing it was, 1,000 years or so ago...I'm sure he would have approved!

Swinton also relocated to Station Road after 42 years at their previous premises on Chorley Road and Barrow left their old ground at Roose to move into Craven Park, developed at a cost of £7,500. Funds were raised following an appeal by Commander Charles Craven, chairman of Vickers Armstrong, the local shipbuilders, after whom the ground was named in honour.

Whilst there wasn't a great deal of other coming and going of grounds during the 1930s - wholesale development was not the order of the day during such lean times - there was some tinkering.

One positive development was the opening of the Headingley South Stand in 1931. It's still much the same today as it was then, although it might have had a coat or two of paint since. Shortly afterwards, in 1932, the Main Stand opposite burnt down causing its 3,000 occupants to alight rapidly.

It had only been opened in 1926 and its destruction prompted the present double-fronted stand to be built in its place the next year. The new Main Stand afforded views from one side onto the rugby pitch and from the other onto the cricket ground, as it still does today.

A lucky escape for Naughton Park, Widnes, scheduled for demolition in favour of council housing on the expiry of its lease in 1931. A reprieve came as fans chipped in and, together with a 10 per cent grant from the RFL, raised the £3,250 required to buy the freehold.

Having played there since 1901, in 1933 Salford bought the Willows (named after a row of trees behind their north stand) from the landlord, Groves and Whitnall brewery.

Times were hard in Humberside and to raise funds Hull KR sold their Craven Park stadium to the greyhound racing company who also used the facilities, then took a lease back. Wakefield's Belle Vue got a 900-seater stand in 1932, since demolished, and Castleford's Wheldon Road (the Jungle is a place for wild animals and creepy crawlies as far as I'm concerned) got a new main stand, the current one replacing the original that burnt down in 1935.

St Helens also toyed with the idea of greyhounds but the proposal succumbed to resistance from the public and church, together with a loophole in its deeds, and the plan was eventually consigned to the doghouse.

Early Bath

Every sport can lay claim to its own catch phrases and clichés. My favourites include 'up 'n' under', 'head and feed' (not cannibalism, I may add) and 'early bath', the latter being shorthand for a sending off.

Talking of Castleford, as I just was, when a player receives his marching orders at their Wheldon Road ground he could be forgiven if he ends up holding a cool pint of beer rather than standing under a hot shower as across from the stadium is a famous watering hole, called the Early Bath.

In all likelihood any dismissed transgressor of the Rugby League rulebook would need a quick wash and brush up first, but I can't help wondering if any such naughty lad ever dared to sneak out of the ground and into the Early Bath to sup a quick pint of best whilst his teammates battled on in his name on the field?

Incidentally, the Early Bath was also once HQ to the Lock Lane amateur club. No doubt some of you could spin a few yarns about the local pubs associated with Rugby League grounds. In fact, maybe even scope for a book?

Sweet tooth

Time for another profile of a familiar character associated with my game. First showing himself in 1932, no trip to the game, especially in Wigan, was complete without the company of my old pal from the Wm. Santus works.

A friend to children and adults alike, especially miners, the top-hatted toff became a familiar face in the crowd and around the perimeter of the Rugby League grounds of the north west. He always had a smile, whatever the weather - or score - and never said a word.

Ladies and gentlemen, a Wigan institution, Uncle Joe, of mintball fame.

Time, gentlemen, please

Talking of toffs, what about my Cumberland fullback 'Gentleman' Jim Brough? Jim had played rugger for England at Twickers and showing his versatility had trialled for Liverpool FC as a goalkeeper before crossing codes to sign at Headingley in 1925.

A physical fitness fanatic and possessor of poise, grace, a raking boot and a perfectly-timed tackle, the suave Mr Brough could be considered unfortunate in that his career coincided with Jim Sullivan. Although the two men's styles contrasted Jim usually got the nod for the British fullback jersey. Nevertheless, the tweed suited, plus-four favouring city type was honoured to lead the 1936 Lions tour down under.

Retiring to take up a business appointment with printers Waddington (of Monopoly fame) in South Africa, Jim returned at the outbreak of war, taking the field again at the age of 38.

After 19 seasons, Jim then applied his considered and calm style with a move into coaching, briefly at Leeds then back home with Whitehaven and Workington, who he duly led to Championship and cup finals. Jim's pedigree was of the right stuff to see him selected as the first travelling coach of the Lions, taking them down under in 1958 to deal with the Aussies in a highly successful tour I'll tell you about later.

Player, captain, coach, manager, winner and probably the best £600 Leeds ever spent, James Wasdale Brough, a true gent.

Back to base

As you might have noticed, I like to note what my colleagues in other sports got up to, so here's a long forgotten story from 1936 that I promise I'm not making up.

Anti-expansionists and those opposed to modern marketing nicknames please take note!

The Yorkshire Baseball League was established by John Moores (of Littlewoods Pools fame), President of the National Baseball Association, in an attempt to establish baseball as a major summer sport in England.

Playing from Crown Flatt, Dewsbury Royals Professional Baseball Club were founder members together with Bradford City Sox, Greenfield Giants, Hull Baseball Club, Leeds Oaks, Scarborough Seagulls, Sheffield Dons and Wakefield Cubs. All of the teams played either at the local Rugby League or greyhound stadium.

Dewsbury's first professional game was on Saturday 9th May 1936. The *Dewsbury Reporter* noted that:

> *"Local sportsmen will have their first opportunity to see the game that is all the rage in America at Crown Flatt this weekend when Dewsbury Royals, the newly-formed baseball team, will play their first game with Hull in the Yorkshire League. Players have been busily practising all week under the direction of WT Graham who has played the game in Canada."*

A large crowd turned out to watch the game. The *Reporter* noted on 16th May 1936:

> *"Probably 80 per cent of those who visited Crown Flatt last Saturday to see Dewsbury Royals play their first League baseball game came out of curiosity. Even*

as things turned out, a bitterly raw afternoon, with an icy wind with rain at times, most people would have their appetites whetted, for there was no doubt about it, the game made some appeal. Compared with the usual sporting spectacles at Crown Flatt, bad as they were last season, I do not think baseball is as thrilling as Rugby League football, but when Heavy Woollen District people are sufficiently versed in the laws as to appreciate the finer points of the game, and, more important still, when some of the Dewsbury players themselves understand its possibilities better, the game should command a good following."

The inexperience of the team, allied to the fact that Dewsbury's foreign professionals were not always available, led to the team struggling. Whereas other clubs in the league had imported professionals, Dewsbury in the main had to field local players. In fact, Dewsbury lost their first nine league games until 11th July when Dewsbury got their maiden win against Scarborough Seagulls 54-6.

Despite improved performances, crowds at Crown Flatt fell away and without the financial backing that other clubs enjoyed Dewsbury found it difficult to attract quality overseas players and struggled financially.

The summer of 1936 was the first and last for professional baseball in Dewsbury as the Royals finished the league season in seventh place with a record of three wins (Bradford, Scarborough and Sheffield) and 11 losses, dropping out of the Yorkshire League and being replaced by York Maroons.

Despite the demise of Dewsbury, professional baseball thrived in the region and the league expanded in 1938 to include teams from Lancashire. The same year players from the Yorkshire-Lanacashire Major League beat the United States Olympic Baseball team and could thereby lay claim to being World Amateur Champions.

Sadly for professional baseball, as with Rugby League in France, World War II brought about a sudden halt to proceedings after the 1939 season. Unfortunately the game had not fully established itself, therefore after the war it only resurfaced in areas such as Hull, London and Liverpool where the game had firmly established roots in the pre-war era.

I wonder if they took the rugby posts down or played round them?

Storm warning

As the decade ground on, far from the grimy north of England, continental Europe was becoming a restless place. The people of several nations fell under fascist dictatorships. Mussolini was already in power in Italy, Hitler took control of Germany in 1933, eliminating his opposition soon after, as did Salazar in Portugal. Franco led an army revolt in Spain in July 1936, overthrowing the democratically-elected government and promulgating a vicious and destructive civil war.

Sir Oswald Mosley founded his black-shirted British Union of Fascists, not without support from those within the British 'ruling classes', notably the heir to the throne and the 2nd Baron Rededsale and his daughters Unity and Diana Mitford.

Despite its glorious isolation, Britain was also in constitutional turmoil. The long reign of King George V ended with his death in 1936 leaving the dashing Edward VIII to ascend to the throne. His reign was short-lived and parliament had to pass a bill allowing his abdication as the constitution could not recognise his proposed marriage to an American divorcee, Wallis Simpson. The reluctant successor was King George VI whose coronation at Westminster Abbey on a rainy day in May 1937 was a popular celebration amongst a weary and anxious public.

By 1939 Neville Chamberlain had returned from Munich with that famous 'piece of paper' in his hand, a declaration that Herr Hitler had no aggressive intentions, a contract that literally wasn't worth the paper it was written on. The tinderbox of central Europe was bone dry and awaiting the spark that would set the continent, then the world, ablaze. British Ashes in another sense awaited.

Summing up the thirties

I think it's fair to say that by the end of the 1930s my game was fulfilling it's role as a mass spectator sport in the north of England and, via public broadcasting, was beginning to get the public recognition we all deserved.

Regular Wembley appearances and the continued success of international tours added a little prestige and gravity to my achievements. Foreign travel was a long and tough effort, but well worth it, especially to Australasia where my skills were very much appreciated and well worth the mammoth administration required.

However, more stalled attempts at expansion, especially in London, were a frustration. I never seemed to be able to get more than a brief foothold outside the usual northern counties where I'd spent my early years.

The fleeting sightings of a mysterious and fascinating phenomenon - Rugby League clubs outside the north - was matched by another controversy of the time. A new road around the western edge of Loch Ness caused an upsurge in sightings of Nessie, buoyed by the famous *Surgeon's Picture,* taken in 1934.

Sadly, like Rugby League's expansion into Wales and London, and progress in France, the rare and elusive dream sank without trace, gurgling below the waterline as it went and dismissed by cynics as fraudulent nonsense and a physical impossibility - although believers always suspected its time would come again...

6

1939-1950
WORLD WAR TWO

After only 21 years of peace, the face of the world changed again. At 5am on Friday 1st September 1939, Poland's fragile peace was shattered as the Blitzkrieg or 'lightning war' struck. In a precise military operation German forces crossed the border. Tanks and motorised troops raced over the hard-baked ground, sculpted after a glorious summer, with support coming from screeching Stuka dive-bombers. An occupation force of one and a quarter million men swept swiftly into Poland and nothing there could halt the advance.

As early as 5.33am that crisp autumn morning, Berlin radio broadcast the threatening proclamation and loudspeaker vans bedecked in swastikas barked out the news as they raced through the towns awakening a sleepy nation. Later that morning, Hitler addressed the Reichstag in Berlin informing the assembly of events.

Unable to gain any ground by diplomatic means over the following days at 11am on 3rd September 1939, Prime Minister, Neville Chamberlain addressed the nation by radio and, in a strained and tired voice, advised that Britain should consider itself at war with Germany. I shudder as I think back to it.

Wailing sirens soon sent people scurrying to their air-raid shelters, the first of many false alarms caused by a friendly plane carrying two French officers across the south coast.

The public accepted this sudden activity soberly with little flag waving, as had been the case in World War One.

Whilst some countries committed themselves to action in defence of freedom, others such as Sweden and Switzerland remained neutral. For the next seven months the uneasy state became known as the 'Bore War' in Britain, *Drole de Guerre* (funny war) in France and as *Sitzkrieg* (armchair war) in Germany as no one seemed in a hurry to fire the first shot. Eventually and tragically, mother earth soon turned red as force met force in a hideous bloody conflict that lasted six catastrophic years.

As air-raids began on mainland Britain, large silver barrage balloons akin to a shoal of friendly whales became part of the landscape in helping protect the skies. Night time blackouts, whilst giving no clues to enemy bombers, proved to be a disaster on the home front as people tripped and stumbled their way along. Painting kerbstones white didn't prevent many injuries and road fatalities doubled. During inclement weather some balloons would have to be cut from their moorings and consequently their mooring chains caused havoc to roofs, chimney pots and trolleybus cables. It wasn't until 17th September 1944 that street lights were turned on again after five long years of war.

To protect town-dwelling children from the hazards of air-raids they were evacuated to the country adorned with gas masks and baggage labels. Journalists reported a strange quietness after the exodus of children. Arriving at often unknown destinations, tired and hungry, many were fretful of possibly never seeing their parents again. In shameful scenes, children were to be confronted with 'pick-your-evacuee' as families haggled over who to have, with the more sickly and grubby ones being left to last. In tenements, due to the lack of proper sanitation, it was still common practice to urinate on newspapers indoors and 'townies' from backstreet Britain were accused of other unpleasant practices such as thieving, bed wetting, swearing and general smelliness. Teachers had to go with the children to try and keep some normality in their education.

As the war progressed from land to the Atlantic the German U-boat campaign against the allied merchant fleet caused a worrying food shortage. Money was invested in creating food additives and methods of preservation such as canning which helped to preserve the nation's reserves.

Food rationing started on 8th January 1940 with adults limited to four ounces of bacon or ham, 12oz of sugar and four ozs of butter or margarine per week. In July the butter/margarine allowance was increased to six ozs but cooking fat and tea were added to the list. Meat became a restricted food with each person having only one shilling and 10 pence-worth per week. Offal was not rationed and therefore very much in demand. If you were invited to someone's house for dinner it was accepted that you took your own food to cook.

As the war dragged on other foodstuffs such as jams and preserves, tinned fruit, biscuits, dried fruit, eggs and cheese became rationed or restricted by a points system. Imported fruit such as bananas and oranges disappeared altogether and things we take for granted today, such as sweets and chocolate, were controlled by a coupons system.

Restrictions were placed on restaurants and a maximum price of five shillings (25p) per meal was imposed. The Ministry of Food set up communal kitchens, soon given the name British Restaurants, to supply good, nourishing and inexpensive meals to the general public which became a great asset to vulnerable towns such as Hastings, from which so many women had been evacuated.

On the kitchen front, women showed great ingenuity in finding ways to extend and enhance the limited food supplies. In fact the Second World War greatly helped the cause of women's liberation due to them having to take on many more tasks, such as working in factories or on the land, replacing the men who were at the front.

To maintain morale it became important that everyone 'mucked in' together and the public was fascinated to learn that even the bathtubs in Buckingham Palace each had five inch watermarks on them to help save water.

One of the strangest contributions to the war effort came from Waddingtons, the Leeds-based board games and playing cards manufacturer who supplied these to a captive market – the soldiers, sailors and air crew held in German prisoner of war camps. The company inserted a map of Europe, printed on silk, into the board or card, providing vital information for the servicemen attempting to escape from the camps.

In the early years of the war, table tennis experimented with using phosphorescent balls so that they could play under reduced lighting and Wembley Arena painted its glass roof black at a cost of £300 so that they could stage events at night.

Until the 1940s the only effective treatment for tuberculosis had been rest and fresh air in sanatoria located in the countryside. In 1944, the powerful antibiotic streptomycin was developed, followed by several others, which brought an effective cure. For example in 1946 some 900 girls between the ages of 15 and 19 died of TB, although by 1961 this had been reduced to nine.

Tough times indeed, but somehow, adversity proved a unifying bond amongst society.

Stop start season

The 1939/40 season had promised an awful lot from yours truly. The New Zealand tourists had arrived and a fine season was in prospect.

Wigan, Dewsbury and Bradford Northern were all gearing up to play a big part in the next decade of the game's history, all cut short by the events of the outside world that would be foremost in everyone's lives for the next six years.

Of course that's not to say your old friend Rugby League was conscripted and sent to the front. At the age of 44 I was young enough, but there were some thrilling matches to be played and even a get together with the Rugby Union boys!

Anyway, enough from me for the moment, the one thing I've never been short of is characters with a few tales to tell. To help me convey the experiences of the time my pal, Sam Grundy, interviewed one of my finest players and ambassadors, Trevor Foster MBE, about his wartime memories and time on tour to the Southern Hemisphere after the war.

Trevor's career spanned the thirties and fifties so I can think of no better man to recall the best moments of the forties.

"For four or five weeks after war was declared everything seemed to close down. Nobody seemed to know for definite what was going to happen. However, after a bit of time, Yorkshire and Lancashire Leagues were set up. The Ministry of Labour had let it be known that they wanted the game to go on and the men in charge didn't need telling twice. One thing that cropped up though was that most players were called up into the forces and some happened to get stationed in different places.

"Players could still play for their teams provided they had permission, but some men ended up guesting for other clubs. Some clubs even closed down and their grounds used for other purposes. This happened at Salford and Swinton. At Wigan the army took over part of the ground and had ack-ack guns installed there. Plenty of players now had no club but there were soon plenty of people looking for their services.

"Dewsbury was one of the pioneers of getting guest players and Eddie Waring's skill in recruiting guests made the Dewsbury team into a good side. They had players travelling from as far afield as Scotland and Ireland to play for Dewsbury. Eddie would offer to pay over the odds for their services and as a result he became a popular man with players! This may have been just match pay of four or five pounds.

"One man to sign with Dewsbury, Alan Edwards, was stationed a long way off in Scotland with the RAF and other men to play for Dewsbury included greats such as Vic Hey, Jim Sullivan, Gus Risman and Roy Francis. These new players brought in big crowds and more money, so it wasn't long before other clubs followed Eddie's example and got players guesting for them.

"We sometimes lost players to active service and you often didn't know who would turn out as not much notice was given by the forces. I remember one game at Keighley where a certain well-known player from Cumbria had come over on leave that day to play for them. He was in the dressing room ready to go out onto the field when military police arrived and placed him under arrest. He hadn't been on leave at all but had gone AWOL just so he could play. Fortunately for him the MPs saw the funny side and allowed him to continue before taking him back to barracks, albeit in cuffs!"

Call up!

On 2nd September 1939, every man between the ages of 19 and 41 was called up for some kind of national service. The day after the British and the French declared war the Australians and New Zealanders followed suit.

This presented the touring Kiwis with a bit of a problem. They were 12,000 miles from home and about to embark on a Test series versus Great Britain. Over £5,000 had been invested into the tour with little prospect of any return now. The tourists had managed two club games, against St Helens and Dewsbury, winning both. The journey home through U-boat infested waters didn't hold much appeal and as a result the 26 players and managers placed themselves at the disposal of the Army. Some ended up filling sandbags in Harrogate in preparation of air-raids but they eventually made it back home later in the year.

During the first weeks of the war players were being paid as amateurs. At Bradford Northern, Trevor remembers pay being around 10 shillings expenses per game: "A lot of players were up in arms about this new pay structure, many relied on their rugby pay to supplement their ordinary wages. When the rugby pay dried up many men were left broke, with nothing to pay the rent or to look after their families."

This situation soon came to a head and resulted in a strike by Halifax, Huddersfield and Bradford Northern. The League had to promise to come up with a solution and they did with the announcement of a flat £1 fee with an extra five shillings if the man had to break time from work to play. Some salary cap! No wonder Eddie Waring was a popular man paying his recruits as much as £5 a match!

Wartime restrictions

Unlike the Great War, the authorities decided that the country was at a greater risk from air-raids and as a result ground capacities were cut, most stadia limited to 8,000 fans at any one time. Odsal, being the largest Rugby League ground, had its huge capacity cut to just 15,000 per match and also became a site for some rather interesting activities, as Trevor remembers: "As a player in the Wartime League the war was always in the back of the mind. Plenty of air-raid warnings disrupted everyday life and at Odsal the club offices were used as an air-raid warning co-ordination office. Around thirty telephones linked with other offices around the north and they all rang with reports of air-raid activity at 11.00am and 3.00pm each day.

"The British public endured rationing as a fact of life until the 1950s and in 1941 regulations tightened even further. To prevent the wealthy from buying all the other supplies a system whereby everyone had 16 points for four weeks was introduced for tinned foods, rice, peas, tomatoes, condensed milk, treacle and biscuits. Bread, beer and tobacco were never rationed but even beer was watered down until it had no more than two thirds of its original alcohol, so it became harder to drown your sorrows than before!

"It became difficult to get a square meal due to rationing. Rugby players tend to have big appetites and I was no different. I lived in digs with two old ladies at the time and they struggled to get a good meal regularly. It helped quite a bit if you knew the local butcher well as he might slip you something extra. The black market offered another place where you could get some extra food if you knew the right people and most tried to get what they could.

"At Odsal part of the stadium was converted into a market garden to grow extra vegetables and sometimes the produce was used as a supplement to a player's match pay. All over the country people were urged to dig for victory and it was no different here. The market garden produced peas, potatoes, beetroot, cabbages and tomato plants. Sometimes they grew so much produce the surplus was given to the general public in the area."

Elsewhere across the Rugby League empire, Belle Vue stadium,

Manchester home to Broughton Rangers, had the only operational speedway track during the war. Unfortunately the Military took over use of the field and Broughton had to move out though the speedway continued despite many riders being in the Army as despatch couriers. Broughton played ten games at Edgley Park, Stockport, and even took their own posts from Belle Vue for good measure.

Not necessarily an League ground but one that has staged more than the odd game in the past, Burnden Park, Bolton was used by the Department for Food as a food store, with massive amounts of supplies stored in the Burnden Stand.

RL 'does its bit'

The early years of the war didn't go too well for Britain and her allies. In 1940 the evacuation of Dunkirk took place and over 300,000 soldiers were rescued from the beaches. Many soldiers found themselves back in Britain at hospital camps and transit areas while the authorities decided where to post them. Headingley was one of those places. Hundreds of soldiers ended up camping there in the weeks after Dunkirk before being moved to more permanent premises.

Rugby League land comes up again with Vickers of Barrow being overwhelmed, working flat out to build and replace lost 'X Craft' used in attacking enemy warships moored in protected anchorages. These were towed to the vicinity of their target by submarine and then released, notably against the German battleship *Tirpitz*. Great secrecy surrounded the site locations with Broadbents of Huddersfield being one such company to be tasked with the work. Shortly after she was adopted by the city of Leeds in 1941, the aircraft carrier *Ark Royal* was sunk off Gibraltar. The people of Leeds raised millions of pounds for a replacement ship during 1942, an association that continues to the present day.

Bombs away!

Fancy sending the Luftwaffe to attack my playing stadia! The old

City Road ground in St Helens had a near-miss after one missile failed to explode nearby and in fact embedded itself in the crater it caused. Maurice Bamford's autobiography paints an interesting picture of a bombed-out Kirkstall Road in Leeds. However, what about the poor old Boulevard taking a direct hit, reducing the main stand to rubble and destroying most of the club's files and records. Wouldn't like to think what the 'Ole Faithful' would have done if they could have collared the pilot, I think they may well have drop kicked him across the Humber!

The Local authorities in Hull attempted to map every bomb that fell on the city, mainly so that the location of any unexploded bombs might more easily be identified and indeed just outside of Hull are the remains of a Second World War bombing decoy at Cherry Cobb Sands, Holderness. Lamps were hung from wooden poles, with the light shining down onto artificial pools of water underneath. The pattern of lights would hopefully resemble Hull docks when viewed from a passing Luftwaffe aircraft, and so trick the bomber crews into attacking empty mud flats and farmland safely away from the city.

Nevertheless, during the 100 actual bombing-raids from 823 alerts, Hull was hit badly and the official statistics at the end of the war made for grim reading.

Of the pre-war housing stock of 92,660 some 86,722 houses were damaged or destroyed (93 per cent.) People made homeless numbered 152,000 and the Luftwaffe's activities caused 1,200 deaths and 3,000 injuries.

The great irony was that although the local newspaper would show a photograph of an easily identifiable, local landmark, they could only describe: "a bombing raid over a north east town."

One lone bomber over-shot its original target (probably Liverpool Docks) and ended up ditching its bombs not too far from Wilderspool, landing in a nearby field that was holding a school fete.

The Germans 'redesigned' Old Trafford, of course. It's a long story, but if it hadn't been for that, and Manchester City's subsequent hospitality, Manchester United may never have got back on their feet again.

Despite the best efforts of the Luftwaffe to disrupt my league programme I soldiered on. Several northern towns were bombed, especially those near industrial targets. One game between Hull and Batley was abandoned during the second half when the aid-raid siren sounded.

Trevor remembers how war was always in the back of the mind: "Although Bradford suffered little bombing during the war there were an awful lot of air-raid warnings and false alarms. This kept everyone on their toes and made you often wonder if games were going to be interrupted."

With the coming of the 1941/42 season, only 17 out of the 27 professional clubs that existed at the beginning of hostilities maintained themselves in any state to continue operating and the separate Yorkshire and Lancashire Leagues had to be amalgamated.

Bradford Northern, winners of the Championship in 1939/40, had been building a strong team and 1940/41 saw them pipped at the last by Wigan.

Salford had been one of the clubs that ceased to function during the war so, what with him being stationed near Bradford, Lieutenant Gus Risman ended up guesting for Northern. Bradford already had the basis of a great side and Gus added a lot of flair, and as one of the icons of the game at the time, played very well at centre and stand-off. Very much a master of all situations on the field Gus earned himself plenty of honours, including the 1941 Yorkshire Cup. Curiously, Wigan had played in the Yorkshire Cup that year, losing to Leeds 9-3 at Central Park.

With Eddie Waring behind the scenes, the emerging Dewsbury club took everyone by surprise to take the 1941/42 season.

Nobody would have predicted the outcome of the 1942/43 season though, an infamous episode, never again to be repeated in Rugby League history.

Now, it has often been said that your good friend Rugby League is prone to shooting himself in the foot from time to time. To this I have to say that sometimes it's nothing to do with me. For some reason a great many people I've been involved with over the years have made some pretty odd decisions, although often well intentioned. Well, the 1942/43 season was one such calamity, so let my old pal Jack Bower take up the tale.

"It all happened in the Championship play-off where the top clubs played each other to decide the Championship winners. Bradford Northern had finished third and won their first play-off game against Huddersfield. Their next game pitched them against Dewsbury and it was this match that caused the problem.

"Northern beat Dewsbury but afterwards the Dewsbury committee lodged a complaint saying that Northern had played an ineligible player. The rules of the day were that a club could only pick a player in the play-offs if they had appeared four or more times for them in the previous season. The lad in question, Sandy Orford, had played for Wakefield and 'guested' for Northern in only three games.

"The RFL decided to disqualify Northern and left Dewsbury to carry on in the competition that they went on to win by beating Halifax in a two-legged final.

"Unfortunately for them, their victory was short-lived as Dewsbury were found to have fielded an ineligible player themselves. Ironically the offence had been in the game against Bradford Northern the same one in which they had complained!

"The RFL were left in a quandary having to decide whether to replay the whole Championship finals or not. As it was, Dewsbury were given a reprimand, stripped of their title and the whole Championship declared null and void. To my knowledge there's been no other occasion when this has happened."

By the way, more eveidence that summer rugby isn't necessarily a new concept as in 1940 a Lancashire Rugby League summer cup competition took place.

Half a cup

With the unsettled War League programme and some clubs temporarily discontinued, my Challenge Cup stuttered along as best it could through the conflict, although one year, 1940, it wasn't played at all. A big day out at Wembley was a waste of resources and neither appropriate nor safe, especially with doodlebugs raining down on the capital, so I brought my final back up north.

The likes of Bradford, Huddersfield, Leeds, Wigan and Dewsbury all staged the final during the war years and late forties and in fact those same clubs pretty much monopolised custody of the trophy between them.

In 1943 and 1944 the final took an interesting twist, being decided over two legs, although needless to say with limited players and competing clubs and with priorities elsewhere the cup's appeal at the turnstile dipped to as low as 15,250.

After hostilities ceased back to Wembley I went, although the jamboree took a couple of years to get back up to speed. Having matched its old level of attendance in 1946, ticket sales smashed through to 77,605 before hitting the hitherto unprecedented high of 95,050 in 1949, the sort of popularity I was happy to get used to.

Au revoir

At the end of the war we all had to find it in ourselves to forgive and forget, although this was a task I wasn't sure I could manage. You see if some people had got their way, in France at least I wouldn't be around to forgive anyone.

To my mind, the Germans did it all the wrong way round in 1939. Having invaded France round the Maginot Line defences, through Holland and Belgium, they concerned themselves with the strategic bits like Paris and the Atlantic and Channel coasts. Anyone in their right mind should have been more interested in the middle and south where the weather is better, the wine flows freely and they play Rugby League.

Anyway, with the bits that could be used to control the high seas and launch an attack on Blighty under control from Berlin, the rest of France was given leave to govern itself, as long as it stuck to Nazi approved policies. A seat of government was established at the spa town of Vichy under a military leader, Marshal Henri-Philippe Pétain.

The ease with which the French had again surrendered their *liberté* had been a national embarrassment and moves were put in hand to knock the French youth into shape. A policy of 'sport for all' became the magic wand that might just put some vigour back into the doleful French general public, and that meant doing it, not just watching it. This meant all sport reverting to amateurism and the professional, elite clubs and institutions were the sacrificial lambs, especially that mongrel game from that scruffy lot in the north of England.

Petain's government saw me as a modern and innovative sport and my players somehow associated with the left-wing Popular Front government that had come to power in France in 1936. I just didn't fit with Fascist sports philosophy that rejected professionalism in favour of playing for honour and pride alone (where have I heard that before?) If this wasn't enough I fell victim to back-stabbing and lobbying from powerful figures within Rugby Union close to the Vichy regime. Sadly, kicking a man when he's down is human nature for some.

Having been the first sport that could point to the exact date I was born, I now became the first sport to have a death sentence passed on it. In December 1941, by a stroke of Petain's own pen, I was summarily abolished. Not just dissuaded, shunned or disapproved of, actually abolished. A governmental decree was signed, my assets were sequestrated for the use of the French Rugby Union and playing my humble *rugby a treize* game became illegal, just like theft or murder.

Even after the war finished and I'd struggled back on to my feet, I wasn't allowed my proud *rugby a treize* name back, I had to be satisfied with *jeu a treize* (game for thirteen) and only got the right to call myself 'rugby' back in 1993.

My French cousins never got their assets back, and it's still impossible for anyone studying to become a state sports instructor to take Rugby League as their option. Some clubs, just like back in the 1930s, still struggle to get access to public playing fields.

The rotten beggars have still got my brass, the miscreants know who they are and what they did, but still no-one has ever apologised, so I hope you'll understand if I just hesitate a little longer before forgiving and forgetting. I don't mean to dredge up the past, but sometimes you've got to get things off your chest. It's not a crime to tell the truth, unlike playing my game in France was.

Rapprochement

A different story in Britain, thank goodness, where during 1943 and 1944 the two codes enjoyed something of a *rapprochement*. With the country at war it seemed sensible that the differences between the codes should be put aside and players, both amateur and professional, could play rugby together again - Union of course!

Lads who had played Rugby League all their lives could now try that other game. Others that had 'seen the light' could play their old code again without discrimination. How kind! Now before I get all sniffy about it there were a couple of games played later in the war that I'm particularly proud of...so I'll let Trevor Foster fill you in.

"The idea to have a couple of games of Union between a Rugby League side and a Rugby Union side was very popular and captured everyone's imagination. The games were to be played at Union rules though, so the League team needed to include a few ex-Union players like me. The first fixture was at Headingley and proved hugely popular and as a result there was a great desire to follow it up. However, it soon became apparent that the Union men were less keen.

"One great player in the Union side by the name of Lieutenant Jackson had represented Scottish Public Schools and The Army. He was very quick and strongly built and impressed a lot of people including the Leeds secretary who scurried into the dressing rooms after the match to offer him terms to turn professional! He was politely turned down.

"Robin Prescott was a front rower in the 1944 match alongside Bob Weighill and these two men went on to achieve positions of great responsibility in Rugby Union in the future.

"I captained the team that day in the absence of Willie Davies, who unfortunately couldn't get leave from the RAF. Those of us with experience playing Union soon adjusted to it. I remember my old colleague Stan Brogden getting one try for the League XV but the thing that struck me was the total lack of animosity between the two camps that day.

"It was a shame that these games weren't carried on after the war. Most of the players were for it and it would've been very popular with the fans but the old school tie prevailed and the RFU no longer wanted anything to do with us League types."

League men 'rehabilitated'

It wasn't just during the cross-code games that League players took part in Rugby Union. The Home Unions often picked League players for their internationals. Let Trevor tell you more...

"I remember down in Swansea, Wales played England at Rugby Union and at this time the barriers had come down between the two games. Gus Risman and I played with Bleddyn Williams and Hadyn Tanner who were well known Union players at the time.

"They made Gus captain, quite an honour although he was always first choice. Later on in the war the Welsh team played Ireland in Belfast and Gus again captained the side. He marked the great Irishman Jackie Kyle and it was 'poetry in motion' to watch them both as they were amazingly skilful players.

"After the war, Jackie Kyle became a surgeon and I remember the first Rugby League season in 1945 he made an unexpected visit to the Bradford dressing room before one game. He just popped by to say 'hello' but he'd have been a good signing had he wanted to make the switch."

These were strange days indeed, none more so than when League players took part in Rugby Union games staged on Wigan's hallowed Central Park. Lancashire played Yorkshire in aid of the British Red Cross Society in March 1941, Yorkshire having at least ten professional players in a game they won 15-8, with a 'Unionesque' nice round attendance figure of 6,000. Twelve months later, in 1942, Lancashire beat Yorkshire 22-6 and, in April 1943, the Royal Air Force played the combined Services in aid of the RAF Benevolent Fund.

In 1943, a Rugby League representative team played a similarly comprised Rugby Union team under Union rules and beat them 18-11. However, although League players were allowed to play Union during the war the 'honour' was not reciprocated, even with the thaw in relations Union players weren't allowed to play League.

That said, the Welsh Services International Rugby Union team of 1942 contained Gus Risman, Trevor Foster, Willie Davies, Ike Edwards and Alan Edwards who had all played League previously. The England Rugby Union team featured such as Ernest Ward, Jimmy Stott, Roy Francis (oddly, a Welshman), Stan Brogden and Johnny Lawrenson.

Counter attack!

The British Army played the French in Paris in 1944, a fixture organised to raise the spirits of the French. The team arrived by plane a few days beforehand and on the Friday were boarded in a barracks just outside Paris, due to be driven to the famous Parc des Princes the next day. The war seemed all but over by then but events took a dramatic turn as the match progressed.

Leading towards the end of the second half, a strange atmosphere began to build in the crowd. Various shouts and cries came from the supporters but they seemed to have nothing to do with the game. As the game finished news arrived of a German counter attack that had forced a bulge in the Allied front. Obviously the crowd had already got wind of this and became worried that Paris may be in danger again.

Trevor recalls: "On leaving the field we were hurried away through the streets of Paris. On every street corner there seemed to be a boy selling newspapers with the news of the counter attack and which made us pretty nervous. Upon arrival at our barracks we learnt that all non-essential flights had been grounded so the team had to stay the night in France. It was a frightening experience and certainly put things into perspective, the game of rugby we'd just played was suddenly at the back of our minds."

More memories. "In 1945, just after the end of hostilities, we happened to play the South Africans at Alamein. The South Africans then as now were a great rugby playing nation and had some very talented players. I was stationed in North Africa at the time and had the honour of captaining the team in this game. At this time, though, many players were more bothered about getting home to their loved ones than playing rugby, and when they found their transportation home had been put back a few days some members of the South African squad rioted in protest.

"There was quite a rumpus in the Egypt Hotel where we were all staying and after the reception some rather drunk and disgruntled South Africans picked up a taxi outside and turned it over in the street."

The Indomitables

With the war petering out the Rugby League authorities made a momentous decision to tour Australia and New Zealand in 1946. It would be an arduous tour over five months and, after circumnavigating the globe, would bring home the Ashes. For those fine outstanding British players the rewards and achievements would enter the annals of history by becoming the only Great Britain team to play a Test series against Australia and remain unbeaten. I wondered if the ambitious schedule colud turn into reality with so many players still active in the services and scattered worldwide? Nevertheless the RFL organised trial matches that enabled the selectors to choose a squad. Let the great Trevor Foster continue his epic tale.

"I can still remember how elated I felt on opening the letter saying that I had been selected. Better still my teammates Frank Whitcombe, Ernest Ward, Jack Kitching, Willie Davies and Eric Batten had also been picked.

"Having assembled a squad the one problem remaining centred on transporting us 10,000 miles around the world. Shipping remained at a premium for other urgent matters. Luckily the Australian government lobbied their British counterparts to provide transport.

"They argued the tour would provide a much needed boost to morale and foster the recovery of people after the war. A sigh of relief all round then to hear the announcement that berths on the aircraft carrier *HMS Indomitable* had been allocated, due to sail to Australia.

"Obviously the team had to undergo a pre-medical and not without a hiccup! In those days it would be impossible to send out a replacement for an injured player so everyone had to be 100 per cent fit. My Bradford teammate, Frank Whitcombe appeared a little forlorn prior to seeing the doctor. He had mentioned about a leg injury that hadn't quite healed up. Concerned about the medical he went into the surgery with a brave face and came out twenty minutes later beaming from ear to ear! 'What happened?' we asked, 'no problem,' he replied, 'I just showed them my good leg!'

"Uniquely, this tour had reporters travelling with the party and one journalist, the popular Eddie Waring, became organiser-in-chief. For instance, with 11 Welshmen in the party he assembled a Welsh choir to entertain people on board and at various theatres in Australia. In his journalist capacity he had a room set up with a telephone and express mail facilities so he could get his reports back to England quicker than ever before. The party felt indebted to Eddie, a real player's man and well-liked.

"Thanks to my experience as an Army PT instructor I got the appointment of physical trainer for the tour party and it fell on me to get the rest of the players up from their bunks at 7.00am for a 'loosen up', resulting in my life being threatened on many occasions, especially by people like Frank Whitcombe, a huge burly man, even by Rugby League standards!

"As for the journey, the sun shone all the way and it felt very invigorating passing through the Mediterranean and Suez Canal. On the canal shores soldiers watched us go by, they knew the Lions were on the *Indomitable* thanks to coverage in the press and they called out to us on the boat, 'I'm from Dewsbury', 'I'm from Leeds', 'I'm from Barrow!' Truly, a wonderful experience. Rugby League was news in very far-flung places that year.

"The food on board the *Indomitable* differed completely from what the players had been used to in wartime. Unlike the rationing at home we found the food plentiful and very good quality, which included fresh meat, fruit and vegetables, things not seen for six years, just the job for 26 hungry players. I remember the biggest appetites on tour belonged to the biggest men. Frank Whitcombe and Ken Gee being the props could certainly eat and they took full advantage of the fare available. As another bonus the duty free drinks proved very popular, particularly the whisky at 4d a tot.

"When ordering a drink each player gave a number which they had been issued. Being teetotal, I didn't use mine but that didn't stop a few of my teammates making the most of it by ordering a few with my number. All good fun on the ship down.

"The journey continued out into the Red Sea and past what was then called Aden and now Yemen. This provided a stop-off to top up on supplies. To pass some time away different sports were played on the huge flight deck, nearly the size of a football pitch, and it's there a scary incident happened!

"During one of these games it so happened that the ball went over the side of the ship into the sea, something like sixty feet below. Immediately my Bradford teammate and winger Eric Batten leapt over the side into the sea to retrieve the ball. He landed in the water, swam over, collected the ball and then back to board the ship.

"Back on deck he received a summons before the Captain who tore a strip off him. Apparently the sea off Aden is shark-infested and Eric could have been eaten, though he hardly looked shocked by finding this out.

"Our journey continued on to Colombo in Sri Lanka, the last port of call before Australia and a regular haunt for the Navy. After 29 days sailing, we arrived at Fremantle in Western Australia.

"The whole journey had been on wonderfully calm seas. Our diet had been excellent and thankfully nobody suffered seasickness. The Navy had treated us really well. During this time the players had all bonded as a team and stood very well prepared for the Ashes series."

Dry land

"No sooner on arrival we got wind that an Australian ship due to ferry personnel back to England had broken down. Next thing, the *Indomitable* received orders to discharge the tour party and travelling priests and take on the personnel bound for England.

"We were put in a naval camp in Fremantle and stayed there for a week. To while our time away the lads organised a match,

Reds versus Blues with the tour party of 26 divided into two teams. Eddie Waring took the whistle and a good crowd came to see the match. The lads donated the money made from this game to the *HMS Indomitable* charity.

"After a week had passed by we then faced the ordeal of a 2,600-mile rail journey to Sydney, something not common back home. The train had a special galley or cookhouse and each player being issued with a knife, fork and spoon and a tin plate. Every mealtime the train would stop and food would be cooked and served. The only drawback was a lack of beds resulting in the little ones sleeping on the luggage racks and the rest of us in the seats and on the floor.

"Arriving at Sydney after a full week, hundreds of people gathered there to greet us and at this point somebody had the idea of sending our biggest men off the train first in order to impress the Australians. First off came Frank Whitcombe followed by Ken Gee then a few more burly forwards, simultaneously an Australian voice in the crowd called out: 'That's it! No more food parcels for England!'

"While I stood on the platform a chap came up to me and said, 'The night I left Newport fifteen years ago, I had a pint in your mother and father's pub.' It had been a terrific welcome, ten years since the last Great Britain tour, and what with the war being in between too it meant so much for everyone there to be back enjoying sport again."

Sydneyside

"Our hotel in Sydney overlooked the Sydney Cricket Ground, which in those days staged many a Rugby League match. Very handy for us, the players didn't need any transport to go and train each morning, as we just walked over the road. The party also received a lot of visitors including family and friends who had emigrated over there. The two weeks before the main business of the tour began gave us more time to work on our fitness and patterns of play. Remember after the long journey over on the *Indomitable* we were already very fit and this helped even more.

"After a titanic struggle we pulled through by a narrow margin in our first match, against New South Wales, the premier state side at the time. Many in the 60,000 crowd at the SCG had camped overnight to ensure getting in, such was the enthusiasm displayed for our visit.

"Our second tour game fell on a Sunday afternoon at Wollongong, 60 miles outside of Sydney. Unfortunately, during that game I got a knock on the knee when it accidentally came into contact with an Australian player. It became rather swollen and I had to come off. The injury didn't clear up too well and I perhaps should have rested it rather than continuing to train. Whilst still keen to play it got worse so I remained on the sidelines until the last few weeks of the tour when I regained my fitness. This came as a disappointment but I didn't feel homesick or anything, with so much going on and everyone feeling part of the team whether they played or not.

"The first Test against Australia in Sydney was a terrific match and one of the most intense struggles. The Australian players I most remember include the skipper, a man named Jorgenson an excellent centre threequarter, and my opposite number in the NSW game, the great Arthur Clues. During the game versus New South Wales he'd picked me up and knocked me from pillar to post all afternoon that day whether I had the ball or not!

"The first Test set before 64,000 fans ended as an 8-8 draw, with tries from Whitcombe and Horne and a goal from Risman, a good result for us as it now meant the Australians had to win the next two Tests to regain the Ashes. Great Britain had held the Ashes for the past twenty years or so and the lads felt pretty confident of keeping it that way after the first Test.

"One incident that happened on tour surrounded our fullback, the great Martin Ryan, not only a great player and the first attacking fullback to run at defences with the ball in hand but also a good looking man with a great singing voice. He'd already used his talent to great effect on Australian radio that had made him a big favourite with the locals. Being of Irish descent he liked to sing old Irish songs and the Aussie radio got him to do some when promoting the tour.

"Anyway, he became ill with appendicitis just as the party was due to move up to Brisbane for the second Test. Obviously he couldn't come with us so he stayed in a nursing home. The papers found out about this and printed a story saying that he felt lonely in this place after the team had moved to Queensland and asked for people to go and visit him. Visit him they did, the next day over 200 people gathered outside this nursing home, mostly girls! Good looking lad, though!

"Up to Queensland for the rest of us and although mid-winter it felt warm and sunny enough to train in shorts alone. It seemed great weather all year round. As in New South Wales we had been entertained lavishly in Queensland but our minds remained firmly on the job in hand, to win the second Test and so retain the Ashes. We didn't want to be the only team to go out there to lose.

"Up in Mackay we beat a local team 94-0 and Ernest Ward kicked 17 goals, the backs sharing 20 tries between them! Another game saw us beat Ipswich despite penalties being 18-0 in the locals' favour! Obviously some local referee tried to give their boys a bit of a helping hand.

"On the day of the second Test, the coach to the ground left at 1.00pm for the 3.00pm kick-off but, upon setting off, it soon became obvious that it wouldn't be possible to get there in time, such were the huge crowds making their way to the ground. The bus had to take us back to the hotel where the players quickly jumped into taxis with a police escort, thankfully arriving there in time at the second attempt.

"The match at Brisbane again saw a terrific contest with Britain at their best in securing a handsome win, 5-14, with Bassett going over for a hat-trick.

"After the second Test the party travelled back down to Sydney for the third and final Test. The Lions won that game too by a clear margin of 7-20 with Bassett just missing out on another hat-trick. By this time the Aussie crowd had seen enough with a lower turn out of 35,294. That result meant that the *Indomitables* were the first British touring party to go on an Ashes tour without losing a Test match against Australia, something that had never been done before or since.

"With the Australian leg of the tour completed we had a new experience, flying the six hours over the Tasman Sea from Sydney harbour to Auckland in a big seaplane. In the event the party split into two so the seaplane didn't carry the whole team at once. Obviously nobody wanted to lose the whole team in an accident. On arrival the pouring rain contrasted with the weather in Australia.

"With all due respect to New Zealand at the time, the players looked on the last part of the tour as a holiday. We'd had a very hard tour in Australia, won the Ashes and now wanted a bit of a rest. It poured rain the whole time but the welcome was very warm. We were well received by the Maori people and visited a lot of schools where the children sang for us, treating us like royalty.

"Next came the only Test match of the New Zealand leg of the tour at Carlaw Park. Surprisingly, although in terrible conditions of mud and pouring rain we just lost out in a tight match. Another loss followed this time in a game against a local team but the Lions managed to win a further five during that part of the tour to save any further embarrassment.

"At the end of the tour, Ernest Ward finished as top scorer with a 101 points from five tries and 43 goals.

"Finishing joint-top try scorers were Eric Batten, who like Arthur Bassett followed his father's example, having toured in 1910. Both Eric and Arthur scored 18 tries each."

Homeward bound

"The journey home proved as eventful as the journey out there, leaving New Zealand on a steamship bound for the United States with forty GI brides on board with us.

"Our voyage home set off across the Pacific Ocean, through the Panama Canal before getting the final ship from New York to England. On the evening of us leaving New Zealand the girls arrived to get on board, a very tearful farewell for them as they were leaving their families behind. Many of their families stood on the harbour waving goodbye, adding to the emotional scene.

"Once we'd set sail we got dressed for dinner in collars and ties but didn't see any of the girls, as they were obviously very upset, but after a few days they got to know us all and joined in playing games on the deck of the steamship. The funny thing was a rumour started to go around that they'd decided that they didn't now want to go to America but wanted to go to England with us!

"On arriving at Panama, the ship went through the great locks, a marvellous sight. You could see fish all around the boat as it went through the canal before docking at Panama City. We were allowed to go ashore for two to three hours for a look around there, but this nearly caused a diplomatic incident.

"The ship was due off at 11.00pm and all were aboard apart from Frank. He hadn't arrived and the rest of us became rather concerned that he might be left behind in Panama. Watching over the side of the ship up the quayside, eventually along staggered Frank, rather late and obviously a bit worse for wear. He'd apparently had a pint or two ashore and as he approached the gangway he picked up a signpost next to it and threw it in the water. At that very moment a Panamanian policeman walked by and saw what happened. This policeman was a huge man, bigger even than Frank, himself 6ft tall and nearly 19 stone, and he came over, grabbed Frank and put the handcuffs on him.

"With ten minutes to departure it looked as if Frank would be left 10,000 miles from home. Luckily, one of the Australian reporters on board with us, a certain Harry Sunderland, went down the gangway and talked the policeman into releasing Frank, but it was touch and go for a while.

"The boat managed to set sail from Panama, albeit a bit late due to Frank's antics on the quayside, however 24 hours from New York we got news of a shipping strike. The ship had to divert to Halifax, Nova Scotia in Canada, a great upset for the girls on board who had expected to meet their fiancés.

"During the time away there was a lot of correspondence with our families and loved ones. The post was very important to keep us up to date with life at home. The tour party arrived back six months after we'd originally set off on the *Indomitable*.

"On arrival back at Tilbury docks, the party was greeted by the directors of our various clubs and several RFL officials, all being very happy with the tour as whole. Some of us went back to our clubs immediately and others got extra time off to meet up with their families, something we all looked forward to.

"Record attendances ensured a profit of over £6,000 and this meant players received a bonus of £123 on top of a wage of £1.10s a week on board ship and £2.10s a week on land.

"It had been the tour of a lifetime and something I'll never forget. The *Indomitables* came back a very proud party of players. Nobody felt homesick at all during the trip despite the fact that some players didn't make the Test teams, including myself while I was injured. The players all became firm friends for life after that. I felt privileged to have played with great players like Willie Horne, a master at stand-off, and Gus Risman whose speeches as captain got the best out of the team. Another great personality was the great Workington forward Ginger Hughes, father of Emlyn Hughes the Liverpool and England footballer. Ginger didn't get in the Test team but still made a great contribution. He liked a joke too, always creating fun around the place. This made for a good atmosphere and made being part of the touring team a very enjoyable experience.

"Although the players had been away for six months our clubs accepted the fact and considered it prestigious to be contributing players to the Great Britain team, the Ashes tour being regarded as the highlight of the game only coming around every four years. There was no animosity from the clubs at all, even though it meant missing a few of the opening matches of the following season.

"There had been much talk amongst the British players of staying in Australia and playing for an Australian club side and behind the scenes a lot of offers had been made. Both Ernest Ward and I received offers. South Sydney approached me but I decided to stay in Bradford as Northern had built a very powerful side and stood on the verge of honours. Many players had been away from home because of the war and wanted to get back to normality and as a result opted to turn down the Australian dollar. In the years after the war Bradford had successive trips to Wembley so it felt great to be at home!"

As the players adapted to life back home in Britain the new

Labour government embarked on the process of introducing some social welfare provisions.

During 1946 legislation for the National Insurance Act came onto the statute books guaranteeing an old age pension for everyone. The compulsory scheme took a weekly contribution from the worker and on their retirement returned a weekly pension starting at 26 shillings a week or 42 shillings for a married couple. Everyone became entitled to sickness and unemployment benefit.

1947 and the coldest winter

1947 saw a very cold winter for Britain, demand for coal and electricity was so large that all fuels were severely rationed. For some weeks it became illegal to use electricity in the home between 9.00am to midday and 2.00pm to 4.00pm.

Many factories had to close due to lack of coal. Bread and potato rationing had been brought in and in almost all cases allowances were lower than during wartime. The demob suit issued to each serviceman the day he left the forces did little to keep out the cold.

Trevor continues: "There were a lot of postponements of matches but bigger clubs would call in supporters to put straw on the pitch to protect it from frost. Often adverts were put in the local papers to attract fans to help. The clubs would provide hot drinks to those that helped out.

"On cold days, we often had to use a bit of 'fiery jack' to keep the cold out. The assistants in the changing room, what are nowadays physiotherapists but then were just the man in the street, really used to help rub down players with it. In terms of playing equipment not many players had padding but a few wore scrumcaps.

"I used one once at the Boulevard as my ears were becoming a bit sore so the kitman gave me a nice gleaming white scrumcap to wear. Well that made me 'the target of the night' and I was knocked from pillar to post. The bright white scrumcap certainly helped them see me coming. Needless to say I didn't wear it again.

"Boots were much heavier in the 1940s as there weren't the lightweight materials available that there are now. Two men on the staff, Dick and Maurice used to make sure the boots were well looked after and clean for each game. Each Friday they'd spend the day looking after the boots and making repairs."

Box of tricks

During the 2004 Bradford versus Saints Challenge Cup match, I met up with two lads from Bradford, Phil Beverley and Henry Caigill. After a good chat about times gone by, Henry kindly loaned me some old memorabilia including programmes and newspapers from his box of Rugby League bits and pieces.

Pride of place has go to our cherished Trevor Foster once again, who at the ripe young age of 89 is still keeping time at Bradford home games. Rummaging through the offerings I came across Trevor's Souvenir Brochure 1938/1955 priced one shilling. Included here is one of several press reports that I hope doesn't cause the great man too many blushes.

From the *Daily Herald*: "When youngsters talk of forwards in the days to come, the old 'uns will talk of Trevor Foster – one who has hands as misleading as a gifted half-back; one who kept his head when the going was fierce and gave science preference when strength alone might just have been as successful; one who was universally admired as the shining example of the scheming and spectacular school as compared to the 'bull-at-the-gate' type."

Trouble at the BBC

The good old BBC comes in for plenty of criticism from my adoring fans in modern times, who often feel my game is sold short, but is it a latter-day problem? Not if you read an article entitled "Cap, Bells and Blunderbuss" in *Rugby League Review* all those years ago!

"In grand array the would be muzzlers of *Rugby League Review* have been paraded in these columns during the past year. From the referee who let the cat out of the bag to the president who guarded his cakes, they have proved a motley crowd. Now the ranks are joined by no less a force than the BBC in the person of (to quote his own words) 'the well known sports journalist and broadcaster' – Mr Kenneth Wolstenholme. While many others have darkly hinted at dire consequences to our person, Mr W. has issued an ultimatum and appears in no doubt over its acceptance. We are not even offered the choice of swords or pistols, but simply ordered to prostrate our unworthy carcass at the feet of the great panjandrum."

The gist of the problem stems from *Rugby League Review* daring to criticise the standard of the BBC's reporting of Rugby League on *Sports Special* presented by Mr Wolstenholme. To quote further from the article: "It will be remembered this particular article (they the BBC) contrasted the services given by newspaper men in the Saturday evening sports editions with the 'mess' and there is no other word – made by the BBC with their sports coverage."

After threats from Mr H. to the *Rugby League Review* the reply forthcoming was thus: "If Mr Wolstenholme is unable to stand criticism, let him ask for his cards and return to the 'numerous newspaper contracts' which he assures he has held down for more than 24 years. The *Review* has no intention of apologising to Mr Wolstenholme with fresh evidence emerging from RL radio commentators that they, the BBC, are incapable of dealing with the game and request Mr Wolstenholme apologises to the whole body of RL listeners."

Saturday only, by government decree!

Moving on to a programme I picked up gives another insight into times gone by. The Halifax versus Leeds official souvenir Cup Final programme printed for the game on the 6th June 1942 at Odsal, Bradford has some meaty comment.

In what amounted to just a folded-up piece of paper priced 2d it only had one page devoted to previewing the game. After an introduction to how the respective teams won through there was an interesting piece about playing on a Saturday:

"Everyone is asking what the prospects of Rugby League Football

Like Hunslet and Huddersfield before them, Swinton won 'All Four Cups' in 1927/28 - and then went one better by adding a fifth - the Salford Infirmary Charity Cup. Proudly displaying their haul, they are pictured at their Station Road ground. (pp133)

A rare picture of the first Challenge Cup Final to be held at Wembley. Here, a scrum collapses as Wigan and Dewsbury battle out the 1929 showpiece event. Wigan won 13-2 in front of a crowd of 41,500. (pp122 & 414)

In 1934, Jean Galia introduced Rugby League to France. The growth was rapid - within five years the French had 225 member clubs and their national side defeated England to win the European Championship. (pp146)

Jim Sullivan joined Wigan from Cardiff and became the most prolific goal-kicker of all time - in 928 career games, he kicked 2,687. One of the greatest defensive fullbacks the game has seen, he was also handy on attack, crossing for 96 tries. He kicked the first-ever goal in a Rugby League match at Wembley, when he led Wigan to victory over Dewsbury in 1929. A triple tourist in 1924, 1928 and 1932, he retired in 1946 but remained at Wigan as coach for another six years. (pp135)

The 1948 Challenge Cup Final was the first to be televised - and the first to be attended by a reigning monarch. Here, King George VI shakes the hand of Bradford Northern captain Ernest Ward. Northern lost 3-8 to Wigan.

Gus Risman was born in Cardiff to Latvian parents in 1911. A talented sportsman, he was touted by Tottenham Hotspur FC but decided on a rugby career and agreed to join Lance Todd's Salford in 1929. He enjoyed a career which spanned a quarter of a century, playing 873 games and scoring 4,052 points. He was central to Salford's great success during the 1930s, winning the Championship three times, the Challenge Cup once and the Lancashire Cup four times. He left in 1946 to join Workington, who had entered the League the previous year. In eight seasons as player-coach, he played 301 games for the Cumbrians, guiding them to Championship and Challenge Cup success. (pp179)

The Lance Todd Trophy was first presented to the Challenge Cup Final man of the match in 1946, when Wakefield's Billy Stott (above) was the recipient after guiding Trinity to a 13-12 success over Wigan. Lance Todd was the 1907 New Zealand 'All Golds' tourist who became coach of Salford from 1928 to 1940. He was killed in a car crash in 1942. (pp75)

In the inaugural Rugby League World Cup, Great Britain defeated France 12-16 in the final at Parc des Princes, Paris. Skipper David Valentine lifts the trophy. (pp218)

The 1954 Challenge Cup Final Replay at Odsal between Halifax and Warrington attracted a world-record crowd of 102,569. After ending 4-4 at Wembley, Warrington emerged from the replay victorious by 8-4. (pp202)

The 1952 Challenge Cup Final between Workington Town and Featherstone Rovers was the first to be televised across the nation - in 1948, the year of the first televised Rugby League match, the final had been broadcast only to those living in the Midlands.

In 1958 Great Britain defeated Australia 18-25 in the Second Test at Brisbane with only eight fit players on the pitch. Captain Alan Prescott played for 77 minutes with a broken arm. Here, 'Captain Courageous' is carried round the Sydney Cricket Ground after his men secured a 1-2 series win with a 17-40 victory. (pp216)

Billy Boston joined Wigan from Neath RUFC in 1953, and made such an impact that he was selected to tour Australia with Great Britain after playing just six games. For his club, he became a prolific try-scorer, crossing 478 times. He went to Wembley six times, winning three finals, before leaving Wigan for Blackpool Borough in 1968. (pp209)

Brian Bevan was born in Bondi, Australia, in 1924. In 1945 he boarded HMAS Australia as a naval stoker and headed for war-time Britain. He made contact with Bill Shankland, a 1930 Kangaroo, who suggested he try his luck at Leeds. They rejected the 21 year-old, as did Hunslet So he travelled to Warrington, where he scored a try in a trial match. The rest, as they say, is history. In his first season at Wilderspool he scored 48 tries, and within four years had overtaken the club try-scoring record. He went on to register over 100 hat-tricks, and won every available honour in a 16-year career with Warrington. (pp207)

are for next year, and the answer to that question will certainly be
materially affected by the lead given officially by the Government,
as to what they wish clubs to do. If they think that the staging of
Football matches on Saturdays only is in the best public interest, let
it clearly say so. No doubt they will have realised that the Saturday
afternoon visit to a football match is the relaxation and pleasure of
many thousands of workers who throughout the week are putting in
long hours doing essential war work. Although your guess is as good
as mine, it is with certain confidence that I feel that, difficult as the
staging of Rugby League Football may be next season, ways and
means will be found to carry on."

In the field of play

Like everything else post-war, paper was in short supply and in
another programme of basic simplicity for Workington Town
versus Hull I found no comment on the game in general, although
it did have a diagram of a Rugby League pitch on the back. This
well-informed effort no doubt intended to help any converts to
understand the field of play.

Station Road Epitaph

Once again, the *Rugby League Review* comes up with the goods in
December 1948!

"After the Lord Mayor's Show...' This was my first thought after
watching the club match at Swinton which followed the two
'specials' played on the same turf – the Second Test and the
Lancashire Cup final.

"Not for a long time have I seen such a depressing game. The
lowest attendance and receipts of the tour – 5,000 spectators who
paid £650 – probably accounted for some of the initial depression.

"When the teams turned out with a funeral-like march, with
the crowd demanding the 'War Cry', it appeared as if the tourists
were going to miss the ceremony. However, I am assured by
Captain Wally O'Connell that they had no such intention.
Apparently the Australian 'War Cry' was the best on tour, and in

the author's words had more life in it that the match."

Cheeky blighter!

So, my friends, I hope you enjoyed a dip back in time and back the cuttings and magazines go into the box for future generations to rediscover.

Post-war hardship

Uncertain times for all after the end of the war. I put away a copy of the *Sunday Express* from 2nd June 1949 to look back on in later years myself, and reading it today reminded me of some of the hardships and worries of the post-war age, and some of the lighter moments.

Headed "What Stalin intends to do," one of a series of reports from a defecting Soviet colonel, Grigori A. Tokaev, warned: "Do not underestimate your peril. You in the west have left to you at the most five years and possibly as few as three years of peace, security and superiority. It will take the Politburo that long to complete the development of a practical atomic bomb." Chilling words indeed.

Worksop Rugby Club ordered fifteen jerseys via the Board of Trade, who gave permission to the manufacturers to make them, but the club only received eleven, being told they couldn't have the extra four unless they ordered another eleven. "The Board of Trade only think of soccer," complained the club spokesman, a Mr Wheeler.

Petrol was rationed to enough for 90 miles per month and a Leeds man appeared in the city's magistrates court for attempting to sell water, telling his victims it was black market 'white petrol.'

A report announced at a United Nations meeting at Lake Success pointed to better harvests of wheat, maize and rice so "the quality of bread should improve, rations should be increased and it may be possible to lift any restrictions of foodstuffs."

On the subject of agriculture, an advert for Fordson Major tractors advised that: "ploughing with two horses costs 15 shillings per acre, half the cost with a tractor."

On the radio, there was a choice of North, Light and Third stations, offering programmes such as 'records', 'reading', 'dialogues', 'familiar music' and the real showstopper 'The Archbishop of Canterbury.'

Monkeys were being used to pick tea in the Szechwan province of China and Jose Ruez, a professional hunter in Portuguese East Africa, had reportedly shot 200 elephants in two years and recently nine elephants in fifteen minutes. Not sure he'd get away with that now!

Try disallowed!

One St Helens half-back of the Second World War period is remembered for a disallowed try.

Breaking through on the burst, 50 yards from his opponent's line, Morris sped towards the posts. With only the fullback to beat he neatly sidestepped to score under the sticks, a better try one could not wish to see, and the referee had a perfect view as he followed Morris to the line. There could surely be only one decision, but without hesitation the ref signalled 'no try'! There was no question of a forward pass as no pass had been made, there was no knock on, no obstruction, and the ball had been correctly grounded, so why did the ref refuse to give what seemed a perfectly good try?

Well, it seems that as Morris received the ball it became deflated. By the time he reached the line the ball was well down giving the ref had no option but to disallow the try. I have no idea what Law 50[h] says today, but at the time it instructed that the referee must whistle as if the ball is out of play if the ball becomes deflated.

Strangely enough, the same problem occurred when Wigan toured France after the war, about 1946 or '47 as I recall. The ball became flat during one of their games and with no spare available the game was stopped while scouts chased around the town's sport shops to find a replacement!

War Years summary

The Great War had been a setback for civilisation as a whole, but

World War ll hit me as hard again. Had the world learnt nothing?

The ruined economies and infrastructures across the world left a terrible legacy and one which would take a lifetime to rebuild. Never mind the horrors of Burma, Stalingrad and Pearl Harbour, close to home lay ruins of bombed out streets and buildings, some of which, out of commercial reasoning or respect, have never been rebuilt to this day.

Amongst the tragic waste of human life many young men, rugby players amongst them, died serving their country. War Leagues disrupted my growth and the French game was abolished by the French collaborationist government decree. Just look where it is now compared to what it could have been.

The walls between sport had temporarily come down, but just as quickly gone back up again, as heavily fortified as the one in Berlin. Oppenheimer's bomb had obliterated the Japanese cities of Hiroshima and Nagasaki and cast a shadow for the prospects of future world peace. Although the fighting had stopped the Cold War between the political ideologies of the free west and Communist Eastern Europe and China had broken out in earnest. As Winston Churchill warned in 1946 after being booted out of office by Clement Attlee's 1945 Labour landslide election: "From Stettin in the Baltic to Trieste in the Adriatic an iron curtain has descended across the continent."

Whilst I'd been in suspended animation waiting for normality to return I had managed a little progress, edging up into Cumbria and putting down roots at Derwent Park, Workington in 1944 and setting up shop at the Recreation Ground, Whitehaven in 1948. Years of lost opportunity though.

Once again, time to pick myself up, dust myself off and, together with the rest of the country, start all over again.

7

1950-1960
THE THRIFTY FIFTIES

As the decade progressed, the fifties turned from an austere beginning into, for me at least, a time of largesse and middle-aged spread. The stress of life eased and times were good both on and off the field of play. I finally began to prosper.

The Second World War had finished only five years previously and the era began with an austerity not seen since. Food and clothing rationing continued with housing still in short supply and often in a poor state of maintenance.

On the positive side, unemployment queues shortened with labour needed to re-establish the country and its economy. I recall that most married women did not work in those times although after the war many women wanted to keep their independence, having kept the wheels of industry turning in the factories and on the land. They had coped well with daily life during the war in that they had to be breadwinner, raise the family and cope with daily administration. On the other hand, many returning soldiers, especially ex-prisoners of war were left with a sense on hopelessness coupled with a feeling of being 'redundant'.

Most young men had to serve a two-year compulsory period of National Service in the armed forces.

Cigarette smoking, the norm for men but not for women, hadn't yet been linked to cancer or heart and chest disease, however, improvements in social circumstances proceeded quickly. The world's first National Health Service, introduced in 1948, had already made a great contribution to the improvement of the public's health, but struggled to cope with the large number of chest and lung complaints. Smoke from coal fires, used to heat almost all houses, combined with fog to make 'smog', which killed 4,000 people in 1952. The 1956 Clean Air Act measures helped to clear up the 'pea soupers' and smogs but couldn't stop the damp winters. Other domestic heating was by way of paraffin lamps and stoves, which caused many problems with nightclothes catching fire. (By the way, does any reader remember using the old earthenware pop bottles as bed warmers?)

Britain and Holland suffered tragedy with the 1953 North Sea disaster although with the public only just getting over the horrors of the war to some extent the events have escaped the history books. Folk just didn't want to talk about the loss of life and massive scale of destruction.

The combination of high tides and gales started in Cumbria then worked its way down the east coast, seaside towns and villages suffering most as huge waves and flooding caused widespread destruction and the loss of over 300 lives in Britain and 1,800 in Holland. Pre-fabricated houses designed as a temporary, cheap option after the war were decimated with many washed away, although in some cases they came to the rescue as floating debris made makeshift liferafts.

The post had to go regardless so the mail ship *Princes Victoria* set out for Larne, Northern Ireland in atrocious conditions. Four miles from her destination she bore the brunt of a series of huge waves and sunk, all women and children lost, as well as all crewmembers with only 43 survivors. The officer sending the Morse messages stayed true to his post and lost his life with his body later found on the Cumbrian coast. No respite for local fishing boats sent out in the storm regardless, their owners more concerned with catching fish than the safety of the crew, some never to return with much loss of loved ones.

Queen Elizabeth ll was crowned in Westminster Abbey on 6th June 1953. Broadcasting had helped to involve the bulk of the population and although to own a television set was a rare achievement, 'open house' and street parties were organised turning the Coronation into a socially inclusive occasion. Of the adult population of Britain, numbering about 36,500,000, around 56 per cent watched the Coronation on television, some 20,400,000 viewers whilst radio had 11,700,000 listeners.

News arriving on the eve of the coronation announced that the British expedition to Everest, led by Lord John Hunt, had been successful. The first two men to the top were a Kiwi, Edmund Hillary and a local Nepalese sherpa, Tenzing Norgay who reached the summit on 29th May. Such is the nature of mountaineering that although one man leads and another follows, the effort is considered a team one and the conquest is regarded as shared. Failing to respect this, the media were determined to force one or the other to claim the first footfall on the summit and years later Tenzing wrote that it had indeed been his colleague, but sadly the public clamour had by then soured one of mankind's great achievements.

In spite of the general post-war austerity we all felt there was something of a feeling of relief and release after the ordeal and hardship of the war. Concern surrounded the dark goings on in the communist Soviet Union and in 1951 two spies, Burgess and Maclean, defected to Moscow, taking British state secrets with them. Winston Churchill became Prime Minister, overseeing the British response to the Cold War, atom bomb tests in the Monte Bello islands.

In 1953 the United States and the Soviet Union both tested thermonuclear devices within nine months of each other. The 'Doomsday Clock', an idea by *The Bulletin of Atomic Scientists* to symbolically represent humanity's proximity to nuclear destruction, moved the closest it has come to midnight, symbolising the zero hour of an apocalyptic nuclear attack, just two minutes away. (The farthest it has been set from midnight is

17 minutes away in a wave of optimism at the end of the Cold War, in 1991. The current time is seven minutes to midnight last set in 1998.)

As a public outlet for concerns about the worry of nuclear destruction the Campaign for Nuclear Disarmament was founded in 1958.

Some cheer arrived with the 1951 Festival of Britain and 1954 saw the end of food rationing in Britain although supplies were still short. The *Daily Telegraph* and *Morning Post* published a regular series of menus suggested by Egon Ronay advising how to: "feed a family of four appetisingly and well" for £4 and 15s a week.

No supermarket trolleys to contend with, of course, there being no self-service shops or supermarkets yet. Restaurants were too expensive for many although Lyons Corner Houses proved popular, snappy service coming courtesy of waitresses called 'Nippies.'

In the early fifties, Mr and Mrs Average had lino on the floor and if they could afford it there would be a carpet in the middle. They didn't have a washing machine, television, car, telephone, computer, double glazing (who remembers Jack Frost on the windows during the cold winter weather?), central heating, a fridge or freezer. Bread didn't come sliced and toasting forks were common, as there were no such thing as toasters. One would place the bread on the end of the fork and hold it close to the fire, absolutely delicious! An amazing fact is that today's video recorder alone has more computing power than existed in the whole world in 1950.

Radio remained the mass media of the time with the *Dick Barton* series as popular then as *James Bond* is today. In the days before play stations, children's entertainment came from such as *Rupert, Biggles, Just William* and the *Famous Five* books by Enid Blyton. William Golding wrote *Lord of the Flies* in 1952. The National Anthem ended every evening's cinema performance and people respectfully stood until the end.

Cultural change loomed just around the corner and one landmark date was 12th April 1954. That day bandleader Bill Haley recorded *Rock Around the Clock* with his Comets, so becoming the grandfather of a new style of music, rock 'n' roll, and the first popular singer to sell a million records, mainly to his 'Teddy Boy' followers.

Ruth Ellis was executed in 1955, the last woman to receive the death penalty in Britain.

Sport remained a tonic, as ever, and on 6th May 1954 Roger Bannister became the first man to run a mile in less than four minutes, in fact 3:59:4 at Iffley Road, Oxford in front of 3,000 spectators. Sadly, in 1958, 23 Manchester United players were killed in a plane crash at Munich airport.

Despite intermittent problems such as the 1956 Suez Crisis, the struggle for control of the Suez Canal after the British Army left Egypt, prosperity gradually improved throughout the decade. By 1959 the then Tory Prime Minister, Harold Macmillan, went into the General Election with the slogan that the British people "never had it so good." Economic growth stood at over three per cent a year and wages continued to steadily rise. A coal miner typically earned £7. 15s a week, whilst a police constable had an annual salary of about £445.

The *Daily Mirror* of 24th August 1956 quoted a Lowestoft housewife: "we often daydream of what we could do with £10 a week". She commented on her husband's allowance: "the average pocket money allowed by wives is 25 shillings, and that's often got to pay for fares and lunches." House prices held firm and, above all, everybody was in work, and all this with low inflation.

Package holidays had yet to arrive with Gatwick airport only being opened in June 1958 and Heathrow amounting to only a collection of huts. Still no motorway travel in the early fifties although by 1959 the Mini had gone on sale and part of the M1 had opened. One could hire a bicycle but beware, cycling at night with no lights meant a 10 shillings fine, or 50p in today's terms. Not only that but air at a garage was free.

Just before the start of my 60th year I staged an event that I mark as one of the milestones of my life. During those years I had thrilled so many people, drawing bigger and bigger crowds to my game in the post-war years. In that respect would the 1950s disappoint? Dr Jack Whittaker helps me rack my brain for details.

The 1954 Odsal Replay

Warrington and Halifax stood proud as the two leading teams of the 1953/1954 season, and both won through to Wembley, although neither had a particularly easy passage as Halifax scraped past Wigan 2-0 in the third round and Warrington won tight games in the second round and the semi-final.

The final took place on a fine Saturday afternoon before a crowd of 81,841 but the rugby didn't match the weather and the crowd saw one of the dreariest of all Wembley finals, a defensive game starving the talented wingers on both teams of possession. There were no tries and the scoring extended only to two Halifax penalty goals in the first half to which Warrington replied similarly in the second half.

The replay had to be delayed for eleven days to allow the same two clubs to play Championship semi-finals. Halifax had finished top with Warrington second, both teams having won all their 18 home games to set up a Championship final between them.

This no doubt increased interest in the Cup Final replay, but no one foresaw the phenomenal crowd that converged on Odsal that day.

Twenty five-mile traffic jam

The chaos surrounding the Odsal replay was not predicted, and seemingly least of all by the stadium management.

With the replay scheduled for late on a Wednesday afternoon and the previous ground record being 69,898, most estimates had been for a crowd of under 60,000, fewer than half those that actually gained entry. The railway authorities must have known these estimates as they provided only six excursion trains from Warrington with no special trains whatsoever from other towns. This lack of suitable rail transport no doubt forced thousands of fans to travel by road.

Throughout the day, vehicles of every description poured into Bradford with the queue stretching for miles. Robert Gate's book *There Were A Lot More Than That* describes the scene in the hills above Ripponden on the afternoon of the 5th May 1954:

"There was a seemingly endless cavalcade of motor vehicles winding slowly and anxiously down over the moors from Oldham and Rochdale. Those towns are 10 to 12 miles from Ripponden, which is six miles from Halifax, and from Halifax to Odsal is another good seven miles. Imagine that, a continuous line of traffic snaking from Oldham to Bradford, 25 miles across the backbone of England."

Similar, although smaller, queues stretched east to Leeds and south east on the road from Wakefield, this game clearly amounting to more than a domestic affair between the finalists. These supporters had better luck than those in the main jam, and although progress took time, access to Odsal from these directions was not obstructed.

Two hours before kick-off time most fans coming from the direction of Halifax found it impossible to reach within two miles of Odsal except on foot. Thousands of spectators abandoned their cars to walk to the ground, but on arrival found even more chaos. By kick-off there were 1,239 coaches parked around Odsal, together with an estimated 9,000 cars.

Gatecrashers

The length of the turnstile queues made entrance to the ground extremely slow. One result of this mass of humanity was the collapse of fencing surrounding the ground through which thousands of fans found an easier entrance. Whether this had been a deliberate act or simply the inevitable result of pressure from the crowd has never become clear.

One group that travelled to the match had some good fortune. On nearing the ground the driver of their mini-bus became increasingly agitated by the traffic congestion. His passengers, who by this time had probably had a fair bit to drink, made his mood no better by their friendly ribbing. Having parked his bus, the driver leapt out first out shouting, "as I haven't been able to have a drink I'll make damn sure I'll be first in the ground." He duly ran to the turnstile queue, well ahead of his passengers, and hurried to pay his admission. Just as he entered the ground the fence collapsed and his mates stepped through the hole without paying. The driver's comments are not recorded and how his passengers travelled home is not known either, but it may not have been on the bus in which they arrived.

Although the gates had been shut half an hour after kick-off, spectators still squeezed into the ground through the broken fences.

They probably felt themselves luckier than another coachload who arrived so late that they didn't think it worth going into the ground, staying on their coach and listening to the game on the radio. Their return journey sounded even worse, jammed for several hours in the traffic leaving the ground.

Players' Views

Arnie Stevens played as a centre for Warrington in the Wembley final and as first reserve at the Odsal replay. He gave me his insider's view of fifty years ago.

"We knew it was to be something special as we had to have a police escort from our hotel in Ilkley. The changing rooms then were at the top of the slope, and although we could hear the crowd, we could not believe our eyes when we came out to go down to the pitch. I had never seen so many people in one place in my life; it was as though every Rugby League supporter was there, and more coming in.

"The game was a classic, from end to end, and after the drab game at Wembley it showed what the two teams were capable of. With the massive crowd it took us nearly forty minutes to get from pitchside back to the dressing rooms.

"Halifax had fielded a strong side in both the Wembley final and the Odsal replay, and were favourites to take the Cup. The team's playmakers were the famous halfback pairing of Dean and Keilty, a combination that had won many matches for Halifax."

Writing almost fifty years on, this is Ken Dean's memory of the replay. "It started like any match day. I went to work in the morning, home for lunch, a quick shower and change of clothes and down to Bull Green in the Halifax town centre, where we always picked up the coach.

"All the lads were there on time as usual. Frank (Dolly) Dawson, our coach, would not allow any player to be late or he immediately dropped you from the team sheet, and that meant no pay. By this time everyone was remarking on the amount of traffic about, particularly coming down King Cross Road from Lancashire, and meeting up with all the Halifax supporters. The need for a police escort to get us through to Odsal was quickly decided.

"On arrival at Bradford the scene was amazing. A large crowd had been expected, 60,000 or more had been mentioned. Most Halifax supporters got into the ground, but many from Lancashire gave up hope and listened on the coach or car radio. Amazingly there was no serious injury recorded in the crowd, but it is said that quite a lot saw very little of the match."

The attendance of 102,569, at the time a world record for any form of rugby football, was exceeded only by estimates of the 'real' attendance. The police and Odsal officials put the crowd at 120,000 and other reliable observers at 10-20,000 more. The game had to be played with the overflow of spectators sitting around the pitch, so close that a path through them had to be cleared for goal kicks taken from near the touchline.

The game itself was a much more exciting affair than the earlier Wembley final. Warrington scored two tries, one a spectacular try from scrum-half Gerry Helme late in the game deservedly clinching the Lance Todd Trophy and a win for Warrington, 8-4.

With the passage of time it is easy to forget that the game itself was contentious with several disallowed tries. There was plenty of comment in the press for some time after the game, but there we have it, a Warrington win, or if you prefer it: 'Halifax was robbed'!

Ever since my birth in 1895 I have had the pleasure of generating healthy debate among players and spectators alike, and it seems that the result of the Odsal replay was no exception. Just imagine if I had had the benefit of a video replay in those days, but who in the crowd would have been able to see it!

Cumbrian cups

What else did the Challenge Cup in the 1950s offer? No team can be said to have dominated the competition although Wigan did well with wins over Barrow, Workington Town and Hull. Warrington treated their fans with successes against Widnes and Halifax.

Perhaps the most memorable feature of the cup in those times came in the great performances from some unfashionable teams, emphasising just what a great competition the Challenge Cup had become. Top marks go to two teams from the somewhat remote part of the far north west, Barrow and Workington Town.

Worky entered the Rugby League in 1945 and by 1952, inspired by their captain, the 41-year-old legend Gus Risman, amazed everyone by not only reaching but also winning an exciting 18-10 final over Featherstone, themselves taking their first Wembley bow.

Although never again were they able to reach those heights in the cup, Town came close as losing Wembley finalists in 1955 and 1958.

The somewhat older Barrow club had come agonisingly close to cup success many times. Back in 1938 the Shipbuilders lost at Wembley to Salford and in 1930, 1935 and 1949 were losing semi-finalists.

Again reaching Wembley, Barrow lost the 1951 final to Wigan 10-0 and in 1952 they proved themselves one of the most consistent Cup teams in the years around the War by again reaching the semi-finals, only to be edged out by arch-rivals and eventual-winners Workington Town.

Finally, success and revenge with defeat of Workington 21-12 in the 1955 final, arguably the greatest achievement in the history of the Barrow club, although they have since repeated the triumph of an appearance at Wembley.

I can look back on the fifties as one of my finest periods, with countless great players established or emerging. In 1988 I decided it was high time to recognise and celebrate a selection of the very greatest. The 13 lads commemorated in the Hall of Fame today include no fewer than seven who played at their peak in the 1950s. Take a bow Brian Bevan, Billy Boston, Neil Fox, Vince Karalius, Alex Murphy, Gus Risman and Tom Van Vollenhoven.

Among these heroes are two of the greatest wingers of all-time, Brian and Billy.

The Great Bev

Brian Bevan is, and probably always will be, my most productive try scorer with 796 tries in the first-class game of which 740 were scored for Warrington, where he spent the major part of his long career.

Bevan, born in Sydney in 1924, first played as a stand-off at primary school, but following injury his father thought the wing a more suitable position, apparently not because of his frail frame, but because as a junior New South Wales sprint champion he certainly had the required pace. His father took him to all the big Rugby League games at the Sydney Cricket Ground and, on the way home young Bev would side-step the telegraph poles *en route*, developing the ability to step off either foot.

He followed his father by signing for Eastern Suburbs between 1941 and 1946, although his war service limited him to only eight first-grade games, in none of which he scored. He was soon to make up for that with a vengeance.

Shortly before the end of his wartime service in the Navy, he was transferred to a ship heading to England for repair. On arrival he made contact with Bill Shankland, a friend of his father, who had played both for Eastern Suburbs and for Warrington and earned his living as a golf professional in Leeds. Bill introduced Brian to both the Leeds and Hunslet clubs; neither gave him even passing interest so Bill suggested trying his old club, Warrington. The rest, as they say, is history.

Although he will always be one of my greatest wingers, Brian's appearance was the very antithesis of greatness with his thin frame and spindly legs taped up with bandages around his knees.

To add to the impression of frailty, Brian looked much older than his years, having premature baldness. These negative impressions were soon put to rest when he got the ball, for he was not just a try-scoring machine but a great player who excelled in almost all aspects of the wingers' craft.

Bev played in 688 first class games, rarely failing to score, with three or more tries on a staggering 101 occasions, including six tries in a match four times and seven in a match twice. He topped the Warrington try scoring list in each of his 16 seasons, except for 1956/1957 when limited by injury and scored more than 50 tries in a season nine times. During Brian's most prolific season, 1952/1953 he managed 72 tries, just short of the all-time record of 80 set by Rosenfeld before World War One.

Perhaps one of the best ways to try to appreciate his greatness, now that we can no longer see him play, is to read what his colleagues and opponents said about him.

Jim Challinor, his centre partner at Warrington: "A superb sidestep he had, but what really used to make even the most experienced players grasp at thin air in the tackle was his change of pace. He had a sudden fantastic acceleration that no one could anticipate."

Harry Bath, the Warrington captain and fellow Australian: "He dazzled his opponents so many times, and turned the result of a match so often, that many deeds that would have lived forever with another player have been forgotten."

Clive Churchill, the great Australian fullback and captain: "At the peak of his career he was a phenomenon. I've seen him gather the ball behind his own goal line, pierce his way through all 13 opponents, and race the full length of the ground for a scintillating try."

Bernard Ganley, Oldham and Great Britain fullback: "I have been left standing by Brian more times than by any other player. I never was able to get him in a tackle. Whenever he had the ball I used to look round for help for I knew it was hopeless to try and take him single-handed."

Lewis Jones, Leeds and Great Britain fullback: "Time and again opponents, myself among them, could have sworn that the Warrington flyer was going full bat, only to find him producing a last-second surge of pace to leave them and the spectators breathless."

Brian Bevan died on 3rd June 1991 in a Southport hospital aged 66. Tributes to his greatness poured in from all over the world, including one from his opponent and great rival Billy Boston who said: "Brian Bevan was the greatest I have ever played against. He was a real gentleman. No one will ever get near his record."

Brian is honoured by his statue, which now stands outside Warrington's new Halliwell Jones stadium.

King Billy

William (Billy) John Boston was born in 1934 in Cardiff's Tiger Bay docklands, the middle child of seven. His father came from West Africa and his mother from Ireland. As a child he attended the small South Church Street school in Cardiff's Butetown which has the amazing record of contributing two players to the Rugby League Hall of Fame, for Gus Risman had been a pupil there some years before Billy.

Billy's ambition was to play Rugby Union for Wales, so it is perhaps surprising that his career in the Welsh game was confined to junior and district rugby in Cardiff together with an occasional game for Neath. Maybe the selectors missed his fabulous talent, and supporters of that game in Wales had to wait until 1986 to see the first black man play in its international colours. Billy's decision to 'go north' was probably quite unconnected with this but in passing I can note that the first black man to play Rugby League for Wales did so 50 years earlier, in 1936.

Billy signed for Wigan not long after his 19th birthday in 1953. At that time the great Wigan team of the post-war years was breaking up and their coach, Boston's fellow Welshman, the legendary Jim Sullivan, was scratching his head to come up with something that would help to renew his team's success. In Billy Boston he found the ideal catalyst.

Such was his impact that, still 19 and after only half a dozen games for Wigan, he was selected for the 1954 tour of Australia and New Zealand. In view of his limited experience, he was chosen for the less important fixtures of a gruelling 32-game tour and wasn't selected for the first Test in which Britain suffered a disastrous defeat.

Billy's chance came in the second Test and he seized it with both hands, scoring two tries and helping Britain to victory. He played in all the remaining Tests in both countries, finishing with a record 36 tries in only 18 appearances in Australia extending this to 50 from 26 matches on the New Zealand leg of the tour. In doing so Billy equalled Jim Leytham's record of four tries in a Test match, set in 1910, which he repeated in the first Test in New Zealand.

When he began playing Billy weighed 12 and a half stones but, as he matured and gained weight, he acquired the strength and ability to burst out of almost any tackle, with exceptional speed, a body swerve and a fine pair of hands.

Billy's career with Wigan finished after 15 seasons in 1968 but he came out of retirement to play 11 games for Blackpool Borough in 1970. In all Billy chalked up 571 tries in first-class matches, the most by any British player at almost a try a game for Wigan, 478 in 488 appearances, and 24 for Great Britain in 31 matches.

In three seasons he scored 50 or more tries, with 60 in 1956/1957. Over the years there have been many tributes to Billy Boston, but one of these seem to me especially apt. Billy's schoolmate, Gus Risman, in his autobiography said of a young Billy: "He has speed and handling ability right out of the ordinary and I have yet to see any player with the same ability as Boston for bursting out of a half-tackle.

Many is the time opponents think they have got him nailed, but somehow or other he can throw tacklers off and not lose a split-second. He is incredible and will most assuredly develop into one of the greatest players of all time."

A deserved tribute to one of my greatest, yet most modest players, who has given so much to me and to the Wigan club that he continues to regularly support with a passion.

Alexander the Great

Saints faced a hectic end to their 1956 season. Having won through the Challenge Cup rounds to face Barrow in the semi-finals, the tie ended 5-5 before a crowd of 38,897 and just four days later 44,731 fans gathered to witness the replay as the Saints triumphed 10-5 to book a date at Wembley. This lead to the Saints reversing a Championship semi-final defeat by Halifax and revenge over the Thrum Hallers at Wembley 13-2 in taking the cup home to the glass town for the first time.

In a challenging period after the Barrow cup semi, the Saints had to travel to play both Workington and Oldham away. In order to give their troops a rest the club played virtually a reserve side in the final league game at home against Whitehaven allowing the chance of the first step on a path to stardom for one of the greatest half-backs ever. Take a bow, Alexander James Murphy.

Born in Thatto Heath on 22nd April 1939, Alex took no time to earn his nickname 'Mr. Magic', impressing the Saints coach, the great Jim Sullivan, even before he could sign for the club. On leaving St Austin's school he was invited to train with the first team squad, and knowing Alex he wouldn't have felt out of place.

On the eve of his 16th birthday, after a final of a local cup competition, St Helens Chairman, Harry Cooke whisked him up to the Saints boardroom to offer terms of £80. Alex did not hesitate although there had been stiff competition for his signature. In fact, Alex had to be smuggled out of the ground in an MI5 type operation as four other clubs representatives waited in the wings.

A sum of £80 had to be the bargain of the decade. In his first full season 1957/58 he scorched in for 27 tries as the Saints finished runners-up in the league behind Oldham and even further rise to fame came before he had even won county honours.

The jubilant teenager was a shock choice for an outgoing Kangaroo tour, alongside five of his teammates. Selected at just 18 years of age, Alex became the youngest player to tour, going on to play in all three Test matches and his outstanding form helped Britain wallop the Green and Golds. In fact, after the final Test Alex picked up one of many beer glasses that had been thrown at the British team and in a spontaneous gesture toasted all four sides of the ground. Alex was growing up quickly.

Alex went on to become a legend during his playing career, eventually taking over the captaincy of his hometown club. It is difficult to select just one game that stands above the rest but the 1966 Challenge Cup third-round tie must be up amongst them. Saints trailed Hull KR with time almost up but not one to give in, Alex hoisted a massive up and under towards Hull KR's posts and, quick as a whippet, regathered for the winning try to take Saints to Wembley for the first of four trophies in the season.

Between 1961 and 1974 Alex appeared in four winning Challenge Cup finals for three different teams, St Helens, Leigh and Warrington, player-coach for three of them, and then between 1975 and 1989 coached Warrington, Wigan and St Helens to Wembley.

'Murph the Mouth' also presided over a long stint as an outspoken summariser on BBC television.

Love him or hate him, Alex was indeed a man of magic.

Visit the outstanding Saints Heritage Society's web site for a glowing biography on Alex Murphy although if you're unsure just how great he was, just ask him yourself, I'm sure he'll tell you...

National Service and Rugby League

As the Roman militarian, Vegetius stated in his *Epitoma Rei Militaris* (General Rules of War): "Let him who desires peace prepare for war". This was the reasoning behind the post-war conscription of civilians known as National Service.

Although the Labour 'landslide' government of 1945 favoured withdrawal from commitments to Empire, clearly some military support would be needed to fulfil Britain's responsibilities in a world still unsettled by conflict and change. The National Service Act was passed in 1947 to become effective on 1st January 1949. At first the obligation on men was one year, then 18 months and from 1950 two years, after which one had to serve three years as a reserve.

One Rugby League player to do his National Service, Alex

Murphy (what, him again!) went on to star for the RAF XV. Rugby Union I'm afraid, as I was still banned from the armed forces. Still, Alex flew my flag as being instrumental in enabling his team to compete with the Army and Navy in the inter-Services tournaments. As well as turning out for the RAF at Union he would double up playing Rugby League for St Helens the same week. Good lad.

For those not in the know, there were some decent perks to be had as a serviceman with time off for sport encouraged, as no doubt many more of my family who were called up for service discovered.

Ashes lost after thirty years

As the decade began, Great Britain, unbeaten by Australia for thirty years, reigned supreme and were favourites to maintain this superiority as the touring team departed down under in May 1950.

On paper the touring party of 26, captained by Bradford centre Ernest Ward, looked strong with a record eight players from the mighty Wigan club. However, judged on the results of Test matches the tour amounted to a disaster.

Keen defence enabled the Lions to hold out for a 4-6 win in the first Test, but in Queensland the tour fell apart as a 15-3 defeat in the second Test and a succession of injuries in the club games left only 14 men from which to choose the team for the decider.

Thus it came to pass in Sydney on 22nd July 1950 that Britain's thirty-year hold on the Ashes came to an end with a 5-2 defeat, but experiences in Queensland had soured the tour and undoubtedly contributed to the loss of the Ashes. Problems began as soon as the team entered Queensland with the inexplicable targeting of the scrum-half Tommy Bradshaw, both on and off the field. In the second Test both Tommy and his Wigan colleague, prop forward Ken Gee, were dismissed for using 'insulting language' to the referee. The official had disallowed what seemed like a perfectly fair try by stand-off Dickie Williams and when a second try was not awarded Bradshaw, the mildest of men, records that all he asked the referee was: "Is that a sliding try, Sir?" His dismissal and subsequent suspension, the first ever imposed on a touring player in Australia, ruined his tour and played on his mind for years afterwards.

Britain's misery continued in New Zealand with the loss of both Test matches and a very much wounded Lion returned home in the autumn of that year.

In keeping with my booming fortunes domestically, my game in the 1950s continued to show unexpected development internationally with each season bringing a Test match series, either at home or abroad.

In 1952 the Kangaroos took their turn to visit Britain, captained by the legendary fullback Clive Churchill. These post-war tours were very demanding with the 30 or so senior clubs all wanting to play against the tourists and 1952 continued the trend with games against seven clubs before the first Test at Headingley. The tough introduction to the tour seemed to have exhausted the Kangaroos who lost 19-6, their only points coming from penalty goals.

Prior to the second Test they faced a further seven clubs, playing some exciting rugby, but again seemed jaded in the following Test match which Great Britain won easily 21-5. Once again the Ashes returned to these sceptred isles.

Away from the Tests the tourists progressed better, defeating a further five clubs in addition to both Lancashire and Yorkshire and by then they had scored a record number of points for a touring team in Britain and carried this form into the third Test winning easily by 7-27.

The 'Roos had also conceded the lowest points by a touring party, but tours stand or fall by the Test match results and this side is remembered in Australia as the side that lost the Ashes having held them for only two years after a 30-year drought.

The 1953 Kangaroo tourists visiting New Zealand became the first Aussie side to fly out by aeroplane, predecessors having all set sail on the foaming brine.

A backward step for the 1954 Lions who hold the unenviable record of being, up to that time, the poorest team to represent me down under, winning only 13 of the 22 games played in Australia.

They started badly, losing two and drawing one of their first five games before the first Test in Sydney in which they were comprehensively thumped 37-12. The tour recovered in Queensland with six consecutive wins leading to victory in the second Test, 21-38, but the tourists fell into further disrepute as their game against New South Wales had to be abandoned. The referee Aubrey Oxford, having had his fill of the constant brawling and foul play, quit the game in the 56th minute and never officiated again. The showdown final Test in Sydney saw Australia recover the Ashes with a 20-16 win.

Although the Lions fared better winning two of the three Tests on the New Zealand leg of the tour, like the Jowett car works in Bradford that ceased production that year after a glorious run, 1954 saw the Lions a bit clapped-out.

One point to note is that the first Irishman to play for Great Britain, Tom McKinney turned out that year, a good while before the next one, Brian Carney in 2003.

Following the exhausting 1952 tour, the Kangaroos elected to play only 19 games in Britain in 1956. For their sake, this was perhaps as well as they had a shocker, particularly in the club games, the low point being their 24th November thrashing at St Helens by 44-2. All six Saints forwards, Prescott, McCabe, Terry, Silcock, Gaskell and Karalius, scored tries. The tourist's poor form affected the gates at Test matches, which saw an aggregate of 63,649, the lowest attendances since the War. Whilst Britain won the Test series 2-1 once again recovering the Ashes, perhaps more importantly for the Kangaroos, the tour was a financial disaster the Australians going home with a loss of over £8,000, a large sum in those days.

In terms of results, the 1958 Lions were the most successful British team of all-time. Of the 21 games played in Australia, 19 were won with one loss and one draw. But the tour had started badly with discontent among the management, which included a coach for the first time, remember 'Gentleman' Jim Brough? On the field there were several poor displays early in the tour, particularly a draw with a very weak Western Districts team who should have been easily dispatched. These performances led to a comprehensive 25-8 defeat in the first Test at Sydney.

Progressing north to Queensland, the Lions got back on track with several huge victories and arrived at the Brisbane for the second Test needing to win to save the series. In terms of heroics for many the game ranks alongside that of the 1914 'Rorkes Drift' Test (the one that finished with only 10 fit players), a game known thereafter as 'Prescott's Test.'

Prescott's Test

Born in Widnes on the 17th June 1927 Alan Prescott signed for St Helens from Halifax on 11th January 1949.

During an illustrious career he was to don a Saints shirt 404 times, gain 14 Lancashire County caps, represent England on 12 occasions and have the honour of playing 31 games for Great Britain. Captain and Lance Todd Trophy winner of the successful Saints Wembley cup final win in 1956 could well stand out as his finest achievement but not for Alan Prescott! His heroic deeds on the 1958 Australian Tour would go on to be remembered for many years after and gain much respect for the British bulldog spirit.

Great Britain, led by Prescott, had lost the first Test in front of a massive and partisan crowd of 68,777 at Sydney Cricket Ground. It had to be all or nothing in the second Test at Brisbane's Exhibition Ground. The omens did not look good as the referee that day was Darcy Lawler of NSW, reputed to be a 'Pom hater' supreme. It was common thinking amongst the Lions that he would leave no stone unturned to ensure an Australian victory.

The scene was set on the 5th July with the majority of the 32,965 crowd thinking only of an Aussie victory. Within three minutes more dark clouds hung over the Brits as captain Prescott fell heavily in a tackle breaking his arm between wrist and elbow. What followed next defines what sporting heroes are made of. After telling the coaching staff that he had suffered a break, Alan simply had the injury strapped up and went back on the field to continue. Still no substitutes in those days.

Bad to worse after eight minutes when Warrington centre, Jim Challinor was dumped heavily on his right shoulder. Taking advice from the touchline to soldier on as long as possible he played out the match with one limp arm.

Ten minutes in and the storm clouds had burst as Eric Fraser, the Warrington fullback, received a kick on his elbow and although saying little about it, continued in immense pain. Surely this was too much for any team to take and expect a win but...

Dave Bolton, the Wigan stand-off was next to suffer a cruel blow after 19 minutes when a crunching tackle forced him to see out the rest of the game from the touchline having broken his collar bone.

More adversity followed as Vinty Karalius, later nicknamed 'The Wild Bull of the Pampas', suffered a bad injury to his back that resulted in the loss of much of the use of his legs. At this 20-minute mark he had indeed been playing like a wild bull with some ferocious tackling.

Despite all this trauma Great Britain somehow led 2-10 at half-time via tries from Challinor and Sullivan and two goals from Fraser.

The half-time interval in the British dressing room resembled a casualty ward, overcast with an air of disbelief as the other players realised the extent of their captain's injury. Medical opinion decreed that he should not resume for the second half but Alan feared all could be lost. Alan's own decision went against medical advice and he duly took his place on the field of play.

Prescott had to keep changing playing positions to try and protect the broken arm from further aggravation and in doing so made the crowd aware of his injury resulting in a strange silence. Even if in the end his presence only inspired his destitute teammates it did the trick.

Eventually it was Karalius, playing at outside-half, that created the finale that clinched the win, scored by 19-year-old Alex Murphy, the youngest player ever to tour Australia.

The Poms held on to battle home 18-25 followed by amazing scenes at the end, as captain marvel Alan Prescott with his right arm in a sling was proudly held shoulder high by his jubilant teammates.

Great Britain went on to claim the Ashes in the final Test at the

Sydney Cricket Ground by Britain's biggest winning margin against Australia 17-40 before another huge crowd of 68,720. That game was not without controversy as the partisan crowd, displeased with what they saw as poor refereeing, temporarily stopped the match with a bombardment of bottles and anything else that they could find to throw at the hapless official.

The first World Cup 1954

For some time, I'd hoped to spread my international wings by bringing together my various national teams in a World Cup. Debate among those that cared for me had indicated wide support for this competition and in 1954 my dream became reality when the world's Rugby League family gathered together in France for the very first World Cup tournament of any code of rugby.

The World Cup concept was predominantly a French initiative. Now France had been a hot bed of Rugby League growth and, despite the best efforts of the Vichy government and the French RU only a few years before, it was becoming so again.

Paul Barriere, my French boss, wrote to the other three main playing nations in 1953 with his idea of a World Cup Series and it was also suggested that the USA be invited to participate. An experimental American All Stars team, mainly based on gridiron players had toured Australia in 1954 but came in for a few hidings so their involvement wasn't pursued.

Great Britain had toured Australia earlier that year and a gruelling tour had left many key players injured and exhausted with little appetite for further intense international competition. In consequence, the squad that left for France appeared weak, with only three of the 1954 Lions in the party. Dave Valentine, Huddersfield's Scottish loose forward, captained the team, the only other Lions being Gerry Helme, Warrington's scrum-half, and Phil Jackson, the Barrow centre.

Great Britain, New Zealand, Australia and France each were to play the others once in a league-type tournament with the side topping the table winning the cup.

To the amazement of just about everyone, the young Great

Britain team saw off the fancied Australians 28-13, going on to draw with France 13-13 (the best turnout of the competition of 37,471) and finished by beating New Zealand 26-6. France had also overcome the southern hemisphere sides. The final league table left Great Britain and France both with five points, Australia two points whilst New Zealand finished bottom with no points at all. A play-off, in effect the first Rugby World Cup Final, was necessary, scheduled for Paris on 13th November 1954.

All the matches had produced five-figure crowds and, although outside the rugby heartland of south west France, 30,368 fans converged to the Parc des Princes in Paris to witness a battle royale. The inexperienced British lads had been given little chance of success yet in a close-fought contest Great Britain took the first World Cup final 12-16 and in the process made a little piece of history.

The competition was an outstanding success prompting the Rugby League International Federation to register the name 'Rugby World Cup' as its trademark, no doubt hoping that this would discourage others from copying the title. Alas, recent experience shows that not to be the case.

These days it seems a sportsman doesn't actually need to win anything to merit an award in the Queen's New Year or birthday honours list.

Given that my game produced the first British team to win a World Cup in any major sport, and to this day none of my heroes or administrators have received 'owt', please permit me to acknowledge them myself: -

Jim A. Ledgard (Leigh), David Rose (Leeds), Phil Jackson (Barrow), Albert Naughton (Warrington), Mick Sullivan ((Huddersfield), Gordon Brown (Leeds), Gerry Helme (Warrington), John Thorley (Halifax), Stan Smith (Hunslet), Robert Coverdale (Hull), Don Robinson (Wakefield), Basil Watts (York), David D. Valentine (Capt.) (Huddersfield)

Australia staged a second World Cup in 1957 and with no play-off final scheduled the team finishing top of the league would take the cup.

Aussie duly dominated the whole affair winning all three of their games to finish top with six points whilst Great Britain, France and New Zealand ended up with two points each.

Although a tremendous success financially, Great Britain, as defending champions, had a torrid time with only one victory and that against a poor French team 23-5, nevertheless attracting 50,077 neutrals to the SCG.

The British party was far too small for an event of such importance with only 18 players. To make things worse several lads were injured in the France game, so that Britain's next game against Australia again at Sydney, ended up a one-sided affair with a 6-31 thrashing, Britain tryless, although the game did feature the best crowd of the competition at 57,955.

Matters deteriorated further when Great Britain capitulated 21-29 to the weak New Zealanders, the Kiwis' only win in the competition.

Unfortunately all this early promise of bigger and better international events fell flat. Future World Cups were blighted by ever-changing formats and no consistency in time scale so after a cracking start to my World Cup career the land of plenty declined to a "should we have a World Cup or not?" and the concept done bigger and better by other sports. I'll fill you in later.

New clubs for old

Every decade of the 20th century saw new clubs join me to play at the first-class level, but unfortunately only a few of these clubs survived long term in the toughest of all sports.

For every Featherstone Rovers (1921) or Castleford (1926) there have been a couple of dozen teams that weren't as durable, often after a promising start at the top level. When a team underestimates the demands of my professional game, both on and off the field, it's sad to see their demise. On the other hand, since the First World War none of the teams that established the Northern Union had folded.

Sadly, just before the start of the 1955 season this happened when Belle Vue Rangers withdrew from the league. Originally Broughton Rangers, they had been one of the most successful sides of the early years of the Northern Union, winning the Lancashire Senior Competition in 1897 and 1899. Rangers then won both the League Championship and the Challenge Cup in the 1901/02 season and the Challenge Cup again in 1911.

Rangers remain the most successful of the founder members to call it a day, caused by the management of Belle Vue Gardens, primarily a pleasure park and zoo in south east Manchester, withdrawing the use of the ground where Rangers had played since moving from The Cliff in 1933.

Of my other founder members, six had withdrawn for various reasons in the years before the First World War. They were Tyldsley (1900), Liversedge (1901), Manningham (1903), Stockport (1903), Brighouse (1906) and Runcorn (1915), and although Manningham and Brighouse had fielded strong teams for a time, the others achieved little success. Although Rangers never repeated their early achievements, they had always played competitive rugby with several players achieving selection at international level. Indeed, they were unlucky to narrowly lose the Lancashire Cup Final to the powerful Wigan team in successive seasons 1947 and 1948.

On a more optimistic note, the fifties era saw three new teams join with Cardiff and Doncaster in 1951 and Blackpool in 1954.

Sadly, Cardiff resigned after only one season and Blackpool Borough struggled on for many years with little success. In 1987 Blackpool moved to Wigan as Springfield Borough, a decision which proved disastrous with crowds falling below 550 for the last eight games of the 1987/1988 season.

Then began a merry-go-round of name changes and relocations. First Chorley Borough at Victoria Park, Chorley in 1988/1989, Trafford Borough at Altrincham from 1989 to 1992, back to Blackpool as Blackpool Gladiators in 1993 and at the end of the 1992/1993 season the Gladiators finished next to bottom of division three. The RFL then decided to relegate three teams to revert to a two-divisional system and Blackpool's league status was lost after a struggle, in one form or another, to survive in the professional game for almost 40 years.

In the twenties and thirties, new boys Featherstone and Castleford had discovered just how hard it is to establish a team in first-class Rugby League, but their plight was nothing when set alongside that of the Doncaster club in the years which followed their formation in 1954. Donny's first season promised a lot finishing 11th in the 31-team league, but they then failed to finish higher than the bottom five in any but two of the next 33 years.

Doncaster's remarkable persistence, I'll tell you about their appearance on the telly a bit later, was finally rewarded when they were promoted as second division runners-up in 1993/94 and for a brief moment after two games temporarily topped the first division.

Although Donny's ground, Tattersfield, fell victim to creditors the Dons re-established at Belle Vue, Doncaser Rovers' soccer ground. Let's hope those long years of toil are replaced by some overdue success.

The Welsh League 1949-51

When players were given the opportunity to switch codes without even moving from their roots there was no telling what might happen to the Union code in Wales.

The time was right for the formation of a Welsh Rugby League, which began in prosperity. Not a word which one would associate with the Welsh working man of 50 years ago, but there can be no doubt that conditions had improved rapidly for the vast majority of people in Wales in the years after the last war. Welsh economic output rose by 23 per cent between 1948 and 1954 compared with an improvement of 18 per cent in Britain as a whole.

As in England, attendances at sporting events reflected the post-war hunger for entertainment, and were further boosted by Welsh success on the field. Rugby Union was a major beneficiary, especially for the Penarth Road-based Cardiff club, which regularly provided the bulk of players for the national Union side. Of course, in the absence of Welsh clubs, Rugby League was unable to benefit from this upsurge of interest in sport, but international Rugby League played in Wales between 1945 and 1950 had attracted large crowds. The time seemed right once again to try to establish a foothold in the communities that had provided so many fine players to the professional clubs.

The Rugby League Council had voted to give the substantial sum of £1,000 and a promise of further support to a development fund. No doubt they were persuaded by three games played in Wales in late 1949 between St Helens and Huddersfield, the last of which saw a crowd of 29,000 at Abertillery. Regrettably, and in keeping with their long history of animosity towards me, the Welsh Rugby Union retaliated early with their secretary stating: "My Union intend to fight the challenge of Rugby League." They did so with some speed, suspending William Hughes, an official of Blaenau Gwent RUFC, for helping the Abertillery District Council to organise the game.

There can be little doubt that this aggressive opposition to Rugby League was motivated by the large numbers of Welsh Rugby Union players that had 'gone north' over the years.

Of the eight clubs, Aberavon, Amman Valley, Bridgend, Cardiff, Llanelli, Neath, Welsh Dragons and Ystradgynlais, on paper Cardiff, who had recruited several professional players, was the strongest side, the others each fielding only one or two players with professional experience.

Support for the league was patchy, with Cardiff attracting the largest crowds of 2,000 to 5,000; satisfactory but not remotely able to compete with the numbers watching the city's Rugby Union and soccer clubs. In these terms, the most encouraging development was at Ystradgynlais, where a team composed entirely of Rugby Union players attracted crowds of over 2,000, more than the entire population of the village at that time.

The Welsh League faced many problems, not least of which was the difficulty of finding grounds on which to play. Furthermore, prospective supporters of my game had seen the standard of the top clubs in exhibition matches in South Wales and understandably wanted to see Welsh sides able to play against them. In consequence Cardiff and Llanelli made successful applications to join my first-class ranks beginning in the 1951 season.

The second season of the Welsh League began in 1950 with eight teams, Blaina having replaced Welsh Dragons. Inevitably, interest was focused on the two aspirants to my professional game, Cardiff and Llanelli, and while Llanelli again had a strong season, Cardiff were unimpressive suffering defeat at the hands of the other sides in both cup and league games. In spite of this lack of success, Cardiff was confirmed as a full member of the Rugby Football League on 30th April 1951. I can't recall what happened to Llanelli's bid, but enthusiasm for the new game had waned rapidly in the second season.

Cardiff Rugby League Club 1951-52

Cardiff's election to the Championship raised hopes for the game in Wales, which unfortunately were quickly dashed, in no small part because they started without forwards capable of making the step up to the first-class game.

Five different hookers were used in the first six games, and the two prop forwards were changed in each match. The realisation that even survival at the top level was unlikely came in their next match when they were thrashed 72-5 at Central Park by the great Wigan team of that time. Another 13-66 hammering at home to Barrow, Challenge Cup finalists that year, followed.

Problems on the field continued, made worse by a failure to play a settled team, and with each defeat came yet more changes in personnel although initially crowd numbers at home games, though modest, were adequate to ensure financial survival. With repeated heavy defeats attendances fell with only 200 at the Barrow game.

Some stability came with the return to Wales of Ted Ward, the Wigan centre and former Great Britain captain, bringing a few wins against weaker sides. The moment was lost and even successes on the pitch didn't improve attendances much and Cardiff withdrew from the league at the end of the season.

With five wins they had finished one place above the bottom

side Liverpool City, but in 36 games they had conceded 1,024 points, an enormous number in the days of three point tries and only the Liverpool City team of 1906/07 has a worse record.

Cardiff was readmitted to the Welsh League, but with dwindling interest from the south Welsh public and no clear purpose the venture folded at the end of the 1954/55 season.

Workington - where there's a will, there's a way

A look at the Workington Town website at the end of the 2003 season summed up wonderfully the family spirit that exists in my sport.

"We have reached the end of a year when a lot of people did not give us a hope. We have to thank the local players who have stuck to their task all season and have worked hard, and the travelling players who have come into the club and fitted in well.

"We have to thank all the staff at the club from the back room staff, match day stewards, bar staff and administration staff who have all pulled together to keep things going. Obviously, the sponsors are a major help to the club and a massive thank you goes out to them.

"And then there are the fans. What can I say? Thank you just does not cut it. I know we probably have not agreed on a number of issues, and I can understand a lot of the frustration that they have gone through but that hard core of fans are what the club is all about. They are the people we have to work hardest for. I have heard some of them, this season, saying, 'that's my lot I won't be back!' but come the next home game there they are in their usual places. To them a heartfelt thank you because if it wasn't for you we would not have a club."

However, all was not gloom for Workington. After admission to the league in 1945, Town quickly became something of a force, moving from Borough Park, home of Workington Town FC to Derwent Park in 1956.

Town shared Borough Park with Workington FC for their first 11 years, and their cosy relationship got particularly close in 1952 when the football club were due to play Oldham Athletic and Town were ordered to complete their Challenge Cup quarter-final by the same weekend. Sunday rugby was unheard of, so after the Reds' 2.00pm game finished it was all hands on deck with only one hour for the groundstaff to clear everyone out, erect rugby posts, mark the pitch and admit the Town supporters in time for a 4.45pm kick off. Seemingly living a charmed life, Town went on to win the cup that year defeating Featherstone Rovers, 18-10.

Champions in 1951 with a runners-up spot in 1958, close to glory again in 1955, defeated by local-rivals Barrow in the Challenge Cup final. Another Wembley trip in 1958, although no glorious homecoming as Wigan won the cup that day 13-9.

Yet a list of results doesn't quite tell the story of this Cumbrian coastal outpost that in the fifties would send the cold shivers down the spine of many a visiting team and supporter alike. Whenever the Challenge Cup draw was made, 'Workington away' was the one to avoid. Derwent Park was no ground for the faint-hearted.

Also in 1952 Town recorded their highest crowd, 20,403, for the visit of St Helens. Good times and certainly a far cry from the few hundred that attended in 2003, as the club tried desperately to find it's feet in National League Two and build a team to grab back some of the glory that Cumbria is crying out for.

It's hard to see the day when another Workington Town player wins a Great Britain cap to go alongside such past names as A Ackerley, E Bowman, P Charlton, B Edgar, Les and Peter Gorley, N Herbert, Phil Kitchin, W Martin, V McKeating, A Pepperell, I Southward, Arnie Walker and G Wilson. But there again with the diehard support that they have it may not be that long before teams are once again saying: "Good grief, Workington away!"

The great one-eyed God

Although a BBC television service had been broadcast from Alexandra Palace in London since 1936, few homes owned a television set. They were expensive relative to earnings and most people either read the news in the daily papers or listened to the radio. Entertainment outside the home still usually included a weekly visit to one of the many local picture houses most of which showed news programmes, such as Pathé, and short feature films on current affairs.

Television spread rapidly and widely after the death of King George VI in 1952. Many people wanted to see the televised state funeral and almost everyone watched the coronation of his daughter, Queen Elizabeth ll, in 1953. At the time Britain's sole television broadcaster was the BBC, using just a single channel for a limited time each day. As telly caught on, cinemas declined and closed or transferred to other uses.

My debut appearance on British television came on 10th November 1951 as I took my bow on the BBC broadcast of the second Test between Great Britain and New Zealand from Station Road. A last-minute penalty saw the home side triumph by 20-19, and the BBC quickly decided that it wanted more.

Accordingly, my next appearance happened two months later with my first league match when BBC cameras were present at Central Park for the 2.15pm kick off between Wigan and Wakefield Trinity on 12th January 1952.

That day's *Yorkshire Post* announced: "BBC want to know northern TV tastes. The audience research chief of the BBC, Mr Robert Silvy, is appealing to northern TV viewers to tell him their likes and dislikes so that he can discuss whether northerners tastes differ from those in the south." The correspondent opined: "The Yorkshireman does not want 'cloth cap' TV and feels that the north v south complex which now tinges television controversy is mainly a figment of the southern imagination."

Incidentally, elsewhere in the same paper under the heading, "Rugby League hampered by mudlark", Alfred Drewry wondered whether: "it would not be best to close down altogether between December and cup tie time with the exception of a Christmas pipe opener?"

That year also saw the first televising of the Challenge Cup final, Workington Town versus Featherstone Rovers, although that would be the only final shown for the next six years, as the RFL feared the impact television would have on attendances, a very real concern at the time.

Whether screening my Challenge Cup final actually did have

an adverse effect on the attendance was open to question. The 72,093 attendance for the 1952 final had dropped by over 18,000 from the previous year when Wigan and Barrow had played but the downturn was probably due more to the respective populations of the finalists rather than television.

This wasn't the line taken by my then RFL secretary Bill Fallowfield, who persuaded the RL Council to withdraw the facility the following year. Fallowfield also had some harsh criticisms for the amount the BBC was offering for the television rights, as well as for commentator Eddie Waring whose knockabout approach risked ridiculing the sport. For viewers outside the game's traditional heartlands, Eddie's entertaining commentary probably added an element of identity to the sport that many 'down south' still knew little about.

Although the Challenge Cup final became off-limits, the BBC were still able to show other matches. However, Fallowfield wouldn't have been impressed by the impact on attendances that some of these had and neither did the compensation received make up for the shortfalls at the turnstiles. In 1955, the BBC offered £350 to cover the next Challenge Cup final, or £480 for three years (somewhat short of current figures!)

In his *Official History of Rugby League*, Geoffrey Moorhouse notes the drop in attendances when matches were televised. An England versus France international in November 1953 saw the league programme crowd total drop by half, while the coverage of the 1954 World Cup final between Great Britain and France saw them down by over a third.

Selected club matches were televised each Saturday throughout the season, and thus Rugby League suddenly became available to huge audiences, although this interest didn't result in the spread of the game outside my northern heartlands as I'd hoped.

Although traditionally professional sport had been played almost exclusively on Saturday afternoon, the development of floodlights in the 1950s extended the opportunity to play the game at other times. I didn't mind, I'd play anywhere anytime and Rugby League was one of the first sports in Britain to grasp this opportunity. On 31st October 1951, Bradford Northern switched on their new floodlights, illuminating proceedings for 29,072 spectators to see their heroes beat the New Zealand tourists 13-8. I must say, compared with today's technology these were mere flickering candles and few clubs were prepared for their costly installation. At Bradford, the novelty wore off quickly and only 8,568 spectators watched the tourists defeat Wales under those same floodlights a few weeks later.

A few other clubs experimented with the novel idea and Leigh spent £4,100, a huge sum at the time, equipping their Hilton Park ground with lights. Their enterprise was rewarded when their first two floodlit games realised £3,328. Other clubs were slow to follow the example set by Bradford and Leigh, and while a few representative games were played under floodlights, league games remained Saturday afternoon fixtures.

September 1955 saw the launch of ITV and the new channel was quick to add Rugby League to its line up. The launch of Granada and ABC from the Winter Hill transmitter above Bolton was still six months away when London weekday contractor Associated-Rediffusion broadcast a knock-out competition featuring eight leading clubs (Featherstone, Huddersfield, Hunslet, Leigh, Oldham, Wakefield, Warrington and Wigan) played under floodlights on various London football grounds. Warrington defeated Leigh 43-18 in the final at Loftus Road; the participating clubs being paid £400 for their troubles.

This modest competition was the catalyst to convince my other clubs to install floodlights and by the end of the decade almost all my leading clubs had followed suit.

My attitude towards television can't have been helped by the effect that the televising by the BBC of the third Test between Great Britain and Australia in 1959 had. Apart from hitting the attendance at the match itself, which was 20,000 lower than Central Park's capacity and the lowest of the series, there was an even more dramatic effect on the rest of the day's fixtures, with Leeds, York and Bramley all suffering their lowest post-war attendances. For this, the RFL received just £1,250, which was less than half the gate money lost from the Test alone.

Many of my clubs took against television, indeed the RFL wasn't alone as the Football League backed off regular live coverage of soccer after a goalless draw had been shown by the new ITV on a Saturday evening in September 1960. During 1966 Wigan refused to appear in their third round cup match at Odsal, receiving a fine from £500 by the RFL. Before the decade was out, 16 clubs (more than half of the professional teams) resorted to legal means in an attempt to get television banned from the sport, even though by that time the value of the television rights had soared to £200,000 over a three-year period.

Apart from this financial involvement, the BBC was also following Associated-Rediffusion's lead with the launch of its own floodlit competition, first staged in 1965, of which I've got a story or two to tell you later.

Voices of dissent

I've always had a patchy relationship with the press, so it's not surprising I've done my own thing and had more than a few magazines and papers of my own published.

Anyone taking even a passing interest in me knows that there is always vigorous debate about the direction in which I should develop. The international game, salary cap, Super League expansion, rule changes, play-off arrangements, the number of overseas players allowed, the range of debate seems endless. But it was always thus, and I have regarded this as a vital sign of my continued health.

The 1950s were no exception, even though there were far fewer Rugby League newspapers, magazines and internet message boards about as there are today!

After the War, the publication of magazines wasn't easy, and a visit to a local newsagent would reveal shelves that held only a few titles. Of course, there were more daily newspapers than today as, at a time when hardly anyone had a television set, they were the main source of news. An idea of the cost of publishing a weekly magazine can be gauged from the launch in 1950 of the *Eagle*, a boy's comic that achieved cult status for a few years. Hulton Press, the publishers, spent £30,000 on pre-launch publicity, a massive sum to advertise a comic which cost 3d (one and a quarter pence in today's money.)

Naturally, Rugby League could not compete with that sort of investment, but there were a few weekly magazines that had a format similar to what we now call 'fanzines'. The newspaper *Rugby League Review*, published weekly, was one of the outlets for debate both for fans and journalists. The 100th edition focused on the future of the game, that is to say, my future. There is nothing new under the sun, and the hot topic in that issue concerned whether I should concentrate my development in Britain, especially in my heartlands, or spend precious resources in introducing the game to other countries.

The editor, Stanley Chadwick, had a bit of a bee in his bonnet about what he saw as a waste of valuable resources by the game's administrators, and in this centenary issue he showed no mercy in his criticism.

He began by listing the developments that he considered 'stunts'. See if you can spot anything that is topical over 50 years later!

His list was Experiments with the Laws of the Game, Welsh Clubs, A World Cup Competition, Development in London and the south of England, exhibition games in South Africa, an Italian tour and plans to take occasional games to the USA. Stanley thought that all of this was making a laughing stock of our game. He continued: "not until the future of every senior club is no longer in doubt, and the need for periodical financial assistance is removed, shall we be able to turn our thoughts to extending the game's sphere of influence." Now where have I heard that recently?

Some Rugby League writers have interpreted Chadwick's opposition to the RFL's development plans as part of the animosity that existed between him and Bill Fallowfield, the longtime secretary of the RFL. This vendetta reached it's climax before Mr Justice Stable at Leeds Assizes in July 1952, when Fallowfield was awarded £300 damages for libel by Chadwick and his publishing company, as a result of articles published in *Rugby League Review* between 1948 and 1950.

Chadwick was not alone in his criticism of the RL Council. In the same issue, Tom Longworth, the respected Rugby League journalist on the *News Chronicle,* a popular daily newspaper in those days, wrote that the club chairmen and the Rugby League Council were responsible for putting the interests of a few powerful clubs before the development of the international game. Well, who would have thought club chairmen would do that?

The same issue of this magazine also contained an article that criticised the excessive number of scrums, which at the time were spoiling the game as a spectacle. There were also concerns about the standards of referees, and particularly the variable interpretation of the rules of the game.

The author was the Rev. Frank Chambers, in his day a respected referee who had played for Huddersfield pre-1895 and for several seasons under Northern Union rules. He wrote: "with wisdom and patience the evolution which has been at work for over half a century will continue, until the whole world of sportsmen will recognise our game as the greatest and finest of all manly sports." That hasn't yet happened but we can all share the sentiment!

Looking back, more than fifty years on, much of this criticism may seem negative. The problems were really not that big, at least not for the leading clubs. The same issue tells us that the 'Match of the Week' was Leeds versus Wigan at Headingley and the crowd was typical for a big game in those days, at 32,000!

Red card for a spectator

I have always been proud of the way in which the millions of my spectators have supported me for over a century, showing passion for their team and yet also a standard of behaviour which is the envy of some other sports. I have never seen, nor do I anticipate seeing, the sort of hooliganism that occasionally has spoilt soccer matches in recent years, but there have been times when a few individuals have disgraced themselves with standards of behaviour below that which I have come to expect.

You may say that it was always thus, but one respected referee of the 1940s and 1950s told me of an incident that you might find amusing. He wouldn't tell me which teams were playing but, as referee, he was well aware that this was a real 'needle' game with passions raised to fever pitch on both sides.

"There was a huge crowd and seats were placed in front of the grandstand, against the railings and not far from the touchline. On one of those seats sat a big man wearing a fine camelhair overcoat with an orchid in his buttonhole. He was evidently 'somebody' and clearly wanted to demonstrate this. Alongside him sat a woman in furs, bejewelled and wearing sprays of flowers.

"The game began, robust yet fair, and I had no trouble in the first half. What happened during half-time I don't know, but immediately on the restart dirty play began and I knew that I was going to have a difficult time.

"If a player more than once broke rules such as offside or obstruction I would always have a word with him, but I never cautioned for deliberate foul play. Rugby League is a hard game and dirty play may endanger the recipient, so whenever I came across gratuitous violence I always sent the perpetrator from the field.

"Now in this match, within a quarter of an hour I had three or four men back in the dressing room and it still didn't seem that the violence was going to cease. While I was concerned with this, and was trying to steady the players, it occurred to me that much of their wildness was due to the frenzied yelling of the crowd. It seemed to have gone to the players' heads. Foremost among the howlers was the affluently dressed man on the touchline, even though for much of the time he wasn't sitting in his seat. For during the greater part of the second half he was on his feet, gesticulating wildly and shouting at the players using language that you won't find in the *Oxford English Dictionary*. I felt that he was largely responsible for winding up the players to fever pitch, and I knew that something had to be done. But what could be done?

"Scarcely had the thought passed through my mind then the ball went into touch in front of him. As the scrum was being formed he went into overdrive screaming obscenities at the players. I had no choice but to stop the game and I said to him, 'You are inciting the players to dirty play by your actions and your language. Therefore I have no alternative but to dismiss you from the ground.' I suppose that I should have expected his response which was to tell me to mind my own business and get on with the game. At that point the chairman of the home team came up to ask what was the trouble. I told him that I had given our friend five minutes to leave the ground and that three had passed already. It was a critical situation but I have seldom seen a more pleasing sight than this 'hooligan' being escorted from the ground by the club officials with the crowd jeering him on his way.

"The game resumed, the crowd behaviour was impeccable and not a single unworthy incident occurred again."

A Rugby League referee needs the patience of a saint, the hide of an elephant and the eyes of a hawk, preferably two pairs. Quite why they subject themselves to such a weekly ordeal I can't imagine, but although a good moan about the ref is included in the admission money, we're always pleased that someone volunteers to do the job.

One way to cure the blues!

Another old friend, Chris Westwood, recalled an anecdote from his childhood the other day.

"I was five-years-old and know exactly when it was in late October. How can I be so sure? My sister was born the month before on 15th September 1954. It was my mother not my father who took me to my first game.

"My father, with whom I spent many happy, miserable and often poignant hours behind the sticks subsequently, was unavailable as he was at work, getting in all the overtime that was going down the pit.

"More than the odd thought did occur that he could be directly below where we stood at Post Office Road. New babies cost money, as I found out myself thirty years later.

"My mother, my infant sister and I would turn up at Post Office Road, come rain, shine, blizzard or hailstorm. My sister would be pushed through the knots of people in one of those prams that had huge back wheels and small front ones, and ornate curled handles.

The bodies of these prams resembled the gondolas on fairground rides.

"Once your baby brother or sister had graduated to a pushchair the wheels became ideal to help manufacture a trolley, bogey or tut-tut or whatever the regional name is for those home made wooden go-karts that kids would career down the steepest hill you could either find or dare risk going down. That's if the pram hadn't been passed on to a relative with a new addition to the family.

"There was something strange about the way my mother pushed the pram through the throngs of people, an almost manic urgency. I could hardly keep up with her. Her actions were focused entirely on getting to the game and if someone had their shins clipped by the pram, well she didn't even notice. Getting to the ground as soon as possible was all that mattered.

"Because of the pram we couldn't go through the turnstiles like my mother, who had to pay. The gateman would instead open the big wooden gates at the side for us, the ones they opened at half-time to let kids in free and to let everyone out at the end of the match.

"The terracing at the railway end at Post Office Road in those days consisted of permanently wet, greasy railway sleepers, embedded in shale. At the top of the terracing was a flat area of this shale, which was actually spoil from the pit, used when the ground was originally built. My mother, with me in tow, would patrol, pushing the pram up and down this area for the entire match. She would shout and scream at every real and perceived offence committed against a Rovers player, or wrong decision by the ref. Her voice would echo across the largely empty terracing. People would look round quizzically and leave her to it.

"After the game, we would walk back to our home much more slowly and calmly. It was a kind of exhausted calmness, as if there was nothing else left to be angry or in pain about. Once back to the home comforts she would quietly change my sister's nappy and get the tea on and wait for my father to arrive back to a moderately serene home atmosphere.

"The following year my sister was in a pushchair. To my disappointment (one that I almost still live with), heightened by the fact that I'd told the other kids in the street that I'd be inheriting those wheels, the pram had gone to a heavily pregnant aunt and now I was going to the match with my dad in the 'traditional' way. We never missed a game and the screaming and shouting never let up throughout the match, including half-time, for the whole season. And, yes, I was scared sometimes.

"Every couple of weeks or so I go to my mother's for lunch; mashed spuds rise from the plate like *cumulus nimbus* clouds before a storm, braised steak stretches out to the horizon, four kinds of veg and gravy that could make the dead walk. You know what I mean; 'your mam's dinner', as opposed to 'lunch at your mum's'.

"After we finish we do the crosswords in the papers and talk about stuff. She tells me who's dropped dead in Station Lane outside the butchers, her latest bingo win, things like that. I sometimes ask her about things that happened when we were kids that we didn't understand at the time, or general 'remember when' type episodes of yesteryear.

"On one of these visits, I asked her about my bizarre introduction, with my baby sister, to Rugby League. She laughed and said, 'well I suppose nowadays they can give you all sorts of medication, but back then you had to find your own way of dealing with post-natal depression.'"

The Irate Mother

Another pal, Jack Whittaker recounts a tale from the fifties.

"It used to be said that mothers breed only rugby football players in Featherstone. And it was one of those mothers that prevented a serious incident during one of those friendly fixtures that Featherstone used to have with Castleford. In this particular game feelings were running high as a Featherstone player of some ability had done the unthinkable and joined Castleford, for whom he was playing that day.

"In front of the main stand was a bench on which were seated several women, one of whom was nursing a very young baby. Towards the end of the game the Featherstone forwards executed a move not seen in today's game as they dribbled the ball at speed towards the Castleford line. The 'traitor' in the Castleford ranks stopped this forward rush by kicking the ball with some force into touch, but unfortunately straight into the women sitting on the bench.

"The nursing mother, leaving her baby on her neighbour's knee, ran onto the pitch and made straight for the offending player, looking like some Amazon, and breathing out threats and curses. Realising that he was her target the offending player took to his heels and with the woman chasing him round the ground the crowd were entertained for a good two minutes before the officials were able to escort her from the pitch. Later she claimed that the ball had hit her baby, but perhaps she should have thought of that possibility before taking a seat only a yard or two from the pitch. We don't know whether in later years the baby was able to even the score with Castleford."

The ref is not a homer!

A final story for this decade from Reg Parker who recalls the scene in the early fifties as Barrow travelled to play York.

Officiating that day was none other than Syd Abram, who you might recall from earlier as the first player to score a try in a Wembley final for Wigan. The lad packing down with Reg in the second row was Jack Grundy whilst at loose forward was Harry Atkinson. As the game progressed and yet another scrum formed, Harry made a request of the whistler, 'Syd, make sure the York scrum-half puts the ball in straight.'

After several repeats of this from Harry, Syd retorted that as a referee he should be addressed as 'Sir'. Somewhat bemused, Harry replied: 'but I call you Syd at work!' 'No matter,' came the reply from Syd, enjoying his position of authority, 'it is to be 'Sir'.'

"You've guessed it, as the players packed down once again, Harry pleaded to the ref, 'Sir Syd, please ask the York scrum-half to put the ball in straight.'"

Our refs have always commanded respect, but it usually stops short of knighthood!

Finished with the fifties

I've no doubt about it, the fifties were a boom-time for Rugby League, my golden age in my golden years.

After 65 years of setbacks and fighting for survival against circumstance and so many who would see me fail, finally I'd had some sustained success that I could look back on and be proud of. Surely I had finally arrived?

The fifties had blessed me with a host of top-notch players and I even featured regularly on national telly!

The post-war hunger for live sport of any kind brought me bumper crowds and prosperous times early in the decade but by the end of the fifties I had a nagging doubt or two. What had I put aside for my pension? Even with my successful World Cup adventure, internationally and even around parts of these shores I still wasn't as well travelled as I should have been.

Despite better times, some of my grounds hadn't had much attention with not much regard for the comfort of my players and paying supporters.

With my northern provenance I suppose I seemed a bit rough around the edges for many, although that was how most seemed to like me. No pretensions, airs or graces but maybe my lack of ambition would let me down as old age advanced?

8

1960-1970
THE SWINGING SIXTIES

The 29th August 1960 was an important day for me, my 65th birthday, the day most people retire gracefully.

I'd had a lifetime full of event and emotion, lots of fun and very rewarding, but most of the time a damn hard slog.

I had no intention of stopping but what was in my pension fund to look forward to? I've never been wealthy, in cash terms at least, but over the years I'd accumulated plenty of goodwill. I'd got a huge family and lots of friends to look after my best interests when I needed them in the years that were to come - and holiday homes all over the world!

Sounds of the Sixties

The sixties were a fashionable time, Mary Quant, fab gear on the Kings Road and Carnaby Street, the Mini and drainpipe trousers. Everyone's favourite Christmas holiday viewing *The Sound of Music* and the 1963 war classic *The Great Escape* dug in for a long innings.

December 1960 saw the pilot of Tony Warren's drama based on everyday life in Salford. With the working title of *Florizel Street* the schedule only extended for 12 episodes and the terrace would be knocked down in a 13th if it wasn't a success. A name change helped and *Coronation Street* is still with us 4,000 episodes later.

Elvis was in his pomp, *All Shook Up*, prompting a run on the national stocks of Brylcreem with the groovy British response being Cliff and the Shadows (who ended up as enduring as me, selling 21 million records since 1958.) The Beatles and the various Merseybeat groups were the lot your father wouldn't approve of, but the Rolling Stones were the type your mother didn't like either. The Stones played free in Hyde Park and there were more 'psychedelic happenings' at Woodstock and the Isle of Wight.

Where were you on 22nd November 1963? Everyone remembers. President John F Kennedy was in Dallas, Texas, where he met his end by an assassin's bullet, although some would say there was more to the incident than met the eye.

Now what happened in 1966? Hmmm, ah yes, Bobby Moore lifted the Jules Rimet Trophy, the World Cup of association football, and don't you forget it! I'm never allowed to, even though my Rugby League World Cup success came first.

I've always believed the adage "don't put off tomorrow what you can do today," but I've been swimming against the tide with that as the same year Barclay's bank introduced the first British credit card. That'll do nicely.

Although compulsory National Service ended in 1960, world affairs continued in the same tense vein as the fifties, with a particularly worrying time being the Cuban Missile Crisis. The American presence in Vietnam continued fighting communists, a war many people felt they had no business being involved with.

Campaign for Nuclear Disarmament members marched to the British government's nuclear research base at Aldermaston, Berkshire each Easter and at its height in the 1960s, tens of thousands demonstrated calling for Britain to voluntarily give up its nuclear weapons and to refuse to allow the USA to have theirs based on British soil.

The 'Space Race' set the USA against Russia in pursuit of a

propaganda coup. Russia got the first satellite into space with its *Sputnik*, but the USA got the main prize in 1969 when with "one giant leap for mankind" Neil Armstrong set foot on the moon.

It's often said that if you can remember the sixties, you can't have been there. Well, my memory needs jogging from time to time so I'll tell you a tale of the fab and groovy sixties with the help of Dave Dooley and a few of my other friends.

Vision On

Along with so many of my sporting cousins, the sixties could not match the preceding decade with regard to paying spectators. Nevertheless, the age of the mass media found me performing on a national stage for the first time. No longer was my act restricted to the northern boards, thanks to television, my teams, players, referees and stadia became part and parcel of our mother tongue from Pontefract to Penzance.

When I reflect on those heady days of fortune and fame, I still can't decide whether I had really become a 'television sport' as opposed to a 'sport on television.' Whilst housewives (yes, you could still call them that in those days) up and down the country could inform you that Billy Boston played for Wigan or Alex Murphy was a bit of a cheeky monkey, the number of fans trundling up to watch those celebrities dwindled as the decade sped on. Notwithstanding, come quarter to four on a Saturday afternoon I was centre stage in millions of British front rooms, even though my players appeared only a few inches high.

Eddie Waring, Eddie Waring, Eddie Waring is a bum
Eddie Waring, Eddie Waring, Eddie Waring is a bum!

They say that 'familiarity breeds contempt' and so it was with my public voice and chief representative in Great Britain. This contemptible insult in song was readily heard on many a Rugby League ground in the mid-sixties. Sung to the tune of *My Darling Clementine* this simple refrain reflected and reinforced two up and coming aspects of popular culture in the country of my birth. First was the emergence of chants and singing at sporting venues, which first hit the heights at Anfield, as the great Liverpool teams emerged in tune from the shadows of their blue neighbours. Secondly, the predilection of the British press and population to knock any public figure who had the misfortune to be successful or famous, or even worse, both!

There were those who worked through the decade and those who lived through the decade. It has got to be said that this was the first era when free time and spare money were coincidental for the man and woman in the street, but mostly the man. Many a bloke worked five and a half days and finished midday on Saturdays. At that moment of emotional release he could call at the local on the way home, go to the match or join a new breed of couch potato and watch television. Inevitably, Saturday afternoons would mean BBC *Grandstand* with yours truly in all my blazing glory. A 14-inch black and white set that would put him back £60 or he could enter the world of commercial bureaucracy and rent a set from Rumbellows for a few bob a week.

Love him or loathe him, Eddie Waring was popular, prolific and, most important of all, he was an enthusiast for Rugby League. For many a youngster Christmas would see the serious *Eddie Waring Annual* accompany the comic perennials of the *Beano* and *Dandy*. My public voice was distinctive in tone, pitch, dialect and accent.

The antithesis of the manufactured BBC sports commentator, Eddie was genuine, emotional and confident; some would say northern.

As a celebrity he was satirised and stereotyped. Waring was blessed with catchphrases from my game. "It's an up and under" or "he's gone for an early bath" entered the formula talk in pubs and filled the mouths of empty impressionists. Yet these glib references make a feeble attempt to characterise the importance to my game of the 'Dewsbury Trilby.'

Eddie's job was to sell me to a nation of couch dwellers. This involved the impossible task of perfectly matching information, relationship building and entertainment. Who could ever forget the high-pitched screams that accompanied Len Killeen's successful 65-yard penalty goal in the 1966 Challenge Cup final for St Helens against Wigan? Talk about banshees waking dead dogs. This was the man who made household names of Billy Boston, Alex Murphy, Don Fox and Mick Sullivan amongst many others. When my older fans say that there were more characters in the sixties, this might have a great deal to do with the fact that these great players were in the nation's face on a regular basis. When I was a lad in the early 1900s if you were to tell me that one day I would be watched by five million people every week I would have accused you of madness on the scale of Rasputin sawing a pygmy in half at the University of Insanity. Eddie Waring had meaningful relationships with housewives the length and breadth of the country in the 1960s, albeit vicarious in nature.

Eddie Waring, my public face, my distinctive voice, one of my greatest devotees. I miss him dearly.

Teams of the times

As the decade began, the British were suffering from an acute bout of schizophrenia. The generation gap was much talked about and there was a love amongst the youth for all things American. Yet everyday life was equally dominated by traditional British culture, teenagers were happy supping Tizer or Jusoda whilst listening to Elvis Presley on Radio Luxembourg and your first pint would be mild or bitter, a bit like the weather. I lived through ten years of extreme severe winters and sizzling summers, Acker Bilk and Captain Beefheart, *Steptoe and Son* and *Bilko*, women on the rise and men on the moon, Wigan, Wakefield Trinity and St Helens as opposed to Bramley, Doncaster and Blackpool Borough.

As money and opportunity for many people proliferated I felt greater competition for my attention. I began to feel a little schizoid myself. On the one hand, millions of people regularly watched me on television including some of my faithful who had obviously exchanged my stadium seats and terraces for a coal fire and a square box. They say things go in cycles and I have experienced many deserters, especially in the thirties, but this was different. It was as though an alien force has entered my kingdom and enticed my followers to stay in, as though the speckies had gone soft. It was a good job the players hadn't!

Many of my great contests in the sixties were captured on the small screen. The 1961 Challenge Cup final produced a try of such great quality that it accompanied the *Grandstand* credits for donkeys' years. The classic length of the field inter-passing move between Ken Large and the legendary Tom Van Vollenhoven was my visual catchphrase. Those 10 or 12 seconds encapsulated my very essence, the speed, skill, collaboration, co-ordination and brave defence that separates me from everyday ordinary experiences. That sensational try sealed the victory for the Saints and a universal reference point for any subsequent great touchdown. Moreover, it confirmed my status as a fantastic spectator sport worthy of a mass-media audience.

The vanquished in the 1961 Challenge Cup final participated in a classic showpiece event just four years later. In those days a good old War of the Roses provided a healthy context for any major final and the open nature of the 1965 Challenge Cup final between Hunslet and Wigan generated a pulsating contest that left the result in doubt up to the final whistle. Very often most of my disciples, quite naturally, only remember the great tries, tackles and kicks from a match. Those blessed with great memories, or even a video recorder, can relive the passion of the forwards battle where most matches are set up for a win or loss. That particular day two great packs demonstrated the gritty defence and handling skills that characterised all-time great players like Brian McTigue and Geoff Gunney. This created the space for the headline takers like Lake and Shelton to complete sparkling team moves. As Wigan prevailed by 20-16, even the Lance Todd Trophy was awarded jointly to Ray Ashby of Wigan and Brain Gabbitas, the Hunslet stand-off, such was the parity of the teams and the contest.

As the decade ended, fresh teams were challenging the dominance of the old guard as Castleford and Salford mounted a serious campaign for silverware. These teams brought a smile to my face and brought back memories of other great teams in yellow or red from the thirties.

Castleford came to prominence in the mid 1960s. They were

often regarded as a 'Cinderella' team from a small but homely town and ground. Cas emerged very much as a television team as my popularity on the small screen spread to the 'snooty' BBC2 in the form of the BBC2 Floodlit Trophy.

Clubs had to have floodlights installed as these games were played on Tuesdays with a 7.30 p.m. kick-off to comply with the television schedules and Cas were keen to succeed in this minor competition, and indeed won the first three finals (1966, 1967 and 1968). Inspired by a hard pack of forwards and their talented half-back combination of Hardisty and Hepworth, the team matured into a side that were to carry off the Challenge Cup in 1969 with an 11-6 victory over Salford.

The beaten finalists on that particular day had built a high-profile team by plundering the valleys of Wales and combining Welsh gems like David Watkins and Maurice Richards with high-class league signings in the shape of Colin Dixon and Paul Charlton. The resulting team was rich in footballing skills and the crowds poured back to the Willows. Clubs capitalised on their newly-installed floodlights to experiment with Friday night fixtures for league matches. This measure suited some clubs but other communities were still very much in favour of the traditional Saturday afternoon kick-off.

Another team to hit the heights in the sixties was Swinton. The Lions of Swinton, their nickname derived from their local White Lion pub, had a proud heritage, particularly in the 1920s and 1930s when they collected four championships, two Challenge Cups, three Lancashire Cup victories and five Lancashire League titles. Their Station Road ground was heavily in demand for internationals and domestic competition finals and semis. In the early sixties, the town of Swinton was buzzing as a team was constructed to challenge for the top honours in my game and their first title for some considerable time, the Lancashire League competition, came in the 1960/1 season. Their backs included diamonds like Ken Gowers, Alan Buckley and John Stopford, whilst their pack boasted international class players like Dave Robinson, Graham Rees and Bill Bretherton. Albert Blan, who read my game with ease, magnificently led the team and applied team tactics with great flexibility as matches progressed and unfolded. It was always a thrill for me to see the trains pull into the Swinton station on big match days and watch a mass of bob caps and scarves spill on to the platform. As rattles revolved, nerves were temporarily settled as supporters bayed and rallied their teams. They ascended the station steps for the shortest of strolls into the Lions' den. Two hours later, many of these fans trudged miserably back to their awaiting carriages with the bitter taste of defeat in their mouths.

The Lions' trophy haul might have been greater in this decade had it not been for their misfortune to be paired with St Helens in no fewer than five cup finals between 1960 and 1964. The Saints beat Swinton in four Lancashire Cup finals and a Western Divisional Championship final during this time. Nevertheless, the Lions roared on to greater success.

In an effort to sharpen up competition at the top, the 1962/3 season signalled a return to two divisions. Swinton emerged as champions following one of the craziest seasons my game had ever known.

Deep freeze

Ah yes, winter rugby. By the time the campaign approached Christmas just 11 league rounds had been completed as a result of the introduction of divisional leagues to pad out the season and club incomes. From 29th December until more temperate conditions in early March the next year we had 156 matches postponed, all of which needed re-arranging, meaning that the season had to be extended into June. In the interim of the handful of games that were playable, one at Castleford needed the pitch thawing with fifty braziers. Three fixtures at Widnes were made possible only by spraying the pitch with £500 worth of anti-freeze, which ruined the pitch and poisoned the players!

When the season resumed on 9th March, clubs had to complete 19 league fixtures and their Challenge Cup commitments by playing two or three fixtures every week. The division one title was decided over the Easter weekend when Swinton met their nemesis, St Helens in both home and away fixtures. A refined game plan and some precocious tactical kicking enabled the Lions to complete a fabulous double over their Lancashire rivals and secure a stranglehold on the Championship. Hunslet edged Keighley to secure the second division Championship. The following season witnessed the Lions retain their title losing only five league matches in a magnificent campaign. *Crackerjack!*

One of the most pleasing aspects of the decade was the manner in which my honours were distributed amongst the clubs. Seven different clubs won the Champions tag; Wigan, Leeds, Huddersfield, Swinton, Halifax, St Helens and Wakefield Trinity and the same number carried off the Challenge Cup; Wakefield Trinity, St Helens, Widnes, Wigan, Featherstone Rovers, Leeds and Castleford.

With one third of my clubs winning a major trophy of some sort, interest was maintained throughout the competition. If you consider teams like Workington Town winning the Western Divisional Championship, Hunslet, Hull KR, Bradford Northern and Hull carrying off the Yorkshire Cup together with a Warrington victory in the 1965 Lancashire Cup and the dominance of Castleford in the BBC2 Floodlit Trophy, then the widespread celebrations kept most supporters' expectations and dreams alive and kicking.

The Dreadnoughts

One club more than any other in the 1960s caught the imagination of the public as they rose to claim more major final success than any other. They were the wonderful Wakefield Trinity side that ruled the roost for much of the decade. In total they waltzed off with three Challenge Cup victories, two Championships, three Yorkshire Cup finals and three Yorkshire League titles. In my youth Trinity had won the Challenge Cup in the 1908/9 season when quality players like Kershaw and Newbould had graced their colours. More recently they emerged as a strong force immediately following the Second World War when the team battled to a second Challenge Cup final win over Wigan by 13 points to 12.

However, the sixties would prove to be Trinity's most successful and protracted period at the top of the Rugby League tree. Their powerful pack of forwards, smart half-backs and classy threequarters characterised this outstanding team. The 'Dreadnoughts' at the start of the decade featured the elusive butterfly Gerry Round at fullback, the creative Harold Poynton at stand-off, rock solid international forwards in the likes of Jack Wilkinson and Don Vines and were led by one of the smartest players ever to play my game, Derek 'Rocky' Turner.

As if that line-up wasn't enough, Trinity also paraded the greatest points scorer I have had play my game, remember the lad from the Sharlston 'Village of Fame', the irrepressible Neil Fox.

Animal Magic

Neil was very much a modern player. His 6 ft and 15 stones physique, nowadays a prerequisite for the position, was unusual in 1960. Notwithstanding this physical advantage over opponents, Fox was a natural footballer with superb positional sense, immaculate timing and a lovely pair of hands.

In a long career of 828 games at centre threequarter for Wakefield, Bradford, Hull KR, York, Bramley and Huddersfield between 1956/79, 'Hall of Famer' Neil amassed a world record 6,220 points including a winning streak of 95 games between March 1958 and May 1960 in which he scored in every one of them.

In his Wakefield days he managed to score an incredible 272 tries and went on to an all club career total of 358 tries. This places him on the top shelf of try scorers in my game with only my elite band of wingers and Ellery Hanley to keep him company. The powerful centre would have gained all domestic and international honours even if he had not been one of the greatest goal kickers in the history of my sport. Neil booted an incredible 2,575 goals over.

In the 1959/60 season, Neil crossed the tryline 37 times and kicked 171 goals for a total of 453 points. He finished the season as the game's top goals and points scorer. Neil also featured in the 1960 Challenge Cup final at Wembley when Trinity blasted Hull with a record 38-5 victory and we witnessed Rocky Turner receive the Challenge Cup from the Queen. Fox helped himself to two tries and seven goals for a Cup Final record haul of 20 points. Neil and the club repeated this success two seasons later when Wakefield defeated Huddersfield 12-6 in a close encounter. That season the club had its most successful campaign ever winning the Challenge Cup, Yorkshire Cup and Yorkshire League but losing out to Huddersfield 14-5 in the Championship final. That campaign also proved a pinnacle for Neil as he netted an incredible 456 points, only ever surpassed by two players Lewis Jones (496) and David Watkins on two occasions (493 and 476).

The Championship that had eluded the Belle Vue club throughout its history finally arrived in the 1966/7 season when Trinity defeated St Helens in the Championship Final replay by 21-9. The Championship winning team had changed considerably from the heady days earlier in the decade apart from the talismen Neil Fox and Harold Poynton, the latter having assumed the club captaincy. Another player who graced my game from South Africa also bridged the decade, namely Gert 'Oupa' Coetzer. This direct running back added flair to the side. Another star, who would later join Neil Fox in the record books, was the powerful second rower Bob Haigh. Bob managed somehow to score 40 tries in the 1970/1 season, a record for a forward.

The Watersplash Final

Speaking of Trinity and Foxes, Neil's brother, Don also played a vital role for the Belle Vue team in the second half of the decade. Don was a fine player in his own right with excellent footballing skills usually exhibited from the loose forward's berth. He will forever, live in people's minds for the closing seconds of the 1968 Challenge Cup final between Leeds and Wakefield Trinity.

In a game that should never have been played the players had to cope with a flooded Wembley surface that reduced scoring opportunities to a minimum as the ball either hydroplaned like a skimming stone or fell motionless like a grounded wrecking ball at the end of a shift. As the watery lottery approached its final swallow dives, John Atkinson seemed to have sealed victory for the Loiners with a late try. From the resulting restart the gliding figure of Trinity winger Hirst hoofed on a puddled ovoid, and the ball finally halted over the Leeds tryline under the sticks. The leaden-footed Leeds defence watched agonisingly as the Wakefield will o' the wisp dived on the football to leave his side just one point behind with a conversion to come from in front of the sticks.

It is said that most of the spectators and players from either side couldn't bear to watch Don's attempt at goal. On any other day it would have been a simple task but a sodden ball, Wembley's watery and unfavourable surface and his collapsed boot conspired to slice Don's goal attempt wide of the right hand post. As the 'poor lad' sunk to his knees irrelevantly wiping his face with a drenched jersey, the Leeds players danced and skipped past him to the tune of their last-minute pardon and the referee's final whistle. The greatest of dramas are not scripted.

This Sporting Life

That moment beautifully links to another Trinity-based drama some five years earlier as not content with a regular slot on the nation's small screens, I finally became a movie star. Please bear with me whilst I go somewhat introspective in true art critic fashion.

David Storey's novel and screenplay examines the trials and tribulations of Frank Machin, a miner desperate for fame and public acclaim on the Rugby League playing field. Lindsay Anderson's direction beautifully explores the darker side of life in a northern town that drew on influences that were both typical and stereotypical but always absorbing. The obsessions at the time with class, kitchen sink dramas and the exploration of the psyche of men challenged by new values were acted out against a black and white context of simultaneous success and failure.

I suppose I cannot complain at my portrait in these respects, it's just I was very uneasy at the time with the lasting impression. Richard Harris, who was one of my greatest fans, played the lead role magnificently. His surly manner and barked dialogue dominated the film to such an extent that people might well be forgiven for walking out of the cinema believing that the majority of my players were self-obsessed and puerile. Nothing could be further from the case. The film attributes Machin with a string of unappealing characteristics.

He was a restless soul searching for acclamation almost at any human cost. Harris beautifully portrays the self-reliant, cocky individual who signs on for a £1,000 fee (you could more or less buy two Mini cars for that amount in 1963) and beautifies match reports that mention and glorify his name. I am not saying that there weren't players of my game who portrayed these characteristics, but these were the exception rather than the rule. By contrast his teammates were self-assured, comfortable in company and above all loved the game they played. If you could compare Machin and Neil Fox, the only similarity was the haircut!

Fox was very much part of my culture and tradition, Machin an outsider in every sense who just happened to reside in my heartland. Nevertheless, he was credited with the best line in the film. When asked by a reporter how it felt to be a star of Rugby League, Machin responded with authority: "We don't have stars in this game, that's soccer!"

This truism demonstrates how my players view themselves. Even now, decades into the mass media and communications era, few Rugby League players are comfortable in front of a camera or reporter's notebook. Most prefer a low profile existence off the pitch keeping their feet, heads and egos in the real world.

The other main theme that was investigated by Storey and Anderson was class. Unlike my representatives on Earth down under, thinking that one person is better than another is very much an English characteristic. My game provides easy situations for this exploration of the relationship between directors and players. Whereas there are not many Machins in my world, the values, attitudes and *modus operandi* of more than enough Rugby League club directors like Weaver, the chairman of the City RLFC in the film, are still evident.

There are those directors who still operate like meat traders, with little regard for my players as human beings. Weaver wants to own the players rather than develop them as people.

Our best clubs have long realised that the best people and strongest characters also make our greatest players, sadly this is not the case everywhere. In the sixties some directors routinely interfered with team selection, such was their arrogance and apparent superiority. This particular attitude was even more pronounced in their relationships with supporters. The boardrooms and 'inner sanctums' of the club heirachy were and are maintained to keep the riff-raff out.

The class system is still alive in many minds. I'm not trying to conclude that the young men who so nobly play my game don't need a guiding hand every now and again, but it's more the case of grooming, character building and personal development being the driving approach rather than patronage and diffidence.

On a lighter note the action shots from the film were generally well done apart from the tries that were arranged for Richard Harris. It must have taken great guts and determination on behalf of those extras to make those half-hearted attempts at tackles on the Irish actor!

This Sporting Life painted a monochrome landscape where life is a struggle on every corner; reality is grim but only if you are a loner. This was not the decade that I lived through and witnessed. Work was hard at the time but it was the first era of disposable income for the working person. The music was vibrant and British. Summers sizzled and fashion moved apace. Cheap package holidays, progressive programming on television, fine novels and fabulous films raised people's horizons and ambitions. Moreover, there were some fabulous games of Rugby League with the result of many a game very much unpredictable.

Pack men

By God, there were some hard men playing my game in the sixties. 'Brian' seemed to be a popular name for a couple of these graduates from the School of Hard Knocks.

Those who had the pleasure to witness the 1962 Ashes Tour would recall instantly two hard 'Brians'. Brian Mc Tigue played my game gloriously from one of my least glamorous positions, prop forward. This Wigan gem was the connoisseur's forward. He combined hard running with clever footwork, brilliant ball handling and terrier like tackling. He was the cornerstone of the great Wigan pack and a mainstay for his national side. When it comes to hardness however, there was a lump of Cumberland granite who was way off the Mohr Scale.

Of course I'm talking about Brian Edgar, the scourge of the Aussies on that Ashes Tour. A perfect foil to his fellow county man, Dick Huddart, a Whitehaven stalwart who had the speed of a gazelle and a jackhammer hand-off. With Rocky Turner, Workington Town stalwart Herbert and masterful hooker Bill Sayer, a platform was built that warmed the cockles of any Cockermouth heart.

The sixties abounded with Rugby League 'packs of aces' that resulted in some of the greatest ever contests at a time when the winds of change blew through society and through me as the time was ripe for substantial rule and image revision.

On the slide

As crowds declined, I felt an internal pressure within the walls at Chapeltown Road to open up the game and sure enough, changes were duly rung season by season.

Although I was an emerging television star, Bill Fallowfield the secretary of the Rugby Football League used to maintain weekly records of the weather and my match attendances, along with programme details of BBC *Grandstand* and other major sporting events in a valiant attempt to explain the decline in attendances.

The Challenge Cup finals drew capacity crowds when Saints, Wigan, Leeds or Salford reached Wembley, my showpiece was in good shape, but the Championship finals reflected a declining pattern. The 1959/60 final between Wigan and Wakefield Trinity attracted a record 83,190 crowd to Odsal Stadium, in sharp contrast to the 26,358 who witnessed the 1969/70 final between Leeds and St Helens at the same venue.

Between the same two seasons the Yorkshire Cup finals,

remarkably between the same two teams, Featherstone Rovers and Hull, and both matches played at the same Headingley Stadium, declined in attendance from 23,983 in 1960 to 11,089, 10 years later.

Of greater concern to me was the steady decline in weekly league games as this declining income stream threatened the financial stability. The reigning champions as the decade commenced were St Helens who boasted an average home attendance for all games of 14,426 spectators during the 1959/60 campaign. By the end of the decade the Saints were still at the top of their game, winning more competitive games than any other club during the period, waltzing off with two Challenge Cups, one Championship, seven Lancashire Cup victories and Lancashire League champions on no fewer than five occasions. Nevertheless, in the last season of the decade their home support had fallen to an average of 6,505 diehards.

Happening scene

In order to win back some of the supporters who'd walked or crawled to their couches, my administrators introduced a few rule changes that fundamentally altered the way in which I worked and was presented. These 'nips and tucks' included substitutions being allowed for players injured before half-time from 1964 and from 1966 the five yard offside mark at the play-the-ball, four-tackle rule and 'double penalty' (kick for touch and tap restart.)

As well as exploiting Friday nights and floodlights, my first Sunday league games were played on the 17th December 1967 in fixtures involving Leigh versus Dewsbury and Bradford Northern against York.

I even became popular with eggheads, as the first university match between Leeds and Liverpool in 1968 was followed by the Universities Rugby League Association being formed one year later, very much a case of crash barriers replacing class barriers.

Many of my players and supporters felt that I was suffering from innovation fatigue, come to think of it I did need my summer break more than ever!

Cavern Club

Bradford Northern had been on the wane for a while and a dire playing record from 1961 to 1964 only compounded the situation. In fact, out of a total of 90 games played, only nine were won with two draws. The lowest point came against Barrow on 23rd November 1963 when a grand total of 324 fans stood like lost souls on a desert island that was one corner of the Rooley Lane embankment, near the old dressing rooms. A far cry from the 102,569 plus in 1954 and the 56,476 crowd who attended the Huddersfield game in Northern's Championship-winning season of 1951/52.

The Rugby League authorities were contacted and informed that Northern "would not be fulfilling the remainder of its programme in this the 1963/1964 season" and the club duly went out of business, their last match being against Leigh on 7th December 1963. One for the quiz buffs in that wingman, Dlambulo, scored the last Northern try before their demise, whilst fullback Beevers kicked the only goal in the 5-33 defeat by Leigh.

Those few diehards who attended the game would have been unaware of the dire situation facing the club until the front page of the *Telegraph and Argus* on Tuesday 10th December had a headline that announced "End of the road for Northern!"

The first paragraph stated: "Not only the people of Bradford, but the whole Rugby League world were shocked to hear of Northern's plight and the decision to give up playing forthwith."

"And there's more," as the comedian Frank Carson used to say. Realising the magnitude of the loss of the city of Bradford to the game, clubs rallied each offering a player to assist in Northern's rebirth, and as we know now, what would Rugby League be like without Bradford?

Apart from Bradford, the game in the sixties was remarkably stable in league terms, despite the dwindling crowds of the latter years. This was a decade when no other clubs left or joined the competition. The same 30 clubs provided continuity and stability. Indeed the only change was cosmetic as Liverpool City changed their name and ground location to Huyton.

Run rabbit run

Meanwhile, down under in Australia, I witnessed the greatest monopoly of the Australian competition ever as the St George club continued their amazing run from the mid-fifties. From 1956 to 1966 St George won every single Grand Final, a run of 11 successive victories. At the time their playing captain was also the coach.

They mastered the art of rebuilding teams over a protracted period whilst still maintaining their position at the top of the Aussie tree. Ably led and tutored in succession by Ken Kearney, Norman Provan and Ian Walsh, their playing staff included great names such as Wilson, Lumsden, Bath, Gasnier, Raper, Langlands and Huddart. A fabulous record crowd over 78,000 watched the 1965 grand final between St George and Souths at the Sydney Cricket Ground, home to so many domestic and international classic matches over the years. The losers that day, Souths, built a side that was to dominate the competition for the next five years winning four finals and losing the unforgettable 1969 grand final to Balmain.

That game went down as the greatest upset in Aussie Rugby League history as nobody gave the Tigers a wildcat in hell's chance of defeating the Rabbitohs, who paraded no fewer than 12 internationals. The then Souths skipper, John Sattler, now confesses that his team were far too cocky and allowed Balmain to grind out an unfancied victory whilst the Tigers players were accused of feigning injury in order to disrupt the free-flowing moves of Souths' lethal attack. Balmain's offence was masterminded by former Wigan stand-off Dave Bolton who added a pair of drop-goals to two goal kicks by Len Killeen and a try by Syd Williams. In my game the lesson of never underestimating your opposition is one that needs relearning every season.

Cock a doodle doo!

The Ashes were Green and Gold coloured during the sixties, but it didn't all go the Aussie's way.

Whilst Eric Ashton's Britain claimed the main prize in Australia in 1962, choking an aggregate turnout of 500,335 paying spectators, they couldn't beat the Kiwis, who made the Poms swallow comprehensive defeat in both Auckland Tests.

Aussie came to Britain the next year, 1963, and like that August's Great Train Robbery, took them back, starting with a floodlit Test at Wembley, the first for donkey's years. Only 13,946 supporters were on hand to see Reg Gasnier's hat-trick against a 12-man Britain.

By the time Bobby Moore lifted the FIFA World Cup in 1966 the Lions had already taken a 3-0 flogging down under, even losing six of the midweek games against such as Central Queensland and Northern Division. The Kiwis were easier this time, a straight eight for the Lions, including both Tests at Carlaw Park.

Gasnier's men again came ashore in 1967 and after a successful opening Test win for Britain at Headingley the RFL took the second Test to London again, but this time to the White City Stadium that had been built for the 1908 Olympics. The floodlit match proved more popular than the previous visit to London, at Wembley, this time with 17,445 inside, but still not the big payer the RFL had hoped for.

Over the Channel to France for the Aussie tour, and something of a turn-up. I shouldn't have been too surprised as France were perfectly capable of beating New Zealand and Great Britain during the sixties - and they did - but a draw in Marseilles and losses in Carcassonne and Toulouse sent the 'Roos back home with a cockerel crowing in their ears.

On Safari

Last time I went on safari in earnest to a new country was when I set foot for the first time in France during the thirties.

In the face of bitter SARU opposition, my homeward-bound British and French touring parties at the end of the 1950s and early 1960s had stopped off in South Africa to play a handful of exhibition games. I didn't much like South Africa, it was run by nasty people, riven by apartheid and rugby of any sort was the preserve of the white man, but boasted some good players making their fortune overseas.

Nevertheless, by 1962 the first South African club matches got under way in an attempt to get a club structure off the ground, and a team thought worthy of international competition was raised.

In 1963 South Africa embarked on their debut overseas tour, playing two Tests in Aussie, losing both 34-2 at Lang Park (10,210) and SCG 54-21 (16,995), but surprising New Zealand 3-4 at that former Chinese market garden, Carlaw Park. The Kiwis took some lustre off the achievement claiming the game didn't have Test status as one of the team they had fielded was really an Aussie. Spoilsports! With two wins from seven matches against local sides in Australia and another against Wellington from three regional games in New Zealand all looked set to prosper but sadly the whole thing fizzled out, strangled by lack of investment and the opposition of another code.

Still, I'm never beaten. A resurgence of interest saw two games against the former Soviet Union in 1992, in Johannesburg and Pretoria both won by the Russkies. Further, the South Africa Rhinos made an appearance at the 1995 World Cup, playing England at Headingley, Australia at Gateshead and Fiji at Cougar Park, Keighley (or Lawkholme Lane as I grew up with it.)

Frequent attempts to regenerate interest have seen the Wales team tour there in recent memory and all is not forsaken.

Pasta masters

I've always been partial to a plate of spaghetti and the odd ice cream so I'm pleased to tell you of my next adventure.

Efforts to get Rugby League going in Italy date back to the 1950s when, founded by dissatisfied Union defectors, the Italians set up their own domestic club Rugby League competition.

The Azzuri toured Britain twice, playing six British club sides in 1950 and another seven in 1954, losing to them all but not disgracefully. Still, Rome wasn't built in a day.

The peak of my *Italian Job* came, not with Michael Caine "blowing the bloody doors off" - that was later in the decade - but on successive days in January 1960. The mighty Kangaroos played two games against my Italia thirteen at Padua (15-37) and Treviso (22-67), each attracting over 3,000 spectators. In terms of public awareness Italy now seems pretty much lost to the Unionists, so let them get on with it. *Que sera sera*, whatever will be will be (actually, that sounds quite catchy, I'll remember that!)

However, far from dead, England and France played an exhibition game in Venice in 1982 and towards the end of the century the Italia RL boys were back. Revived in 1995 by a couple of passionate enthusiasts, Mick Pezzano and John Benigni, Italy made appearances at various 7's and 9's competitions in Sydney and Fiji, the Mediterranean Cup and then the 2000 Emerging Nations World Cup (beaten in the final by BARLA.)

Although an away trip to Rome or Florence looks a distant prospect as the Azzuri are mainly comprised of second generation Italians living in Sydney, join me in raising a glass of Frascati in a toast of good luck to the Rugby League. From little acorns mighty... err olive trees do grow!

Howay the Lads

As an Australian tour manager, broadcaster and journalist, Queensland-born Harry Sunderland did more than most to promote my game at international level.

He managed three Australian teams to tour Britain between 1929 and 1938, and was instrumental in helping to introduce the sport in France in the 1930s and Harry also made an attempt to introduce the game to the United States.

Harry's lasting mark, however was his influence in establishing the Lance Todd Trophy awarded to the Challenge Cup final Man of the Match.

The great administrator died in England in 1960 aged 74, honoured by the Premiership, later grand final man of the match award. This prestigious award goes to the man of the match in the championship play-off final voted by members of the Rugby League Writers Association.

The first recipient of the Harry Sunderland Trophy was Terry Fogerty of Halifax in 1965. In better days for the club Halifax had overcome a Saints team 15-7.

Only two players have won back to back Harry Sunderland awards with Widnes' Alan Tait in 1989 and 1990, while Andrew Farrell achieved the same honour in 1996 and 1997. Chris Joynt also took the title twice in 1993 and 2000.

When the wheels came off

Geoff Lee pictures the typical 1960s scene, Dewsbury v Halifax at Crown Flatt on a wet and muddy afternoon. On the sidelines waited a St Johns Ambulance man and his colleague, a young apprentice, probably making his debut, on hand in case of emergency, armed with a brand spanking new metal stretcher with all mod cons, i.e. wheels.

After a while a Dewsbury player got laid out, prostrate at the far side of the field. The ref waved the stretcher on and our two heroes set off, with the lad at the front running faster than the older bloke could, but both holding onto the stretcher.

The screws that held the whole thing together mustn't have been tightened properly and slowly the front half slipped away from the back and just as they reached the middle of the pitch it collapsed in a tangle, both medics finishing up in the mud. Hilarious, well the crowd thought so, particularly when the injured player got up and the young lad limped off with a bad ankle.

The final is over and glory gone!

Think of the cliché of Rugby League and you'll probably conjure up an image in your mind's eye of a pit town in the 1960s. Chris Westwood told me another couple of anecdotes from his youth during just such an age.

"Most of what I'm going to tell you takes place in the early 1960s, just as I was becoming a teenager, but the story is about the 1920s. Every Saturday morning, I would earn my pocket money by doing the family shopping, whilst my mother cleaned up, scouring the front step, shaking the rugs, cleaning the windows and black leading the Yorkshire range.

"Actually I'm lying, we'd moved to a coal board semi at the other end of town by the sixties, but you can't beat a bit of Hovis advert stuff to get people feeling nostalgically historical. I did do the weekend shopping for my pocket money though.

"I hated it. To Darnton's bread shop for a dozen scufflers (you can keep your barm cakes), the Co-Op, divvy number 6134 since you ask, for cheese (cut with a wire), sugar (bagged up in the shop in that folded blue paper) and soap (Rinso being favourite.) Then to Asquith's butchers for the meat. Ralph and Luke Asquith knew what meat my mother would want, so the onus wasn't on me to choose the Sunday joint, thank God. At every shop large women in grubby raincoats would push in front of me and the shop, whichever it was, would have to be almost empty before I was served.

"Whenever I made this miserable trip up and down Station Lane I would notice this man. His hair was grey but still thick even if it was closely cropped. He wore trousers and a jacket that were obviously from a suit, but which didn't match. The cloth shone with wear on the elbows of the jacket. His shoes weren't down at heel, they were down in every way, but still an attempt had been made to polish them. His old cardigan was shapeless, whilst his shirt was minus the collar that was in them days a separate item that you attached to the shirt.

"He needed glasses, that was obvious, as he closely examined the change in his small purse with screwed up eyes. He wasn't shopping for a family, that was clear. You'd hear him ask for two ounces of bacon, he'd buy one bun in Darnton's and small amounts of tea and sugar in the Co-Op. He'd put his purchases in a small string shopping bag and walk to the next shop not shuffling but almost, still trying to muster up a purposeful stride, and now and again correcting his stoop. It was clear that this man had pride.

"Every couple of weeks my father and I would go to Sammy Lowe's barber's shop for a haircut. That isn't stating the obvious, you could still get a shave and a singe at Sammy's if you wanted one. My father would sit and gossip about goings on at the pit, they'd always be 'working in watter' in parts of it, and of course there'd be speculation about that afternoon's Rovers' game. We weren't engaging in father and son 'bonding', that was hardly necessary, it was just convenient and my dad could make sure that I had the right kind of haircut. No quiffs, no square neck and he had to be able to run his finger up the back of my neck and feel the bristles. God only knows what heartache he was in for as the sixties really got up a head of steam, and my adolescence really kicked in?

"We stepped out of the barber's into the lane straight into the path of the old man I've been telling you about. We stopped to let him pass and my dad muttered 'ey-up' to him, like you still do in Featherstone. 'That's Jimmy Rudd', he said and left it at that, knowing that my curiosity wouldn't let his comment hang in mid-air for more than a moment. 'Who's Jimmy Rudd, dad?' I asked. My dad didn't know that I'd been observing and wondering about this man for ages, perhaps instinctively knowing that there was something different about him. So he took his time answering, unaware that I was dying to hear what he was going to tell me as he paused to light a Woodbine. 'Jimmy Rudd was the first man to kick a rugby ball at Wembley. He played stand-off for Dewsbury in the 1929 final and he kicked the game off. It was a scandal. Dewsbury didn't play fancy football, but they had a good pack. They were told to change their style to make the game better to look at with it being the first Wembley Final, and that was why they lost.'

"Jimmy Rudd disappeared into Cawson's chemists at the bottom of Station Lane. My dad and I made our way home to have some dinner before going to the match and I was left with a memory that still affects the way I think about things, a memory that revolved around ordinary people doing extraordinary things then becoming ordinary people again."

Grandad has the last say

"For the last couple of years of his life my grandfather hardly spoke. He sat in an old chair in the corner of the living room occasionally spitting into the fire, the smoke from his foul-smelling pipe catching the rays of sun that filtered through the kitchen window.

"As a child I managed to see and enjoy the last years of his energy, sprightliness, and mischief. Down the pit at 13, third battle of Ypres at 30 and everything that followed for working class families that came after it.

"After he retired from the pit he took a job hosing down Bullock and Sons buses on the night shift. I'd sometimes see him set off for work in his oilskins and Sou' Wester, looking like a lifeboat man with a hell of a long trip to a call out.

"On Saturdays, I'd go to Schofield's for his tripe and pigs trotters, the latest in a long line of grandchildren to get the job. Then to Tommy Keenan's off-licence with an empty quart pop bottle, which Tommy filled up (illegally I suppose) with enough Tetley's to see Grandad through the weekend. He'd give me a swig of 'wallop' as a reward.

"His name was Josiah. He was a quiet man on the surface. Gran used to say 'ee he sits there like an old sheep. He never used to get mad with anybody, even though you could see he was inside.'
Think of the 'enforcers' in Rugby League who have been the sweetest guys you could meet off the fields, but would rip people apart as part of a day's work on it, and you get some idea of where my grandad was probably coming from.

"He became too old to hose down Bullock's buses, and gradually descended into what I guess was his dotage. Whoever was handy would take him outside to the lav once or twice a day. He'd come back and people would ask him how it went. 'Fair to wind', was the usual reply and he'd return to his thoughts, his eyes sometimes looking more watery than mere wateriness.

"I'd known he'd played in the early days of the Northern Union, when he was a member of a club based in a somewhat disreputable working men's club in Purston Park called The Crow's Nest, which had been headquarters for local junior rugby. I came into Gran's after a Rovers game one Saturday afternoon for a cup of tea so stewed you could stain teak with it, but would have kept Captain Oates alive.

"Grandad turned to me and at first I thought it was for me to take him to the lav, but it wasn't. 'When I played in't Northern Union I were a dirty player', (he didn't say anything stronger, obeying the miners' tradition of never swearing in front of children).

'Me and my pal were always getting sent off for something. In the end they suspended us *sine die*, which we assumed meant forever. One night we went for a pint of wallop at the Junction and had a few. We decided to do something about the situation. My mate worked in the joiners shop at the pit and the following day he borrowed two saws. That night we sneaked into the ground and sawed t'goalposts down. If we weren't laikng, nobody were laiking.'

"He laughed until he started coughing uncontrollably. He spat into the fire, looked at me with mischief in his watery eyes and drifted off into his reverie."

Sixties end

As I look back on the sizzling sixties, a broad smile appears on my face. The decade brought many of the happiest days of my life and despite losing some of my allure I was looking fitter and faster, thanks to a few facelifts and a sprinkling of Old Spice!

Yet, the swinging sixties had swung away from me a bit. The boom time of the fifties with my massive popularity and great players was hard to live up to and I'd given it my best effort, but I felt a little decline was inevitable.

Never mind, I'd had some fun and delivered one timeless sporting moment, although for maybe the wrong reasons, with Don's miss at the watersplash final, the poor lad.

To paraphrase John Lennon's sentiments of the time: "All we are saying, is give League a chance". With the seventies just around the corner, I needed all the help I could get.

9

1970-1980
NORTHERN SOUL
OR LOST SOUL?

Like so many of my older supporters, do you look back on life gone by with rose-tinted glasses? When the memory drifts back to our earlier years we recall with affection the happy, carefree days but gloss over the harder times. However, during periods of worry and strife it appears that the world we stand on is about to collapse underneath our feet and swallow us down into a chasm.

When middle age dawns it is often accompanied by a feeling of restlessness. Called mid-life crisis it picks you up like a whirlwind and splatters the thought patterns into oblivion as one gets the urge to do the most outrageous things in fear of the body clock suddenly winding down. I read an interesting article recently that suggested people as young as thirty something are now suffering mid-life crisis. That's well before life has taken off in my book! But why all this doom?

From a relative period of calm in the sixties life for me went into rapid decline. Deserted terraces, money worries, a lack of self-esteem, creaking bones, loss of get up and go. Pity the well-man clinics hadn't yet arrived to sort me out. Yours truly was heading down the toboggan run of life sharper than Arkwright's till on *Open All Hours*.

You are what you eat they say, so could it be something in that foreign grub that arrived in the seventies, such as the burgers, curry and lager that people seem to thrive on nowadays? I say there is nothing like a good old Yorkshire pudding, Lancashire hot pot or Cumberland sausage washed down by a smooth pint of Tetley or Black Sheep. For the older reader, anyone remember 'bubble and squeak', the Sunday leftovers fried up for dinner on Monday? Now that was a treat indeed.

If not my diet, at least I had my family all around me so maybe it could be the day job that was getting me down?

Anyway, let's reminisce a little before contemplating my own personal mid-life crisis.

Dancing the night away

Looking back in time we sometimes wonder how we ever managed, however, some things do make a comeback such as the trams in Manchester, cobbled town centres, fashions and house decor. We try to get rid of the past yet hark for many bygone values.

With power cuts, the miners strike and three-day week, the job in hand certainly suffered during this period and did place my life in limbo. It's times like this when you find out who your friends are. Still, life had to go on with the hope of brighter days ahead. I'm pleased to say my family kept on enjoying itself and many took advantage of the free coach trips to Blackpool that nightclub owners there would lay on from various north west towns to drum up business during quieter periods. Famous venues for revellers included the Cavern in Liverpool, Wigan Casino and Bolton Palace where you could tune into Northern Soul or *Saturday Night Fever.*

Speaking of music, compact discs hadn't yet been invented, so one had to do with crackly vinyl records of the last knockings of the Beatles, Slade and the Bay City Rollers.

A change from the seventies staples of Mud, Queen, T-Rex and Roxy Music, two versions of *Una Paloma Blanca* were in the charts the same week of 1975. *The George Baker Selection* and Jonathan

King were the guilty parties, and before you ask it was about a wedding dress, not a cocktail. In fact in 1973 the biggest-selling chart act was, believe it or not, *The Wombles*! Punk came and went.

From memory, hot pants caused the odd a wink or two on the dance floor and for the blokes 40-inch flared trousers. Crombies and Chelsea boots with the zip-up sides were amongst the 'in things' in fashion, and who would own up to going out on the town dressed in a Ben Sherman, Dr Martens, kipper tie and turn-ups? Some razzle-dazzle there. Talking of which, remember the fluorescent jackets that illuminated children on their journey to school?

National Fire Service greatcoats wouldn't have been appropriate in the summers of 1976 and 1978 when nature turned the heat up quite considerably. In one of the heat waves we had an invasion of French ladybirds that lay siege to Southport with many a car owner unable to see through their windscreen. Nowadays the French have resorted to different tactics by laying siege to ports.

As a strange coincidence, as this is being written, Britain recorded the hottest day on record when the 100 degrees Fahrenheit barrier was passed for the first time, on Sunday the 10th August 2003 at Brogdale near Faversham. *It 'aint Half Hot Mum*!

Milk came in Egyptian type pyramid containers, chocolate in Aztec bars, which I presume came from Peru, and memories are also made from natty acrylic star jumpers, tank tops and Mk 1 Cortinas. Wagon Wheels seemed twice as big as they are now and colour telly arrived with BBC2. Green Shield gave a new meaning to stamp collecting, enough of which could earn a gift such as a nice new Chopper bike. Pubs used to close mid-afternoon to allow the weary landlord some respite.

Times were tough when you could buy a terraced house for £3,800, which now represents ones quarterly expenditure bill. A holiday abroad in 1970 would typically cost 36.5 guineas and good value too. Mind you that wouldn't get you to Clacton-on-Sea these days.

Now popular within the 'millionaire' community, Chris Tarrant started his career on *TISWAS*, and a family night's viewing featured Pan's People, the *Partridge Family*, *Starsky and Hutch*

(BBC's favourite repeat), *Ironside* and Esther Rantzen's *That's Life* programme, a campaigning one but with a sense of humour, especially for comedy vegetables. Who remembers hiding behind a cushion during Saturday teatime whilst watching *Dr Who*?

Viewers of children's television would remember the intrepid presenter John Noakes playing Rugby League with Castleford. The *Blue Peter Annual* 14th Edition, on every child's Christmas list in 1977, featured the classic quote: "There was no turning back now - in five minutes time I would be out on the field," and a rather *risqué* team bath photo.

Folk weren't used to walking into lampposts whilst using their mobile phones as street corners still featured public call boxes, now fast becoming a thing of the past. Very few of them worked but always looked smart, bright red with heavy doors on them, well mostly as the odd door or two would sometimes go missing (who would want a red phone box door?) Not all were alike, though. Over in Hull, most phone boxes were creamy white and a little village called Kings Moss in Lancashire had a bright green one to match the surrounding countryside. A little old lady in the village would place fresh flowers inside every week.

What about 'Telephone Booth Stuffing' that became popular in 1970? It actually started in South Africa when 25 students packed into a booth and announced it a world record. The craze soon spread worldwide, including Britain, with some folk going on diets to try and achieve a new record. When the fad waned 'Volkswagen Stuffing' took over.

By the way, what did happen to Spangles, those colourful, square-shaped sweets with a dimple in the middle?

Nationwide

Well, there are a few memories from round our end, but what were the current affairs events that got people talking during the seventies, and who was in the news?

January 1970 witnessed the first Boeing 747 landing at Heathrow airport. Now there seems to be a jumbo jet roaring overhead every minute. IBM launched floppy discs that have themselves become old technology, whilst a farming programme replaced *Monty Python's Flying Circus* in the Midlands region. Apparently this new anarchical TV comedy was not well received in certain circles, least so amongst Brummies.

The Vietnam War escalated whilst the Israeli government agreed a US plan for a ceasefire in the Middle East. It appears 30-odd years later nothing much has changed with conflict still everyday news. A cyclone and tidal wave in Bangladesh killed approximately 300,000 people.

What of 1971? Decimalization was introduced and certainly gave some elderly people a few monetary problems, with even yours truly getting his shillings wrong.

Philips launched the VCR in time to capture the *Two Ronnies* as they arrived on our television screens. The 'optically challenged' Ronnies Corbett and Barker drew enormous television audiences, usually around 17 million viewers, with their array of characters.

There were less people out of puff with fags at £1 for 20 but disappearing from our screens was cigarette advertising, banned as the Public Health Cigarette Smoking Act came into force, steering advertising money towards sponsorship of televised sporting events, such as motor racing, snooker, darts and...Rugby League.

The world watched agog as the unmanned *Mariner 9* blasted off on an epic journey from America to Mars on 30th May and when it arrived on 14th November later that year it became the first space probe to orbit another planet.

How about the tatty raincoat worn by Peter Falk, alias *Columbo* the cigar chewing detective who arrived in 1972? However, you would have had to watch by candlelight as there were frequent power cuts brought on by the miners strike that was challenging the closure of the pits and the Prime Minister of the day, Edward Heath.

Wrinkly stockings took a bow out on the Yorkshire Dales in 1973 as worn by Nora Batty in *Last of the Summer Wine*. Ever popular, gentle entertainment, it's still running, the longest-lived comedy series in the world.

The USA and Vietnam agreed a ceasefire at a meeting in Paris, whilst in the art world the Spanish artist, Pablo Picasso, died at the age of 91 and Sydney Opera House opened its doors that October.

Celebration turned to sporting tragedy when the Bader Meinhof terror gang murdered Israeli athletes at the 1974 Munich Olympic games, a dark side of what should have been a festival of athletic unity. Returning from outer space, 19th December witnessed NASA's *Apollo* mission ending with splashdown as the most recent astronauts to walk on the moon.

Facing certain impeachment over the 'Watergate' affair, Richard Nixon became the first president of the USA to resign, Gerald Ford stepping into the breach the following day as the first unelected President.

Tragedy in 1976 when over 25,000 people in Guatemala were killed during an earthquake, whilst in and around Tangshan in China another 650,000 people died in another devastating tremor. The supersonic aircraft *Concorde* entered commercial service that year after much controversy, it being built at vast public cost and then 'sold' to British Airways for just £1 a plane.

Not only was 1977 the Queen's Silver Jubilee but lo and behold a British tennis player in Virginia Wade actually won the Wimbledon singles title and was presented with the trophy by Her Majesty the Queen. Heady days for tennis, with a coincidence in that Richard Lewis, later to become Chief Executive of my professional arm in 2002 and ex-lawn tennis player, was actually playing on an adjacent court to Virginia.

The 'King of Rock', Elvis Presley, passed away at the age of 42 in his Memphis, Tennessee home. Many distraught fans could not come to terms with the news and for many years after still believed he was alive. *Star Wars* hit the big screen with plenty more outer space adventure.

Louise Brown made history by becoming the first 'test tube' baby to be born in Britain during 1978 whilst near Brest, France, the oil tanker *Amoco Cadiz* also made history by making a mess with the worst oil spill ever.

In 1979, history was made when 'there is no alternative' Margaret Thatcher was elected Britain's first woman Prime Minister, crushing Labour's Michael Foot in the General Election. The 'Iron Maiden' certainly was a formidable figure whilst taking on the Trade Unions, EEC and Soviet Bloc countries during her term in office.

For whom the bell tolls

In Rugby League, 1970 saw the head-high tackle clamped down on, whilst in 1971 the six tackle rule was introduced into the Sydney Premiership competition, having been four previously. By 1975 the six-tackle rule had become universal.

Hard to believe it was so recent, but independent timekeepers were only introduced in 1972, the ref having more than enough on his plate. To indicate 'time up' each club supplied a timekeeper and when the 80 minutes elapsed gave a blast on a hooter, siren or in South Sydneys case, rung a rather fine brass bell. I thought the hooter idea most appropriate, harking back to 'clocking off' the shift at factory or pit.

The drop-goal was reduced in value from two points to one in Aussie in 1971 and the same rule was adopted in Blighty in 1974.

International standardisation resulted in metrification being used on pitches and posts. Goal posts were to be 5.5 metres apart and crossbars 3.05 metres from the ground instead of 18ft 6ins and 10ft 6ins. I suppose teams also felt more threatened as opponents reached their 22 line as opposed to the 25!

Three cherries

One reason for my decline in popularity could be attributed to many top stars flying the nest to Aussie pastures new, enticed by the poker machine-backed clubs that could offer bigger incentives than the metricated, dreary old pound.

A steady stream of British players, starting with Barrow's Test centre Phil Jackson in 1960, began to arrive in Australia. In 1963, Derek Hallas moved from Leeds to Parramatta and the Dewsbury star, Mike Stephenson downed his plumbing tools to become the first British player to defy the RFL's warning and sacrifice his Great Britain career for one at Pernrith, west Sydney, starting a flood.

Other great players followed like Castleford's stand off Alan

Hardisty, a little whippet if ever there was one, (whoops! Shouldn't mention whippets here should we?), towering Phil Lowe from Hull KR to Manly, Steve 'Knocker' Norton and Gary Stephens both Castleford to Manly, Bill Ashurst of Wigan to Penrith and the mighty Mal Reilly to boot, a tough nut for Manly.

Shorn of many of my stars, it did seem like I was having a closing-down sale.

Meanwhile, back in England, several clubs faced insolvency and the RFL at Chapeltown Road organised loans to a maximum of £20,000 per club to keep the strugglers afloat. Whilst no doubt some money did go on trying to emulate the Australian type gambling fund raising schemes, high Income Tax and a 15 per cent levy on club gates payable to the RFL's central funds compounded matters. Wigan created the loudest fuss, being a big opponent of this extra burden.

The climate improved a little for the lower clubs when in the 1973/74 season two divisions were re-introduced, only first division clubs facing the levy.

Surprisingly, Hunslet were the only club casualty of this dreary era, the first holders of 'All Four Cups' in 1907 now gone with the wind. The depressing effect of the closure of the nearby factories and foundries and slum clearance in this industrial area of south Leeds certainly accelerated the clubs demise. Good folk were definitely strapped for some 'readies.' Hunslet's last game at Parkside, soon after redeveloped into industrial units by Leeds City Council, took place on 21st April 1973. Stalwart captain Geoff Gunney was the last Hunslet player to leave the field of play that fateful day, but he led the way in resurrecting the New Hunslet club four months later at the nearby Elland Road Greyhound Stadium, resplendent with 'tuning fork' posts.

Someone evidently did have the same idea as the Aussie Leagues entertainment complexes that underwrote the game there, as giant social clubs sprung up across the north in the late sixties and thrived through the seventies. The Batley Variety Club, Sheffield Fiesta and Wakefield Theatre Club offered entertainment giants only usually seen on the *Parkinson* chat show. Why get excited about a visit by Whitehaven or Widnes (no disrespect) when a weekend's entertainment could now feature Shirley Bassey, Tom Jones or Neil Sedaka, and chicken in a basket to boot?

Money, Money, Money! (with apologies to ABBA)

Well then, what of the sparse and depleted crowds in the seventies that did manage to make an effort as I entertained? Certainly my talents weren't appreciated over at Knowsley Road, with attendances ranging from 2,500 to 5,000 and fewer still on 'brass monkey' winter Sunday afternoons. Fans huddled together on the Popular Side of the ground for a morsel of warmth with a wee dram of whiskey or flask of pea soup, whilst the Eddington Stand was akin to count the fans in one minute.

Meanwhile over at Headingley, barely 5,000 to 6,500 hardy souls would turn out for a similar event, not a lot for a big city club. I definitely had a few more of the "Rugby League is dying" brigade echoing their opinions in those 'good old' days. I must say it was a worry and I did consider taking my pension!

With such thin turnstile takings in the seventies deep concern for my welfare became evident after the 1974/75 season when the combined match attendances totalled just 800,000.

As a saving grace in 1971/72 several commercial organisations came to the rescue with welcome financial assistance. Ever-reliable Joshua Tetley gave support to the tune of £4,000 in backing the Lancashire Cup, later becoming the Burtonwood Brewery Lancashire Cup in 1976 then followed by Greenall Whitley's Grunhalle Lager. Esso, then John Smiths brewery, sponsored the Yorkshire Cup.

A new cup competition was born, accompanied by a welcome cheque for £9,500 from the manufactures of John Player cigarettes. The new Players No.6 Trophy changed name three times, first to the John Player Trophy, then the John Player Special Trophy and finally the Regal Trophy.

By then Silk Cut had butted in by sponsoring the Challenge Cup, whilst Stones Bitter pumped money into the senior championship. Forward Chemicals lent their name to the 1978 Ashes series.

Shirt and short sponsorship eventually spread to my individual clubs but not without the odd argument or two with the BBC who were loath to allow advertising on the pitch.

The old Access card was in danger of overload and there is no doubt in my mind that this generosity in exchange for some valuable publicity helped my bank balance immensely in keeping the wolves at bay.

The growth in commercialism coincided with a new, slimline leadership for me in 1972 when a meeting of 26 club chairmen decided that I should be administered by a smaller body than the full council of the 30 clubs. When Bill Fallowfield decided to retire as my secretary in 1974 after almost 30 years in the job the Executive Committee (as it was now called) had the task of selecting a new captain to take the helm and guide the ship to calmer waters.

From a list of fifty applicants David Oxley, the favoured candidate of the then Salford and RFL Chairman Brian Snape, became the successor taking a starting salary of £4,500 per annum plus a car allowance and annual expenses of £600. Some weeks later, David J. Howes came on board as my first public relations officer. This partnership lasted for several years and became as famous as Laurel and Hardy. Not suggesting that they were comedians, of course, but David did have a good wit about him and helped many in the game to raise funds via the popular *Sunday Mirror* Roadshows, as my good friend John Huxley - Rugby Football League media manager - will now fill you in.

On the road again

The *Sunday Mirror* Rugby League Roadshow was born one Saturday night in the well-known Manchester watering hole, Swan With Two Necks on Withy Grove. I had been appointed to replace George Dawson as the *Sunday Mirror's* Rugby League correspondent, whilst in the same sportsdesk reshuffle the legendary Dewsbury-born 'Angry Man' columnist Peter Shaw had moved up the ladder to become the northern sports editor. Peter was anxious not only to raise my profile within the sport but also to place the paper on a higher plane with Rugby League fans. During a break from the Saturday night production duties we hit on a solution over drinks, as all good journalists do.

I was tasked with finding a 'vehicle' by which we could promote not only Rugby League but also our newspaper. At the time we were closely connected with the Castleford club, its players and some who now played for Huddersfield. "Get yourself over to Cas and see what would work," was the instruction and, diligently, I set about the task. Eddie Waring, another former *Sunday Mirror* columnist, had made a name for himself by running Rugby League nights that included personalities, films and quizzes. His format was taken off the shelf, dusted down and polished. After borrowing the Challenge Cup from the Rugby League it was off to the Castleford Civic centre for our very first on-stage event. The night turned out to be a treat and so another show was introduced.

In October 1974, David Howes had been appointed the Rugby League's first ever Public Relations Officer and, as part of his duties, we came into contact. That contact became more frequent as I tried to impose my own stamp on the *Sunday Mirror* column. He was seeking a way in which the game could interact with fans away from the pressures of game day and to help keep fans connected to the sport and its stars. It was his fertile, creative mind that, part-fuelled the Castleford Civic Hall show and went on to fashion the format that was to serve the Roadshow so well throughout its 11-year, 100-show lifespan.

The central plank of Howes' scheme was to offer the show to a player's testimonial committee, thus guaranteeing that there was more than one reason for coming to see it. Allied to that, the show keyed into the emotion of being a fan so that they could contribute to the evening in many ways.

The next element of genius Howes brought to bear was the assembly of a team of show participants around which the whole four-hour event was constructed. The fulcrum of the show has to be the front man and Howes went for the mellifluous tones of broadcaster and journalist Keith Macklin. The Widnes-born media star's distinctive voice had long been associated with Rugby League and, although he had fronted television programmes such as *Songs of Praise*, the fans knew that when he spoke Rugby League was in there somewhere.

The *Sunday Mirror* Roadshow was, if nothing else, a major fundraising device. The central cash generating member of the team was none other than former Wakefield Trinity, Featherstone Rovers, Oldham, Carlisle and England utility-forward Mick Morgan, who would later be voted 'Man of Steel' in 1982 whilst at Carlisle.

Quick-witted and razor tongued, 'Morgie' ran the best memorabilia auction in sport and spattered his patter with earthy humour, a wide range of sporting and Rugby League knowledge and an insistent auctioneering style that was to prove irresistible to beneficiaries and their committees.

The first show was staged in Hull for Hull KR beneficiary Paul Rose, the uncompromising international forward, and it set the trend of fun and entertainment. Part of the inaugural Roadshow team was the guitar-playing, Neil Diamond tribute ace John Kendrew from Castleford but, after a few shows had been successfully staged, an international player joined the ensemble; St Helens and Great Britain scrum-half Neil Holding. Irrepressible Neil had a talent for mimicry as he had demonstrated on children's television show *Junior Showtime* and that, allied to a wicked sense of humour honed in the Saints dressing room, saw him join the act in seamless style.

The format was simple; the first half opened with the latest Rugby League video and then Keith Macklin would conduct interviews with the club's great and good. That enabled many players to finish their training commitments and arrive in time to support their club mate by joining in the fun. The second half opened with a knockabout Rugby League quiz usually based on a popular television quiz of the time.

The two teams were a mixture of players and fans. How the fans enjoyed seeing their heroes display their knowledge of Rugby League - or lack of it! Teams were asked to undertake unusual tasks such as providing mimes from which their teammates had to guess players' names, referee signals and other diverse subjects.

Usually the Roadshow undertook ten shows a season and

covered virtually every club in the League with the exception of Swinton for some unknown reason. Perhaps their players never stayed around for the 10 years or 300 games necessary to qualify for a testimonial? Such was the popularity of the event there usually were some disappointed players each year who failed to win a booking.

One favourite memory is the night we went to Barrow to help Eddie Syzmala's benefit. The heavily-tattooed England hooker never let the huge toothy grin leave his face all through the evening. We all enjoyed the moment when David Howes attempted to be more than light-hearted with famed Rugby League tough man Frank Foster, who was not in the mood to have the joke on him at any stage in the interview in spite of all David's efforts. David had labelled Frank as 'Val Doonican' because the former Barrow coach was wearing a patterned jumper and Foster was not amused. He lifted the shocked Howes up in a bear hug and suspended him over the 12-foot drop from the stage!

There were anxious moments too. When we wanted to celebrate Steve Norton's testimonial we utilised a well known nightspot in the middle of Hull. Normally we could rely on players being with us by the time the video presentation was starting but, on this occasion, both David Howes and myself were left pacing anxiously in the foyer, as there was no sign of the players by the time the video presentation was closing. That left us with no interviewees and, worse still, no stars for a huge group of fans. Eventually Steve and his teammates were located in the pub across the road with the legendary loose forward leading his teammates in a song. The players, when they eventually arrived, were, of course, superb but it all went to prove the best-laid plans are sometimes fallible.

Trips to Cumbrian clubs had their own special attraction for besides the warm welcome that awaited you on the West Cumbria coast you could key into the special passion the Cumbrian fans have for the game. We cheered some of the greats like Arnold 'Boxer' Walker, John McCracken, Paul Charlton and Sol Roper. On another occasion, the Cumbrian post-show drink was in a nightclub. We took along our two beautiful personality girls but, unfortunately the venue was past its best and dancing was hampered by your feet sticking to both the carpet and the dance floor!

One moment that never failed to thrill was revealing how much the lucky beneficiary was to receive from the evening's entertainment. After just a few Roadshows the trend of raising £1,000 and more was established. This was a considerable amount of money in those now far off days and the look on the face of the player when Keith Macklin announced the final amount always made the effort worthwhile.

Sometimes it was hard not to be caught up in the emotion of it all, especially if we had succeeded in raising an inordinately large sum of money for a particularly deserving player. There wasn't a dry eye in the house when we went to Batley for Paul Storey, who went on to coach at the Bulldogs. That night the Roadshow yielded more than had been raised in the rest of his testimonial.

Some players got carried away with it all too. 'Boxer' Walker gave away a treasured England jersey for auction at one show in Workington and we hurriedly negotiated a behind-stage deal with the purchaser to make sure he got it back.

Although other media organisations and clubs have run their own versions of the *Sunday Mirror* Rugby League Roadshow they have never quite succeeded in delivering the same atmosphere and sheer joy of the original team. The decision to end the series was taken, reluctantly, by David Howes and the Mirror Group promotions department.

They wanted to go out at the top having raised more than £250,000 in 100 shows during more than 10 years. Players' testimonial years were starting to become a thing of the past and, although there was still a demand for the Roadshow team to continue, it was judged to be the right time to retire.

1895 Club

Around this time a group of enthusiastic supporters set up a pressure group to fight my various causes debating on a weekly basis at the Nags Head public house just down the road from St

Helens RLFC. Even then the media coverage I received was not of the highest standard and a 10,000 signature petition was compiled calling for better coverage by the BBC and handed over on the morning of the 1976 Challenge Cup final.

Other issues on the frontline were the freedom to play my sport in the armed forces and colleges and universities.

However, some didn't 'play the game', notably those in charge of my clubs who thought fans should be seen and not heard and eventually the group faded. I do still believe however that some good did arise from this little acorn of support.

The group has restarted as 1895 International, aimed at fundraising and assistance principally for international development of the game. Good Luck, I say.

Bring on the Dons... Another Bloody Sunday

Excuse the language, dear reader, but the title above relates to Doncaster RLFC whose moment of infamy came with a one-hour Yorkshire television documentary following their plight on and off the field during their rock bottom 1979/80 season. Desperate for any sort of win, having received losing pay for what seemed an eternity, the programme showed that life is not just about the top dogs.

To help with the story several fans from the totalrl.com internet message board chipped in with their memories.

First up, 'Fartown Till I Die' recalled "the opening sequence was utter class, hard drives from forwards and bone crunching tackles, all in slow motion to Prokofiev's *Montagues and Capulets*. Very parochial really, but also very much a reminder of just what this great game of ours is really built on."

'Simac1967' added: "Geoff Fletcher always played without his wig. He would put it back on after the game. In one notorious incident during an away game at Fartown, Huddersfield wingman and prankster Graham Swale sneaked into the Huyton dressing room and purloined the said hairpiece. Apparently Geoff didn't see the funny side. The incident made *Look North* news."

Geoff Fletcher, of course, coached Huyton at the time, in fact 'Piggy' Fletcher was a true character in my game, seemingly

Chairman, Head Coach, accountant, grass cutter and kit washer all in one, all this above the day job as a pig farmer in St Helens. Rumour had it that Geoff used to put his wig on back to front if his team lost so no one could recognise him!

Next up 'PrinceCharlesForKing' chipped in: "one hell of a documentary. Wonderful images of miserable fans thinly scattered across crumbling terraces in the driving rain. You just thought to yourself, "why on earth do they bother?" One of the first times that I became really aware of RL and I was hooked."

'Hornetto' carried on: "Fulham get a mention in the narrative. Rochdale Hornets feature quite heavily with footage of an eminently forgettable 10-3 cup win in the early part of the programme. I'm the kid in the red jacket jumping around on the Railway side of the Athletic Grounds. It's a great window on the era when I really got my teeth into Rugby league (I'd been going since 1971, but at 15 and 16 you start to work out what it's *really* all about)."

Next comments came from 'cjb'. "It was filmed during the 1979/80 season but was not shown on television though until a year after. It appeared on Yorkshire Television on 8th April 1981. The opening slow-motion sequence was Donny versus Swinton (18-33), other games shown were a first-round cup tie away at Rochdale (lost 10-3), Featherstone at home (lost 0-31) and then the big one, Donny versus Huyton, 24th Feb 1980 (WON 6-3!).

"My interest in all this is as a Huyton supporter. Geoff Fletcher's pre-match team talk was pure class. It starts off: '*Anyone, who's come here today, who thinks we've come to lose, tell me now, cos we've got lads here who'll go on in yer place. Ah don't want to hear you've got a bad head, a bad foot, a cold, after. Tell me now and we can alter, cos if yer goin' on that field today ah want yer to go on to win. Anyone who thinks ther gonna lose, there's no point even trying. Now there's only one thing what wins these games, tackling, Anyone not prepared to tackle shouldn't be on the field. You've got to go in like a lunatic and knock em down, ah want em putting down and really knocking down.*'

"He then has a go at a few individuals over there previous performances, telling one player: 'Yer attacking prowess lately has been absolutely none, ah don't know what the hell's going on there, but yer defence is perfect, now lets have some attacking from yer.' Next in line for a tongue-lashing is Bob Goulding (the dad of Bobbie Goulding junior) telling him: 'Na then, poser. Yer forget Widnes, yer forget Salford, yer playing with Huyton now! Yer do as we do, yer run hard and straight, yer a big fast lad.'

"Huyton scored first (0-3) then Donny scored just before half-time (3-3). Then cometh the hour cometh the man, as Tony Banham came off the bench about 20 minutes from time to score the decisive winner (6-3).

"The Donny players were on £60 a man to win, and it showed them drinking champagne in the club after, still wearing their mud splattered kit."

Finally, 'rhubarbtriangulist' still has his Huyton versus Donny appreciation pin badge.

The Red Devils of Savile Row

The Willows, Salford's ground since 1901, got its name from a row of trees that stood on the site and further seeds were sown in the late sixties as Salford assembled a team that wouldn't look out of place in Savile Row, but were they a cut above the rest?

A quiet, steady climb up the league table during the mid-sixties culminated in collaring sixth position in 1968-69, their best league position since 1949-50. After a 30-year gap the twin towers of Wembley beckoned once more only for Castleford to thwart their cup quest at the last hurdle in front of 97,939 supporters.

Brian Snape had taken charge and wasted no time in recruiting from the very best rugby talent either code could offer. David Watkins, the Welsh Rugby Union fly half and British Lion switched codes in October 1967 for a reported £16,000, creating a shock wave that reverberated right down to South Wales. In fact, David was later banned as a spectator from Cardiff Arms Park. Unsettled at stand-off he later switched to the centre position with devastating effect and gave his all in 407 appearances kicking a world record number of 221 goals in 1972-73, as well as taking other points and goal records from Gus Risman.

Another player to blossom was Chris Hesketh, who failed to make the cut in his Wigan days, but went on to amass 452 games for Salford, with his 23 appearances for Great Britain being a Salford best. Personal honours were to follow for Chris with the captaincy of both Salford and Great Britain and, like Watkins, he received the MBE.

The ex-England Union international, Mike Coulman signed from Moseley RUFC for £8,500 in October 1968 giving sterling service completing 463 games and scoring 135 tries, a record for a Salford forward.

More headlines in the *Manchester Evening News* on 19th December 1968 confirmed Salford had captured two current Rugby League internationals in wing threequarter Bill Burgess from Barrow (£6,000) and Halifax's Colin Dixon. It took a record transfer fee of £11,500 to persuade Halifax to part with Dixon although unfortunately for Burgess a shoulder injury curtailed his career in 1970.

Salford flourished the chequebook in breathtaking fashion, breaking the transfer record three more times. Paul Charlton arrived from Workington for £12,500 in October 1969, £13,550 secured the services of Eric Prescott from St Helens in September 1972 whist £15,000 went Featherstone's way in August 1975 for Steve Nash. Charlton broke the try-scoring record for a fullback in crossing for 33 tries in 1972-73 as well as representing Great Britain 18 times.

Another Welsh Rugby Union player, Maurice Richards, signed in October 1969 becoming a great favourite and creating club history by amassing a record total of 297 tries during his 498 starts.

Sharp as a needle, speed man Keith Fielding signed from Moseley RUFC in May 1973 for £8,500, and broke the club's try record with 46 touchdowns in his debut season. Add in a youthful Ken Gill and one can see a Rolls Royce side emerging.

It had been a long time between drinks as the league title had eluded the club since 1938-39, although matters were now ready to change as Salford completed their 1973-74 league programme top with 47 points, just one ahead of St Helens. Within weeks of Salford's achievement the other Red Devils, nearby Manchester

United, got relegated from their first division. Another title sewn up in 1975-76 with just the whisker of one point separating them from Featherstone, who in those days were a force to be reckoned with.

Sadly the star-studded team couldn't grace Wembley in the seventies although Lancashire Cup success arrived defeating neighbours Swinton in 1972.

The historians must ponder why this Salford team didn't achieve more silverware. Three runners-up spots on the trot in the Lancashire Cup, defeat to Leeds in a solitary Players No 6. Trophy final and a runners-up spot came against St Helens in a Premiership final, although a replay over Warrington did see the BBC 2 Floodlit Trophy buttoned up and winging its way to the Willows, but little consolation.

Salford's status as a pool of talent was recognised at Test level for the Aussie tour in 1974 when Hesketh, then club captain, Charlton, Dixon, Richards, Gill and Watkins all travelled beating the previous high of five picked for the 1936 party.

To sum up, whilst a great era for the fans to witness such a smart and attractive team, and two outright titles can't be sniffed at, having cut their cloth the Savile Row team didn't quite deliver as they should have.

Footnote:

During the last game of the 1976-77 league season between Salford and Leeds a tragic injury took the life of the Leeds player, Chris Sanderson. Chris suffered a broken neck late in the first half, causing the game to be abandoned, never to be replayed. A rare occurrence but such tragedy certainly puts matters into perspective.

Here is an account by Phil Stockton of what he can recall.

"I was in the crowd that day. As I remember it there was a scrum, which collapsed, and it appeared someone had gone down injured and was subsequently stretchered off. There was a long delay and initially impatience by the crowd as we didn't know what had actually happened. Eventually there was announcement that the game was to be abandoned and I think they did state that a player had either been seriously injured or had died.

As the crowd left the Willows you could have heard a pin drop. It was very eerie to be in such a moving mass of people without a word being said and in such a collective state of shock. The saddest day in Rugby League I have ever experienced."

Syd Hynes of Leeds eventually dedicated their Challenge Cup win that year to Chris, which was a very moving gesture, worthy of both men.

Whilst Ray Gent was handing out book publicity flyers at the Saints versus Salford game in 2004, a Salford fan not only confirmed the story but said it took him 20 years to bring himself to attend a live Rugby League game again.

Widnes, Cup Kings

Nestling alongside the River Mersey and amidst its chemical factories is Widnes, the jewel of Cheshire. Synonymous with Rugby League to many, Widnes had a golden era during the seventies as glittering cup final appearances became routine and the trophy cabinet regularly in use.

Losing the 1971 Lancashire Cup final to Wigan became a distant memory when at last success came not once or twice, but thrice with a hat-trick of Lancashire Cups as the Red Devils of Salford succumbed twice and then Workington Town yielded to the Chemics. After a year off, Widnes again triumphed over Workington Town twice to complete five Lancashire cups after a drought of nearly 30 years.

After a 10-year gap the black and white rosettes came out again at Wembley in 1975 as the Chemics headed for a capital day out in the 'Smoke' and success over Warrington, 14-7. Big Jim Mills charged over for Widnes' only try, whilst Bevan replied with one for the Wire. The difference in the end was the trusty boot of Dutton with six goal kicks plus a drop to his credit.

Not all plain sailing as Widnes withered when the *Dads Army* from St Helens produced a classic win in a near 100 degree heat wave. They don't like it up 'em! The red-hot favourites floundered in the white heat of Wembley to the tune of 20-5 as standpipes appeared across parched Britain. No Widnes ribbons the next year either, losing to Leeds, 16-7.

Onward to the 1979 final versus Wakefield Trinity the Dreadnoughts sunk, going under 12-3.

It was pick 'n' mix in the John Player Trophy with Widnes tasting defeat in the 1975 final at the hands of Bradford Northern with the gate a poor 5,935 and not much cheer from a score of 3-2. The 1976 final faired better with Hull and Widnes combining to produce a crowd of 9,035 with the Chemics taking the cup 13-19. Widnes and Warrington next exchanged pleasantries in back-to-back finals with one win apiece that at last attracted five-figure gates.

More glory to Naughton Park via the BBC 2 Floodlit Trophy in 1979 against St Helens but not before two reversals from Leigh and Bramley, a famous story I'll tell you later.

Bradford spoiled the Widnes party in the 1978 Premiership Final 17-8 and the biggest prize of all as Widnes at long last claimed their very first championship in 1978.

Bradford and Featherstone got into a spot of bother as that season came to a close. With a couple of matches left, the only outstanding matter was the runners-up position, with Northern and Saints the candidates. Both sides could reach second spot by winning their last match of the season if the other team slipped up in theirs. Just 48 hours before these matches kicked off the players at Featherstone Rovers (Northern's opponent) went on strike after a boardroom argument had split the directors and brought about the chairman's resignation. The players stood behind the chairman and refused to play the last match unless he was reinstated. No invitation forthcoming, the players carried out their threat. The RFL took a dim view of the affair and fined Featherstone for their players' actions.

With the Premiership play-offs a week away, the RFL had to act quickly and awarded Bradford second place overall despite St Helens winning their last match and finishing one point ahead of Northern.

Using the percentage system that had been in force from 1905/06 to 1929/30 Northern rated a success percentage of 75.86 per cent from their 29 league matches whilst St Helens score from

30 games was 74.99 per cent. Fancy going back to rules used in the 1900s!

Well done Widnes on a supreme effort during the seventies, with more to follow.

Bradford Northern reborn

In contrast to the fortunes of poor old Hunslet, fair play to Bradford Northern.

After their travails of the previous decade, Northern pulled themselves up by their bootstraps and found success again in the seventies as champions in season 1979-80, Premiership Trophy winners in 1978, landing the Yorkshire Cup against York in 1979 and taking home the John Player Trophy twice.

Add also beaten finalists in the Challenge Cup twice, runners-up in the Championship once and twice beaten finalists in the Premiership, a Lazarus-like rise from the last decade's demise.

Challenging time

Whilst pondering over the Challenge Cup in the seventies I wonder if tradition saved my bacon? I seem obsessed about it but crowd receipts were my bread and butter and mercifully the average attendances during the depression held up well at 86,622 compared with the turn-outs in the sixties which had averaged 87,356 per final.

The crowds at Wembley were certainly higher than finals these days, with the lowest of the decade being 72,395 for the clash of Featherstone and Bradford in 1973 and the highest in 1978 when Leeds and St Helens played before 96,000. This was strange indeed when you consider that club games could barely raise a smile. A seat at the mainly-standing Wembley cost all of £6.50.

Plenty of variety as the decade witnessed seven different clubs holding the Challenge Cup aloft.

Time for classy Cas to encore with successful return trips to Wembley and not only did they defeat Wigan in front of 95,255 but kept the Lancashire outfit tryless in a 7-2 result.

In an era of shocks little Leigh took perhaps the biggest scalp in 1971. Starting the game as 1/5 on favourites and on a reputed £5,000 a man winning bonus, the Loiners lost the services of Syd Hynes who achieved the unwanted mantle of the first player sent off in a Wembley showpiece following a clash with Alex Murphy. Folklore says Murph winked at Hynes as he was stretchered off, although he claims it was a blink. Murphy got two drop-goals and the Lance Todd Trophy although Leeds supporters felt he better deserved two black eyes and an Oscar. Nevertheless, Billy Thompson's dismissal of the Leeds captain 15 minutes from time wouldn't have changed the 24-7 result which was well beyond the Loiners by then and the shock win for Leigh was well deserved.

Kick-off a few moments early enabled Graham Rees to score a try for victorious St Helens in the 1972 final versus Leeds before the official three o' clock start.

In January 1972, British coal miners went on strike for the first time since 1926, the dispute lasting for seven weeks with a state of emergency declared. To economise on electricity, Edward Heath's government reduced the working week to three days. As a result of the strike miners' wages increased to amongst the highest in the British working class and the country was forced to recognise how important coal was to the economy.

By 1973 inflation and other workers settlements meant the miners had dropped from first in the industrial wages league to 18th. Throughout the country, relations between the industrial unions and the Government were hostile as national pay restraints were introduced to help stabilise the beleaguered economy. The miners realised that the poor economic situation and soaring oil prices caused by the Arab-Israeli War could be used to their advantage and in late 1973, the miners once more voted to take industrial action if their pay demands were not met. In February 1974, the miners duly came out on strike again. Within four weeks a state of emergency involving a three-day week had to be again declared. Prime Minister Heath called a General Election hoping that the electorate would support the government's attempts to deal with the deteriorating industrial relations situation, but the Conservative Party was defeated. The new Labour government reached a deal with the miners shortly afterwards.

Thus it was a great day for the underdog at Wembley in 1973 as the pit village of Featherstone, already embroiled in the coal strike struggle, socked it to the Bradford city slickers 33-14.

Coached superbly by Peter Fox, this unfashionable club had done the business at Wembley with an early 17-point blitz. Peter could now stand tall amongst his more illustrious brothers Neil and Don. A tough, no-nonsense Yorkshireman who possessed a warm, inner affection for my sport had shown the rest that one doesn't necessarily need a fortune in the bank to produce a winner, as his homespun outfit recruited mainly from the amateur ranks did him proud.

The try heroes for the Rovers that day were John Newlove twice, Vince Farrar, Mick Smith and Hartley with Kellett kicking eight goals and Nash one. Steve Nash and Alan Rhodes played hero's parts. The game produced a then record eight goals for fullback Kellet with the 47-point total eclipsing all previous Wembley finals, with receipts of £125,000 another high.

John Robinson, at the *Sunday People*, summed the Featherstone spirit up:

> *"Take a bow Peter Fox, team builder extraordinary! The likely lads of Featherstone took Wembley by storm and no-one can be prouder than coach Fox, the man who put the team together for next to nothing. Though Featherstone's points blitz destroyed a lot of competitive interest, Northern came back courageously in the second half to make it an all action final."*

Many more tributes poured in as the club basked in the glory. Featherstone had never shone so brightly in the limelight!

The next final saw Featherstone at Wembley again, but this time overpowered by Warrington, who then relinquished their hold on the cup to Widnes, the baton in turn passed to St Helens who took over polishing duties.

Leeds then took back-to-back cups having appeared in four finals, making one of the finest come backs ever against St Helens

Karel Tom Van Vollenhoven
made his name in South Africa,
where he starred for Northern
Transvaal and the Springboks.
He joined St Helens in 1957, and
scored 392 tries for the club
before retiring in 1968.

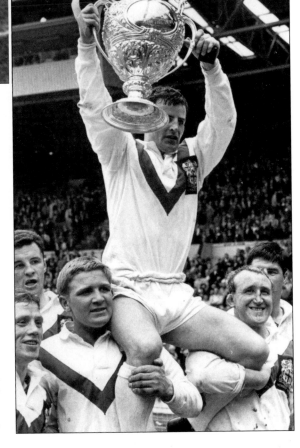

Alex Murphy signed for St Helens on
his 16th birthday in 1955, and went
on to score 275 tries in a 19-year
career. He won the Challenge Cup
Final in 1966 with Saints, and was
back at Wembley with Leigh in 1971.
He became player-coach at
Warrington the following year, and
led them to Wembley glory in 1974.
(pp213)

Neil Fox was one of the game's greatest centres during his career with Wakefield Trinity, and has scored more points than any other player in the history of the game - 6,220 from 358 tries and 2,574 goals. He spent the twilight of his career as a loose forward, and for a decade was an automatic selection for Great Britain. (pp250)

Vince Karalius was a hero of the 1958 Second Test win at Brisbane. Playing through injury, as did many of his colleagues, he destroyed the Australian pack with ferocious tackling despite suffering a back strain early in the game that made it difficult for him to walk, let alone run. (pp218)

Great Britain won the 1970 Ashes in Australia after coming from 1-0 down to take the final two Tests. Cliff Watson is pictured leaving the Sydney Cricket Ground with the Ashes Trophy, and, inset, with captain Frank Myler. (pp302)

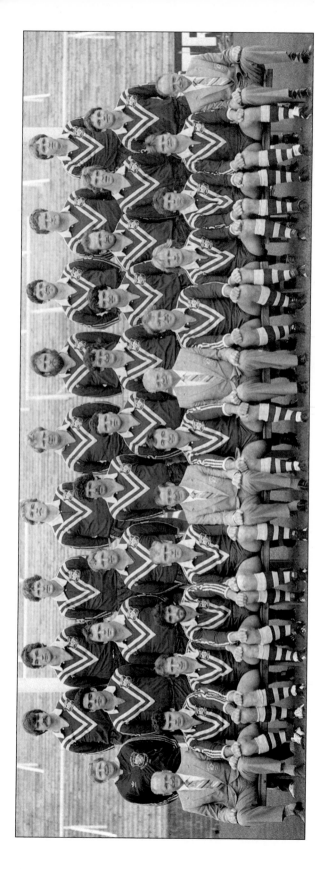

The 1982 touring Kangaroos were dubbed 'The Invincibles' after sweeping all before them and returning home unbeaten - the first tourists to achieve such a feat. In all, they won 15 games in Britain and seven in France. (pp316)
Back row, L-R: John Ribot, Paul McCabe, Gene Miles, Don McKinnon, Ian Schubert, Eric Grothe, John Muggleton, Craig Young, Greg Brentnall.
Middle row, L-R: Frank Stanton (coach), Mal Meninga, Rod Morris, Rohan Hancock, Rod Reddy, Les Boyd, Ray Brown, Greg Conescu, Ray Price, Brett Kenny, Wayne Pearce.
Front row, L-R: Alf Richards (trainer), Chris Anderson, Steve Mortimer, Steve Ella, Steve Rogers, Frank Farrington (manager), Max Krilich (captain), Tom Drysdale (manager), Wally Lewis, Peter Sterling, Kerry Boustead, Mark Murray, Dr Bill Monaghan.

in 1978. Down 12-5 at half time they gave their all in keeping a clean sheet in the second period whilst scoring nine points themselves to secure the cup, 14-12. There was anguish in the final minute for the red and white contingent after Noonan dramatically dropped the ball with the Leeds try line at his mercy.

We are the Champions

In Ron Pickering's schools athletics programme, children competed in beanbag races and suchlike, each edition finishing with everyone jumping in the swimming pool on Ron's command of: "away you go!" Just as contrived was the process for finding Rugby League champions between 1969 to 1973. Clubs had to win through a 16-team play off as a lop-sided fixture list meant the 30 clubs often only met once in the 38-game season.

In the final league placings for 1969/70 Leeds finished nine points ahead of Castleford and a huge 13 in front of third placed St Helens. The blue and amber faithful in an Odsal crowd of 26,358 came away shell shocked when their team failed to take the league form into the final play-off going down 24-12 to Saints.

The next year's final ended in drama at Station Road, Swinton, when a Saints late drop-goal attempt sailed wide to Wigan's corner flag with the quick-witted Billy Benyon beating all before him to catch the ball and go the length of the field for a sensational try. Wigan, having finished two points ahead of St Helens in the regular season, were distraught and a crowd of 21,475 left gasping as Coslett brilliantly converted the try from out wide to make it a score of 16-12.

Registering their last league title of the century, Leeds extracted revenge over St Helens in the 1972 Championship final, which turned out to be a close shave at 9-5 after the Saints had beaten Leeds the week previously in the Challenge Cup final, 16-13.

Dewsbury caused a mighty upset after securing eighth position in the final league table of 1972/3. The Heavy Woollen side sent their support into raptures by trimming the tales of red-hot favourites Leeds by 22-13. In a fine, two 'T-R-Y' performance, latter-day Sky Sports commentator Stevo was voted the man of the match to claim the Harry Sunderland Trophy. And rightly so.

With the top-16 play-off finals ending their days in 1972/73, the RFL introduced the club Championship as a gap-filler. Simply taken up to raise money it ran out of steam in the first year. All clubs participated in a complicated merit table based on league results. An encouraging crowd of 18,040 did produce excellent gate receipts in seeing Warrington take the trophy over St Helens by 13-12.

In between two Salford titles, the Saints squeezed one more in before the tiny village of Featherstone took on all-comers to claim their very first Championship. Widnes and Hull KR rounded the decade off, claiming a title each.

A final flurry

To wring some more revenue out of the paying public the RFL introduced a new end of season competition in 1974/75. The league structure had taken on a new format with the Championship trophy awarded to the team topping the regular season league table but with the play-off system having been a real money-spinner, the 'powers that be' didn't want to lose the extra revenue, hence the Premiership Trophy arrived.

Played after the Wembley final, it extended the season by a couple of weeks. Depending on the final league placings the top eight clubs competed in a mini knock-out competition with the last two remaining teams playing a final.

A good turn out of 14,531 for the first final gave the concept a healthy start and an average crowd of 16,126 for the first five finals were respectable and turned out to be a catalyst for the event to take on a 'grander' style in the eighties.

One season wonders

A rum do. In season 1973/74, Captain Morgan came on board with a new trophy, based on the first-round winners of the respective county cups. Warrington came out top again against Featherstone

4-0, their prize £3,000. Unfortunately, my bosses consigned it to Davy Jones' locker after one season.

St Helens participated in a one-off tour to Australia in 1976, the first British club entertainers to laik their talents down under. Queensland beat the Saints 21-15 before 11,000; Eastern Suburbs won 25-2 with 26,856 attending and then onto Auckland in a challenge match won by the home team 20-13, attracting 13,000.

I'd been a real patchwork with endless experiments and chopping and changing, for example my 1973/4 season contained no fewer than six different knock-out competitions. No wonder my support was drifting away, I floated like a rudderless ship in a sea of inconsistency.

Turn off the lights!

The BBC 2 Floodlit Trophy had little impact on my fans during the seventies. The competition didn't exactly set the house on fire with the average attendances not rising above 6,600.

Saints win over Dewsbury 22-2 caught a cold with the lowest final turn out of 3,858, a far cry from the sixties when 11,200 spectators was a good average.

Low scores were the order of the day and one final, Salford versus Warrington, even ended scoreless, with an average for all finals of just over 14 points. In fact, 240 minutes of effort produced a miserable two tries in the first three contests, pretty much draining whatever interest the competition had started with.

The last final did finish on a high, with 18,500 fans seeing Hull beat Hull KR 13-3, although in those days a Hull derby could get that crowd playing tiddlywinks.

I suppose Castleford enjoyed it more than the rest of us, winning three times.

Pretty dire looking back on the facts but something different in a BBC Floodlit Final that was played in the afternoon daylight! My friend Cliff Spracklen, chairman of my supporters association (RLSA) and a champion of the Bramley club's cause will now explain.

Winter of discontent... but not for Bramley!

December 1973 was a joyless time for many, with the 'winter of discontent' of power cuts and strikes as Christmas approached, but loyal fans of Bramley were celebrating early, on December 18th to be precise! That was the day that Bramley won the first-ever trophy in the club's long history.

Never having figured in the list of honours, the Villagers had nevertheless contributed to the history of the game. The first-ever test case on broken time featured a Bramley player, England international Harry Bradshaw during 1893, two years before the decisive split of 1895. Bramley also helped in the establishing of the game in France and provided players for the French 'Pioneers' when the latter suffered injuries whilst touring Britain, but the Villagers had to wait until 1973 for their maiden trophy.

The BBC Floodlit Trophy was self-explanatory. Played as a knock out on Tuesday evenings, with games shown live on BBC 2 and a final on a December evening, it didn't always catch the eye as the most glamorous of competitions. That said, what would clubs give today for live terrestrial television exposure?

Bramley was making its debut in the competition, by virtue of not having floodlights installed until that year. Ironically, floodlights were not to play much of a role in the final outcome. This was the winter of strikes, power cuts and the 'three day week' and to conserve power supplies electricity was rationed. Young couples sat huddled in the all-electric council flats, listening to transistor radios by candlelight, and hearing parents reminiscing about the wartime black-outs. Fish and chip shops did enormous business, as many had no means of cooking during power cuts.

Non-essential lighting was restricted to conserve supplies, and floodlit sport was axed by Government decree. Instead, professional sport had to be reorganised to midweek afternoons for the first time in years.

The deal with the BBC stood and the schedules planned so after much deliberation the BBC Floodlit Trophy continued as normal, the only difference being some games had to be staged in the afternoon and delayed highlights shown later that evening.

The Villagers were on the up at the time, led by experienced ex-Hull FC star Arthur Keegan, and had qualified for promotion to the first division, the league having been divided into two divisions again.

Super League fans in the 21st century would be incredulous at little Bramley's achievements, beating Wakefield away in the first round and Castleford at home in the second. The Villagers' success warmed the hearts of fans used to a diet of only ever making up the numbers.

First division success came too, but even the most diehard fans must have thought their number would be up in the Floodlit Trophy semi-final, having drawn the mighty St Helens. Fortune favours the brave and in an afternoon game at a packed McLaren Field, Bramley frustrated the Saints and emerged 13-7 winners to reach their first ever senior final.

As the Floodlit Trophy wasn't one of the older established ones, there would be no neutral venue with home advantage decided by the toss of a coin. The other finalists, the mighty Widnes, duly won the toss and the game scheduled for Naughton Park at 2.15pm on the afternoon of Tuesday 18th December.

On home soil the Chemics had to be clear favourites, but against all odds and assisted by a converted obstruction try the Villagers' heroic but controlled effort sealed the game and a 7-15 win. A film producer could not have created such a romantic story.

They were dancing in the Barley Mow that night, the historic pub adjacent to the McLaren Field and site of the old changing rooms.

Names like Arthur Keegan, Johnny Wolford, Keith Bollon, Barney Ward, Jack Austin, Graham Idle, Dave Sampson are all respected in the game. They and the other amber and black stalwarts brought a warm glow to some of the game's hitherto starved, but now celebrating, supporters in that cold winter of discontent.

This was no mean team and later that season they also reached the John Player semi-finals and retained their first division status with a win over Leeds at Headingley, of all places.

In 1973 Bramley was a contented place to be.

War of the Roses

Who did win the War of the Roses anyway, and who were the scallywags that started the bother? Before going on to my version, if you have a moment, I will fill you in with some juicy facts from the original.

Fought between 1455 and 1485 the Roses were essentially dynastic struggles between the various descendants of Edward III, each having rival claims to the throne. Edward III had married his children off to the heirs of the most powerful nobles in the land in the hope of strengthening his family. In the long run, instead of strengthening the Crown this had the effect of fragmenting loyalty to it.

By 1433, corruption of the Ministers of the Crown saw revenue from the royal estates dwindle to about £9,000 a year, a fraction of which found its way into the pockets of the ruling clique, leaving the burden of government squarely on the taxpayers' shoulders.

In 1455, rivalry between groups of nobles turned to violence with a victory for the Duke of York over the royal party at St Albans. These were wars of extermination, every victory being followed by a crop of murders and by confiscation by the Crown of the lands of the defeated.

The Battle of Bosworth, fought on 22nd August 1485 by a mere handful of men on either side, ended the Wars of the Roses. Lancashire and Yorkshire people, in as far as they were involved, were merely tools used by nobles fighting to gain wealth and power for themselves.

Whilst on the subject, I'll tell you about my dual 'Roses' genes as it is not always easy to distinguish oneself in these parts, especially in the little border town of Todmorden that nestles quaintly in the Pennine hills.

In 1888, due to local government changes, the town was transferred to the West Riding of Yorkshire. Not that the friends of Lancashire will have any of this Yorkshire pudding nonsense, as they insist the west part still belongs to Lancashire. To confuse matters even further the local Town Hall has a frieze with Lancashire and Yorkshire emblazoned on it in equal measure, whilst the postcode and telephone numbers come under Lancashire!

Now surely the crème de la crème has to be the fact that the local cricket club is the only Yorkshire club to play in the Lancashire League and in fact has both the white rose and red rose embroidered on the club caps.

Lancastrians and Yorkists may view the rival side of the Pennines as a foreign land, but are united in one thing, Rugby League.

Thorny subject

Having now read about the real wars, I'm afraid Roses games in the seventies didn't exactly catch the public imagination.

In the 1975 clash, held at Wigan, barely 700 spectators 'squeezed' into Central Park. I wonder if the fans were allowed a 'take home' of the surplus pies? Only joking, my friends from Wigan, although I dread to think of all those wasted mushy peas.

There wasn't much cheer on the rounds with just 1,219 at Keighley in 1974 even worse than the game at Castleford in January 1971, which only attracted 2,000 hardy souls to what could be described as a New Years wake.

Public and player apathy didn't help the competition in terms of a bit of spark, in fact an average of around 3,000 paying customers during the seventies was pretty poor. If this had been my only competition then I may have gone bankrupt.

The County Cups

One topic of debate in 2004 centred on whether the historic county cup trophies should be dusted down, polished up with Brasso and restored for professional competition again.

Contested by the amateurs in modern times the idea behind this concept would be to raise extra revenue for the lower professional clubs.

Sadly, to continue the theme, crowds in the seventies on both sides of the Pennines went down like a lead balloon. Average attendances in Yorkshire Cup finals in the sixties had produced a healthy 15,471 with Lancashire fairing even better at 20,688. Out of interest, the Hunslet versus Hull KR final in the sixties encouraged 22,742 outdoors and the Saints versus Swinton final over the border attracted 31,755 welcome customers. No final in either county produced less than a five-figure gate.

By the seventies, folk really did fall out with me with averages of 7,281 and 8,524 respectively. In monetary terms, a huge dent in the bank balance and the doom and gloom decade gave rise to only three finals attracting five figures.

One saving grace in that teams not in the top echelon these days got a crack of the whip in past finals of these two decades, being Leigh, Swinton, Workington Town, Oldham, Rochdale Hornets, Featherstone, Hull KR, Dewsbury, Hunslet, Halifax and York.

So my friends this confirms the sad fact that the seventies were indeed a depressing time for me, but...!

Around the world

"Nothing ventured, nothing gained!" Browsing back through this chapter confirmed I lacked some self-esteem in certain areas. One can either succumb and give up the ghost or ride out the storm. Rugby League is built out of a sterner pedigree, so why let events on the home front stop the world going round?

I decided it was still imperative that I maintained an affiliation with my cousins in continuing to move the international game forward. The world should be my oyster and this is where I journeyed in the hope that the domestic front would hold up and shake itself out of the doldrums.

Now I will admit that the international aspect of my life has never quite climbed its Everest in terms of successful tournaments, so having four World Cups during the seventies did get me checking my pulse. The heart of the matter is that events since have seen me back-pedal more than once.

In a competition staged entirely in England, Australia didn't actually dominate the 1970 World Cup but, like a barnacle on a ship, stuck to the task and came good at the crucial time to take the spoils despite having won only one qualifying game. Great Britain had held sway in a four-team league format, topping the table on six points, three wins out of three, whilst Australia, New Zealand and France finished with one victory each. Australia cemented second spot having a better points difference over New Zealand and France.

Attendances were par for the course in a competition staged in dreary England with the France versus New Zealand game attracting a mere 3,824 diehards in the stronghold of Hull. Only Britain and Australia enticed a five-figure crowd outdoors during a preliminary game at Headingley with a win for the home lads. France gallantly overcame the Aussies in a close-fought encounter taking the game 17-15.

In the final play-off at Headingley Australia prised the cup from Britain's grasp by 7-12, with a half-decent crowd of 18,776 and a bit of a punch up at the end.

The Australian camp had cause to blush after Ron Coote and his players misplaced the trophy until it surfaced 20 years later in a ditch a few miles away on the outskirts of Bradford. Seems like the scallywag who stole it got cold feet.

Britain wrote the headlines amongst the vineyards of France during the 1972 World Cup, a tournament held both there and in England.

Great Britain finished top of a four-team competition to qualify for the final by winning all three games. Australia took second spot having lost just one match 27-21 in Perpignan. Taking maximum points on the rounds Britain prepared for the acid test in attempting to topple the mighty Aussies in a play-off final.

Without wishing to pour cold water on events, the final didn't capture the imagination or arouse the fans interest on a cold, overcast November day, 4,231 being an apology for a crowd in Lyons. Those who did venture out witnessed a tense tussle with the outcome going to the wire in nail-biting fashion 10-10 after extra time. The day belonged to Britain, however, after receiving the trophy due to a better playing record in the qualifying rounds. No 'golden point' needed. How it might have been different if France had managed to reach the last stage when a game at Marseilles attracted 20,748 paying customers against New Zealand, secured by France 20-9. New Zealand finished bottom of the qualifying league table having not won a match.

No doubt there were many heroes but non-more than the great Clive Sullivan the then Great Britain captain and Hull FC winger who scored a try in the final as did Mike Stephenson, with Terry Clawson kicking two goals. For the record O'Neill and Beetson scored the Australian tries, whilst Branighan kicked two goals.

Master of his trade, Sullivan, achieved the distinction of being the first black player to captain any British team in a major sport. This was a far cry from when Roy Francis parted company with his first club due to new manager Harry Sunderland taking issue over the colour of his skin! To add insult to injury, Roy was acrimoniously cast into the international wilderness with the selectors ignoring his claim for the 1946 Risman touring party as, in those days, Australia operated a colour bar.

If you had believed my Aussie cousins the 1972 World Cup would have winged its way down under because they believed the French referee ruled out an Australian try when ahead 5-2 after 25 minutes. Georges Jameau, one of France's most experienced whistle blowers disallowed an amazing try by Graeme Langlands after a kick through by half-back Dennis Ward. The respected referee blew for offside although checks on films indicated that Langlands had committed no offence. However, my mates from Oz, the cup came over here and that's that.

Now, Rugby League is partial to a bit of travelling but the 1975 World Championship (rather than cup), made me feel like a journeyman, being staged from March to November and taking in both hemispheres! In a round-robin competition including the daffodil of Wales, plus England, Australia, New Zealand and France, battle commenced on the 2nd March at Toulouse as the French entertained the reinstated Wales. A crowd of 7,563 turned up probably more out of curiosity with the game favouring France 14-7.

Suffering battle fatigue the competition limped into Salford (in

England!) for its last match like a wounded soldier returning from the trenches on 6th November, when Wales took revenge 23-2 with some people trying to spot the fans. A sparse crowd of 2,247 posed a few questions.

Before completely running out of steam, in between I visited Headingley, Brisbane, Sydney, Christchurch, Auckland Warrington, Swansea, Perpignan, Odsal, Bordeaux, Marseilles and Wigan. It all seemed an anti-climax when Australia finally topped the table with 13 points ahead of England on 12 and so claimed the trophy with no play-off. In between I think many people had become bored with the tournament long before November, struggling to keep track of what the position was as it meandered through its nine months. At least I got my passport stamped a few times!

The aftermath caused deep concern with the announcement that the competition lost each competing country £10,000. The England game against France in Bordeaux summed up the problem, 1,581 tickets sold doesn't quite appease the bank manager.

Phew! What a competition that was. Someone pass me the headache tablets!

Having reviewed the unwieldy arrangements of 1975, cosmetic surgery became a necessity resulting in a more compact format for the 1977 World Cup held in Australia and New Zealand. Unfortunately, Wales were shunted to the sidings (England having disappeared also, reverting to Britain.) Australia ended the preliminary rounds undefeated on six points ahead of Britain on four. In a very close, exciting final encounter Australia squeezed home 13-12 in Sydney. Tries for Gill and Pitchford with two goals for Fairbairn weren't quite enough. The Sydney crowd of 24,457 certainly wasn't up to standard for the Aussie Rugby League capital either.

To briefly sum up, whatever the mixed bag of the various competitions and formats I couldn't be too critical, at least my international pot kept simmering.

International round-up

Great Britain journeyed down under in 1970 for a Test series and returned with the Ashes.

It didn't look rosy for the Poms after the first encounter, Britain suffering a crushing bombardment 37-15 in front of 42,807 fans at Brisbane. However, Britain fought back valiantly for victory by 7-28 as 60,962 turned up in Sydney. Another bumper crowd of 61,258 also in Sydney witnessed the Pommies taking home the spoils, winning 17-21.

Taking all before them in New Zealand enabled the side to achieve a better record than any of its predecessors, just one loss in 24 outings. No other British team would take the Ashes during the remainder of the century.

Britain staged the next Ashes series during the dark days of 1973 as Graeme Langlands led the 13th Kangaroos on tour for a much shorter trip. The Brits sprinted out of the traps first in securing a victory over the arch-enemy 21-12, a game held at the insistence of Australia at Wembley.

The Aussie management had hoped for a profitable day, sadly not so with Wembley unable to muster a five-figure gate, actually 9,874. The short-lived glory came to an abrupt end as the Aussies ensured they retrieved the Ashes in two close encounters 6-14 at Headingley (16,674) and 5-15 at Warrington (10,019). Roger Millward crossed for the only British try, while also kicking a goal.

Apart from the Test team only St Helens managed to knock the Aussies down a peg, 11-7.

Ultimately unsuccessful, down under again in 1974 under the captaincy of Salford's Chris Hesketh the Lions drifted to a 2-1 series defeat, although all games finished tantalisingly close. Led by Langlands, participating in his sixth series, the first Test fought out at Lang Park didn't quite match the occasion. Langland's goal kicking plus a try by Orr secured a 12-6 result in a dire game (30,280.)

Bravery came to the fore during the second Test in Sydney after John Gray, the Wigan hooker, suffered a horrendous kick in his face requiring five stitches. Playing on with a closed eye and dislocated finger endeared him to the crowd and his fine hooking qualities and accurate goal kicking performance helped Britain level the series, tries for Chisnall, Gill and Dixon contributing to a result of 11-16 (48,006.)

Close but not close enough in the decider at the SCG. Setting a record of 104 points total from all his Test matches, Langland's teammates carried him shoulder high after a dramatic last 22-18 win. Whilst 55,505 had turned up for the third Test, held once more in Sydney, the series had lost much of it's appeal with overall crowds down around 30,000.

In a reversal of the Aussie situation the international game in England confounded the critics with an upsurge of interest for the 1978 series. Wigan enticed 17,644 fans to Central Park for the first game and fortunes continued to rise with 26,477 flocking to Odsal, which turned out to be a best for 15 years in spite of live television coverage.

With one close win each under their belts it was time for a shoot out at the OK Corral of Rugby League, i.e. Headingley. Bursting at the seams with anticipation the 29,627 crowd eventually left for home disappointed after Britain capitulated 6-23. Widnes entered the history books, to this day holding the honour of being the last club side to scalp an Aussie touring team.

A case of down under and down and out in 1979 for a 'Close Encounter of the Test Kind', although not close enough as Britain lost convincingly, making history of the best forgotten kind by going under in all three Tests for the first time.

Disappearing like the volunteers into Steven Spielberg's alien spaceship, what happened to the crowds? Brisbane attracted 23,051, whilst the two games in Sydney were fought out in front of 26,837 and 16,854, the total attendances in all three matches sagging to an alarming 66,472.

Now at the time that number would be considered excellent if staged over here but for a country where one Test alone could once attract a similar number it represented a sudden and worrying lack of appetite by the fans, and resulted in the tour venture suffering a financial loss.

Bring on the Kiwis -
Reasons to be Cheerful, Part III

Great Britain and New Zealand clashed in four Test series in the seventies, down under in 1970, '74 and '79 and in England in 1971. In the 1970 series, played in New Zealand, the Poms won out 3-0, two games at Carlaw Park and the other at Addington Showgrounds, Auckland.

The 1971 series amounted to a win by two Tests to one for the Kiwis, their first series win against Great Britain for 63 years. As for the public interest in Blighty, it was a mixed bag with the lowest attendance being 3,764 for the first game in 1971 at Salford, with a score of Great Britain 13 New Zealand 18. Further poor crowds at Castleford's only ever Test (4,108) and Wigan (5,479) amounted to rock bottom for Test Rugby League in Britain.

Recovering from that loss Great Britain won both the 1974 and 1979 series, again 1-2 on the same Auckland grounds as 1970 to show overall dominance during the decade.

Nevertheless, turnouts held up reasonably well in New Zealand though with a few estimated 20,000's and the highest accurate crowd number being at the very first game of the decade at Auckland when 15,948 witnessed Great Britain winning by 15-19.

The rivalry with the Kiwis has never been quite on a par with the Aussie clashes I'm afraid.

La Belle France!

As Britain joined the EEC, despite the original opposition of French President, Charles de Gaulle, strangely enough there wasn't much other cross Channel fraternity as only six matches ever got organised, and all in the early part of the decade.

Great Britain suffered defeat 16-8 at the Stade Municipal, Toulouse in the first encounter of 1971 before a decent crowd of 14,690, with the return giving the spoils to Great Britain 24-2 at Knowsley Road (7,783.)

Following on in 1972 Great Britain won a tight game in Toulouse 9-10 then thrashed the Frenchmen 45-10 at Odsal (7,313.)

Finally in 1974 it was 5-24 to Great Britain at the Stade Municipal, Grenoble, *Les Rosbifs* overcoming both the French team and the ref who awarded the home team an incredible 26-2 penalty count. The return game drew the curtain on the decade's cross-Channel ventures, 29-0 at Wigan.

Deserved glory for France though in 1978 as France beat Australia in a two-game Test series, with success at Carcassonne and Toulouse, something I'm not sure the Tricoloures will do again for a while.

Swansong

International Rugby League made a welcome return to Wales in 1975 after a break of almost a quarter of a century, and the locals were not to be short-changed for action in a brutal World Cup game against Australia. Three major brawls erupted at the St Helens, Swansea ground to stir the passionate 11,112 crowd. Such colossal names as Arthur Beetson led Australia from the front, whilst Tony Fisher, John Mantle and Jim Mills for Wales were never ones to take a backward step.

One brawl ended up over the touchline into the grandstand and involved several officials including Graeme Langlands. In between the fighting there was some great Rugby League with classy teenage Aussie Ian Schubert helping himself to three tries in only his second international, and with it the Man of the Match award. Final score 6-18 to Australia with a draw in the punch-ups.

Finally, although the crowd was announced as 13,000, being adjusted downwards to 11,112, Ray Gent tells me that there seemed more like over 20,000 on. No doubt the gatemen had an influence on matters, having been guilty of similar fishy practice in a game against France in 1947.

Split personality

Life isn't just about professionalism, so it's about time I took a look at the amateur scene.

Peace and goodwill arrived in 2003 with the re-integration of the professional RFL and the British Amateur Rugby League Association to unify the sport back into a single governing body, a far cry from the early seventies when you could say I suffered from a split personality. During this era, in fact 1973, BARLA formed, with just a modest £25 in the bank.

Before the split there had been plenty of friction between the amateur clubs and the RFL over many issues to do with the perceived neglect of the amateur game. No doubt the early pioneers couldn't have envisaged the Queen opening new prestigious BARLA offices in Huddersfield, just around the corner from my birthplace I may add, seven years later.

Initially 155 teams affiliated but BARLA's influence quickly spread to include worldwide tours by their amateur representative sides. By 1990 the Association's National Cup attracted 221 entrants although it still retained its roots in the industrial areas of the north.

One amateur club, the mighty Pilkington Recs, played against my professional sides in Challenge Cup competitions no less than three times during the seventies. In 1976-77 Castleford took a deep sigh of relief having edged a thriller 22-23, whilst a year later Wigan avoided blushes all round in the same competition by squeezing home 4-10, both matches taking place at Knowsley Road, before five-figure crowds. The 1979-80 season gave Pilks another shot at Wigan after being drawn out of the bag in the John Player Trophy with the result being none too comfortable for the pro's, 9-18 again at Knowsley Road. Pilks now play their home games at the old St Helens Recs ground at City Road.

East of the Pennines in 1972, West Hull formed having been once known as Birds Eye and playing in the first division of the Hull Works League, although with little immediate success. They then moved on to the Hull and District League playing such awesome teams as Ambassador, Embassy and British Oil and Cake Mills (later Ace Amateurs.)

Ambassador and Embassy were amongst the most feared of all amateur sides and an indication of just how formidable they were came in a television interview with former British, European and

Commonwealth heavyweight champion, Richard Dunn. Richard had defeated Henry Cooper and fought the great Muhammad Ali but when asked if he had ever been frightened whilst boxing he gave a classic reply stating that he had only ever been scared once in his life, whilst playing prop for Halifax White Star against Ambassador! It had been so physical and tough that he quickly scurried to his car after the game and locked himself in until the Ambassador players had changed and left.

As well as being a success at the time of writing this book, West Hull won all before them in season 1974/75 including both RFL and BARLA versions of the Yorkshire Cup, League title, Council Cup, South Yorkshire Shield, BP Sevens and York Sevens. West Hull descended from the Cawoods club who had became the first modern day amateur side to beat one of my professional teams, Halifax 8-9 in the first round of the John Player Cup in the mid-seventies.

One example of the unsung heroes within the amateur game is the Shaw Cross club, tucked away a stones throw from Dewsbury's Ram Stadium. Not for nothing was Shaw Cross awarded the National Sports and Arts Foundation Sports Club of the Year in 1999, beating all other community sports clubs everywhere else in the country.

Running 14 teams at 12 age groups, plus a girls team and hosting social players, the clubs *alumni* include Mick Sullivan, Mike Stephenson, David Ward and Rocky Turner, amongst others, and three current Super League players in Lee Gilmour, Keith Mason and Nick Fozzard.

The open-age coach, Mick Turner, has taken his men on pioneering tours to South Africa three times and, wearing his other hat as coach to the BARLA Lions for the last nine years, his lads became the first British Rugby League team at any level to return unbeaten from a tour to Australia. Another feather in Mick's cap came with his BARLA Great Britain beating the full French team twice.

Serving as club secretary for 53 years, Douglas Hird has organised exchange coach trips to Rugby League clubs in the south of France each year since 1970, offering over 1,400 young people the opportunity to see another part of the world, meet other young sportsmen and helping many a young lad along the straight and narrow. Like so many similar volunteers throughout the amateur game Doug seeks no reward, other than the satisfaction of a job well done, but has deservedly received the BEM for services to the community.

On such men is our game built, and they exist wherever Rugby League is played.

It ain't easy

Colin Hutton tells a story from this vintage.

"Whilst England Manager in the late seventies we were returning home from a game in France on a very miserable evening. During the coach journey back from Heathrow to Leeds I got talking to the late Harry Vomersley from Bradford Northern and also the late Bill Oxley from Barrow. The topic of conversation turned to Rugby League and in particular coaching.

"Frank Foster's name was mentioned as he was familiar to us all and at the time coached Barrow, indeed the longest serving coach in the league. During his playing days as a second row forward from the Cumbrian mould, Frank's reputation had him down as one of the hardest players in the game.

"Unfortunately Barrow were suffering from the yo-yo syndrome of promotion and relegation. Harry Vomersley remarked that though they had spent plenty of money, they were not getting much value yet Frank had kept his job. This prompted Bill Oxley to remark that it wasn't that easy. 'We have decided to sack him three times at board meetings but no one dare tell him.'"

In a Leaguer of its own

Whilst getting the old feet up one Monday after a hard weekend at work, I thumbed through an old copy of the *Rugby Leaguer* newspaper from the early seventies, which was the only weekly publication dedicated to my game at the time. Here are a few snippets, but not much cheer amongst them.

Cold winds blow and we shall have snow. Missing from today's game, quite happily, is the aftermath of a bad winter. One club 'snowed under' was Blackpool Borough who had suffered controversy about taking a home game to Warrington. To avoid another postponement against Bramley a game went ahead with three inches of snow on the pitch. According to the report, the game was as dire as the weather.

One heading on the front page read: "Fixture pile-up leaves Barrow in spot." Due to the adverse weather Barrow were left with eight fixtures to fulfil before the end of the season as opposed to what should have been three.

The law of the land intervened as another interesting leading headline told us: "'Never on a Sunday,' law making life tough for an amateur club." The newly formed amateur club, Altash, was forced to play all their games away because of a byelaw, which banned Sunday football on council fields in St Helens. Because of the difficulty in finding players the club had left its home in Kirkby, near Liverpool, and moved to St Helens. However, games had to be played on a Sunday to compete against teams of a similar suitable standard.

England lost their bottle but were in the money as they flopped against France 14-9 in Toulouse. England still won the revived triangular tournament by the skin of their teeth and 0.38 of a point average. The only player to emerge with any credit was Castleford's second row forward Brian Lockwood who came on for the last 10 minutes. Doesn't say much for the rest of the players. Apparently when England's Alan Smith scored a try it led to bottles, coins and even a stone being thrown on to the pitch. I suppose the Francs, as their locals used to have, made up the losing pay.

The good old letters page featured a J Smith from Prescot, Lancashire, most concerned about the lack of personalities in the game, bad arrangement of fixtures, lack of amenities at grounds, as well as poor BBC coverage, also complaining about football results being shown when a game is on live. Food for thought, as these issues still occupy fans' minds today.

On the results page, Blackpool Borough weren't exactly crowded out, attracting 950 good folk to the seaside town to watch them lose to Swinton 16-20, an improvement after recent results against Warrington and Bramley. Interestingly, Bramley was battling for a top-16 league position in order to qualify for the Championship play-offs. Elsewhere, 2,450 witnessed Keighley having a home reversal to Huddersfield, 5-10. The biggest crowd in the results section was the 6,320 who witnessed Wigan beating Workington 20-5.

Not much for sale in the adverts section, although there was a semi-detached house for sale in Penmaenmawr in North Wales at a reasonable price of £5,100, whilst Subbuteo rugby was advertised as the 'replica of Rugby League and Union football.' Surely the *Leaguer* wasn't touting an amalgamation of the two codes?

Finally, the price of the *Rugby Leaguer*, pre-decimalization, was 7d, something for you young un's to work out!

Seventies summary

There was a great deal of industrial conflict in the early seventies as the working classes sought better pay and conditions. In these difficult times it wasn't only yours truly who was suffering.

The strike-ridden seventies, with its images of picket lines, typified the decline in the manufacturing, mining and other heavy industries in the working class areas in the north, but for the increasing middle class horizons were broadening faster than ever.

A meal out at a Berni Inn or Beefeater with prawn cocktail, steak and chips and Black Forest gateau, accompanied by a nice bottle of liebfraumilch, was the height of new-found sophistication. The likes of Laura Ashley and Habitat, even MFI, had brought affordable fashion and design to the High Street.

Never mind the Cod War dispute with Iceland, North Sea oil and gas were flooding ashore and Britain was now in the European Economic Community, as it was called then. Package holidays to the far off exotica of the Canaries, Spanish Costas and Greece were becoming within the pocket and aspiration of many.

The public perception of Rugby League for many amounted to a barging contest between mud-splattered northern blokes on a windswept paddock in a remote northern pit town with a stereotype commentator wailing clichés about 'early baths' and 'oop and unders' with scrums being 'half a ton of rugby.'

Whilst a trip to Wembley was always a popular day out, poor old 'thud and blunder' Rugby League increasingly seemed to belong to a bygone era, and just didn't fit the bill as times changed within the areas of leisure available to the man in the 1970s street. The grim northern *Likely Lads* had become the suburban *Good Life*.

Entertainment and lifestyle choice was available from an ever-increasing list of sources, not just the ramshackle local Rugby League ground, which itself seemed not to have seen a coat of paint for decades.

Some mornings I had woken up and wondered if it was all worth it as by the age of 75 I'd certainly gone thin on top and needed more than a walking stick for support. I'm afraid my game had stood still for too long and stagnated. Rugby League needed a kick in the backside and it wasn't long into the eighties when it was to get one from the 'Invincibles.'

10

1980-1990
GREED IS GOOD

Social conditions in the eighties could be summed up by one word, 'Thatcherite' (and that doesn't mean a Cotswold roof repairer!)

Under the government of the 'Iron Lady', free enterprise ruled the roost with the state seen as an obstruction. The future of the country was entrusted to the new breed of young, upwardly mobile professionals, 'Yuppies.' The London Stock Exchange had been deregulated in a 'big bang' and publicly owned companies such as British Telecom, British Airways and British Gas were privatised, helping to create a 'shareholder economy.' Tell Sid! Council house tenants qualified for massive discounts as local authorities were compelled to offer public housing for sale under 'right to buy' legislation. "Rely on yourself, look after number one" was the motto.

Trade Unions were regulated to water down their effectiveness and the whittling away of industrial dead wood (and plenty of live as well) saw unemployment quickly rise to three million.

The credit boom and conspicuous consumption of the few stuck in the craw of the many. With pits under threat from government closure, Arthur Scargill and his National Union of

Mineworkers threw down a challenge in a long and acrimonious strike. Some declared it a government victory over the tyranny of those who would bring the country down for left-wing political ends. Maybe it's wiser to say that all parties took a heavy defeat.

An uneasy Britain had its own threat of terrorist violence from the IRA and the fascist government in Argentina saw its chance and caught Britain off guard to occupy the Falkland Islands in 1983, territory the Argentinians considered more rightfully theirs. With much flag waving, a task force was despatched to reclaim the islands but as usual at great human cost, not least when the aged battleship General Belgrano was sunk with the, possibly unnecessary, loss of over 300 Argentinian lives.

Political change elsewhere saw the fall of the Berlin Wall in 1989 and its domino effect across many former Eastern Bloc countries which had been governed by communist ideologies of varying severity, watched over by the USSR. With the regime change came easing of the Cold War and the nuclear threat that had been at the back of everyone's mind for so long. With the reduced spending on weaponry a 'peace dividend' was promised, but never showed up, at least not in my pay packet.

1989 saw student protesters for democracy massacred in China's Tiananmen Square with worldwide news reels showing a lone student defiantly standing in front of oncoming tanks.

Assassination was at the forefront in 1981 as attempts were made on US President Ronald Reagan and the Pope. Two bodyguards killed Indira Gandhi, India's Prime Minister in 1984.

Trouble captured the news in 1986 as the US bombed Libya, the Chernobyl nuclear disaster caused world panic and the *Challenger* space shuttle exploded. Two air disasters in 1988 with Pan Am flight 103 being blown up over Lockerbie, Scotland and the US shooting down an Iranian airliner as the Soviets had done to a Korean civilian airliner over its airspace in 1983.

In 1987, there was an amusing story of a West German pilot landing unchallenged in Russia's Red Square, something akin to breaking into Fort Knox. New York's Stock Exchange suffered a huge crash, whilst criminals found life more difficult with DNA testing being used for the first time.

Africa was in a terrible state and the harsh famine there and his perception of governmental inactivity prompted rock star Bob Geldof to organise a charity concert, *Live Aid*, at Wembley and JFK Stadium, Philadelphia on 13th July 1985.

Worse to come as Africa saw the spread of the HIV/Aids virus which quickly assumed epidemic proportions.

On 6th March 1987 the seven-year-old 'roll-on-roll-off' car ferry Townsend Thoresen's *Herald of Free Enterprise* left Zeebrugge, Belgium, for her regular four-hour crossing to Dover. The bow doors had been left open as the man who was supposed to check them had fallen asleep in his cabin. Just half a mile outside the harbour, she began to take in water and list violently rolling onto her port side, against a sandbank. Of the 500 people on board, 193 lost their lives.

More trouble at sea as, on 24th March 1989, the *Exxon Valdez* oil tanker grounded on a reef in Prince William Sound, 40 miles off the Alaskan coast. It dumped 11 million gallons of crude oil into the waters and contaminated about 1,300 miles of coastline. The *Exxon Valdez* spill was not the biggest in the world, but was by far the deadliest to wildlife. The wreck of the *Titanic* was located during 1985 and a few artefacts retrieved, a postcard menu being auctioned at Sotheby's in December 2003 for £28,800.

After 437 years lost at sea, Henry Vlll's ship, the *Mary Rose*, was raised from its watery grave.

Bringing a whole new range of traffic jam possibilities, the 120 miles of misery that is the M25 London Orbital motorway opened, along with other 'big stuff' that typified the decade, such as the Channel Tunnel (started in 1987, completed in 1994) and the redevelopment of London's Docklands, all symbols of free enterprise investment.

Technology and the media's own revolution raced ahead of most people's imaginations. Not only were the first mobile phones becoming widely available, they were actually portable. On New Years Day 1985, Ernie Wise made Britain's first cellphone call. By 2002 most people in Britain and every sixth person in the world owned a mobile.

Microsoft Corporation continued to computerise the world

and made Bill Gates the richest man on earth. No longer science fiction, the computer became an everyday worktool. Sinclair launched the first personal computers, with the ZX81, a simple machine for £100, followed by their next innovation, the C5, a battery powered deathtrap car.

Changes in printing technology, such as computerised print setting rather than the old 'hot metal', were introduced into the newspaper publishing world. News Corporation owned the *Sun, Times* and *Sunday Times* amongst others and had set up a new works at Wapping, resulting in large labour losses. Wapping became another watchword for industrial action with further bitter conflict. The reduction in production costs saw several new national newspapers come and go in the *London Daily News, Sunday Correspondent, News on Sunday, Today* and *European,* whilst the *Daily Star, Sport, Sunday Sport* and *Independent* (with every Leaguie's favourite correspondent, Dave Hadfield) survived.

Launched in November 1982, Channel 4 only transmitted programmes for a few hours each day to begin with and although I have rarely featured in their programming, I've certainly made plenty of appearances on Sky television, who introduced a four-channel service using the Astra satellite in late 1989.

Comedy and entertainment became politicised and rallied against the Thatcher government by such as the Red Wedge movement, UB40, comedian Ben Elton and the satirical puppetry television programme *Spitting Image.* On the other hand, pop music tended towards the 'disposable' with Stock, Aitken and Waterman-produced acts such as Bananarama, Kylie Minogue and Rick Astley.

The music world vibrated with grief on 8th December 1980 with the news that John Lennon had been assassinated outside his apartment near Central Park, New York. In 1981 millions watched the Royal Wedding. The one and only *E.T.* landed in view of cinema goers in 1982. Vegetables became popular in 1983 with the one and only cabbage patch dolls taking a bow.

Icons of the age included the infernal puzzle of the Rubik's Cube, the boxing pantomime act Frank Bruno, the gull winged de Lorean car, the Brinks Mat robbery, the American soap opera

Dallas and Queen's anthem *We Will Rock You,* which regularly returns to haunt us to this day.

Unlike today, soccer languished in the doldrums. The 39 deaths at the Heysel stadium disaster of 28th May 1985 before the European Cup final, violence and a general yobbish public image directly led to English clubs being banned from European competitions.

As if the Heysel tragedy wasn't enough another shocking event that would have a further knock on effect in the sporting world had befallen the city of Bradford a few weeks earlier on 11th May 1985. The old wooden stand, scheduled for imminent replacement, at Bradford City's Valley Parade burned down during a game, tragically killing 56 people. The dated structure was largely unchanged from when Manningham RLFC had played there before changing codes to Association Football just after the turn of the century.

Insurance premiums rose by as much as 500 per cent and in doing so placed a strain on many sporting grounds, with some having to close unsafe sections due to the stricter requirements of Local Authority Health & Safety regulations.

Worse to come on 15th April 1989 as BBC's *Grandstand,* hosted by Des Lynam that day, was interrupted by news flashes from the FA Cup semi-final played at Sheffield Wednesday's Hillsborough Stadium, that built up a picture that shocked the world.

Part of the match programme notes that day read: "As you look around Hillsborough you will appreciate why it has been regarded for so long as the perfect venue for all kinds of important matches. It is a stadium that benefits such occasions and the large crowds they attract." The picture of the now infamous Leppings Lane end that accompanied the article could never foresee the horror that would befall the innocent supporters simply out for a day's sport. Liverpool had brought a much larger support than Forest but for segregation purposes they were allocated the smaller end. A bottleneck developed as only three gates and seven turnstiles were available to cope with the 10,000 fans due to enter that stand. Inside the ground fans became more and more restricted in movement until the area could take no more. Ninety-six people lost their lives in the crush that dreadful day with many repercussions for ground safety and an inquest into the police handling of the situation to follow.

Points of Order

Although industrial strife played a large part in my birth, my players had no trade union until the Rugby League Professional Players Association was born in 1981, led by Gary Hetherington as its first chairman.

On 1st January 1983 the sin-bin was introduced for domestic games. Originating in ice hockey, where tempers get frayed regularly and a 'cooling off' process is necessary, its adoption into Rugby League seemed like a useful addition to the referees' armoury. The first players 'in the bin' were Trevor Leathley (Huddersfield) and Clive Pickerill (Wakefield) at Fartown. The ref doing the binning was Bernard Walker.

To give more emphasis on try scoring, the RFL introduced the four-point try and also the ball had to be handed over after the sixth tackle instead of the defending side being given head and feed at a scrum.

The Invincibles

My new-found self-esteem suffered a puncture after the Green and Golds turned up to teach the Poms a lesson! Never mind those eighties impostors with the explosives, tanks, cigars and gold chains, the real *A-Team* were the 15th Kangaroo Test side of 1982.

Led by Manley hooker Max Krilich they became the first team to go unbeaten on tour having won all 23 games in Papua New Guinea, Great Britain and France earning the nickname the 'Invincibles.'

Their high-powered play, sublime ball handling skills and fitness of the highest level were to win them many accolades as they swatted all before them in a clean sweep of challenges. The sheer athleticism simply had to be admired and came as a rude awakening, demonstrating that the British game had rested on its laurels for too long and fallen behind.

Even the 3-0 Test result didn't tell the complete story as the inspired team was simply on another planet. Lewis, Meninga, Sterling, Price, Grothe, Kenny, Rogers, Boyd and Reddy to name a few were the champagne and caviar compared to the British fish 'n' chips as they swept the Brits off their feet. .

Britain registered only one try in the three Tests, scored by Evans in the last match, compared to 19 by the Aussies, the worst defeat being 4-40, and the closest game 6-27. Although the British fans had to eat humble pie, many were left with nothing but admiration for such outstanding talent.

Whilst the south transept of York Minster went up in smoke, the smouldering embers of the Lions' Ashes ambitions saw a modest improvement of sorts over in Australia during 1984. Although Britain again lost all three Tests the Lions actually scored three tries, Schofield two and Hanley one, whilst conceding 10. Again, the worst defeat ended 25-8 and the closest Test had a 12-point gap. By *1984* we weren't all being controlled by Big Brother as George Orwell predicted, but it wasn't far off.

Meanwhile in 1986, it was well past being embarrassing as the series started with a 16-38 loss and didn't get any better, the Lions surrendering their Ashes chance and failing to get within 30 points in the next game. Still, six tries to Britain (five of them from Garry Schofield) and 17 to Australia in the series as a whole showed some improvement, but still no sniff of a win.

The British high point of the series came at Old Trafford as 50,583 fans turned out and although Great Britain were well beaten the highlight for the home support had to be a great length of the field try by Joe Lydon.

The margin gradually closed by the 1988 Ashes series as Britain managed eight tries against 11 to Australia but with the series already lost and no Test win over Australia since 1979 things were desperate. I'm pleased to tell you that the drought was broken at the Sydney Football Stadium, a game that also provided two of the better moments of broadcast commentary, at least to Pommy ears.

Kevin Ward and Andy Gregory combined to give Martin Offiah the chance to open the scoring before Phil Ford scooped up a loose ball to scamper 20 metres for a second, leading commentator, Darrell Eastlake, to admire his skills with the immortal phrase "Geez, he's a rubberman."

A Wally Lewis try two minutes after the restart brought the Kangaroos back into it, but the onslaught was resisted before Andy Gregory grubbered past Garry Jack for Henderson Gill to reply. Sam Backo's score brought Australia to within four points before Paul Loughlin sent Gill away for his second leaving Eastlake to call the immortal words on Henderson's post try celebrations "He's doing a bit of a boogie!"

The crowning glory came as Andy Gregory sent namesake Mike on a blood vessel bursting 70-yard run to the posts, to seal a 12-26 victory. Phew, about time. Hooray, Britain had actually won a Test match for the first and only time against the Aussies in the eighties, the last one of the decade.

The disastrous run of 14 consecutive defeats stretched back to 5th November 1978. That Guy Fawkes Night Test match produced a crowd at Odsal of 26,447 when other attractions were on offer, but by the end of the eighties the public had lost it's appetite for easy pickings and the Sydney game featured the lowest crowd from the decade's twelve Tests at 15,994.

As far as the Kangaroo's were concerned our cupboard was bare. I couldn't even gain any solace from other's fate, the Kiwis managed three Test wins over the Aussies during the decade, although Australia did give France a few thumpings.

Pure Gold

Life in England turned to pure gold in September 1983 with the lifting of the ban on English clubs signing Australian players. To whet the appetite of my fans many of the 1982 Australian touring party put pen to paper and like boomerangs returned back to the north of England to play during the Aussie summer, my winter.

Just like a good wine it was vintage stuff. Amongst the dodgy 'taches and mullets arriving on these shores were such revered names as blockbusting centre Mal Meninga (St. Helens), Steve Ella and Brett Kenny (Wigan), the awe-inspiring Wally Lewis (Wakefield Trinity), Kerry Boustead (Hull KR), Peter Sterling and John Muggleton (Hull), Chris Anderson (Halifax), no-nonsense Les Boyd (Warrington) and, later, Gene Miles (Wigan).

Other star names followed after the 1986 tour including the great fullback Garry Jack (Salford then Sheffield Eagles), Steve Roach (Warrington), Bob Lindner (Castleford and Oldham), Martin Bella (Halifax) and many more including some who were unlucky not to tour. While it was great to have such talent serve their skills to an adoring public, the jury couldn't agree whether the influx denied young British talent its chance.

Long live the king

King Wally his name, Rugby League his game. Lewis had to be one of the finest Australian players ever to wear the Green and Gold with distinction. A fine ambassador and adorned like royalty he gained respect from all who had the privilege to see him play.

A career that took in 33 Tests (1981 to 1991) gives an indication of his worth to the Australian cause. This popular Queenslander became an all-time great and on his journey to fame received the highest accolade of the *Open Rugby* Adidas Golden Boot award as the outstanding player in 1985.

Wally's schoolboy career took him on a path to Japan, Europe and Britain being a member of the outstanding 1977/78 touring Rugby Union side. A Rugby League Test debut arrived in France in 1981, while the following year he gained the honour of vice-captain of the touring Kangaroos that played in France and Britain. Although unfortunate to lose his Test spot to Parramatta star Brett Kenny, Wally never again looked back with Kenny being moved to the centres to accommodate Lewis. Wally wasn't dropped again.

Proudly wearing the maroon of the Queensland State of Origin side for the first time in 1980 he set in motion a record of 22 consecutive games of the highest intensity up to 1988. Only an injury prevented him from going on. In this period the Queensland colours were only lowered in two series. In a ground-breaking exercise he led a Queensland team to an historic tour of England in 1983 to take in a three-match programme.

Hull KR proved a tough nut to crack and, in an uncompromising first game, the English club took Queensland close, 8-6. Unfortunately for Wigan (2-40) and Leeds (2-58) Queensland at last found their form. Leading his players from the front with great kicking tactics and accurate, bullet type passing eventually won Wally the Australian captaincy.

King Wally Lewis, a jewel of a player who never took a backward step.

It takes two to tango!

Growing old gracefully can test one's resolve to the limit. A few lucky people don't require the use of wrinkle cream, hair colouring, dentures or slimming clubs, but for the rest of the nation's oldies life takes on a new meaning trying to keep tuned in and tummy tucked in.

Policemen all look so young, making folk my age feel even more clapped out and as for the old thinking cap, advancing years question your ability to remember even the most recent goings on. One friend can't even remember to take his ginkgo capsules that are supposed to be good for the memory cells. Good grief! Now where did I put my spectacles?

All today's music sounds similar, to me anyway, and speaking of the music industry it's fascinating how one minute pop stars captivate their audiences and send fans into a frenzy, only to be forgotten the next.

So how did I survive the depressing seventies only to be born again in the eighties? Even though I hadn't attended one of those fancy health farms, or been on the vitamins, my general health did improve a little and boy what a feeling to be alive again!

A good singsong always lifts the spirits and although not quite on par with *Top of the Pops,* or even *Songs of Praise* come to think of it, my spectacle is enhanced dramatically with a song or two performed by my very own Rugby League choirs. It's spine tingling stuff to raise the hairs on the back of ones neck.

Unfortunately some renditions are a bit *risqué* for my liking and certainly not appropriate for a family book. Two notable exceptions are from Hull FC and Hull KR, both of whom were elevated to gladiator status, rejuvenated in the eighties after years of mediocrity. Battle lines were drawn in the city as the pendulum of success swung east.

Hull last held the Championship trophy aloft in the 'rock 'n' roll' days of 1958 when Workington Town took runners-up spot. Although Hull KR did spiral to the league title in 1978/79 the champagne had remained on ice since the glory of 1924/25. Quite a thirsty wait, methinks!

Challenge Cup success for Hull belonged in the bygone days, their one solitary win before the eighties achieved in 1914 defeating Wakefield Trinity 6-0 at Halifax. Meanwhile Hull KR failed to get on the winner's rostrum at all. So after a rendering of the clubs songs we will delve into the glory years they shared in the eighties.

Here goes with the Humberside Song Contest! Marks out of 10 please.

> *"Ole Faithful, we'll roam the range together, Ole Faithful, in any kind of weather, When the round up days are over and the Boulevard's white with clover, for you old faithful pal o' mine. Giddy up old fella, cos the moon is yellow tonight, Giddy up old fella, cos the moon is mellow and bright, There's a coyote howling at the moon above, So carry me back to the one I love, for you ole faithful pal o' mine..."*

... and from east of the River Hull,

> *"When the red red robin goes bob bob bobbing along, along, There'll be no more sobbing when he starts singing his own sweet song, Wake up, wake up you sleepy head. Get up, get up get out of bed, Cheer up, cheer up the sun is red. Live, love, laugh and be happy."*

Ole Faithful echoed long and loud around my grounds, as the

Black and Whites of Hull turned up the heat on their opponents. Great imports like Peter Sterling, James Leuluai, Dane O'Hara, Fred Ah Kuoi and Gary Kemble combined with the best of British including Lee Crooks and Steve 'Knocker' Norton to produce some awesome displays and help kick-start the Hull revival.

Attendances climbed dramatically at the Boulevard averaging 13,180 in 1981/82. Local coach operators had a field day in transporting the Hull faithful to their away games. However, *When The Red Red Robin* rang out just as long by the Rovers, as these two old adversaries met head to head with the force of a volcano, attracting 20,000-plus attendances.

Wembley Stadium thronged with anticipation in 1980 when a sea of black, white and red swept into town for the Challenge Cup final and a massive 95,000 crowd eagerly awaited the first Hull derby final. A crescendo of noise welcomed the troops onto the field of play and under the heat of the occasion the red side of Hull went on to claim the winners ribbons 10-5, leaving the Black and Whites suffering post-match losers depression and years of ribbing from across the River Hull. Dropping a goal for Hull KR that day was the mighty atom Roger Millward, a snip of a find by previous club Castleford after being caught on camera when ITV used to broadcast junior Rugby League on a Sunday afternoon.

The Robins reached the last stage the following year but relinquished the trophy to the black and white-shirted Chemics of Widnes.

Hull City Council's 1928 plan to build a bridge four miles west of Hull between Hessle and Barton-upon-Humber sunk without a trace after being hit by the financial woes of the great depression of the late twenties and early thirties, but construction finally started in 1973 and, having been opened by the Queen, the first traffic crossed on 17th July 1981. With price inflation during construction and delays caused by ground conditions, labour relations difficulties and adverse weather the original estimate of £28m grew. By the time the bridge opened the debt stood at £151m, due to be paid off by 2032.

Counted amongst the first year's Humber Bridge traffic were many fans headed south to Wembley, as Hull and Widnes gave their all in a classic 14-14 draw in 1982. The midweek replay at Elland Road gave the city a headache or two with an incredible 41,171 fans packing tightly into the ground with *Old Faithful* echoing around the stadium at the finish as Hull took the spoils. A Challenge Cup win for Hull FC, but such an achievement at Wembley eluded them. Hull had worn their home shirt of black and white hoops with white shorts, whilst Widnes had their all white home shirt with black shorts. Appropriately enough, BBC2's much talked about drama that year was the gritty, northern-based *Boys From The Blackstuff.*

In what should have been a walkover Hull then narrowly lost the 1983 final to Featherstone Rovers 12-14, one mighty upset. The bookmakers had earlier poured cold water on the game by declining any more bets on the Saturday morning.

Void of a Hull club for one year the twin towers then witnessed a classic, some saying the best Challenge Cup final ever, at a warm, sunny Wembley in front of the Queen herself! Akin to a bull and matador fighting it out in the bullring, initially first one side and then the other took the game by the horns in nip and tuck style. Legends like the mighty Peter Sterling and James Leuluai of Hull tangled with new wonder winger John Ferguson, supreme Brett Kenny and the ever grinning Henderson Gill for Wigan. In a gripping game of outstanding quality the Cherry and Whites crossed the winning post 28-24. Brett Kenny wrote his name into the history books by becoming the first Australian to win the Lance Todd Trophy.

In a Grand National style photo-finish Castleford took the cup the next season with only one point separating them from Hull KR. Jamey Sandy, probably the smallest player ever to appear in a final at 5ft 2inches tall (or short, as the case may be), seized the day by snatching a great 62nd-minute try and in doing so contributed to some real drama.

With a minute to go, Castleford held a 15-10 lead and were nervously hanging on when suddenly the tide appeared to turn in the favour of Hull KR as John Lydiat sent the Robins support into raptures with a try in the corner to make it 15-14. The crowd waited with baited breath as John Dorahy lined up the conversion but, agonisingly, the ball sailed wide to the great relief of the Castleford support.

More of the same

In the Championship chase, whilst Hull produced the goods in 1982/83 (runners-up Hull KR) the Robins duly took over the reins and kept the title on Humberside in both 1983/84 (runners-up Hull) and 1984/85.

Hull had three bites of the cherry in consecutive years to claim the Premiership trophy yet couldn't overcome the last hurdle. Old rivals Hull KR took the honour in 1981 in a low score of 11-7 that all but emptied the city of Hull of League fans with a full house at Headingley. Hull fared no better against Widnes twice and so were left with an unwanted hat-trick. To put the tin hat on it, their arch-rivals took on the challenge to 'come on down' and beat Castleford in 1984 by 18-10 but lost the year after to a Mal Meninga-inspired Saints, 36-16. Who could forget Meninga scorching away for a length of the field interception try? Once again Hull fought through to the last final of the decade but Widnes had the Indian sign over them for a third time.

Battle stations prepared, the two Hull giants locked horns in the 1982 Regal Trophy final and in front of a passionate throng of supporters at Headingley, Hull triumphed, 12-4. Revenge was sweet for the Robins who gained a victory in 1985 at Boothferry Park, Hull City AFC's ground and, in doing so, nilled their deadliest rivals 12-0. However, the following year Hull KR handed the cup over to Wigan in a close game 11-8.

Hull had a mixed bag in the Yorkshire Cup in the eighties, winning three on the trot by overcoming Bradford Northern and Castleford, as well as thrashing the Robins 29-12 in 1984 when 25,243 fans again squeezed into Boothferry Park. Castleford took revenge 31-24 in 1986. Whilst the Robins had lost to Leeds in 1980 in a close call, 8-7, they gained a victory in 1985 against classy Cas.

The BBC 2 Floodlit Trophy bade farewell in 1979/80 with the last final held at the Boulevard. A record 18,000 turnout gave the competition a rousing send off. The home support weren't let down in their first ever final with their Hull favourites finishing off Hull KR. The latter did take home the cup in 1978 in a win over St Helens.

Six tantalising derby finals, passion of the highest order, classic moments and plenty of drama was all the city of Hull could ask for.

Elsewhere…

Whilst the Challenge Cup seemed dominated by Hull FC and Hull KR, Widnes and Wigan who made up 14 of the 20 finalists of the decade between them, with St Helens 'up for the cup' on two occasions (both lost), there was success for other dark horses.

Like rank-outsiders in the Grand National, Castleford, Featherstone and Halifax all confounded the bookies by forging past the favourite on the rails to each claim Challenge Cup glory.

Featherstone caused a major upset by taking the scalp of Hull in the 1983 final, 14-12, as did Castleford three years later over Hull KR, 15-14. These were the days of 90,000-plus crowds at Wembley, swaying, sweating, swearing and singing, squashed solid like sardines in generally disgusting yet happy conditions.

The 1988 Challenge Cup semi-final had trench like defences with Halifax and Hull FC failing to score in the shoot out, 0-0. It was equally tight in the replay, going Halifax's way 4-3, with the only try of the game scored by Halifax's Tony Anderson. The blue and white hoops of Halifax failed to get rolling on the big occasion with Wigan taking it at a canter, 32-12. Not since Wakefield strolled in the park in the 1960 final against Hull, 38-5, had a club taken a tonking by more than 20 points.

Out of interest, after the Wakefield rout of Hull the following two finals of Wigan versus Saints and Wakefield versus Huddersfield both finished 12-6, the first duplicated scores.

Revenge is sweet or so they say. The Wigan faithful had always maintained that Alex had bent the rules in his own inimitable way in the 1966 Wigan versus Saints final that finished 2-21. An offside offence at the time resulted in a scrum down. Now just before the final the Saints made the astute signing of Wigan's veteran hooker Bill Sayer who had greater experience than Wigan's young hooker

Colin Clarke, father of ex-player, now pundit, Phil Clarke. In a period when scrums were properly contested, Murphy allegedly continued to move offside so that the Saints could dominate the game by winning the scrums and gaining possession. The song that day was "Roses are red, violets are blue, the Saints 21, Wigan two." But not in 1989 where no doubt the Wigan mob penned their own rhymes and Saints fans had to say "ouch" after Wigan finally put the record straight gaining revenge over an Alex Murphy coached St Helens side. The halo really slipped off the Saints with a score of 27-0.

The Wembley turnout that year was 78,000, well down on the previous year's 94,273 for Wigan's triumph over Halifax. Nothing sinister, Wembley had reduced its capacity by replacing 40-odd miles of concrete terracing with plastic bucket seats.

Silver service

Glory for the 'Tangerine Machine' of Blackpool Borough, gaining promotion to the first division for the start of the 1979-80 season, which saw them face the drop again. Bradford doubled up that and the next year, securing consecutive Slalom Lager Championships, as it was called then, for the first time since success in 1940 and 1941.

The last time the town of Leigh celebrated the championship crown was way back in 1906 so congratulations to the Leythers in 1982. Under Alex Murphy's guidance, Leigh took further success with the Lancashire Cup that year.

A curiosity on 3rd May 1982 as Bradford Northern captain Jeff Grayshon led his team from the pitch after 56 minutes of a league game against Hull KR.

The referee, Robin Whitfield, had sent off John Millington (Hull KR) and Gary Van Bellen (Bradford), then Steve Hartley (Hull KR) and Dean Carroll (Bradford). The last straw came for Grayshon when Ian Ellis (Bradford) went for an early bath. Grayshon took the can for continual dissent and promptly marched the whole team, or what was left of it, off the field. Bradford received a ban from three competitions the following year, later suspended, and Grayshon took no more part until September. The result, 17-8 to Hull KR, was allowed to stand.

Hull FC, Hull KR and Wigan apart, Widnes also notched up back-to-back Stones Bitter Championships, as the title had become, in 1988 and 1989.

Perennial bridesmaids, St Helens, missed the cut three times with only the consolation of runners-up. Tight at the top with three titles edged by a whisker of one point.

The title of Yo-Yo kings went to Halifax. After finishing rock bottom of the second division in 1978, they improved year on year to become top of the Slalom Lager Championship in 1986 followed by defeating St Helens 19-18 a year later in the Challenge Cup final. In dramatic theatre, Halifax's John Pendlebury somehow dislodged the ball from Saints' Mark Elia after it seemed he was certain to go over in the corner for a winning try. Lance Todd Trophy winner that day, and a second for Australia, veteran Graham Eadie led with style from fullback.

1989 saw Widnes kings of the world, defeating Canberra 30-18 in the World Club Championship with 30,786 inside Old Trafford, and St Esteve 60-6 in the experimental European Championship.

Dwindling interest from players and fans alike saw the end of the County Championship, abandoned after 87 years with Lancashire having won 34 times, Yorkshire 24, Cumberland 16 times and Cheshire once.

The end of season Premiership play-offs were increasing in popularity, keeping the season alive until the end for those in the top half of the divisions. What turned out to be a ground-breaking decision by my bosses was to take the Premiership final to Old Trafford in 1987, home of mighty Manchester United FC.

The previous year's final at Elland Road, Leeds, produced a crowd of 13,683 as Warrington beat Halifax, 38-10. In a reversal for Warrington the following year at Old Trafford, Wigan took their scalps by 8-0. But hey hey, jackpot time with 38,756 fans inside. This chosen venue had never looked back and has become a huge success in later years.

The Varsity Match, Oxford versus Cambridge was introduced in 1981. Rugby League at Oxbridge. Who'd have thought it?

Wigan Casino

After a long nap the sleeping giant of Wigan woke up and started smashing records as freely as plates in a Greek restaurant. The alarm call came with the once-mighty Wigan suffering relegation with Hunslet, York and Blackpool. Fortified by a hearty breakfast of 'humble pie,' immediate promotion saw the Riversiders bounce back and normal service resumed on 29th August 1982 with the attractive visit of Hull FC. Wigan won 23-8 and a Central Park crowd registered at 10,142 made it two five-figure crowds in a row after years of thin turnouts.

Maurice Lindsay had just replaced coach Maurice Bamford with Alex Murphy, and after the game the four Wigan directors, Lindsay, a local antique dealer Jack Robinson, Jack Hilton and Tom Rathbone, announced they were prepared to provide a £120,000 debenture loan to the Wigan club in return for complete control.

There seemed no one able to stand in their way and a resounding majority passed the debenture deal at a shareholder meeting on 2nd November. One shareholder speaking from the floor gave the four men his full backing describing the previous 20 years at Wigan as "a horror story". That shareholder's name? Dave Whelan.

The Wigan juggernaut began to roll with major signings of Henderson Gill (Rochdale £23,000), Colin Whitfield and David Stephenson (Salford player exchange and £60,000), Glynn Shaw (Widnes £30,000) and Mick Scott (Halifax £28,500.) Further, it was announced in October that the club had signed New Zealand Test captain Graeme West, later to become a Wigan legend.

The gamble paid off for the four Wigan directors as Wigan secured the John Player Trophy in defeating Leeds 15-4 on 21st January 1983 before a 19,553 crowd, Wigan's first major trophy for nearly 20 years.

Progress rumbled on as Wigan bulldozed a path to the 1984 Challenge Cup final for the first time in 14 years. On this occasion Widnes outplayed them with a score of 19-6. The destroyers in chief were in fact three Wigan lads in Lydon (Lance Todd Trophy), Gregory who Wigan had rejected as not big enough and an ex-player, Keiron O'Loughlin. Famously, Maurice Lindsay said after the game: "We'll be back".

In the summer off-season, Wigan placed their mark on the game with the signings of the great Brett Kenny, as well as a little known Aussie winger by the name of John Ferguson.

Lindsay and Murphy fell out pre-season, with Murphy being shown the door, legend has it after lamping his boss one. Murphy out, Clarke and McInnes in and true to Lindsay's word, Wigan returned to Wembley and victory in 1985.

More major signings followed including the jewel in the crown, the one and only Ellery Hanley from Bradford, with whom he was in dispute. The deal of cash plus players was to amount to around £150,00. A formidable side now started to blossom with the Lancashire Cup and JPS Trophy next placed in the trophy cabinet.

After Wigan had defeated Leigh in the semi-final prior to taking on Hull KR, another master stroke came with the signings of South African Rugby Union players Rob Louw and Ray Mordt for a reported £75,000. However, there were hiccups in the quest for the next trophy as Castleford knocked them out of the Challenge Cup, unexpected defeat to Halifax in the league, and Warrington beat them in the Premiership. It was time to say goodbye to the coaches Clarke and McIness, whilst welcoming on board Graham Lowe.

At the start of season 1986, £100,000 went to Widnes to acquire Joe Lydon, whilst other big name signings included Dean Bell, Ian Roberts and mighty atom Andy Gregory for £130,000 from Warrington. With Hanley and Edwards already in the fold, Lowe's first year brought success in guiding the club to the Lancashire Cup, the JPS trophy and Premiership. The main prize though was the league title in a record breaking season. Wigan took the title by a massive 15 points and in doing so notched up a record 174 tries, a record points total of 941 and a mean record of only conceding 29 tries and 193 points. Oldham did spoil the party by knocking them out of the Challenge Cup, eventually won by Halifax.

The transformation from the second division seven years earlier to world champions on a big night out on 7th October 1987 became complete as Wigan took on Manly, the Australian Grand Final champions. A partisan crowd of over 36,000 crammed into Central Park to witness a bruising, tryless contest eventually edged by Wigan 8-2. The team consisted entirely of British players apart from non-playing substitute Graeme West.

The scene was set for the River Douglas club to take all before them. Wigan would turn Rugby League from a sport into a business and, to use the catchphrase of the time, it would both cost and earn 'loadsamoney.'

The Spanish connection

Always on the look out for unusual stories I came across an article that got me dancing a flamenco, Rugby League in Spain!

The Santa Eulalia Sharks League Tribe started life in the early 1980s as a supporters group for the Fulham and Kent/Southend clubs, founded by Kevin Martinez and Pedro Pinero who were very keen on Rugby League. Their enthusiasm soon spread amongst their young friends and although there was no history of the game or coverage on Spanish television they soon had plenty of converts. A wellwisher supplied the two boys with video tapes, mainly of the Balmain Tigers and other Australian sides and coaching techniques.

Aided by adults they became the first supporters club in Spain and such was their enthusiasm that they promoted themselves in the Rugby League press, mainly in the *Rugby Leaguer.*

With more support from the *Leaguer* they then amended their name to Santa Eulalia Rugby League Club - the Tigers and later still changed allegiances to the Sharks. Friends from the British Isles also supplied them with tackle bags, rugby balls (League shape of course) and tackle shields.

Fame also came on Ibiza when Don Andrews spotted them training on a beach and wrote an article for *Ibiza Now*. Other photos appeared in *Open Rugby* magazine, *Rugby League Review* and *Rugby League Week*, as well as various fanzines. They also had a mention in *Daily Majorca Bulletin* when they wrote of their hopes that Spain could one day have a Rugby League team.

All good stuff but I wonder what did happen to the lads as they grew up? Anyone out there know? Either way, what of this Fulham crowd?

The Bucking Broncos

The brainchild of Harold Genders, who was a former Rochdale, Widnes and Blackpool player, later appointed Managing Director, Fulham RLFC started life in 1980.

The *Daily Mail* ran a story that took everyone by surprise in that Fulham was to apply to the RFL for membership. Leeds based Finance Director, Brian Dalton confirmed the story, whilst another northerner, Ernie Clay, the club's Chairman, gave the plan his full backing. At an RFL meeting in Harrogate, it was voted 27-0, with three absentees, to accept.

Writer Colin Welland, a diehard supporter of my game, also joined the board, whilst famous footballer Malcolm McDonald, Fulham's Marketing Executive presented a launch plan with an average crowd of 4,000 needed to break even. Ex-Widnes player Reg Bowden was appointed player/coach and signed Roy Lester from Warrington as the first player.

Fulham won their historic *debut* match on 14th September 1981 against Wigan, and attracted 9,554 to Craven Cottage with newspaper reports full of enthusiasm and compliments for the venture (how times have changed). That season, Fulham finished third in division two behind York and Wigan and together with fourth-placed Whitehaven were promoted at their first attempt. Their record was played 28, won 20 with an average crowd of 6,096, against an average crowd for the division of 2,005.

As is often the case, the promoted club then spent the next few seasons yo-yo-ing between the two divisions.

The Fulham FC club had seen the League team as a way of making money, although falling crowds and the costs of running a team most of whom were based in the north of England meant that the days of the Rugby League club seemed numbered. In June 1984 the directors of Fulham FC pulled the plug on Rugby League and announced their intention to put the club into liquidation.

Hanging by a thread for the next few years London's only senior club then suffered a period of name changes, ground moves, more threats of closure and also occasional triumphs and success as to the rescue came fans Roy and Barbara Close, who pretty much single-handedly saved the club.

The National Sports Centre at Crystal Palace was used as a home venue for one season, then the polytechnic stadium in Chiswick became the new home ground in 1985 and would remain so until 1990 and a move back to Crystal Palace.

1991 saw a change of name, as the London Crusaders were born, to widen the appeal to all the capital's citizens, not just those adjacent to the Kings Road. Either way, Fulham was no longer appropriate as the team didn't play there.

Another ground change in 1993 with a move to the Copthall Stadium, Barnet at the bottom of the M1 and the signing of ex-All Black John Gallagher.

In 1994 London Crusaders finished third in the second division and reached their divisional Premiership final. This year also saw the club bought out by the Brisbane Broncos and renamed London Broncos, bringing some stability until the entity was sold on to Virgin. Better times in Super League and the Broncos brightest moments to date with a runners-up spot in the league table and the last Wembley Challenge Cup final led out by a beaming fan, Richard Branson.

For more, try *From Fulham to Wembley*, 20 Years of Rugby League in London by Dave Farrar and Peter Lush or *The Fulham Dream - Rugby League Tackles London* by Harold Genders.

Border skirmish

For over 300 years, life in the borders of England and Scotland wasn't exactly a pleasant experience. Constant cross-border feuding peaked in the 16th and 17th centuries when robbery, livestock raiding, murder, kidnap and arson were everyday occurrences. This constant war or 'border reiving' had little to do with relations between the two countries though, who were officially at peace. The word 'bereave' actually has its roots in 'reive.'

Long after Hadrian had built his wall, other fortifications called Peel towers were constructed of stone with massive thick walls. For extra security there would normally only be one entrance via a double door at ground level, one being an outer iron grating and the other made of oak reinforced with iron. The bottom of the building would be for storage only with access to the upstairs living quarters via a very narrow, curving stair. At the top there would be a beacon to summon help in times of attack. So what has all this got to do with my life?

For someone who has tried to spread his wings far and wide on a professional basis, I must admit Scotland has been a tough nut to crack. I sometimes wonder if there are Rugby League towers to keep me out.

Edinburgh has staged the odd skirmish or two in recent years when 'on the road' games and a couple of Challenge Cup finals have taken place in the tartan territory, as well as a modest amateur set up evident, but no firm prospects of a professional club.

My journey north has always seemed to come to the end of the line at Carlisle.

After Carlisle's first foray into the brave world of Rugby League in 1928, the resurrection came in the off-season of 1981. The then chairman of Carlisle United, James Bendall, now sadly passed away, proposed that a Rugby League club could share facilities at Brunton Park, home to Carlisle United.

It took around £80,000 to recruit a team. Such names as Allan Agar as player coach and his assistant Mick Morgan helped guide the fledgling club and shrewd moves were made in signing such as Jimmy Thompson, Dennis Boyd, Nigel Stephenson and Jimmy Birts although the entire team trained in Yorkshire and was bussed up to Carlisle for the Sunday fixtures.

Carlisle's opening game came in the Lancashire Cup when the new boys gave a good account of themselves in a close match with Wigan, 6-9. In their first league fixture a good crowd of 5,900, still a club record, assembled to see the home club entertain Workington, going down 6-23. Better times followed and Carlisle gained promotion in its first season. Mick Morgan set a world record for a prop in scoring 25 tries and, to cap matters, the football club also won promotion to their division two.

Promotion was not to be the rainbow's end however, with the club struggling to establish itself in the higher division and relegated well before the season's end.

The Carlisle club survived several years and moved grounds many times but, in the end, the eternal struggle proved insurmountable and a merger with Barrow saw the end of the Carlisle club in its own right...for the time being.

The Valley of Death

There's no doubt that the Welsh have a fierce passion for the oval ball, steeped in folklore. However, trying to make them my second cousins has been a different kettle of fish.

Ever since I was born, in-roads have been attempted in the Principality but eventually each has withered away. The eighties proved no different as attempts were made to put a base down in South Wales once more.

In 1981 the RFL admitted Cardiff City to the family with an overwhelming vote by 27-0, to be based with the soccer club at Ninian Park with the great David Watkins as Managing Director and former St Helens player John Mantle as coach. Four top Welsh Union international players were signed in Steve Fenwick (Bridgend), Tommy David (Llanelli and Pontypridd), Paul Ringer (Ebbw Vale and Llanelli) and Brynmor Williams (Cardiff, Newport and Swansea).

The Blue Dragons as they were known attracted a very good crowd of 9,247 for their first match at home against Salford, the final score being 21-26 to Salford. No other game attracted a crowd as good and the club finished the season half way up the league. After the third year there was bad news as the Welsh Football Association put pressure on to eject the club, as they wanted the ground for the round ball only.

A brief, reformed courtship with Bridgend failed miserably and after collecting just two points in 1984/85 failed to reappear in 1985/86.

and others...

I couldn't seem to settle during the eighties, listless days and restless nights. I needed more than Sanatogen as my member clubs chopped and changed causing chaos like a riot at the bingo hall.

After Fulham's bow in 1980, Cardiff City and Carlisle followed the next year, as I just mentioned, joined my second division.

By 1983/84 a new club, Kent Invicta, joined in but relocated to Southend in 1984/85. Huyton changed their name to Runcorn Highfield. Huddersfield added Barracudas to their name.

That year the increase of the second division to 20 teams meant that it would take 38 rounds to play out a full double round robin, which was too many, so a complicated fixture formula was used to reduce it to 28.

To prevent any more of this structural instability, rules were passed to try and safeguard any new entrants. Newcomers had to have £50,000 in the bank and a 10-year lease on their ground. Under these rules Mansfield Marksmen and Sheffield Eagles were born in 1984/85, Bridgend arrived and Cardiff City departed.

There were by now 36 clubs in the two divisions, the largest number since 1902/03. Mansfield struggled from the start before relocating to Nottingham but Sheffield went on to buck the trend and achieve great success due to the remarkable efforts of Gary and Kath Hetherington.

Are you still following me? 1985/1986 saw Bridgend and bottom club Southend Invicta dropping out of the competition altogether and the promotion scheme was changed to three up three down, then the next year two up, four down to reduce the top division to 14 clubs.

Blackpool Borough left the town in 1987/88. There was trouble when they wanted to call themselves Wigan Borough and word was that Wigan RLFC got the Rugby Football League to stop them. Settling on an alternative, they played as Springfield Borough for one season before Wigan Athletic pulled the plug on the ground share and they had to move to Moss Lane, Altrincham to become Trafford Borough. Some of the directors weren't happy with that and the club split with part of it becoming the old Chorley Borough for season 1988-89. Huddersfield promptly dropped their, frankly implausible, Barracudas.

More unrest in 1989/1990 as York left Clarence Street and moved out of the city, adding their new locality to their name, becoming Ryedale-York. Nottingham City replaced the Mansfield Marksmen.

Never a dull moment, although as Groucho Marx once said: "I don't care to belong to a club that accepts people like me as members."

Welcome to the jungle

A rare new arrival into the Rugby League international family in 1982. Papua New Guinea was accorded Test status, starting by hosting two of the game's superpowers at home, an Australia 2-38 defeat at Port Moresby (15,000) and another loss to New Zealand 5-56, again at Port Moresby (13,000.)

Just as *Frankie Goes to Hollywood* in 1984, so Britain visited Mt Hagen, captained by Brian Noble, running out winners 20-36 (7,510). A proposed tour match against a PNG Combined XIII yielded to a visit by Prince Charles. I suppose the local security forces had their hands full as it was.

Nevertheless, the Rugby League-mad Papuans had made their mark and to this day celebrate Rugby League as their principal national sport, the only country on earth to do so.

Fans walk barefoot miles through jungle to get to the game, many arriving with no money and having to settle for a perch in a tree outside the ground. I can quite believe one report of an attempt to sabotage a rival club by planting palm trees on their pitch.

Bon Voyage

Great Britain and France were still playing partners on a regular basis in the eighties, clashing no less than 16 times. I suspect that some of my younger fans might not even know that the game is played across the Channel! There were a couple of high spots for the French but generally the *Tricolours* came out second best. Just two wins and a draw weren't much to write home about.

The start of the decade was quite encouraging and had the powers that be rubbing their hands with glee. An excellent turn out of 13,173 over in Hull witnessed Britain keep a clean sheet, 37-0. Unfortunately, the game in Carcassonne in 1987 had the French wondering what happened to their fans with a paltry 1,968 turning up.

The gulf in playing standards was growing but at least Test match football involving France hadn't been condemned to the scrap heap.

My cousins across the Channel had competed with Britain in the eighties even though they still missed the journey to the South Seas, as well as suffering a cash crisis and poor leadership. There was a cash injection given by Australia, New Zealand and Great Britain on condition that certain standards were re-established.

As with previous years there was still the malice of the French Rugby Union to contend with in that they resented the courts decision to allow the *treizistes* to restore the word 'rugby' in their title.

Compounding their felony the FRU encouraged their own clubs to offer money to 13-a-side players to change codes. The gaffe was blown when a document advising how much *quinzistes* could be paid before tax leaked out.

It was something of a political hot potato as the Home Unions expressed outrage whilst saying very little, especially to the Inland Revenue, about the RFU's own 'boot money'. A French farce to contend with '*Allo 'Allo* the comedy spoof of the *Secret War* drama which ran for nine years from 1982, as French rugby made a mockery of itself.

But what about the Kiwis?

Out of 13 clashes during the decade, the Kiwis won seven, with two going to a draw. Praise where it is due, I say. The Poms did suffer a very first three-Test whitewash in 1984, going down 12-0 at Auckland, 28-12 over in Christchurch and 32-16 back in Auckland.

The World Cup tournament was a strange affair again with it

being played in both hemispheres from 1985 to 1988 with some of the above matches counting as World Cup points. Unfortunately, France failed to meet their obligations in the southern hemisphere matches and so Australia, New Zealand and new kids on the block Papua New Guinea were awarded the points. In the play-off final Australia beat New Zealand 12-25, attended by a record Auckland turn out of 47,363.

Stars and stripes

Harry Sunderland, who played a major role in establishing me in France, reckoned the USA to be the next port of call.

A gridiron player called Mike Dimitrio assembled a team of mainly gridiron volunteers, and the snappily-named American All Stars set out for Australia in 1953. Opening with a 25-34 win over a Southern New South Wales/Monaro team at Canberra, only a handful of wins proved the experiment less than a commercial success.

Nevertheless, games were organised at the Long Beach Memorial Stadium and Los Angeles Coliseum before the home side was thrown to the lions (i.e. Australia) with two defeats in front of modest crowds costing the promoters, which included the RFL, NZRL and ARL a small fortune.

A handful of wins wasn't enough to build on then, but hope sprung eternal and another American footballer, Mike Meyer got the ball rolling again in 1986 and the game has bumped along stateside since. I've got a reasonable foothold with the AMNRL-established league around such places as New York, Philadelphia, Connecticut and Washington DC.

Another body, the USRL, based around Jacksonville, has helped stage one-off challenges, events and training camps for British clubs at, I kid you not, Disneyworld.

The USA Tomahawks have been regular visitors to Moscow and Canada in recent years and always show up when there's a World Cup on.

Easy on the burgers, the Yanks are coming!

Fame Academy

The year 1988 witnessed the Hall of Fame being introduced to honour a selection of great players of the past, splendidly arranged by the game's leading archivist and historian, Robert Gate. The rule was that any player selected had to have been retired at least 10 years.

The inaugural list was, in no particular order of merit, Billy Batten, Brian Bevan, Billy Boston, Alex Murphy, Jonty Parkin, Gus Risman, Albert Rosenfield, Jim Sullivan and Harold Wagstaff. Neil Fox was to be added later, after his qualification period.

One of these days, we'll organise a Rugby League museum worthy of the name, but until then these gentlemen are honoured only at Red Hall. I did have some characters during the eighties though.

Gizmo's moment

One of the most publicised signings of all time was made on 17th October 1983, when Wigan signed Shaun Edwards seconds after midnight on his 17th birthday. The signing featured on BBC *Breakfast Time* a few hours later (yes, you read that right).

In an illustrious career in which Gizmo captained England schoolboys at both Rugby Union and League, he broke records like no player before him in becoming the game's most decorated player ever, in terms of medals won. These included seven Championships, five Premierships, nine Challenge Cups, seven Regal Trophies, three World Club Challenges, five Lancashire Cups and three Charity Shields.

For Wigan, he made 467 appearances, scoring 274 tries in 14 seasons between 1983 and 1997, increasing his tally to 584 matches and 325 tries in three further years at London Broncos and, briefly, Bradford Bulls.

One amazing statistic is that Shaun appeared in no less than 11 Challenge Cup finals which, one would think, may never be equalled. At one point, he was the youngest ever player to appear in a Challenge Cup final, at the tender age of 17 years, 201 days old.

The Black Pearl

Born to be a winner, Ellery Hanley set out on a journey to stardom on 26th November 1978 that would lead him into immortality and fame.

His Rugby League debut came with Bradford Northern, whose fans were set for a treat in a six-year stint that would yield 89 tries in just 126 appearances, a phenomenal effort indeed.

Undoubtedly, his finest season at Odsal came in 1984/85 when he amassed 55 tries in only 37 outings. No matter whether he was on the wing, playing at centre, or even stand off he had a devastating effect on opponents, often mesmerising them with the body swerve of a gazelle.

Who could ever forget his length of the field try against Featherstone? He hugged the touchline with a ballerina balance whilst swatting the opposition tacklers away like flies, all captured on BBC television.

His 55-try effort gave notice to other clubs of his outstanding talent, which subsequently led Wigan to fork out a world record fee of £150,000. From there, Ellery became one of my most decorated players as medal after medal ended up in his trophy cabinet.

Dubbed 'Black Pearl' by his army of fans he went on to represent Great Britain and eventually achieved the distinction of taking on the captaincy.

At 30 years of age in 1991, Ellery set another milestone by becoming a Leeds player for another record transfer (£250,000 cash) and ended up serving the club for four years. His exploits enthralled another new audience with his immeasurable skills and phenomenal upper body strength.

Having coached the Great Britain side against Australia in 1994, the Australian megabucks offered to star players during the battle between the Super League and ARL administrations lured him down under to Balmain in 1996/98, where he had played previously in 1988, before calling it a day.

With a career total of 428 tries over his 498 appearances, Ellery's record speaks for itself.

A huge draw card in his own right, he won *Open Rugby*'s

prestigious Adidas Golden Boot in 1989, the Lance Todd Trophy at Wembley and the honour of an MBE.

Although a quietly spoken private man, who liked to keep himself to himself and the media, of whom he had a strong distrust, at arms-length, there is no doubt that Ellery was an inspiration to a generation of young players.

Before leaving Rugby League for pastures new, Ellery coached St Helens to a grand final win.

Linger a little longer

More, but different. By the time he arrived at Headingley, Ellery Hanley had long since secured legend status, then having been made captain of Leeds (deposing the current Great Britain skipper Garry Schofield) as well as being coach of Great Britain, I suppose he could pull rank on virtually anyone. He regularly explained the decision he required to referees.

Ellery made sure he let everyone know who was boss. It might have been my imagination, but I'm sure that old Ellery delighted in making everyone wait for him. When both teams and officials were lined up and poised for kick off and the assembled Headingley throng's attention was focussed on the proceedings, then and only then would he consider unzipping his tracksuit top and slowly jogging to the sideline to hand it to one of the trainers. When Ellery was good and ready, and not before, could the game proceed.

Not the only slowcoach, I recall Colin Whitfield, prolific goal-kicking centre of Halifax, had a superstition whereby he was always the last man on and off the pitch. He could often be seen shuffling near the touchline until everyone else had taken the field. It was only a matter of time until someone (i.e. Bobbie Goulding) caught him out, lurking out of sight near the dressing rooms long enough for Colin to eventually think that the coast was clear, then to Colin's horror, with a tap on the shoulder Bobbie trotted on past.

Has there been any goalkicker who took longer than that famous son of Humberside, winger Paul Eastwood? By the time Paul had finished contemplating, adjusting himself and generally dithering, enough time to brew up a cup of tea, boil an egg and smoke a cigar had passed. Fair play to him though, Paul didn't miss many either for Hull, Hull KR or Great Britain.

Not so much late as early for Sammy Windmill who used to run the Market House, a well known Rugby League pub in Dewsbury. Sammy played over 70 games for Featherstone Rovers between 1966 and 1983 and became assistant to Allan Agar, coach of the Featherstone team that upset Hull in the 1983 Challenge Cup final. It was therefore a sombre moment before kick-off at the 1989 first-round Challenge Cup match at Bootham Crescent between York, where he also had played, and Leeds, as the public address announced that Sammy had passed away. A minute's silence was impeccably held, as these occasions always are, also observed on Radio Leeds where Ron Hill was due to commentate on the match. No flowers please.

This was all news to Sammy who was at home listening on the radio.

Extensive local investigations into Mr Windmill by one of my younger enthusiasts, Rob Castlehouse, have revealed Sammy to be a bit of a character to say the least.

One theory is that the death announcement was a practical joke, another that Sammy himself announced it. Certainly his pub took plenty of brass that night as customers called in mark their respect with a pint, only to see our hero standing behind the bar with a smile on his face. No one knows what happened to the collection made at the solemn match.

Various reports received suggest that he is now dead, running a boarding house on the east coast (although that might be confusion with Bridlington-based Les Dyl) and living in Spain with a rich widow. I'm sure that's the way he'd like it.

Apparently, Sammy's moment of glory came during an 'A' team match against Leeds when with his team already 50 or 60 points down, he intercepted a pass and went the length of the field unopposed, only to stop 10 yards out and drop a goal. Explaining afterwards, Sammy announced: "I've always wanted to score a point at Headingley!"

Haven't we all, Sammy, haven't we all.

GREED IS GOOD

The one-armed stand-off.

In 1989 Runcorn Highfield suffered a players strike. Coach Bill Ashurst came out of retirement to play against his home town and first professional club, Wigan, in the John Player Trophy first round coming on as a substitute and getting himself promptly sent off after 11 minutes. He received a four-match ban for his trouble and a £100 fine for bringing the game into disrepute. As for the score, his team lost 92-2. Simply can't please everyone in the family.

Talking of Runcorn, one of my internet friends, 'Ronnie 2', tells a tall tale.

Runcorn Highfield had an almost constant turn over of playing staff during the late 1980s. Some were former internationals such as Chris Arkwright, others were one-game Rugby Union trialists, usually listed in the programme as AN Other.

The most unusual signing of all took the form of one-armed Australian standoff, Kerry Gibson. He had been born with a left arm that ended at the elbow, but had become a Rugby League player in his home country where despite having one arm, he could still pass with power and accuracy. Kerry had long been a friend and fellow countryman of Runcorn and Oldham loose forward, John Cogger and John persuaded Runcorn coach Bill Ashurst to let Kerry train with the squad.

Gibson impressed and Ashurst named him as substitute for the Good Friday 1988 second division game with Springfield Borough. An Australian television film crew turned up at Springfield Park, Wigan, to report on the story of the one-armed player who looked like making his debut in the English game. Unfortunately for them, they did not know which player was Kerry Gibson.

As the Runcorn Highfield team bus pulled into the car park, the television crew came to attention. The team had been alerted about the filming and the sense of humour, which went hand in hand with being associated with Runcorn Highfield, came into play. Kerry himself came up with an amusing plan in that as the team alighted the bus every player had his left arm tucked up the back of his team jumper and each of them smiled at the camera before nipping into the changing room. Needless to say, the

343

television crew was thrown into complete confusion by the Venus de Milo of Rugby League!

Lion tamers

Colin Hutton, coach of the 1962 Lions, made me roar with laughter the other day.

"The first Rugby League AGM I attended was held over a weekend at Blackpool. Most of the formal business was dealt with on the Saturday, so as to leave Sunday for 'any other business.' Salford was represented by Les Bettinson who complained about the condition of the Huyton pitch where his club had recently played a cup tie.

"Geoff Fletcher, who pretty much ran the Huyton club single-handed, was none too pleased at Les's outburst saying that vandals at the ground were the bane of his life. He argued that every game had to have a massive pre-match cleaning up operation due to the constant damage.

"Les retorted: 'Why don't you get some guard dogs then, Geoff?'

"I thought Geoff was going to have a fit. With cheeks puffed up he retorted by saying, 'Guard dogs Les! We had a circus near the ground recently and people witnessed lions cowering in their cages that had been terrified by the children, so if the bloody lions are terrified, what good are guard dogs?'

"The meeting ended in fits of laughter."

Fly, Eddie Fly

The world's sporting public took Eddie Edwards to its heart during the 1988 Calgary Winter Olympics, as Britain's first and, to date, last ski jumper finished 56th but not last as one other jumper suffered disqualification.

His 'massive' jump of just 77 metres accompanied with flailing arms and wobbly skis earned him worldwide fame, albeit more for foolhardy courage than sporting achievement, and with it a nice fortune to the tune of £87,000 in the weeks to follow. With saturation media coverage his fortune grew by the end of 1988 to £400,000 from a book, record, endorsements and sponsorship. Everyone wanted a piece of Eddie the Eagle.

Fame is fleeting and the money quickly disappeared, poor old Eddie being declared bankrupt in 1992 thence onto Leicester to study law. Not accident law I hope.

From one Eddie to another...

'Eee's a poor lad!

I mentioned him earlier, one Edward Marsden Waring, a name to this day synonymous with Rugby League.

Born in 1910 and brought up in Dewsbury, he reflected the earnest and rough hewn town in his own human fabric. Not only did he play both codes of rugby, but also was a talented sprinter, as well has having football trials with Nottingham Forest and Barnsley.

From an early age his schoolmaster would edit his Rugby League articles from whence he graduated into life as a journalist with the *Sunday Mirror* and *Rugby League Revew*, before taking another turn on his journey. In the 1930s, Eddie became the youngest manager of one of my clubs, Dewsbury, and with his flair, astute leadership and outstanding determination he transformed the club into a trophy winning team during the war, champions in 1942 and Challenge Cup winners in 1943.

During the fifties a meeting with screen legend Bob Hope in Hollywood impressed on Eddie that television would be the medium of the future and with that advice ringing in his ears, Waring went on to star on the small screen for three decades.

Whilst in many ways an instantly recognisable personality with his own personal style that must have given the game a wider audience, many Rugby League fans felt he portrayed a negative stereotype for the sport. However, as Trevor Foster confirmed in his 1946 *Indomitables* article, here stood a man of great character, charm and wonderful youthful energy.

Waring was a man with a big heart, no matter how he was viewed or what he did in his time, he gave a lot back to the sport he loved. He even paid his own fare on the Australian tour and was regarded in high esteem by the Australians, many of whom invited him to speak at functions.

Eddie rose to the status of a national institution with his trilby and 'unique' commentary for BBC television during the broadcasting of live Rugby League matches. His broad Yorkshire accent warbled into the nations living rooms with catch phrases of "up 'n' under" and "early bath", yet many fans of the game cringed with every word. In fact, many thought it served the BBC's interests to keep him there, so as to give the impression that the sport was just a quirky northern 'cloth cap and whippet' affair.

It didn't help matters when Eddie accepted an invitation to referee the BBC's *It's a Knockout* game show that first aired on 7th August 1966. The first edition was, would you believe, held in Morecambe, which then was a town related to music hall comedy. Hosted by McDonald Hobley with Ted Ray and Charlie Chester in tow as master of ceremonies, the fun and games were held alternatively in Lancashire and Yorkshire and contested by various teams who had different slapstick challenges set before them.

Unfortunately, the television debut of *It's A Knockout* amounted to something of an embarrassment, as referee Eddie Waring recalled ten years later. "The contest was held on the sands of Morecambe in Lancashire and one of the games was a three-legged soccer match, filmed live. Everything had been arranged very well except for one vital detail... the sea. The tide came in and not only was I refereeing up to my knees in water, but also the camera crew were splashing about trying to rescue some of their equipment." Waring stood, as ever, only a moment from disaster himself in that salutary first programme.

Whilst Eddie made eight tours to Australia, and although obviously well schooled in the game, his eccentric style of commentary made him and his sport an easy target for another of the 1970s entertainment giants, the mimic Mike Yarwood.

Actor and playwright Colin Welland summed up the thoughts of many with the words: "while Rugby Union is treated with the importance of a state occasion, Waring reduces Rugby League to the level of mud wrestling." Alternatively, the then RFL Chief

Executive, David Oxley offered the alternative view in that: "he brought a great feeling and a great depth of emotion to the game. He loved the players for their courage, character, humour and athleticism and he never, never held up the game to ridicule."

The line between entertainment and high farce was a tightrope that Eddie straddled daily. For example, I recall on one occasion Eddie's jaunty match preview piece to camera ended with the usual twinkle in his eye, the shot drawing back to reveal Eddie perched on the crossbar. Never mind, it's only Rugby League, just a bit of fun. Would John Arlott, the venerable sage of cricket, Dan Maskell, custodian of all that was right and proper at Wimbledon or Henry Cotton 'the Maestro' of golf, even Peter O'Sullivan or David Coleman for that matter, allow themselves to be put in that position? Hey, it's Rugby League, only a laugh, nothing serious. That's how it was during Eddie's era.

Whilst a household name, Eddie still led a simple life with his wife Mary and son Tony. Perversely, away from the screen Waring lived an excessively secretive life and did his best to cover his footsteps. Story has it that Eddie regarded the Queen's Hotel, Leeds as a sort of post box. No one seemed to know where he lived, but if you wished to contact him, you could write to the hotel and he would phone back eventually. Apparently, he checked the pigeonholes at reception regularly.

More showbusiness came his way, including fabled appearances with comedy giants *The Goodies* and *Morecambe & Wise* in their Christmas shows. His larger-than-life personality and work in writing books and generally championing his beloved sport saw him recognised with the award of an MBE.

All good things must come to an end and in 1981 at the age of 71 Eddie hung up his microphone with a farewell Challenge Cup final, 22 years after his first adventure with the competition, and then the end of season Premiership final between Hull and Hull KR at Leeds. Bowing out with his immortal departing words he bade the nation farewell with: "So there it is…back to David Coleman in the *Grandstand* studio…it's all yours, David lad."

Some likened his departure from the BBC to the removal of Nelson's Column from Trafalgar Square. Eddie could only be followed, as he duly was by dual-coder Ray French, he could never be replaced.

Eddie lived his last years peacefully in his beloved Yorkshire and passed away on 28th October 1986, aged 76.

Whether his contribution spread the game or held it open to ridicule, his unique personality is still mimicked to this day, demonstrating that Eddie Waring has never been ignored or forgotten. Truly a giant of Rugby League.

Glad that's over!

So what of the eighties? All Porches and Samantha Fox down south, where I was still only an occasional visitor, but back up north it was a decade that made me feel like a schoolboy being caned as the Aussies gave me a lesson or two in how to play the game. They had shown that a more professional attitude to training, fitness and coaching could elevate the game from one simply for tough blokes to one for super athletes.

Yet it wasn't all doom and gloom on the domestic front as my players, especially on Humberside, had served up some mouth-watering treats, big occasions and surprise results. The icing on the cake for many fans was to be able to see some top quality play from those Invincibles returning at club level and at least I lived in the public consciousness, even if not treated with the respect I deserved.

I did lose the County Championships, although the competition had sort of lost its legs and become much like the craze of 1984 - a Trivial Pursuit.

Time to head off on my travels again and stride off into the new decade in a more positive frame of mind than I arrived, wobbly-legged. I'll soon be 100 years old and it certainly doesn't seem that long since I told you about Queen Victoria, the *Daily Express* being born, Mafeking and fashionable small shoes that had the chiropodists rubbing their hands from plenty of potential business.

No doubt more challenges lay ahead. In fact, one could say that the biggest test of my life since the heady days of my birth was about to jump out and surprise me!

11

1990-2000
THE NEW AGE

Now entering my nineties, the decade proved a milestone in more ways than one. My own thoughts were that my general health (having just undergone a BUPA check up) seemed a bit up and down. My top half looked in pretty good shape but I couldn't claim to be well all over as my 100th birthday approached and with it a welcome telegram from her Majesty the Queen.

However, it wasn't the fact that I could still get around without the aid of a walking stick but more to the point that some thought my face was out of condition. Maybe a visit to the plastic surgeon would transform my looks and give me a new lease of life.

The macho, power hungry attitudes of the 1980s gave way in the late nineties to the 'new man', sensitive, paternal and prone to the odd tear or two. I get a bit emotional myself sometimes.

The public hadn't taken to Margaret Thatcher's Poll Tax, leading to riots in Trafalgar Square and damage throughout central London. Think back to my 1930s. Has anything much changed?

The Trade and Industry secretary, Michael Heseltine, embarked on a programme of coal pit closures, with a devastating effect on my northern 'heartlands' communities.

Barings Bank collapsed under the losses accrued by one of its Far East derivatives dealers, Nick Leeson, who became known as the 'rogue trader.'

New Labour celebrated the rise to power of Prime Minister Tony Blair after their 1997 election victory over John Major's Conservatives. This had been the first Labour administration since the dark, strike ridden days of Jim Callaghan in 1979. With it came hope of a more egalitarian approach towards my game from government, although I'll let you judge if I've been treated any better by governmental departments and agencies since.

An awkward befriending and glad handing of British youth culture by government, known as 'Cool Britannia', came and soon went. The phenomenon included bands such as Oasis and Blur, the film *Trainspotting* and Damien Hurst's pickled sheep, none of which was my cup of tea. In fact, a part of Hurst's window artwork at the Eyesto'rm gallery in central London was thrown away by a cleaner, who thought it was a pile of rubbish left over from a party the previous night.

A bomb at Canary Wharf in February 1996 galvanised minds in Northern Ireland. All large events during the seventies and eighties carried the worry of bomb scares, including my Test matches, so it came as welcome news when stop-start negotiations culminated in the Good Friday Peace Accord, signed on 10th April 1998. Too late for the 1997 Grand National though, postponed to the Monday and the course cleared, although no explosives were found.

Tragedy in Paris in 1997 as a car crash caused the death of Princess Diana and Dodi Fayed, followed by a nationwide outpouring of grief. Extraordinary scenes of emotion swept the country.

In the sky, Haley's Comet made a once in a lifetime visit and equally rarely, in Britain at least, 1999 featured the disappearance of the sun in a total (if you were in Cornwall) solar eclipse.

Nelson Mandela's 27 years in jail as a political prisoner in South Africa came to an end in 1990, as did the apartheid regime that separated people on the basis of their colour.

Tina Turner became the Queen of Rugby League with her *What You Get Is What You See* hit, adopted as the anthem for the ARL's Winfield Cup. Also, her *Simply the Best* seemed to play out on the public address after every and any big match, a legacy I'm not quite sure we can thank her for...

Born out of Radio 2's sport department in the good old days when, on Saturday afternoons and occasionally midweek evenings, Radio 2 would split to give music on FM and sport on Medium Wave, Radio 5 Live first aired on August Bank Holiday 1990. Radio 5 Live has featured Rugby League since, although maybe not as often as I would have liked.

How are the in-laws?

Before launching into the traumatic and complicated events of the 1990s, a quick word about my relationship with the 'in-laws.'

Incredible though it may sound today, the Cold War between the two rugby codes was still raging. Whilst the two codes rubbed along reasonably well enough up north, the RFU still imposed restrictions that defied both logic and the law. As late as 1995 any player appearing under League rules was immediately 'professionalised' and ran the risk of ostracisation from his Union club.

League was banned in the armed forces and it was a struggle for any student team to get recognition until David Hinchliffe's Sports (Discrimination) Act (1994) opened the door for forces and students to play Rugby League.

High profile Union code switchers still abounded. The lure of playing rugby for a living suited the better players and the opportunity of a famous name convert was a coup for the successful club and a fillip for their fans who on the whole still saw the other code as an enemy bent on League's destruction. I must say that this point of view, with a few honourable exceptions, probably wasn't far off the mark. The likes of Offiah, Gibbs, Devereux, Davis, Bateman, Ellis, Moriarty, Ackerman, Innes, Botica, Tuigamala, Scott Quinnell, Fallon and many others signed over and had successful League careers to a greater or lesser extent.

Some were somewhat less successful. All Black John Gallagher, for example, arrived at Headingley after a £350,000 transfer from the NZRU and never recovered from a shaky start, some clatterings and being stretchered off after a spear tackle against St Helens.

It could go wrong though. One unfortunate, Steve Pilgrim, found himself in rugby purgatory. Having had a run out on trial for Leeds 'A' team (featuring in the match programme as AN Other or A Trialist, as so many did in those days) he was identified, the whistle blown and a ban from Twickenham ensued. Poor Steve didn't make the mark in League so was consigned to rugby oblivion until his Union imposed exile for playing Rugby League expired. Incredible in a civilised democracy, but that's how it was then.

Warrington-born former London Broncos utility-back Adrian Spencer was forced to withdraw from the 1994 Varsity match at Twickenham because he had been an amateur Rugby League player.

Rumour has it that the 1995 Welsh RL squad was refused tickets for a Wales v Scotland RU game and even the Welsh RU prodigal son, Jonathan Davies had been refused entry to Cardiff Arms Park in his capacity as a radio commentator having taken the League shilling. Grim days for sport.

Better news as Rugby Union finally dropped the amateur pretence and went professional in 1995 opening the door for some *rapprochement* and the spectacle of the two 'cross code' challenges between the respective champions Wigan and Bath in 1996. The League fixture was first, played at Maine Road and won by Wigan, 82-6 (Martin Offiah modestly limiting himself to just the six tries). Rumour had it that the Wigan management didn't want Bath humiliated by a 'nilling' but the look on Sean Edward's face when Bath scored their try could have stopped a clock. Bath duly prevailed in the Union rules return match at Twickenham, the score more of a contest at 44-19.

A further thaw in the climate enabled Wigan to enter the Rugby Union Middlesex 7s at Twickenham in 1996, and I allowed myself a wry smile when the Pies brought the trophy back to Central Park.

Whilst the London Broncos were afforded use of Harlequin's

Stoop Memorial Ground in 1995 there were still those in the press who held a dim view of me. I could write a book about my treatment by the media (in fact, I have done) but I'll leave the last word on the end of the Cold War to Michael Herd. In an obviously considered and thoroughly researched article published in the London *Evening Standard* of the time he described Rugby League as: "a game for ape-like creatures watched by gloomy men in cloth caps." Where did you get your manners, Michael?

Domestic Rugby League (pre 1996)

For the first five years of the decade the championship had been Wigan's all the way. At least it was only by points difference over the Saints in 1992 and a three-way tie with Bradford Northern and Warrington the year after.

The inclusion of a new club, Scarborough Pirates, in 1991 brought the number of pro clubs to 36, an equal of the previous record. Time for another reshuffle so the 1991/2 season saw yet another change in league format with a change to a three division structure, 14 in the first and third divisions and, curiously, only eight (home and away twice) in the second.

Scarborough only lasted a year and by the 1993/4 season, surprise surprise, back to two divisions as the bottom three clubs Nottingham City, Blackpool Gladiators and Chorley Borough disappeared to the amateur ranks. Henry VIll has nothing on Rugby League when it comes to wielding the chopper!

The disappearance of Chorley Borough was only temporary as Chorley Chieftains reappeared for the somewhat rushed Centenary season. Always footloose and fancy free, Chorley briefly relocated to Preston North End's Deepdale ground and assumed the more neutral moniker of Lancashire Lynx.

The 1995 Centenary season - Wigan's again - was largely regarded as a bit of a damp squib. Apart from the teams in the 11-club first division adopting old shirt designs there was little else in the way of ceremony or celebration. Perhaps eyes were on the controversial switch to summer and the brass that would come with it.

The competition had again been re-split into three divisions which meant that no sooner had the last winter season finished, then it was time to swap bovril for ice cream for the first summer season (or Super League 1, as we must learn to love it) to start. Little consideration for the players, as usual.

Dwindling Challenge

A little of the Challenge seemed to have disappeared from the Cup as mighty Wigan took on all-comers continuing on from the eighties by winning eight finals in a row. If you were a Cherry and White supporter the annual pilgrimage to Wembley could pretty much be taken for granted. As for the losers it was a case of, "Oh well, we got there didn't we?"

"Get yer records here," as the 1990 Wigan versus Warrington Challenge Cup final broke an amazing 14. Some of these included Wigan becoming the first team to win three successive Challenge Cups, going on to pass Leeds's record of 10 victories and in doing so appeared in the most Wembley finals of 16, as well as Wembley wins in 10. Andy Gregory became the first player to win two Lance Todd Trophies with a little extra in collecting a record fifth medal.

Wigan 28 Castleford 12 in 1992 inflicted Castleford's first defeat at Wembley after their previous four successful visits, lastly in 1986.

Richie Ayres of Widnes got his marching orders, sent off in the 65th minute of the 1993 final against Wigan after using his elbow on Martin Offiah. This game also produced a rare brawl after Bobbie Goulding put in a high and late tackle on Jason Robinson. A good job four subs were used for the first time.

Francis Cummins of Leeds became the youngest ever player to score at Wembley in the 1994 final, eclipsing Shaun Edwards' record by one day to set a new mark of 17 years 200 days. This game proved a money spinner with receipts going over the £2m mark for the first time. However, some animosity must have been brewing up when Wigan Chairman, Jack Robinson didn't thank the coach John Dorahay at the winners' banquet. The next day, Dorahay received his P45 and thus become the quickest coach ever to be sacked after winning at Wembley. In an earlier round in that year's competition, poor old Blackpool Gladiators assumed an unwanted claim to fame. Blackpool hardly laid a glove on Huddersfield who racked up a score of 142-4, a world record for senior Rugby League.

Another record during 1995 when Leeds and Wigan became the first teams to meet in consecutive Challenge Cup finals, also the first final under the 10-metre rule and a first for in-goal touch judges.

With Wembley's capacity reduced to the high 70,000's, and ticket prices on the rise, I was still regularly filling the place.

Ancient and Loyal

The Pie Eaters, Cherry and Whites or Riversiders, to use three of their nicknames, continued to dominate domestic affairs during the early nineties.

Six more championships were to be won on the trot following on from the successful late eighties. Not content with being top dogs in one competition they also won consecutive Challenge Cups from, and inclusive of, 1990 to 1995. It took a huge shock result by Salford to take Wigan's scalp 26-5 on 11th February 1996 and finally bring their magnificent cup run to an end.

Added to the Challenge Cup run, Wigan's trophy haul took in four Regal Trophy finals, four Premierships, one Lancashire Cup and two World Club Challenge games all in the space of six seasons.

The first National Lottery draw took place on 19th November 1994, but a safer bet would be that Wigan would clean up. That year their dominance extended to all five available cups, being the Challenge Cup, Regal Trophy, League Championship, Premiership, World Club Challenge and even BBC Sports Personality Team of Year.

Whilst Wigan were the recognisable public face of Rugby League, there were the doom merchants who felt their virtual monopoly was strangling interest and a change on the winner's rostrum wouldn't go amiss.

Little did anyone foresee that a sea change was just around the corner signalling a brave new era and with it the end of Wigan's dominance. The game was ready to catch Wigan up and go fully professional.

Super League revolution

A case of onto the motorway for some and down the lane for others! My latest revolution started when Maurice Lindsay, the boss of the RFL, received an offer from News Corporation, on behalf of their subsidiary, BSkyB television, that seemed too good to refuse.

My proposed 'facelift' sent reverberations through the Rugby League world with some clubs not too pleased with what the 'surgeon's knife' had in mind.

Part of the deal, announced to the Rugby League Council in a meeting at Headingley on 5th April 1995, would transfer the professional playing season to summertime, and £77m would be available over five years on the basis that some clubs would be merged to make a 14-team league.

These would be Bradford, Halifax, Leeds, St Helens and Wigan plus Calder (Castleford, Featherstone, Wakefield), Cheshire (Warrington, Widnes), Cumbria (Barrow, Carlisle, Whitehaven, Workington), Humberside (Hull, Hull KR), Manchester (Oldham, Salford), South Yorkshire (Doncaster, Sheffield), London, Paris and a second French team. Good grief!

A first division would contain the remaining 11 clubs plus a Welsh XIII, but no Doncaster, who had succumbed to receivership.

The package was voted through by the 32 senior clubs plus associate members Blackpool and Nottingham. Chorley abstained and found themselves out of the picture altogether.

This went down like a lead balloon for the likes of Featherstone, Salford and Widnes who missed the cut and equally spelt commercial disaster for the likes of Keighley and Batley who were already gearing up for expected promotion.

A lynch mob hue and cry ensued. Keighley reckoned their omission would cost them £300,000 and served a writ on the RFL for £500,000, ultimately unsuccessful. The Minister for Sport raised a debate in the House of Commons. Fans of the excluded clubs protested angrily on the pitch feeling that their chairmen had been part of a '40 pieces of silver' carve up and, with passions at boiling point, for some it was one family quarrel too many, giving up their support for the game altogether.

At a meeting at the Hilton Hotel, Brighouse on 30th April the offer was increased to £87m and proposals modified to a 12-team Super League without the mergers. Places were allocated on where clubs finished the 1994/5 season plus London and Paris, although no second French team. There would be two other divisions to include Chorley after all, but no Welsh team. Widnes voted against and Keighley were absent, in congress with their lawyers.

Just as calamitous down under, the Australian Super League break away left two competitions as the predominantly Sydney-based clubs plus Newcastle stayed loyal to the ARL, fomenting a media war, loss of public faith in the game and an expensive and bitter court battle. What a mess, our very own mad cow disease.

The implementation of Super League had created a two-tier system. There were clubs who received a £700,000 grant each season, and those left semi-professional. The gap between was huge. Look at the damage caused to Widnes and Keighley's exclusion and the waste and rancour left by their unsuccessful legal actions against the RFL. In later years Dewsbury and Hunslet's refused bids for promotion showcased the 'haves and have-nots' decision making at the time.

If the game was to achieve its potential it would need committed full-time players. Without being disrespectful, we still had plumbers and brickies playing at the top level on a part-time basis. The money on offer could bring us professional players but in hindsight not necessarily professional clubs. One could say that the likes of Bradford, armed with their new nickname, 'Bulls' took off like *Concorde* whilst other clubs took to the marketing challenge like a duck to concrete. With marketing guru Peter Deakin at the helm, Bradford had the gumption to 'take the Bull by the horns' and sell the club as had never previously been attempted, creating a family spectacle in and around their giant

Odsal bowl on match days. A massive surge of interest in the local community saw crowds flocking in and spending their money on anything with a 'Bulls' logo on it.

Others dragged their feet, notably Leeds who still favoured winter, and some made what could only be described as a dog's dinner of the entertainment that new fans to the game arrived expecting. Some clubs had too much catching up on the field to do to fully concentrate on their off-field activities, others lacked or begrudged committing resources to the new dark arts of 'branding' and 'customer care.'

Luckily, hasty expansion plans (Barcelona and Berlin, for goodness sake) were never rushed through and Cardiff as a naturally-located Welsh candidate could have been a possibility had we really wanted and been committed to their introduction. Newcastle United football club made enquiries, and rumours abounded of moving York to form the basis of a Gateshead 'franchise.'

Major decisions on behalf of the game were in the hands of the likes of Chris Caisley (Bradford), David Howes (St Helens) and Nigel Wood (Halifax) who all wore two hats, being executives of their clubs and also of Rugby League (Europe) Ltd, the body established to explore marketing and financial planning of the new competition. Whilst all no doubt men of honour, the potential conflict of interest for those managing the competition having vested interests elsewhere in the game was both clear and unhealthy.

In with the new - Championship (post 1996)

The Super League era started with a bang. It kicked off at the Charlety Stadium, Paris on 29th March 1996 with Sheffield Eagles the 30-24 sacrificial lambs on Paris St Germain's *debut* in front of 17,873 Parisians. Just as football "came home" with Skinner and Badiel's *Three Lions* Euro '96 anthem, in my game, *When The Saints Go Marching In* became the theme during that first Super League summer season.

Having already secured the Challenge Cup prior to the

culmination of the very first Super League summer season, the Saints continued on the trophy trail by pipping Wigan to the title by just one point (still first past the post, no play-offs then.)

The high drama of a thrilling end of season run in with Wigan unfolded into pure theatre as Saints' travelling army descended on London to take on the Broncos, the points secured with a last-minute try to win the day 28-32. Definitely a nerve-wracking moment as Apollo Perilini looked as if he had scored the vital points but the referee handed it over to the video ref for what seemed like an eternity. Finally euphoria as the red vees' got the decision of a try via the big screen.

More nail-biting tension in a tight-fought match at Castleford, definitely not for the faint-hearted. The final result to the Saints by 16-20 doesn't tell the full story, Cas denied a late try with a wonder tackle by two Saints players when all seemed lost.

It was jamboree time in Paris with perhaps 4,000 Saints fans gathering at the Charlety Stadium to see if their side could get the better of Paris St Germain. Mixing with the Parisians over the weekend was a joy to behold, and in one romantic act a Saints fan proposed to his girlfriend at the top of the Eiffel Tower. There were amazing scenes of red and white favours when the Saints took to the field for their pre-match warm up. The players were simply stunned at the travelling support and their faces of awe summed it all up. Paris were no match and lost 12-32.

Sheffield at home in the penultimate game proved an easy victory by 68-2 and so to Warrington and the newly named Wolves at home, only one point separated the Saints from Wigan. With 18,098 fans packed like sardines into Knowsley Road, Saints took it in their stride with a 66-14 win and with it the very first Super League crown, a single point ahead of their oldest rivals.

Incidentally, the mighty Leeds finished third from bottom just above Paris, although sadly for bottom-placed Workington the relegation trap door opened. For the rest of Super League it spelt the end of those idyllic journeys through the tranquil Lake District to Derwent Park.

The second summer season turned out to be an easy ride for the Bulls from Bradford, who claimed their first title since 1980/81, finishing on 40 points with big celebrations at the Don Valley Stadium, Sheffield. Their nearest challengers were the lads from London who lagged behind on 33 points, themselves four clear of Saints. Paris again finished next to last with the Oldham Bears, playing under their new moniker, went down, went bust and re-emerged without their fur.

Sadly for Parisians and the French game generally, by 1998 their club was told to take a 'sabbatical' from which we all knew they would not return. Some fans were not convinced that the fledgling club had been given enough breathing space to become established, whilst others thought they should never have been in Super League at the expense of 'traditional' clubs in the first place. *Au revoir* to the Eiffel Tower, the River Seine and for the romantics, wine, women and song but come on in Hull and Salford, although without wishing to be disrespectful to the bridge and docks, not quite as alluring as an away trip as Paris in the spring.

A rejuvenated Leeds took Wigan all the way in 1998 finishing just four points behind in the final league table, setting up my very first grand final at Old Trafford, which also made the Premiership competition redundant. In fact, Wigan had thrown down the gauntlet to the Saints in the final two Premiership finals by beating the old enemy 44-14 in the penultimate final before 35,013 and 33-20 in the very last one, watched by a crowd of 33,385.

In what would become the season's finale and grow to a massive draw card for me in recent years, Wigan met Leeds in a rain-soaked final before 43,533 excited fans. With the rain lashing down, Wigan triumphed 10-4 with Jason Robinson nipping in under the posts to score the winning try and break the hearts of the Rhinos.

Poor old Dewsbury were denied promotion despite having won their divisional grand final. Under new stricter rules the club had to undertake a health check regarding ground capacity, support and financial health. Dewsbury supporters could be forgiven if their anger echoed long and hard around the sport although their management knew the reality was that planning consent for the minimum upgraded capacity was not in place, nor the money to build it.

The last championship race of the century featured 14 clubs with Wakefield coming up and the barmy army of Gateshead Thunder being voted in as a completely new entity. For aspiring applicants it had been a three-horse race in terms of Swansea and Cardiff also submitting bids (no lessons learned here from Paris).

Bradford came to the fore again in finishing top of the league five points ahead of the Saints. In the elimination play-off game Bradford crushed the Saints challenge by 40-4 at fortress Odsal, so the Saints had to face Castleford at home to secure a final placing. A comfortable 36-6 result meant the ever cunning Ellery Hanley could lead his troops into one more crack against the Bulls. In another rain effected final before an increased crowd of 50,717 the Saints played their 'get out of jail' card in a controversial game by coming back from a half-time deficit of 2-6 to finally take the Championship, 8-6.

Once again Huddersfield took the wooden spoon but like the previous season had a guardian angel on hand as Hunslet befell a similar fate to Dewsbury. In what turned out to be their only Super League season, Gateshead Thunder, led superbly by ex-Saints coach Shaun Mcrae, finished a respectable sixth with 39 points including a very impressive 32-20 home win against his former club.

Not all my fans liked my new suit, but these things take time to settle down, and the new format meant never a dull moment for the top half of the table, everyone challenging for places until the last game of the season.

Taking on the Challenge

A refreshing change in 1996 as the Salford shock win over Wigan in the earlier stages enabled a 'Wiganless' final as Saints took on Bradford Bulls, and the first major cup to wing its way to Knowsley Road after 20 barren years.

The Saints were narrowly down at half-time by 12-14 and more misery followed for their red and white army of fans as Bradford increased their lead to 12-24 to leave one half of the stadium pondering defeat. Cometh the hour, cometh the man in wily Saints scrum-half Bobbie Goulding. Under a hot, dazzling sun the fight-back commenced as Goulding duly 'bombed' Bradford out of the game. Three times the cheeky half-back launched massive 'up 'n' unders' at the Bradford line. Unfortunately for luckless Nathan Graham, the Bradford fullback misjudged on all three occasions and consequently three tries were scored. With a final score of 40-32 to the Saints, and great relief of the Saints contingent, it was time to shed the bridesmaid tag.

Robbie Paul of Bradford caught the eye of the pressmen and was awarded the Lance Todd Trophy having created his own slice of glory in the supreme effort of scoring a first ever cup final hat-trick, but he would no doubt have swapped it all for a winner's medal.

The 1997 final staged a repeat performance as the Saints triumphed again 32-22 and with it the first back-to-back cup wins for the club. The game did have a proud significance for me being my Centenary final. Who would have thought it all those years ago? Unfortunately, a bomb scare prior to the game curtailed the pre-match festivities and poor Paul Loughlin collected his fifth loser's medal, three as a Saints player and two against the Saints. I often forget that Apollo Perilini and Vila Matautia were the first ever Samoans to win Challenge Cup medals and since then there has been Freddie Tuilagi as well in grand finals.

When all seemed lost in terms of David beating Goliath in a final, up stepped Sheffield Eagles in slaying Wigan 17-8 with Mark Aston taking the Lance Todd Trophy. Wigan were massive (14-1 on with one bookie, I recall) favourites, with many saying Sheffield needn't bother turning up. Yet to their credit the Wigan fans took it on the chin and gave Sheffield a great ovation at the end. Some suggested it was the biggest upset of all time. This final featured a record 11 overseas players, with six turning out for Sheffield and five within Wigan's ranks. All in all a great day for Sheffield who picked up £100,000, whilst Chairman Tim Adams collected at 33-1 on a £1,000 bet on his side winning.

The last final of the decade, and indeed the last one at Wembley, saw Leeds triumph at last after years of disappointment. The Virgin entrepreneur, Richard Branson, minus his tie and grinning every step of the way, led out the London Broncos for their first ever Challenge Cup final. Richard's Virgin Express hit the buffers as his team ran out of steam against a Leeds onslaught to finish well beaten by 52-16. No other team before had clocked up more than 50 points and the record aggregate Saints and Bradford managed a couple of years earlier was short lived as Leeds versus London produced 78 points. The game equalled Huddersfield's effort in 1915 in terms of the highest number of tries in a final by the winner.

Welcome respite for the Headingley men, their first Challenge Cup since 1978, such a long time ago for a big club. Leroy Rivett (Lance Todd winner) created history when running in for four tries to eclipse Robbie Paul's first Challenge Cup final hat-trick in 1996. Such is the fickle nature of glory that Leroy soon became the forgotten man when his form afterwards deserted him. Worse still, he crashed his mate's Ferrari only days after. Ouch!

Who's nicked the family silver?

After saying farewell to the County Championships and the BBC 2 Floodlit Trophy in the eighties, more silverware got 'mugged' from my life in the nineties. I don't suppose old Fagan's little urchins could have pinched the family heirlooms any faster.

The two County Cups fought for with such pride since 1905/06 were destined for the scrap heap, and if that wasn't enough to contend with, the Regal Trophy came to a sad conclusion as well.

Charity became a thing of the past with the Shield going, going, gone, while the Premiership finally faltered.

Other silver items disappeared when gold winner's rings became a fashion item for the Championship winners.

Let's remember a few landmarks from these competitions. It finished 0-0 in the first Lancashire Cup final between Wigan and Leigh (16,000) with Leigh failing to score in the replay as the game went Wigan's way 8-0 (10,000), both games played at Broughton.

Wigan triumphed 21 times including a record six on the trot just after the Second World War, as well as being defeated finalists on 14 occasions.

Again, Wigan went on to achieve the highest ever score of 34 points in a final against a luckless Warrington who mustered eight points in 1985.

The 1953 final between Wigan and Saints attracted the highest attendance of 42,793 at Station Road, Swinton. Anyone remember jumping off the train and straight into the ground at Station Road?

No fanfare of trumpets heralded the last final as Wigan took a tense game 4-5 at Knowsley Road in front of a passionate 20,534 crowd. Wigan, having been successful with two penalties and a drop-goal in the first half, held out as the Saints could only muster two penalties during the second period. The Saints did have the chance of a drop-goal but persisted in trying to breach a resolute defence.

Over in the White Rose county, Hunslet gained the honour of taking the first Yorkshire Cup in the 1905 defeat of Halifax 13-3 (18,500).

Leeds ended up as top dogs with 17 successes, runners-up four times. Bradford 11 Huddersfield 4 took the top attendance prize in 1949 with 36,000 inside Headingley.

One for nostalgists, with the 1922 final between York and Batley attracting 33,719 as York took the cup back to the Minster City by 5-0. How times change.

The farewell final in 1992 witnessed Wakefield taking the honours by clipping the wings of Sheffield Eagles, 29-16.

Whether it was right or wrong, my life had to progress minus some very valuable sponsorship. Money down the drain if you ask me and certainly a far cry from the seventies when sponsorship helped save my bacon.

A Regal event

Formerly the John Player Trophy, the Regal Trophy (not silver I may add) was also destined for the scrap heap in the nineties.

Wigan took four Regal Trophies in the nineties, against Halifax 24-12 in 1990, Bradford Northern 15-8 in 1993, Warrington 40-10 in 1995 and finally St Helens, 25-16. It did seem strange that the Warrington game produced a better crowd than the Saints match, the two attendances being 19,636 and 17,950.

The Wire overcame Bradford 12-2 in 1991, Leeds failed to score against Widnes in 1992 with Widnes clocking up 24 points, whilst in 1994 Castleford were to shock Wigan by 33-2. I don't think anyone at the game or watching on the BBC could quite believe that one.

All in all another sad day as one more trophy disappeared, not least for the BBC, for whom the Regal Trophy was a cheap live sport filler, and easy ratings for Saturday afternoon *Grandstand*.

Charity begins at home

Well, it's not only Madonna who went on a *Holiday* because my bosses at the RFL decided that after the Green and Golds had taken me to the cleaners in 1982 we were all in need of respite and could do with a welcome all expenses paid break.

I actually thought that my leg was being pulled when it was agreed to take the first Charity Shield game to the Isle of Man in 1985, home to the Manx cat with no tail, 180ft Laxey Wheel (made in Wigan of course), the famous T.T. motorbike races and a castle clock with only one finger. Good grief! I could get used to this life.

In the first encounter between the cup winners of Wigan and champions of Hull KR the latter suffered a defeat at the Douglas Bowl by 34-6 in front of 4,066 fans.

The three-legged island became a dream venue for many of my family for the next three years, as Halifax versus Castleford 9-8 (3,276), Wigan versus Halifax 44-12 (4,804) and Widnes versus Wigan 20-14 (5,044) all enjoyed a marvellous weekend away. Sadly, all things have to come home, and just like the Manx Kipper I ended back in Blighty for my next adventure.

Anfield to be precise, home to Liverpool FC, as a decent crowd of 17,263 converged on Scouse country to see Widnes beat Wigan 27-22. The charity adventure then took me to Swansea for some South Wales sea air as Widnes again took the Shield against Wigan 24-8 with 11,178 Taffs in attendance. Well not quite true I suppose, but one can dream.

Gateshead played host next as Wigan overcame Hull 22-8 with

10,248 on. A bottle of brown ale, please! In fact, make that two.

The Charity Shield returned to Gateshead in 1992 with St Helens taking care of Wigan 17-0 before a crowd of 7,364.

My family did get to sample a drop of the black stuff when, after a break in the competition, Wigan met Leeds over in Dublin. Leeds took a thrashing and reports suggested that whilst the Leeds camp sobered up the next morning, Wigan were already back home and on the training park.

As Super League became more serious, the Charity Shield became a distraction and my bosses decided Rugby League had had enough weekends away. Anybody would have thought we were all enjoying ourselves!

The Grand Final beckons

Having run since 1974/5, the scrapyard beckoned for the Premiership Trophy.

Once again, Wigan dominated affairs in beating St Helens three times, with other victories against Castleford and Leeds. The Leeds game had the scoreboard going berserk in a one-way stroll for Wigan 69-24 and cold comfort for the Yorkshire side.

The Saints managed to defeat Wigan in 1992 and in doing so stopped their fieriest rivals from taking a clean sweep of all trophies on offer. Hull and Widnes were once again to meet in a final with it going Hull's way 14-4.

The competition was a breath of fresh air whilst it lasted, especially when the final went to Old Trafford for a big end of season jamboree. A grand day out, but grander things to come with its replacement.

On a final note, Wigan and St Helens competed for the last Lancashire Cup, Regal Trophy and Premiership - all going the way of the Cherry and Whites. By the way, has anyone seen the pots?

New faces

The nineties saw a swathe of new outfits come and, in some cases, go again just as quickly, and I don't just mean the *Spice Girls*.

The ARL Winfield Cup competition increased to a total of 20 clubs, breaking new ground in the form of Auckland Warriors, Adelaide Rams and Perth Western Reds, only the former surviving a later cull.

With the Super League schism in Australia came a second club in Brisbane (the South Queensland Crushers) and the Hunter Mariners to rival the existing Newcastle Knights. Both evaporated when peace broke out and the two Aussie factions reunited as the National Rugby League, but Melbourne Storm survived.

In the European (quickly to become English) Super League new, if briefly lived, clubs in Paris St Germain and Gateshead Thunder. A lovely 25,000 seater stadium in Paris which could have been a mainstay of French RL went to waste.

South Wales didn't get its Super League status, but a short-lived club was admitted to the bottom of the three divisions, in the half-hearted form of one-season wonders, South Wales RLFC.

International boom and bust

I really enjoyed the nineties. It was an eventful and varied decade for the international game and I received some long overdue respect and recognition from within and outside the sport, a time when Tests were often played out live on national television to audiences of millions. The era set the foundations for a real expansion in the stature of international Rugby League but, as so often the case, the momentum was lost by the end of the decade.

March and April 1990 saw home and away games against France, a 4-8 win in Perpignan but an 18-25 success for the brave French boys at Headingley.

Anticipation in May 1990 as the Lions tour to Papua New Guinea and the Pacific Islands departed. Perhaps Papua New Guinea's greatest moment came at the Danny Leahy Oval in Goroka with a surprise win 20-18. The game was suspended in the 14th minute as police attempted to control exuberant locals with tear gas. At least 11,598 got in, many by questionable means! On to Port Moresby where PNG couldn't repeat the feat, Britain winning 8-40 with 7,837 on.

Forward to New Zealand for a three Test series opening with a win for Great Britain 10-11 at Palmerston North (8,073), a second Test win 14-16 at Auckland (7,843) with one back for New Zealand 21-18 at Christchurch (3,133.)

Unprecedented by today's standards, the 1990 season concluded with a visit from the Kangaroos, making a full house of Test opponents that year. Off to a flyer with a win at Wembley 19-12 (54,569) soon turned to a familiar tale with defeats at Old Trafford (10-14) in front of 46,615 and at Elland Road 0-14 (32,500.)

During the tour things got a little heated between the Australian coach Bobby Fulton and BBC reporter Harry Gration after a hard fought, skirmish-ridden game at Wakefield Trinity. Opening by asking if he thought the Aussies had let the Wakefield public down, the interview quickly degenerated as Bozo called into question Harry's understanding of the game, an accusation that wasn't well received by the seasoned BBC journalist.

> *Gration: "Did you feel things disintegrated a bit today?"*
> *Fulton: "That's your opinion. The penalties today - probably you don't know much about Rugby League, I dunno, I've never met you..."*
> *Gration (furious): "What right do you have to say that?"*
> *Fulton (voice rising): "I don't know who you are!"*
> *Gration: "I am asking you..."*
> *Fulton (angrier): "Do you even understand how the game is played?"*
> *Gration (indignant): "Yes, yes I do."*
> *Fulton (raging): "Don't you attack me for the way I answer questions if you want to interview me. If you don't, turn your tape off."*

Harry didn't need to be asked twice. Clunk.

To me, that little exchange typified Test Rugby League between the Poms and the Aussies, keenly contested, entrenched, no quarter. Anyway, the total turnout from the Tests and tour matches aggregated 259,544, a nice little earner.

Early 1991 again saw home and away fixtures against the

French, a win 10-54 in Perpignan and 60-4 at Headingley, as the French game started to fall into decline.

Later that year, Britain returned the compliment to the Kumuls, hosting the PNG side in a one-off Test at Wigan but showed little hospitality on the pitch, 56-4 (4,193.)

Barely a pause for breath as the Lions set off in May 1992 for a tour of the southern hemisphere. First call was a warm-up and gospel spreading exercise at Port Moresby for a 14-20 success over Papua New Guinea, then on to Australia.

The series started badly for the Poms with a 22-6 mauling in Sydney, attracting 40,141 Sydneysiders to the Footy Stadium but cheered up considerably with a famous victory at the Optus Oval, Melbourne 10-33, equalling the British record margin set in 1958. It couldn't continue though and an away series triumph eluded the Brits again as the chance was lost at Lang Park, Brisbane, 16-10.

Ah well, on to New Zealand, where after an opening loss 15-14 at the Palmerstone North Show Grounds Oval the series was drawn with a 16-19 win in Auckland, the last Test the Poms played at the much loved but fast fading Carlaw Park ex-vegetable patch.

There was no doubt about it, the international programme was booming again, and about time. Further proof was at hand later that year.

Where were you on 24th October 1992? Most of us were at the World Cup final at Wembley to set a new crowd record for international Rugby League of 73,631. Who will ever forget the little drummer boy leading out coaches Mal Reilly and Bob Fulton, behind them the two teams, through the chaos, smoke and cannon fire of Tchaikovsky's *1812 Overture*?

The game ended in a 6-10 win for Australia. Foreign Secretary, Douglas Hurd, was on the end of a round of booing by sections of the crowd in the wake of his governmental colleague, Michael Heseltine's, pit closure programme. Even in my old age I'm never far from controversy.

France were fast falling off the pace and another exchange in 1993 resulted in big wins for Britain, away at Carcassonne 6-48 and 72-6 in the floodlit return at Headingley.

Later that year the Kiwi tour of Britain arrived to an explosive start as new boy Jason Robinson scored two on his debut at Wembley in a 17-0 demolition (36,131.) Central Park staged another good British win 29-12 (16,502) and the whitewash was wrapped up at Headingley 29-10 (15,139) where Andy Farrell, now Britain's most frequent skipper, made his debut. A three-nil series to Britain, heady days!

Still running to a reasonably predictable schedule, what turned out to be the last full Ashes tour for a while started with a bang at Wembley for the 1994 Kangaroos. Shaun Edwards was sent off after a dangerous high tackle on Bradley Clyde, leaving a 12-man British rearguard action. Jonathan Davies flew over in the corner just after half-time and the British held on for a glorious 8-4 victory in front of a then British Test record crowd of 57,037. Downhill from there, I'm afraid, an 8-38 reverse at Old Trafford (43,930) then all or nothing at Elland Road. Great Britain 4 Australia 23 (39,468) left Britain a bridesmaid once again.

The Aussies continued their tour on to the Stade de la Mediterranee, Bezieres, for a one-off Test. Not France's finest moment as the 0-74 score was both the worst margin and worst 'points against' total ever at Test level. Around 11,000 saw the mighty Mal Meninga's last game on the Test stage.

The decade had seen something of a boom in Test match attendances though, no doubt assisted by Britain's record of having won four in a row. Nothing succeeds like success.

Elsewhere in 1994, international development continued and bore some fruit for Papua New Guinea who sprung a surprise 29-22 win over France at Port Moresby.

It was all going too well, and it was around now that the Super League war saw the ARL out in the cold. Many clubs and players had sided with the new Australian Super League regime leaving the traditional guardians of the Australian national game with the choice of selecting rebels who didn't want to play in the ARL's club competition, or selecting from a reduced pool of those still loyal.

The Halifax World Cup 1995! A ten-team competition, and one of my better celebrations, appropriately on my 100th birthday. Some truly wonderful matches, new faces in terms of Tonga, Western Samoa and South Africa, a feel good atmosphere and

burgeoning crowds all added up to a tremendous success. The
Wales team became a real hot ticket, selling out their matches and
bowing out only in the semi-final to England at Old Trafford.

In another memorable, misty night at Wigan, 26,263 squeezed
into Central Park to watch England 46 Fiji 0 in a World Cup game
that was granted Test status, getting Fiji's track record started. I'll
always remember a little knot of Fijian supporters singing a
Polynesian lament as the crowd filtered out after a booming chant
of "Fiji, Fiji, Fiji" had thundered round the ground in appreciation
of the islanders' extravagant ball handling. Of such nights are
Rugby League legends made.

The final at Wembley repeated the opening match but a
different result as the ARL-based team overcame England's best
8-16 with 66,540 on hand. To coin an advertising slogan of the time
"Wiz zis Rugby League you are spoiling us." *Excellente!*

An Emerging Nations competition ran alongside, introducing
the likes of Moldova, Morocco and Japan to a bigger stage, also
heralding stand alone Scotland and Ireland (defeated in the final at
a soggy Swinton by Cook Islands) teams and throwing together the
intriguing prospect of USA versus Russia at Northampton.

The alignment of the British and Australian seasons made
further long tours impossible and without the co-operation of the
ARL administration the Aussie team that arrived in Blighty in late
1996 represented only the new Australian Super League teams.
Nevertheless they had enough firepower to complete the
traditional 1-2 series win. All seemed gloom after Wembley, spirits
lifted after the series was saved at Old Trafford but again Aussie
proved too strong in the decider at a sell-out Elland Road.

The games were live on national television and well attended,
all was still looking good, but what a difference three years makes.

After two successful games in the Pacific, 4-72 against Fiji at
Nada (3,000) and 30-32 against Papua New Guinea at Lae (8,000),
the 1996 Lions tour to the Pacific Islands and New Zealand
declined into disaster and a 3-0 defeat. The first New Zealand tour
covered live on British television, via Sky albeit at an ungodly hour
in the early morning, saw a depleted Britain stagger with ever-
dwindling player strength from one defeat to another, 17-12 at

Auckland (9,000), 18-15 at Palmerston North (8,000) and 32-12 Christchurch (9,000.) Modest turnouts neither did the Kiwi team justice nor turned a profit. Things were going into decline.

By 1998 my crown had slipped. I'd disappeared onto satellite telly and my matches were shuffled from prime-time Saturday afternoons to the graveyard shift (in entertainment terms) of Saturday early evenings. The Kiwi tour began at the McAlpine in Huddersfield, the first real Test match there, won by New Zealand and on to the brand new Reebok Stadium in Bolton where a half-time British lead withered away to a heavy defeat. A last-minute drop-goal by Tony Smith (apparently his first ever) earned a draw at Watford which was something, but for home supporters, not a series to cherish.

With the Super League war over and with the French challenge having all but vanished, some reconciliation between the three world powers saw the 1999 Tri-Series staged in Australia and New Zealand. The event was a bit of a damp squib with disappointing crowds and part of the Great Britain party sent home early by the team manager, Maurice Lindsay, in an attempt to save costs, a public relations disaster. Oh, and inevitably an Aussie win in the final over the Kiwis.

Club Tropicana

If the international programme had boomed with a *Wham*, then fallen away again, what scope for international competition for my clubs? A nice little trip abroad always appeals, especially if it's somewhere sunny.

Britain's all conquering Wigan side represented Blighty as in the first three of the four World Club Challenges of the decade. A match up with Penrith in October 1991 at Anfield drew 20,152 for a convincing 21-4 scoreline, overseen by French referee Alain Sablayrolles.

Next up was Brisbane greeted by 17,746 in Central Park in October 1992, but this time a reverse as the Broncos scored 22 to Wigan's 8. Dennis Hale from New Zealand was the ref.

Down Under for a change in June 1994 to ANZ Stadium,

Wigan's 14-20 success over Brisbane leaving the 54,220 on hand dumbstruck.

The World Club Challenge 1997 was a more ambitious undertaking altogether. All the Super League teams in Europe and Australia were involved, being split into four groups then playing home and away fixtures at home and down under. Although the Europeans could point to a handful of wins such as Wigan's home and away wins over Canterbury, Leeds's defeat of Adelaide, Oldham's win over North Queensland, Sheffield's against Perth and, most memorably, London's over Canberra. During the group stages only Wigan progressed and that was due to a quirk in the unwieldy competition format. The difference in standards was pretty evident. The final was contested between Hunter Mariners - in their only season - and Brisbane, the Broncos easing home 36-12 watched by 12,000 at Ericsson Stadium, Auckland.

The early nineties saw the first stirrings of the Greatest Game in Russia and the development initiative was assisted by tours there by Fulham and York.

Let us not forget our *Treiziste* neighbours. The 1998 *Treize Tournoi* was a competition that pitted three of the French teams against two teams from the division one and the leader of division two. After home and away fixtures the top team from the French pool played the best English pool club in a play-off. Villeneuve Leopards beat Lancashire Lynx (the division two representative), 16-10, at the Stade de Toulouse (10,283) with the unusual postscript that one of the Lynx players was shot in a French nightclub during the post-match night out.

Sadly the Tournoi wasn't a commercial success, for the English clubs at least, and the exercise not repeated.

Infradig infrastructure

I've always said the three most important things about my original town centre Rugby League grounds were "embrocation, embrocation, embrocation."

The Valley Parade fire and Hillsborough and Heysel disasters in football had a disastrous knock on effect to Rugby League's aged and often crumbling grounds. The Taylor and Popplewell Reports that investigated those tragedies forced local authorities to impose strict ground safety improvements on sports stadia, with a devastating cost effect for some and condemnation for others.

These factors helped see off famous old grounds such as Fartown, Station Road, Thrum Hall, Watersheddings and Clarence Street, but had the effect of prompting their replacements in the first of a new breed of all-seater stadia, such as the Alfred McAlpine. Crikey, it had got so bad that St Helens had a match abandoned after four minutes when high winds blew part of the roof off, just missing the Warrington winger.

Leeds City Council had compulsorily purchased the run-down Parkside and moved Hunslet into the cavernous council owned Elland Road, home of Leeds United.

United's prolific yet strangely carthorse-like striker, Lee Chapman, famously blamed missing an open goal on the deteriorated playing surface...although Hunslet hadn't even played a match there yet. Happily, by 1995 Leeds City Council had built Hunslet a new home, the South Leeds Stadium, only a quarter of a mile from the original Parkside.

Widnes had played at Lowerhouse Lane since 1884, the ground named for Tom Naughton, the club secretary on his death in 1932. Halton Borough Council invested in new stands in 1996 and 1998 and Naughton Park took its current form, now called Halton Stadium.

My top brass had outgrown the insalubrious environs of Chapeltown Road and moved to the rather more befitting premises at Red Hall on the leafy Wetherby Road, Leeds.

Sponsors and finance

In the era of six-figure transfer fees for players, and prior to substantial television contracts, the game was still mainly underwritten by two factors; fans pockets and the 'working mans friends' of fags and beer.

Sponsors of the era trip off the tongue like a visit to the off-licence. Bass Headingley, Stones Bitter, Silk Cut and Regal. Shirt sponsors included Whitbread, Greenalls, Coors, Tetley, Carling, McEwans, Jennings and Thwaites amongst others. Don't forget our other national brands of British Coal and British Gas.

Later in the decade we got £87m from BSkyB and the curious offshoot of Super League milk as an early attempt at 'branding'.

Clubs themselves began to grasp the nettle by appealing to the family market with their own commercial entertainment bandwagons such as Cougarmania and Bullmania at Keighley and Bradford respectively. Not to everyone's taste, but the razzmatazz served its purpose in attracting younger fans, although only to the better spectacles, sometimes at the expense of more modest local clubs.

Personality clash

A factor of my starring role on satellite television has been the virtual disappearance from terrestrial telly, newspaper and media of many of our publicly recognisable personalities. Ellery Hanley continued to snub the press, even when Great Britain coach and others such as chippy Welshman Jonathan 'Jiffy' Davies, the pugnacious Andy Gregory, 'Chariots' Offiah and Garry Schofield gradually drifted out of the public gaze. However, personalities still abounded within the game.

The affable player turned Widnes then Leeds coach, Doug Laughton, was one such character. Chain smoking his way through the weekly 80 minutes, the redoubtable Doug had some memorable run-ins with the likes of Schofield and Bobbie Goulding. Doug spent money like it was going out of fashion, a one-man recruitment agency for Rugby Union converts.

I recall Gateshead Thunder's mascot, Captain Thunder, gesturing to the skies during a game at Headingley, and a few seconds later actually inducing lightning!

Talking of mascots, Ronnie the Rhino contested the 1997 General Election standing in the Leeds North West constituency and receiving over 140 votes. A few more and Prime Minister's Question Time might have cheered up a bit.

Tough as teak Kevin Ward broke his leg for Saints during a

televised game against Wigan. It was an appalling sight, especially when Kevin picked up the limp limb and put it straight.

In 1990 Mal Meninga, the Kangaroo legend, was voted BBC Overseas Sports Personality of the Year, succeeding world heavyweight champion boxer Mike Tyson.

I wonder how many of our current famous faces are known away from the grounds today?

Chariots

One of the few Rugby League personalities honoured with an MBE, Martin Offiah's list of achievements in his 14 seasons in the game are enough to impress any sports fan. Thirty three caps and 26 tries for Great Britain, five tries in eight appearances for England and a huge collection of all the various medals club Rugby League can offer adorn Martin's sideboard.

Having switched codes from Rosslyn Park RUFC to Doug Laughton's Widnes, Offiah then moved to Central Park for a world record fee of £440,000 as the Wigan management assembled the team that swept all before them in the early 1990s.

Ending his career at Salford, via London Broncos and Bedford RU (and a single appearance for *Emmerdale* in 1996!), Chariots lies third in the all-time list of League try scorers, behind legends Brian Bevan (796 tries) and Billy Boston (571) with 500.

There is debate as to whether this tally should include the 20 tries he scored in two seasons for Easts and St George, in the toughest league in the world. Some statisticians contend the familiar list we see in *Rothmans* - or *Gillette* as it is now known - is for tries scored in Britain or for British teams abroad only.

What isn't in dispute is the Wigan club record (shared by Shaun Edwards with a similar feat against Swinton the same year) of ten tries in a game, against Leeds on 10th May 1992. Another, the unforgettable blockbusting length of the field try against Leeds in the 1994 Challenge Cup final on a gloriously sunny Wembley afternoon, will live in the memory of all who saw it, and it gets played on telly from time to time as well.

Chariots had one function, as a devastating finisher with ball in hand, although Martin has shown some versatility outside of sport and been known to tread the boards in the West End theatre, most notably in *Mothers Day* at the Lyric Theatre in recent years. Talented lad, our Martin.

The Poacher

Within a year of entering the professional game on 14th September 1983 with Hull, Hunslet-born Garry Schofield was a full British Lion, making his debut as an 18-year-old on the 1984 tour.

Continuing to illuminate with his tricky stand-off play, masterful distribution and adroit kicking, Garry re-wrote the record books by scoring four tries at Wigan as Great Britain beat New Zealand in the 1985 Test series.

Schofield left Hull acrimoniously to join his hometown club of Leeds in October 1987 for a fee of £178,250, a move that the Hull faithful never forgave him for. Garry proudly wore the shirt and skippers arm band at Headingley in 250 appearances until his departure for Huddersfield in February 1996, where he made his inauspicious debut in coaching before winding down with short spells at Aberavon RU, Doncaster and finally Bramley on 25th July 1999.

A career that brought legend status, both in Britain and the ARL with three summer stints at Balmain and Western Suburbs, Garry's mantelpiece contains an OBE but precious few other medals, a consequence of remaining loyal to Leeds during the prime of his career, when the Wigan team outshone all. Playing in a record six Ashes series, Garry made a total of 46 Great Britain appearances, a record-equalling tally shared with Mick Sullivan, 13 of Schoey's appearances, between 1991/94, were as captain.

Whilst appearing occasionally in the media, as is so often the case there seems no role within the game for one of its greats.

The Iceman cometh

John Monie is quite probably the most successful coach the game of Rugby League has ever seen. He won Premiership Grand Finals on both sides of the world and is the only man to have coached an English and Australian club which have both won every trophy available to them in a single season!

These remarkable accomplishments were achieved with an unflappable approach to the job and a total dedication to winning, earning him the nickname of "The Iceman."

In his youth, Monie's renowned toughness was honed in the boxing booth which came to town with the rodeo and proved useful with New South Wales country club Woy-Woy, then Parramatta, Wigan and the Auckland Warriors.

Last coaching in England with the London Broncos, it is for his time at Wigan that people remember him, when the club won the league and cup double in an unprecedented four consecutive seasons.

Staying power

One of my venerable scribes, John Drake, knows a thing or two about the publishing world, so he's as good a man as any to recall the evolution of Rugby League newspapers and magazines during the nineties.

The start of the 1990/91 season saw something of a boom in terms of Rugby League publishing. In addition to the long-established *Rugby Leaguer* and *Open Rugby*, fans with deep pockets could now also splash out on one or more of the following new titles. A glossy tabloid style weekly named *Thirteen*, a brochure-style magazine called *Rugby League Highlights*, and to coincide with that year's Kangaroo tour, Australia's flagship paper *Rugby League Week* launched a British edition.

It wouldn't be surprising if many people were now left scratching their heads trying to recall any of the above, as unfortunately none made it to the end of the season. *Highlights* managed two issues, more notable for the number of errors it contained than anything truly worthy of its hefty cover price. *Rugby League Week*, despite a promise to stick around, packed their bags and headed home roughly the same time as the Kangaroos. A shame as this was undoubtedly a publication of real quality, but apparently little dedication to the cause of reporting on the British game alone. As for *Thirteen*, well the title proved prophetic, as there never was an issue 14.

However, two other titles that launched at the same time did manage to display a little more staying power, so much so that both are still around today.

One of those was the new independent weekly newspaper, *Rugby League Express*, a 16-page black and white tabloid sold for 50p, which successfully went for the clearest and perhaps most obvious gap in the market, providing match reports from all the weekend's games on a Monday morning. This was an age when the long established *Rugby Leaguer* was still a midweek paper, appearing on a Thursday and without match reports, while the national press were, well, just as bad at this kind of thing as they still are now.

The *League Express* front page carried a picture of Wigan forward Andy Platt being tackled by Mark Aston and Paul Broadbent who had helped Sheffield Eagles to a surprise 18-18 draw against the reigning champions at Central Park. In that weekend's other First Division games, Bradford Northern were beaten 14-10 at Odsal by Widnes, watched by a crowd of 6,701. Oldham recorded a shock 32-22 win over Leeds, Featherstone and Hull KR played out a 14-14 draw and Wakefield crushed Rochdale 42-6. Names that featured in reports elsewhere in that first ever edition which have since disappeared from the professional Rugby League scene included Nottingham City, Trafford Borough, Runcorn Highfield, Ryedale-York and Carlisle.

In Australia, Penrith Panthers were reported to have reached their first-ever Grand Final with a 30-12 semi-final win over Canberra Raiders, while in a centre-page feature, Widnes star Kurt Sorenson gave his views on the forthcoming season. There were no readers' letters until the following week. Hats off to George Bordessa (Liverpool), J Monaghan (Widnes) and B Lamport (Wakefield) who were the first correspondents to get their names in print, all welcoming the arrival of the new paper.

The only other survivor of this 1990 publishing bonanza was *The Greatest Game!*, a quarterly fanzine billed as 'the Voice of the

Rugby League Supporters Association.' Forget a trip to your local newsagent, the only way you were going to get your hands on this baby was by bumping into an RLSA volunteer flogging it outside the nearest ground on matchdays. For a pound, you got 24 pages of 'from the heart' opinion written by the people you stood next to on the terraces. With an editorial subtitled by a quote from Rugby League guru Jack Gibson - 'don't compromise and don't tell lies' - *TGG!* was setting its stall out early.

TGG! featured articles on ground safety following the Hillsborough disaster, a call for a fairer deal for second division clubs and a grumble at the RFL who were seen as allowing the new satellite TV station BSkyB to call the shots with regard to match scheduling, although the quality of their coverage got the thumbs up. Further in, the BBC were under fire, missed opportunities for Rugby League in the United States were debated and the RFL's marketing strategy (or lack of) was investigated.

To lighten the load a little, 'Jonathan & The King' claimed to be the game's first ever comic strip, and the Sin Bin offered a collection of amusing bloopers from other publications... although *TGG!* featured one of its own on the front cover, mis-spelling the name of Leeds' record signing from Rugby Union. Oops! Still, these days, few people in Rugby League would remember the name of John Gallagher (for it was he), let alone know how to spell it correctly.

Summing up the nineties

Good or bad? Well I suppose it depends on which rung of the ladder you were on in 1996, when a handful of teams were able to become fully-funded professionals and leave the rest of the game in their wake.

Part of my heart is filled with sadness that some of my grand old names are unlikely ever to challenge for the main trophies again. On the other hand, given the parlous financial state of the game prior to the News Corporation cash injection, I suppose it's a blessing we've still got a game to talk about. I shudder to think how I would have coped with a series of bankrupt clubs.

The second 'great split' of my life divided my family into 'haves and have nots' and for many there's still much bitterness amongst those cast adrift.

On the other hand, my change to summer brought me new family support along and marketing opportunities for those with the nous to take them. This doesn't sit well with everyone, although those who count themselves as 'traditionalists' who yearn for the good old days probably couldn't have supported my weary old bones the way they were. I suppose, like so often in my life, I've had to grasp the nettle and seek my fortune where the grass appears greenest.

Have the improved standards and entertainment available at the fast improving grounds of the top echelon of the game catapulted the sport into the public consciousness, appealing to a wider and younger market, or have they only served to produce a vulgar, 'dumbed down' pastiche of a traditional, dignified heritage? I'll let you decide.

A tremendous success with the 1995 World Cup went to waste as the momentum gathered notably in Wales wasn't converted into substantial permanent progress, there or anywhere else.

Either way, never a dull moment.

12

2001 ONWARDS
THE NOUGHTIES

Like a naughty pensioner, I just won't grow old graciously. For one whose end is forecast as regularly as the weather, I'm still kicking and screaming and in fact doing some of the growing up and exploring I should have done in my teenage years.

As ever I've got a few ups and downs to tell you about during the first decade of the new millennium, but after a shaky start I'm pleased to report that your old friend Rugby League has a twinkle in his eye at the moment...

By definition, memories take a few years in the making. Accordingly, these more recent years might not be so cloaked in the mists of time as my earlier chapters, but so much happens so quickly these days that some of the events of the noughties just might have passed you and me by already!

I wonder if the noughties will be looked back on as a golden age of the game? I hope so.

The curates egg that is Rugby League's fortunes continued to be good in parts. After a limping end to the nineties, with its unstable structure, internal wrangling and power struggles, such success as my game had seemed to be despite rather than because of myself. Not long into the new decade a way forward appeared out of the mist.

Whilst standards in the club game had been motoring ahead since the advent of full time professionalism in 1996, it was clear that at representative level the British game hadn't kept pace and needed a good shake up from top to bottom. This started in 2001 with what many people considered an act of heresy, the appointment of an overseas coach to the Great Britain team. Luckily, elsewhere a Swedish bloke had laid the ground for foreign coaching appointments, so the shock of an Australian taking the job wasn't what it could have been.

David Waite, it seems, was a 'systems man' and with his role expanding to Performance Director as Nick Halafihi struck out for pastures new, Waitey set about restructuring the whole shooting match. A logical progression for young players to progress through the ranks was required and this was put in place starting with the briefly reintroduced Roses (I'll never get used to 'Origin') as full international Test trials. This worked down through academy to 14-year-old schoolboy level, giving a total of 18 representative teams from top to bottom.

Retiring players such as Lee Crooks, Denis Betts and Dean Sampson were all involved in the structure, passing on their experience and benefiting themselves from an introduction to representative coaching.

The first signs of success within this structure came in December 2002 as the British schoolboys defeated their Australian counterparts at Knowsley Road and Headingley for a 2-0 win in a series, the first for 30 years.

With still no chief executive in place authority in the game seemed to include some executives wearing two hats. A member club of Super League (Europe), which had started off as a marketing initiative, could well have sway within Red Hall making fundamental decisions on the running of the game's structures. It couldn't be right that clubs run the game so at the end of 2001 an even keel was required at HQ and changes were afoot amongst the game's top brass.

Garry Schofield enjoyed success at amateur level before turning professional with Hull and developing into one of the finest stand-offs in the game's history. He first toured Australia in 1984, and went on to captain his country on the 1992 tour, and in that year's World Cup Final at Wembley. He became an integral part of the new-look Leeds side through the 1990s, and ended his career as a four-times tourist with 40 international caps to his credit. (pp379)

Kevin Ward built a reputation as a fierce prop forward with Castleford and St Helens, and was respected by the Australians for his Great Britain heroics. Indeed, he was one of the few players to be offered a club contract down under, enjoying premiership success with Manly.

Martin Offiah joined Widnes from Rosslyn Park RU in 1987 and became one of the game's true superstars. Moving to Wigan in 1991 for a world-record transfer fee of £440,000, he established himself as the world's best winger.

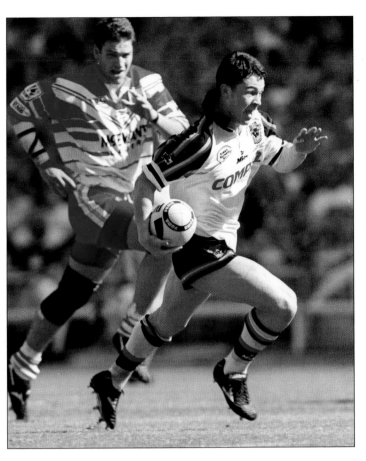

In 1996, Bradford's Robbie Paul became the first player to score a hat-trick of tries in a Challenge Cup Final at Wembley. He won the Lance Todd Trophy, but couldn't prevent St Helens winning the game. (pp364)

To herald the birth of Super League, Fiji hosted the 1996 World Nines. England's Paul Sculthorpe is pictured offloading against Papua New Guinea. (pp369)

Major changes in 1996 saw the professional game switch to summer, the introduction of Super League and the admittance of Paris St Germain to the elite competition. They kicked off the new era with victory over Sheffield at Stade Charlety. (pp360)

In 1998, Super League introduced the Australian system of deciding the champions, whereby top-five play-off culminated in a Grand Final. Wigan were the inaugural winners, defeating Leeds at Old Trafford. (pp362)

Leeds winger Leroy Rivett scored an unprecedented four tries in the 1999 Challenge Cup Final against London Broncos - the last to be played at Wembley before its redevelopment. (pp365)

Australia's international dominance continued into the new millennium, with victory in the 2000 World Cup. (pp396)

With St Helens and Great Britain, Paul Sculthorpe developed into a modern-day great, twice winning the Man of Steel award.

Below, Great Britain's Keith Senior (Leeds) scores against Australian in the 2003 Ashes Series.

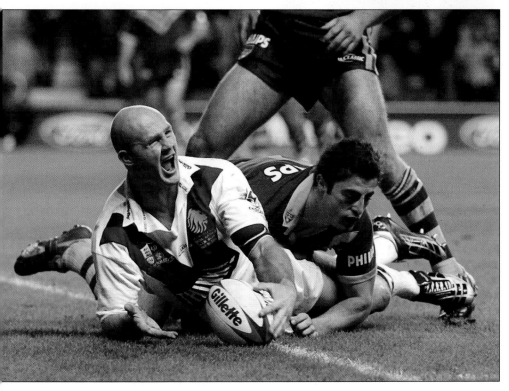

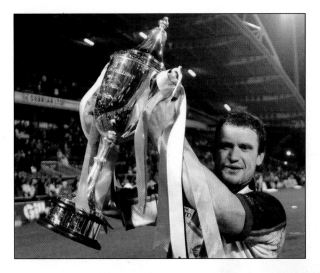

St Helens and Bradford Bulls became the two most successful clubs of the Super League era. In 2003, the Bulls became the first club in the modern game to win every available trophy - the League Leaders Shield, the Super League Grand Final, the Challenge Cup Final and the World Club Championship. Pictured (from top), Jamie Peacock, James Lowes & Paul Deacon and Robbie Paul.

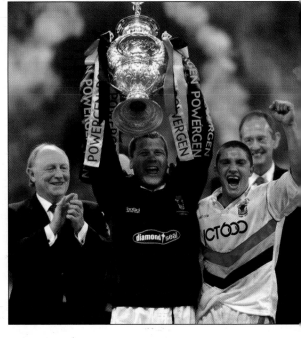

An 'Implementation Committee' led by ex-Halifax director Nigel Wood, who was by then at Red Hall as financial director, had been established to oversee the wholesale restructuring of the RFL's administration and acting boss of the RFL, Aussie ex-ref Greg McCallum, befell something of a coup. Greg had been manfully holding the baby until he heard the news, whilst on holiday in Australia, that his desk had been cleared. A bit harsh, but tough measures were needed. Word had it that accounts had not been signed off for several years, amongst other shoddy management.

Sir Rodney Walker duly stood down from the figurehead position of Chairman of the RFL paving the way for the creation of a new post, that of Executive Chairman. Interviews were held and the lucky winner of the poisoned chalice was the former Davis Cup tennis player Richard Lewis who joined from the Lawn Tennis Association on May Day 2002. No time was lost in appointing a new five-man board of Tony Gartland (general business), Ian Edwards (marketing and media specialist), Maurice Watkins (a prominent sports lawyer) and Nigel Wood (finance.) Stuart Cummings retired from refereeing to take up a technical position, overseeing refereeing and rules.

The BBC had brought us *Walking With Dinosaurs*, but Rugby League still had plenty of its own and amongst the achievements in Richard's first year was the realisation of one of British Rugby Leagues holy grails, the re-unification of BARLA with the RFL. The two administrations continued to run their own competitions and operate in their own respective fields of interest but the single entity quickly proved useful in attracting grant aid and gave the game a unified administration once again.

Another target was the Implementation Committee's recommendation of the restructuring of the respective divisions from Super League and the 19-team Northern Ford Premiership into a new pyramid. The difference in resources and playing standards in the NFP had become polarised with many results a foregone conclusion. Not without resistance from the likes of Hunslet and Workington, the existing clubs plus London Skolars and the reborn York were rearranged into a four-division format. At the pinnacle the existing Super League of 12, then two National

League divisions of 10 each and a new third division comprised of a handful of existing BARLA clubs who would field a 'summer' team, and some of the more adventurous new summer Rugby League Conference teams. Promotion and relegation was possible, except out of the third division, which was to remain as an incubator until standards reached a suitable level.

Every generation tends to see the game through rose tinted glasses, but with professionalism and summer conditions, the noughties saw the club game ratcheted even higher. Handling errors were reduced to a minimum and the game played at an ever quicker pace. It's a far cry from the 'game for gentlemen' I was born out of.

Does it make for a better game though? Opinions vary, but it's no use calling for slower, weaker players who make more mistakes.

"But where are the characters?" I hear some say, at the same time reeling off a list of players many of whom's reputations are safe, coming from a largely pre-television era. Well, many colourful players of yore are still with us, for example, Bamford, Murphy, Schofield, Davies etc are still involved, but now in media punditry. On the field whilst the modern era has produced skilful little 'uns like Adrian Lam, Danny Orr, Robbie Paul and Rob Burrow and tough nut big 'uns like Barrie McDermott, Paul Anderson and Lesley Vainikolo, then maybe the game isn't going too far wrong for talking-point characters.

The much forecast player drift to Rugby Union quickly dried up with only Henry, Jason and Iestyn (household names since playing that game) trying their hand, rather than the wholesale exodus of players and even clubs predicted by some mischief makers in 2001. Keiron and Kris (who they?) were stalked by the Welsh Rugby Union but were persuaded to stay with the assistance of 'Club UK', a slush fund set up to top up the salaries of players who were deemed likely to switch codes.

Interestingly, the drift of coaches and administrators did continue, with the likes of Andy Goodway and Mike Ford joining a growing list of ex-Rugby League men in demand. The brain drain included such as Phil Larder, Ellery Hanley, Alan Tait, Billy McGinty, Clive Griffiths, Steve Hampson, Joe Lydon and Shaun

Edwards amongst others. Conversely, with some of the old guard gone a positive was the renaissance of British coaching talent. At one point in 2000 all 12 Super League coaches were Antipodeans, it seemed anyone with a number in the Sydney phone book would do, but the trend gradually reversed, as trends usually do with the likes of Noble, Cullen, Gregory, Kelly and Harrison *et al* coming to the fore. Come to think of it they would make up a decent pack between them.

Co-operation between the codes is two-way these days. I can always forgive if I get something in return, and the ground and facility sharing now permitted by Union clubs in their new professional era helped enable the Rugby League Conference to expand, and thrive. The Conference started in 1998 with 14 clubs and expanded to 67 by 2004, distributed throughout England and Wales. Scotland continued with its own league growing to eight clubs, and Ireland made a fresh start with their own ten-team Conference competition.

I'm pleased to report that my game has also spread widely through the forces, meeting some resistance at the Sandhurst military academy for a while, although BARLA reported a drift in open age players and teams within the 'heartlands' areas.

More grassroots growth as the student game blossomed to a membership of 64 clubs and the women's game built to 24 clubs. One demonstration of 'girl power' we could have done without came during 2002 as Edwina Currie blew the gaff to a dumbfounded nation on her dalliances a decade earlier with the then Prime Minister, John Major.

Talking of dangerous liaisons, tie-ups between the different codes showed mixed fortunes as Bradford Bulls' takeover of Wakefield RUFC fell through and Saints ditched their marriage with the town's Rugby Union club.

Wigan' s owner Dave Whelan bought the Orrell RUFC club and the single corporate entity of 'Leeds Rugby' fielded teams in both codes.

Internet web sites have helped spread news, fuel debate between fans and speed up the communication process essential in the establishment and expansion of the decade's loudest explosion, that of Summer Conference clubs. More on that later.

A 2001 media petition saw my fans get mobilised and fight back against their perceived misrepresentation and unfair coverage in the papers and broadcasting media. The 30,000 signatures collected gave the petition sufficient credibility to form an Early Day Motion and entry in *Hansard* when presented to Parliament, and provided the ammunition for a complaint (or, in the odd case, compliment) to the editors of Britain's major national and regional newspapers.

May 2002 saw the end of the *Rugby Leaguer* newspaper, as it was bought over and merged with *League Express*. An unhappy and short lived marriage, it re-emerged as *New League Weekly* a few weeks later on 24th June.

The substitute rule changed again, to fall in line with the Australian rule of 12 changes from a bench of four replacements, blood-bin changes to be included. Substitutes benches now resembled Piccadilly Circus at rush hour.

More tinkering as even the ball changed shape, first to a chubbier eight-panel affair for Super League games, rather than the traditional torpedo-shaped design of four panels still used elsewhere in the game, then back to a narrower four panel again.

Sadly, 2003 saw the untimely death of Peter Deakin, the marketing man who played such a revolutionary part in the presentation of the game day event and the re-popularising, if there is such a word, of Rugby League to the local communities, notably Bradford in which he worked wonders. Forty nine was no age.

Brass tax

Whether I like it or not, I'm a business these days, and an expensive one to run at that. A state pension wont pay my way so a bit more financial acumen is needed. The commercial stability of my game has been another roller coaster, with the salary cap gradually taking effect as clubs fell into line (or in Wakefield's case were docked two competition points) after their former largesse. Similar bother for St Helens, Hull and Halifax in May 2003, each docked two points for the previous season's overspending after an RFL audit.

The Super League clubs continued to be underwritten to the tune of £650,000 per year from the News Corporation funding on behalf of their subsidiary, BSkyB television.

Of the original £87 million contractually due over the first five years from 1996, extended to a further five years for £43m more in 1998, the semi-pro clubs had had a share of about £30 million.

When this had dried up, spent on who knows what, the Northern Ford Premiership clubs had to readjust to comparatively leaner times again, with the opportunity of transfer payments for their rising stars having almost disappeared after the Bosman Ruling on players' freedom of contract virtually ended the transfer market. A lucky Challenge Cup draw with a share in a big gate was as good as many clubs could hope for, in exchange for a flogging on the pitch.

The television contracts expired in 2003. After nerve wracking negotiations deals were done with Sky paying £53m for five-year rights to Super League and internationals, with the Challenge Cup being retained by the BBC for a further £12m three-year contract on the proviso that the final moved later into the season.

Ground sharing helped many clubs balance the books, with the summer game allowing all year round revenue when facilities were shared with football (Wakefield and Widnes hosted Leeds United and Everton reserves respectively), Rugby Union (at Headingley) and speedway (Hull KR and Workington.)

Sponsorships during the noughties saw an end to the long standing involvement of Silk Cut, as the Challenge Cup was taken over firstly by Kelloggs, on behalf of their Nutri-grain bars product, then Powergen.

Tetley's continued their long association with the game by sponsoring the Super League, the Grand Final of which continued to grow to rival the Challenge Cup final to create a second focal point of the season.

Arriva Trains first venture was the National Cup, the league-then-knock-out format competition introduced in 2002 for the former Northern Ford Premiership clubs, Arriva taking over from the Buddies soft drinks brand. Fortified by their return, Arriva then announced sponsorship of the BARLA winter National Conference competition.

Match officials bore the prestigious Swiss watchmaker's name of Tissot. The Geneva chronograph manufacturer obviously feeling that precision, accuracy and reliability were synonymous with Super League refereeing...

An unusual one for the GB test team, who started the decade advocating Guinness then the other side of the coin carrying the Department of Transport's 'Think' anti-drink and drive message.

Grounds for improvement

Time and tide waits for no man, and neither does the infrastructure of the game.

During the Blair years, I saw the demise of some of the famous old grounds I have been so familiar with over the decades, and some welcome improvements.

No longer the 'Riversiders' as Wigan's historic home since 1902, Central Park, was redeveloped into a Tesco supermarket. It will take a while for the JJB stadium, owned by Dave Whelan of JJB Sports shops fame, which they occupy in partnership with Wigan Athletic football club, to feel like home.

By the beginning of the new decade Halifax had vacated Thrum Hall, now an Asda, to move in with Halifax Town FC. Their time in the new ground started off well with new covered standing areas behind both sets of sticks but grew to include the embarrassment of a semi-completed stand, which has stood season after season empty and unloved like Halifax's own Millennium Dome. This particular white elephant, a tangle of steelwork concrete and a small patch of seating, stood as a symbol of the hapless financial management of the past, started without the money to finish it. Even the eventual sale of Thrum Hall did not release sufficient funds to restart the construction work.

A farewell also to the venerable old Boulevard in October 2002 as Hull FC hosted the first game of the New Zealand tour as a swan song to the ageing stadium and its notorious Threepenny Stand. The old place, home since 1895, is now replaced by the magnificent

£43.5m Kingston Communications Stadium, located only a drop kick away on what was The Circle cricket and sports ground. Despite the decades of history and legend left behind I doubt few would look back to Airlie Street.

Warrington's new stadium sprung out of the ground during 2003, to replace the historic but aged symphony in concrete and corrugated iron that was Wilderspool, Wire's home since 1898. Legend has it that the name derived from 'wild deer's pool' a creature that, the same as the wolf shown on the town crest, isn't found round those parts much these days. The new ground, named for its first 10 years in favour of local BMW dealer Halliwell Jones in a sponsorship of around £750,000, bucked the 'all seater' trend and caters to the preferences of its fans by comprising 7,000 seats and space for 7,000 more to stand.

The open end at Wakefield's Belle Vue developed a block of multi-storey Portakabins for office and corporate use, affectionately known as the 'Benidorm Flats.'

Another false start for Odsal, as the proposed redevelopment of the whole ground fell through due to delays with planning consent frightening the developer off, having been 'called in' by the Secretary of State for his department's interminable deliberation. In the meantime Bradford City FC's Valley Parade staged the Bulls home matches, not to universal acclaim, and it was a relief to many when the Bulls returned to Odsal at the beginning of the 2003 season.

A deal was struck with Bradford MBC whereby the council were absolved from the responsibilities of their long-term lease, buying themselves out with a lump sum payment to the club. The welcome addition of a new stand at the speedway pit end appeared just in time for the visit of Leeds and the 21,784 crowd that came to watch.

Swinton returned to its own town to Moor Lane, lodging with Swinton FC, before settling at Sedgley Park RUFC after years of exile at Bury FC's Gigg Lane. A far cry from the cavernous Station Road, with its own -and groaning- trophy cabinet, but such is the fate of a fallen giant.

One of the senior amateur teams, Woolston, suffered a

malicious fire at their clubhouse, destroying the building and their irreplaceable collection of memorabilia.

Even Wembley, home to the Challenge Cup final since 1929, saw its last try in 1999, as the long-running saga of its redevelopment continued with the twin towers eventually falling to the demolition ball in early 2003.

Brisbane quit the ANZ Stadium in June 2003 to return to Lang Park (now refurbished and sponsored as Suncorp Stadium) with 46,337 welcoming them home to an unscheduled defeat by Newcastle.

New clubs, old clubs

The constituent clubs within professional and semi-professional Rugby League come and go in number and location. Some define the town in which they play; others barely get a foothold before vanishing into the history books. The noughties were no less turbulent in terms of club 'turnover.'

Mergers. A dark episode. Within the much trumpeted 'elite' Super League the conversion to full-time professionalism was proving unfamiliar territory for some.

Business planning, inflated salaries, marketing, enhanced match day presentations and the scramble between those lower down the table to avoid relegation, with the consequent loss of the wherewithal to pay the full-time players and staff, proved too big a task for some.

Financially struggling clubs Huddersfield, Sheffield, the newly introduced Gateshead Thunder and Hull were forced together into implausible mergers with the incentive of a £1.2m cash inducement. This gave the directors at Gateshead and Sheffield the opportunity to jump ship, leaving two of my development areas with no team and a feeling of betrayal.

The 'senior partners' in these atrocities kept their heads down and after a token effort to add the Sheffield name to the Huddersfield Giants badge and play a handful of games at Don Valley Stadium, the façade was quietly dropped, to the relief of all involved, especially the Huddersfield supporters.

Fortunately, League people are made of sterner stuff and supporters groups at both Sheffield and Gateshead reformed their clubs on a shoestring and kept their dream bumping along.

York Wasps backers gave up the ghost part way through 2002 but through the efforts of its loyal supporters, general fans of the game, the local paper (the *York Evening Press*) and John Smiths Brewery, the club bounced back. All dug deep in their pockets, as York City Knights started the 2003 season in ruder health than recent years before.

London Skolars took their bow in National League Two, having developed a stable structure on and off the field that many longer-established clubs would be envious of, and gaining one win and one draw during their debut season.

New faces in the shape of newcomers Teeside, Coventry, South London Storm, Manchester and St Albans who bravely stepped forward from the ranks to form National League Three. This also featured some of the more familiar names of progressive, established clubs from the existing amateur structure, such as Underbank, Woolston (the inaugural Grand Final winners) and the first season minor premiers, Bradford Dudley Hill.

Bramley's application to re-enter wasn't supported by Hunslet, whose top man, Grahame Liles, complained (in *Rugby Leaguer & League Express*, 20.5.02) that "17 per cent of our season ticket holders come from Morley" (where the Bramley team were to be based). Crikey! That must be nearly 50 people. Never mind, they made it back into National League Three in 2004, together with Essex, Birmingham and Carlisle (back again - third time lucky).

One of my more famous French names overstretched themselves financially and Grand Avignon were gone, leaving only smaller brother SO Avignon to continue the town's association with its principle sport. St Esteve, XIII Catalan and St Cyprien's senior teams merged to form Union Treiziste Catalan, whilst retaining their identities at junior levels.

After a cull of teams in Australia that had seen, amongst others, the South Sydney Rabbitohs ejected from the NRL competition, after a long and acrimonious legal battle they were back for 2002, albeit destined to prop up the table. I might be wrong, but I think the moral here is not to mess people's clubs about?

The year 2001 saw changing times for the Auckland Warriors club. Having been on the financial brink under the original Maori tribal ownership the Auckland club restructured their corporate affairs and re-emerged as the NZ Warriors. After their best ever season in 2002 the Warriors crossed the Tasman to play Sydney Roosters in the NRL Grand Final, boosting their fortunes and reputation throughout the 'Shaky Isles'.

Halifax dropped their not entirely popular marketing nickname 'Blue Sox', in a return to traditional values as their fortunes waned as badly as technology companies on the Stock Exchange. The town's eponymous Building Society became the HBoS bank and never did take up the sponsorship opportunity the club cued up for them.

International rescue

When talking about the noughties in a playing sense, a phrase to send a shiver down the spine of anyone with the game's best interest at heart will be...the Lincoln World Cup 2000. The first 16-team Rugby League World Cup competition experienced mixed fortunes, reasonable highs and terrible lows.

Off to a dull start at a half-empty Twickenham on a rain-sodden Saturday evening, even the opening ceremony was cancelled as a wash out, as Aussie duly beat England 2-22.

Sadly, the competition was slated by a ferocious media attack from the word go and generally failed to fire the public imagination, with a number of poor turnouts in obscure locations like Llanelli, Belfast and Reading. Could have been good if the competition had caught on, as the 1995 World Cup had done, but a potential disaster if it didn't.

Even 'heartlands' games fell short with Australia only drawing 3,044 to Hull for a 110-4 rout of Russia. England - the British team had been split into its component countries, some a bit thin on actual nationals - struggled to attract 5,736 to Knowsley Road in beating Russia 76-4.

England's bid ended at Bolton, outclassed and demoralised 6-49 in a depressing semi-final, marking the lowest ebb in the national team's morale for years.

More brightly, the French group matches enjoyed success on and off the field and some interesting events in the British-based groups arrived in the shape of Lebanon's appearance and the Welsh team coming within a few minutes of knocking out the inevitable winners, Australia, in the semi-final.

A train strike and a ticketing fiasco compounded matters. The wettest October history has ever recorded dampened spirits further and the most ambitious Rugby League World Cup ever concluded with a crowd of 44,329 (actually a record for a game in Britain between two non-British teams) at Old Trafford to see a scintillating Australia defeat New Zealand 40-12.

Contrary to the anticipated profit of £1m, possibly £2m, losses in the order of £1.8m were subsequently announced, causing not only embarrassment but also real hardship within the administration of the RFL.

Stung into a rearguard action, subsequent Test series were scaled down in ambition and staged at medium-sized 'heartland' venues with significantly higher than usual ticket prices in an attempt to maximise revenue and claw back the deficit that had prompted staff cuts at Red Hall. In 2001, a seat behind the sticks at the McAlpine Stadium to see Great Britain play Australia cost £25, the corresponding seat at a packed Elland Road in 1994 had been a tenner.

For the record, the Tests series in 2001 amounted to a nervous win for Britain at Huddersfield, a drubbing by Aussie at Bolton and a battle royale at Wigan, the Ashes being retained by Australia 1-2. A good degree of honour was restored to the traditional looking Great Britain shirt.

An ill-fated one-off Test between the oldest of Rugby League rivals took place in Sydney in July 2002, and a one-sided game saw an ill-prepared Great Britain thrashed 64-10 in front of 31,844. Back to square one...

October and November 2002 saw the popular Kiwis return to British shores for the first time since 1998 with a fuller tour. Visits included Hull FC, England 'A' (at Brentford) and in an embarrassing misjudgement, the Wales fixture was scheduled for the Millennium Stadium which ended up only 10 per cent full. Tests were staged in the new territory of Blackburn (16-30), Huddersfield (a 14-14 draw) and Wigan (16-10). The series ended all-square and the newly-inaugurated Baskerville Trophy, a rather handsome silver shield, was returned to a glass case in the reception area of Red Hall.

After a mediocre adventure to Blackburn's Ewood Park, the aggregate crowds for the three Tests were deemed acceptable at 62,505 (in fact the biggest three Kiwi Test aggregate since 1951 and a far cry from the 13,351 total in 1971.) Television audiences peaked live on Sky at 320,000 and 1.4 million on the BBC highlights the next day.

In a generous gesture the NZRL took only expenses, allowing the RFL to retain the tour profits to help offset the World Cup shortfall.

Played against the massive, blanket media coverage of England's progress to victory in the final of the Rugby Union World Cup, being hosted by Australia at the same time, nevertheless the 2003 Aussie tour of Britain was nevertheless played out in front of three sell-out crowds.

The first Test started explosively at JJB Stadium, Wigan as Adrian Morley, having flown half way round the world to take part from his Sydney Roosters club, became the quickest ever Test sending-off, in the first tackle of the series, 12 seconds in. Aussie squeaked home against the remaining 16, taking the lead only four minutes from the hooter.

Many of the 24,614 bemoaned the controversial Pommy referee Steve Ganson's Test match debut, but it wasn't Steve who made the 'tackle'.

On to the new Kingston Communications Stadium at Hull, which had sold its 25,147 tickets out several months in advance. The keenly-anticipated game also drew a record for Sky, 420,000 viewers live with 1.3 million watching the highlights on BBC the following afternoon, as Aussie clawed back a 20-8 deficit during the last 43 minutes to get home 20-23 and seal the series, leaving the home crowd disconsolate. In a poignant ceremony the memorial to our war hero Jack Harrison had been unveiled prior to proceedings. I think he'd have approved.

On to Huddersfield for the 'dead rubber', although still a sell-out 24,163. With Great Britain & Ireland leading 12-6 with four minutes left on the clock, the never-say-die Aussies stunned all present with two late tries to complete a 3-0 whitewash, 18-12. Britain's best chance for years blown.

At the end of the series, David Waite announced his standing down as Great Britain coach, leaving a much-improved team but a less than distinguished record of three wins (two against Aussie and the only one played against France), one draw and seven defeats from 11 Tests. Bradford coach Brian Noble stepped into the part-time position, no stranger to the international game himself, having skippered Great Britain eight times during 1984.

Ashes aside

Ashes aside, the international programme had continued its somewhat limited and unimaginative theme, given the exotic choice of countries now playing the game. If it wasn't profitable it didn't happen.

Despite the commercial failure, the 2000 World Cup had sparked an appetite amongst the players and coaches for a wider international programme. This cause wasn't helped by a conflict of interest as one of the board of the RFL - I'll leave you to remember who - was also a chairman of a Super League club. A public row erupted as he poured cold water on the international aspirations, preferring an emphasis on the club game at Super League level. This was the sort of blind nepotism that the Implementation Committee had felt bound to act against in establishing an independent board within Red Hall, and rightly so.

A turn for the better as a two-group European Nations Cup featuring the four home nations plus France and Russia brought the curtain down at Wilderspool in 2003 with the two group winners playing out a final, won by England's 'A' team of 'up-and-comers' over France 68-6. The Man of the Match, Wigan's Shaun

Briscoe, received the new Jean Galia Medal, a nice thought.

Sadly, compared to the burgeoning international calendar of the early nineties, the Pacific nations didn't get many invitations. Neither did France who were soldiering on alone in doing their bit to promote and expand the international game with matches against Russia, Lebanon and the Pacific protectorate of New Caledonia (whose Rugby Union structure had switched *en bloc* to League in 2002).

The Greatest Game continued to build in Russia. Rumours and speculation of Rugby League's existence in the former CCCP turned to fact as the Student World Cup opened in Kazan, Tartarstan, to a crowd of 16,000. Further proof, as the 2002 Damart Tour brought Locomotiv Moscow and Strella Kazan to Workington, Hull KR, Dewsbury and Bradford. Russia and Tartarstan hosted games against the USA and the now annual Victory Cup saw Moscow's Olympic Stadium host USA, the BARLA team and the eventual winners, France in 2003. As if to demonstrate the improvisation of the Russian game, the cavernous Moscow Olympic Stadium featured cones instead of corner flags, 'tuning fork' posts and, believe it or not, an astroturf pitch. Keep the League flag flying, comrades!

The Mediterranean Cup was staged for a second time in 2003, won by Lebanon over France, poor old Morocco and new Leaguies Serbia & Montenegro (who actually have a Rugby League pedigree stretching back to Yugoslavia during the 1950s) on the receiving end of some hidings. Nevertheless, progress, and by all accounts well received by the hosting Lebanese public. Yes, that's right, I've got a foothold in Beirut! It's a long walk from the George Hotel!

Not for me a restful winter playing bingo in Benidorm, I prefer to keep busy and set my sights further afield. Embryonic leagues sprung up in such unlikely outposts as Lebanon, the USA and Serbia, some way from the M62. Even Holland raised a team of locals to play the Essex Eels in The Hague.

Domestically, 2001 saw the return of Roses matches under the gruesomely 'Australianised' moniker of 'County of Origin.' Initially a one-off game at Headingley, drawing 10,253 (almost exactly the number at Wigan in 1989 after which the competition had been discontinued) with a 36-24 result, expanding to a two-match series in 2002 at Headingley (36-28) and JJB (22-18), all games won by Lancashire.

Pressure of fixtures reduced the series back to a one off at Odsal in 2003. The 8,258 at Odsal saw Chris Thorman, the first real product of the game in the Gateshead area, equal the Roses Match points scoring record of 20 as Yorkshire shocked everyone with a 56-6 drubbing, against all the pundits' predictions. If not to everyone's taste, this representative match was a good 'shop window' for Chris, as he attracted the attention and a contract from Paramatta Eels and packed his bags for Sydney only weeks afterwards.

Citing lack of support from the clubs, Waite announced the suspension of the competition. All change, once again. Maybe this was a mercy killing, I'm not sure a tribal contest between two counties reflects how widespread I am now, and probably just reinforces stereotypes for those who are still prejudiced against me.

Changing challenge

The stock of my Challenge Cup had been in question over recent seasons as the shift of the regular league season to a spring start seemed to give it the air of a pre-season warm-up competition. What wasn't in doubt, though, was the spectacle of my finals, rejuvenated by a happy, if unlikely accident.

The demolition of my second home, Wembley, and the interminable delay as politicians and sporting committees debated the design of its replacement saw the Challenge Cup finals taken on the road to Britain's regional capitals, first to Edinburgh in 2000, then Twickenham, back to Edinburgh and then Cardiff in 2003 and 2004. This unlikely sequence served as a public relations triumph in exporting the spectacle of my annual carnival to cities, stadia and people who only a few years ago had previously been lukewarm at best, or even unaware or hostile, towards Rugby League.

Murrayfield's first Rugby League game saw a full house of 67,247 as hot favourites Bradford lifted the cup 24-18 for coach

Matthew Elliott, holding off a Leeds fightback, and hastening the end for losing coach Dean Lance. The game had been in doubt as late as 24 hours beforehand as the Water of Leith had burst its banks during the week and flooded the pitch to a depth of three feet. Credit to all concerned who pumped and mopped up. By kick-off, the surface was immaculate.

The preceding semi-final between Hull FC and Leeds had seen an unpleasant end as some spectators in Hull colours had invaded the pitch and pushed a set of posts over. The silver lining to this incident was the realisation that the club needed to clear out its unruly element and look to become more family-orientated, as so many other clubs had become, a mission the club took on very seriously.

The 2001 final at Twickenham was generally adjudged a bit of a damp squib as Saints beat Bradford 13-6 in the now traditional downpour at Rugger HQ. Not a game to dwell on. Talking of one hit wonders, the pre-match entertainment was provided by the 'manufactured by TV' group, Hear'say.

I so enjoyed my first trip there I was more than happy to take my family on a return visit to Murrayfield in 2002. We saw a tight contest between Saints and Wigan, with Kris Radlinski's injured foot being the pre-match talking point. In the end he did play and his flawless defensive performance was the post-match discussion as Kris took the Lance Todd Trophy and held the Challenge Cup as a winner with Wigan 21-12. Another point to ponder was why the crowd of 62,140 had been 5,000 short of capacity, seemingly many Wigan supporters saw a win for the red-hot Saints as inevitable. Take nothing for granted in Rugby League!

One of the semi-finals at Wigan had seen Leeds take a bad beating by Saints, with the most entertainment for the Leeds supporters during the first half courtesy of the stewards' *Keystone Cops* attempts to catch a magpie with a broken wing.

Cardiff 2003 will be remembered for the nip and tuck 22-20 score, the controversy of some impossible video refereeing decisions and Kevin Sinfield's decision to decline a potentially score-equalling penalty seven minutes from time and press for a match-winning try that never came. Sinny had kicked one from the touchline on the hooter only three weeks before to rescue the semi-final for Leeds, and bring on extra-time in a genuinely epic game against the silverware specialist St Helens.

The spectacle of the final was heightened further with the game being played under floodlights, sheltered from a cloudburst by the Millennium Stadium's closed roof and deafened by the 71,212 inside. Robbie Paul stood aside to allow his team's elder statesman James Lowes to receive the trophy from the guest of honour, Neil Kinnock MEP.

An interesting spin-off from this odyssey was the unusual record of James Lowes and Robbie Paul who became the only players to have played in a Challenge Cup final at four different venues.

Cardiff again in 2004, the last spring final before the move to autumn and the repositioning of the big day towards the end of the season. Saints and Wigan won through and with a healthy number of locals filled the Cardiff stadium to it's 73,734 brim. Something of a cloud hung over the Saints, two of their number alleged to have backed their own weakened team to lose against Bradford a few weeks before. In the hope of seeing the cup lifted before he went, Wigan coach, Mike Gregory, delayed his departure to the USA for treatment of a chronic infection that had left him virtually incapacitated. Mrs Sculthorpe's boys, Paul and Danny took opposing sides with Paul, the Saints lad, happier after a steady 32-16 victory.

Times change and even t' owd pot itself, weary with a 100-odd years of polishing with rag and Brasso had developed a touch of metal fatigue and was replaced by a shiny new replica, good for another 100 years or so. One of these days, I'll round up all the various disused cups and trophies and put them in a Rugby League museum. I've never quite got round to building a decent museum, although I did try to get the Wembley Twin Towers moved to Widnes for that purpose, but like everything else it would have cost too much and so they got demolished with the rest of the stadium.

French and Russian teams became regular fixtures in an ever more cosmopolitan Challenge Cup. Games such as Embassy versus Strella Kazan and Leigh versus Locomotiv Moscow began to seem commonplace to British supporters. The best cup run by an overseas team had been in 2001, when Villeneuve Leopards reached Warrington in the quarter-finals.

Super League comes strong

The new decade saw a good sprinkling of 20,000-plus crowds at regular league games, mainly between Bradford and Leeds, two of my more commercially successful clubs of the modern era. The Super League record crowd of 24,020, fittingly, was set at Odsal, the scene of the 102,569 'all game' record for the sport I set in the 1950s.

The regular Super League competition was fought out between 12 clubs, reduced (by those wretched 'mergers') from the 14 that had started it in 1996. Concentration of resources was supposed to bring quality and the dreaded 'I' word, 'intensity'.

I don't know what other sports would entertain this, but because 11 home games don't bring in a big enough income, a few extras were tacked on each year to make 28. From the final table the top five, later top six, then played-off to the last two who contest the grand final to determine that season's champion.

Rather than sitting back and quietly picking up my pension, I thought I'd give the Super League Grand Final a good shove and see what I could make of it. The Grand Final continued to grow in stature year on year during the noughties, with Old Trafford playing host, not always to the delight of the Manchester United manager, Sir Alex Ferguson.

Apparently, the Reds' 1-0 defeat by West Ham in the FA cup one January was directly attributable to the pitch being used for Rugby League. Presumably he meant the 80 minutes of the previous October's Super League Grand Final. As young people these days say, "Whatever."

The 2000 Grand Final could have been entitled 'The Chris Joynt show'. He led Saints to the Super League trophy and winners' rings (a bit of a girly sort of award in my book, what next, winners' earrings?), earning the Harry Sunderland trophy in a 29-16 win over Wigan, with 58,132 making up a very red and white crowd.

Bradford thumped Wigan in 2001 37-6, helped by a Mick Withers hat-trick watched by 60,164, a turn-out quite a bit wider than George W Bush's somewhat dodgy election-winning margin in Florida two months earlier.

Never mind a night out at the bingo for excitement, the 2002 Grand Final, typified the intensifying nature of Super League with Saints edging home 19-18 thanks to Sean Long's drop-goal, later voted (perhaps slightly ambitiously) the 'greatest ever kick'. Bradford's players and share of the biggest Grand Final crowd yet of 61,138 complained over a possible 'voluntary tackle' incident on the final hooter. On another day, it might have resulted in a penalty in front of the sticks that could have changed the result.

With a hunger to match the appetite of the illusionist David Blaine on the last day of his glass box hunger marathon, all 65,539 tickets were snapped up for the 2003 Grand Final, the first to completely sell out. Bradford completed their Grand Final and Challenge Cup double (including the new League Leaders Trophy, a triple) with a 25-12 victory over a flagging Wigan, who had come from third. Poor Terry Newton in his fourth Grand Final, a loser every time.

Following Ranulf Feinnes' ordeal of running seven marathons in seven days on seven continents, another public-endurance marathon had been poor old Halifax's lot. They ended the whole 2003 season pointless as the only two points they won, on the very first weekend, were deducted for a salary cap transgression the previous year, and 27 consecutive losses saw them relegated with a bump.

One unique record goes to Jamie Ainscough of Wigan, who is surely the only player to finish a game of Rugby League with more teeth than he started, acquiring one of St Helens centre Martin Gleeson's in his arm, discovered by x-ray several weeks (and several games) later. Sadly, a subsequent infection forced his retirement in June 2003.

Barry Eaton's metronome kicking brought him a new world record in 2003, kicking 36 consecutive successful goals for Batley.

World Service

The winner of Super League gets the chance to play the winners of the Aussie NRL competition in a one-off World Club Challenge match, which is either a prestigious title or a meaningless pre-season warm-up, depending on how your team gets on.

The World Club Challenge saw a mixed run for British sides with St Helens taking a pasting from Melbourne 6-44 in 2000. The next year, St Helens squeaked past Brisbane 20-18, Sculthorpe and Long chipping two late drop-goals to edge home at a hail-swept Reebok. Only a handful of the 16,041 inside Reebok took up the suggestion made in an advert posted by the Brisbane management in the *Wigan Evening Post* newspaper that Wiganers should turn up and cheer for Brisbane. Cheeky monkeys.

In 2002, Bradford walloped Newcastle Knights 41-26, a downpour soaking the 21,113 hardy souls sheltering inside the McAlpine Stadium.

The start of 2003 saw Saints get their comeuppance against Sydney Roosters, put to the sword 0-38 and disappointing the 19,807 hardy souls who went home from Bolton frozen to the marrow.

Penrith had surprised Sydney Roosters in the soggy 2003 NRL Grand Final, but got a shock themselves at McAlpine, the night before Valentines Day, 2004.

Bradford showed more passion in defending the Panthers out of the game to the tune of 22-4. In doing so, they completed their own modern version of the 'All Four Cups.'

To give the developing grassroots clubs an international dimension, the York 9's was founded. The 2002 competition included such novelties as the French participants from FC Lezignan and Les Hussards de Paris, Kazan, a team based on subcontinental players entitled the South Asia Bulls, and the York Ironsides with the days Civil War theme continued by a display by the Sealed Knot.

Building on this success, the competition was repeated in 2003, this time over a weekend under a flaming June sun. Lezignan were the winners, taking some good cheer home to France. In 2004, a

West Indies representative team won the event, lifting the Fairfax Cup on their debut.

Another competition in bloom was the NFP play-offs, which continued to prosper with five-figure gates turning out to see the promotion deciders. West Hull dominated the BARLA National Conference from the beginning of the decade until Siddal won the 2003 grand final 19-14 at Batley.

Bradford gatecrashed the 2002 Rugby Union Twickenham Sevens, returning north with the pot despite having spent most of the night on a broken-down charabanc straight after a good hiding by St Helens. Not ideal preparation.

Long odds surely on Sale to beat St Helens in a pre-season 'half of each code' money making stunt, but it happened. Neither team scored at the other team's game, demonstrating irrefutably that St Helens are no good at Rugby Union (losing the Union half 41-0) and Sale are hopeless at League (losing the League half 39-0). Glad we've got that settled.

Domesday - the Millennium and all that...

How else then, will we remember the 'noughties', the decade that brought you wall-to-wall David Beckham and the *Ketchup Song*?

Well, if hype was anything to go by, the Millennium bug looked like being amongst the biggest catastrophes in history. As micro chips in computers and machinery all over the planet clicked over from 1999 to 2000, the world didn't stop turning after all. Computers didn't crash, aeroplanes didn't drop out of the sky and hospital wards didn't resemble the control deck of the *USS Enterprise* whilst under Klingon attack. In fact the whole episode passed with barely a whimper, its only legacy being a large number of new Porche-driving computer programmers.

Whilst bad news shouts louder than good, there did seem to be a lot of it. Fuel shortages hit the country as petrol tanker drivers were blockaded into their refineries by users of heavy commercial vehicles who were complaining about the cost of government duty on fuel. 2003 saw the opening of the first toll road since the turnpikes of centuries ago, around Birmingham.

One of the great symbols of national prestige, *Concorde*, tragically crashed outside Paris with the loss of 113 lives, signalling the end of the service two years later.

During 2001, the rural economy was wracked by Foot and Mouth disease costing £1.4 billion in farmer's compensation and costing the economy around £8 billion in total.

Hull's Prescott was put on a charge for deliberate striking in May 2001, but FC fans needn't have worried, it wasn't their full back Steve in the dock. John Prescott, the Deputy Prime Minister, and his right hook were on the fizzer for clouting an egg-chucking protester during the General Election campaign.

New Years Day 2001 also saw the introduction of the Euro, the common European currency intended to bring the participating countries and their dealings with each other a little bit closer together, but sadly world unity was not to be the keynote of the new decade.

11th September 2001 is now a date ingrained in the consciousness of a generation. The catastrophic terrorist attacks in New York and at the Pentagon shook the world and the confidence of many of its citizens.

One minor consequence of the atrocities was the cancellation of the imminent Kangaroo tour to Britain. After desperate negotiations and security reassurances the tour was rescheduled to a truncated three-Test format, to the relief of all in the administration of the British game, for whom the financial consequences of cancellation would have been unthinkable. Also, Lebanon's home debut against the French had to be postponed for security concerns, eventually happening the next year.

In a lighter vein, if that is possible given the subject matter, was the stance of Aussie forward Robbie Kearns who expressed caution that British tourist attractions such as the Eiffel Tower might be targets...

A further terrorist attack on a nightclub on the paradise island paradise of Bali wrought further death and destruction, killing 202 innocents, including the lives of Australian Rugby League players innocently enjoying a post-season holiday.

Rightly or wrongly, the alliance of (mainly silent) partners took action and headed by the USA and Britain sought to wage a 'war on terrorism'. This started in Afghanistan, deposing the extreme regime and pursuing Osama bin Laden the chief suspect of the September 11th attacks, and progressed to a war on the leader of Iraq, Saddam Hussein, intended to disarm 'weapons of mass destruction', of which no trace was found. A big stink as to whether the government had exaggerated the threat from the outset soon followed. Uncertain times for all.

Again, a sombre time at Easter 2002 as the Queen Mother passed away, a constant figure in so many peoples lives, especially those of more mature years. The nation needed a pick-me-up and, thankfully, the summer of 2002 obliged with pageantry and spectacle and a community spirit not experienced for years.

The Queen's Golden Jubilee celebrations, predicted to be a damp squib by our doomsayers in the media, drew two million people to the Mall with processions, music and fireworks. England's presence in the football World Cup, hosted on the other side of the world in Japan and South Korea, and then Euro 2004 saw the nation once again proudly displaying Union and St George flags from every vantage point. The Commonwealth Games (another turkey in waiting, according to our all-knowing media) proved a fabulous and successful sporting spectacle. The country had a cautious smile back on its face.

The ITV digital television service crashed, taking its famous woolly monkey puppet with it. That sounded a warning to overstretched sports clubs as clear as the final hooter at The Shay of the dangers of spending money they hadn't earned themselves before they'd got it.

Cheap air travel had by now become commonplace, giving choice and opportunity to all. It was now perfectly feasible to schedule games such as London versus Warrington in Carcassone and allow French teams the possibility of a home draw in the cup, which Union Treiziste Catalan received in 2002 with a tie in Perpignan against Wigan. St Gaudens also hosted Halifax.

Nostaligia for the 1970s and 1980s in all forms, especially music and clothing, was very much in vogue (although not many were particularly nostalgic for 'retro' seventies Rugby League!).

Tribute bands toured the nation mimicking the originals (and possibly were more popular). Robbie Williams did a passable impression of Frank Sinatra at a black tie 'do' at the Royal Albert Hall.

The new rock 'n' roll, though, was the phenomenon of 'reality television.' This continued to fascinate with 'docusoaps' on every conceivable subject from airport workers, car clampers, a beauty salon, call centre telephonists and vets, together with 'lifestyle' programmes involving cooking, gardening, DIY and even instruction on *What Not To Wear*. Rugby League got in on the act with Yorkshire Television's *Rugby League Raw*, winning plaudits and awards for its gritty behind the scenes coverage of the earthier goings on in the dressing rooms and touchline dugouts of the NFP teams.

The appetite for ever more ambitious and voyeuristic game shows sprung from the Dutch-originated idea of *Big Brother*, and umpteen derivatives followed on involving the Australian jungle, celebrity dieting and pop stars both embryonic and almost pensionable.

Another sign of the times was the amazing turnaround in the life of the Oldham supporter who applied for a job on the door of his team's social club in May 2003. The next week he won £4.3 million on the National Lotto and expressed his intention to join the board instead! Not so lucky for Charles and Diana Ingram, though, hauled before the beak a few months earlier for trying to trick their way to the top prize in *Who Wants to be a Millionaire* with coded coughing. Ahem.

Harry Potter mania at the bookshop and cinema box office and chrome-plated scooters were a must-have delivery by Santa. It seemed everyone had a mobile phone during the noughties, and the craze was to be in constant contact with your mates, sending messages by 'texting.' Not 4 me but OK if U lke that srt of thng.

Whilst Gateshead had survived their fixture list in 2002 with only a solitary draw to show for it, that suddenly seemed a minor triumph in comparison as Jemini, the British entry in the 2003 *Eurovision Song Contest*, achieved yes, I'm afraid, nil points.

My anthem, one I share, curiously, with the Women's Institute, reached the grand old age of 200 in 2004, William Blake's *Jerusalem*. The British space probe *Beagle 2* hit Mars, but then vanished without trace, although the *Queen Mary ll* was launched, the largest passenger ship ever built.

Prime Minister Tony Blair's basic salary was £175,414 in 2003 - less than my top stars. I hear that some soccer players get that every month and someone told me there are 230,000 millionaires in Britain these days. Not surprising, you need the best part of that to buy a house!

So there they are, the noughties, so far. After a turbulent start to the decade the good ship Rugby League looks set fair for a good few years of growth and success.

So what's next?

Well, this is about all I've got to tell you so far, dear reader. You see, not every story has an ending.

I'm not dead yet (despite reports to the contrary for most of my life) far from it, so there's more to come. I can't tell you much more for the meantime, at least not until the sequel to this venerable tome is written around 2104, as this lot has to go to the printer now.

Who knows what's around the corner? With Rugby League it's usually something unexpected and controversial, but I can point you towards some of the important things that are happening which might shape my pensionable years.

The RL Summer Conference is helping the game spread its wings the way it could and should have done during the early 1900s, if it hadn't been suppressed and victimised by those in society who thought my face didn't fit. Not all my new clubs will succeed and some are better organised and capable than others, but there are ever-fewer who can still snub Rugby League on the basis that "they don't play that round here."

My terrestrial telly profile could be better, I seem to have been forsaken for others. At least satellite television and the internet are helping the game reach out to an ever further flung audience, with information plentiful and detailed, rather than the smallest morsel of news tucked at the bottom of the page under the racing results or, worse, nothing at all.

Clubs are waking up to the spectator as a 'customer' who should be treated fairly and with consideration and even useful in becoming involved in influencing events at the club through forums, Trusts and Independent Supporters Associations.

The surroundings I'm played in are getting better, but although some of my stadia are shiny, safe and offering all manner of facilities, some of them lack a little soul and are shared with other sports who often see me as minor partners in the sharing arrangements.

My greatest triumphs? Well, I've always been pretty fairminded, taking players without prejudice as to their background. I'm proud that the first black captain and first black coach of a British national team were in my sport. No apartheid busting invitations offered or accepted by Rugby League, unlike some. I reckon I'm also the first major sport to have had a woman as a Chief Executive of one of its premier clubs.

I'm pretty sure I'm the first British team sport to win a World Cup at anything.

My followers always seem to get along so well with each other, standing side by side in a mutual respect, always with something in common to chat about. All ages, shapes and sizes, I've become a family game with something for all to enjoy.

A lesson for other sports comes from my players, who show such respect for the referee and each other, especially given the endurance, strength and courage that it takes to play the game at any level.

I'm also proud of how inclusive and diverse the game is, from a tribal team in Papua New Guinea or a hill village XIII from the south of France to a team of schoolgirls from Dewsbury, we are all welcome in the same family.

A few words of caution though. The game is rougher and tougher than ever and, to many, it's so much easier to watch than join in. Other safer distractions such as computer games don't help attract younger players and the trend towards litigation and injury claims makes organising any sort of knockabout social game of

Rugby League either a risk or an administrative nightmare.

Whilst it's been the envy of many other sports, I worry about sportsmanship and the role of the referee in our game as well. The poor ref is under scrutiny more than ever in this televisual age and some of our pundits seem to focus on decisions and mistakes of the referee more often than the game itself. I've never seen a referee drop the ball or miss a tackle, so let's get back to a bit more 'Sir' and a bit less of the backchat.

The game's best asset is surely the players, and playing standards are higher than ever. They need to be treated as the thoroughbreds that they are rather than being flogged to death with an endless season of matches. More isn't always better; like chocolate cake, you only want so much.

The players we all admire don't grow on trees, so let's not forget the breeding grounds from which so many of them originate. My National League and amateur clubs have a huge part to play in keeping the game alive in the communities outside of the more glamorous towns and cities. We ignore the game in places such as Keighley, Barrow and Featherstone at our peril.

There's a fine line between embracing change and innovation, something our game has never been frightened to do, and discarding tradition and heritage, principles and events that have been important to the game and its followers over the decades. Make a mental note, swap the temptation for tinkering, be it rule changes, structures right down to the ever changing designs of the playing strips, for a few years of stability. Don't change me too much more, I'm more popular now than ever, if we did but realise it.

My hopes and wishes for the future are the same as they've ever been. I simply want the chance to be played and enjoyed freely and without prejudice as widely around the world as possible. What do you think my chances are?

13

POSTSCRIPT.
A LOOK THROUGH
THE WINDOW

Well, my friends, that's my story for the time being and I hope you have enjoyed sharing my indulgence in this little piece of nostalgia.

Time for me to disappear, I've got the greatest game in the world to attend to and I can't take my eye off it for a minute, but before I go I can't resist a quick look around. Please excuse me whilst I stretch my legs and enjoy a few moments musing round the Founders Bar at the George Hotel.

The walls are adorned with various shirts and photographs looking down on me, of many of the fine and upstanding people who have helped my long and eventful journey and made my game what it is today. It's like a family album!

From before I was born there's an interesting commemorative album photograph of the 1877/8 Dewsbury team; remember, that was the lot that couldn't make their minds up, and one of my forefathers Jim Valentine, the 'Lion of Swinton' dating from 1890.

To Jim's right and above the stone mullion fireplace is a plaque commemorating my birthday, with three players in bronze relief, and to his left is Arthur Bennett, proud trainer of the Huddersfield

RUGBY LEAGUE. IN ITS OWN WORDS

team surrounded with the four magnificent cups his lads won in 1915.

One curiosity is another of the Talents, Douglas Clark, in his wrestling outfit. He was world champ at grappling as well, y'know, and is captured for posterity surrounded by the five England caps he won between 1910 and 1920 and various other trophies.

Remember me telling you about the rugby truce during the Great War? Well at the end of the bar counter, lurking behind the door, is a fine picture of the combatants of a Military War Charity match between Yorkshire and the Northern Command. Strangely, as the game would have been played under Union rules, there are only 29 players (maybe one of the League lads had to take the picture, so couldn't be in it?) plus officials and the ref in shorts, jacket and tie! The date is given as 20th November 1918, nine days after the Armistice was signed. Maybe news travelled slower in those days or the order hadn't reached Headingley to stop fighting the Bosch and re-commence hostilities against my brave Rugby League boys!

One of my favourite pictures is a pile of bodies from Dewsbury and Wigan taken on my first big day out at Wembley in 1929, and another is the Huddersfield team circa 1900 with a fine display of bowler hats and 'taches.

From more recent years there's a packed terrace at Maine Road during a Championship final, 1949 I think it must have been, Warrington and Huddersfield were playing.

Amongst the selection of colourful modern shirts are Great Britain and Australia's, signed by all the players from the 2003 Ashes series, the referee, Stuart Cumming's mauve and black affair from the 2001 Grand Final and a Great Britain under 21 amateur shirt from their 2001 tour to the United States.

So many memories. If you're a hardbitten Leaguie, call in on a quiet day and if you listen very carefully maybe you can hear the place talk to you. Yes, the Founders Bar is a place to feel comfortable in.

Just as the 21 brave club chairmen concluded their business on my birthday, 29th August 1895, and wandered out into the autumn evening towards a destiny they could not possibly predict, now it's

414

my turn to take my leave of the George, step outside and rejoin the bustling world to receive whatever fate may bring me.

I've been in your service for 109 years now, and no doubt will be for 109 more. So, I'll look forward to seeing you at the game next week for another family get together.

APPENDIX

(Based on information courtesy of rfl.uk.com,
made available by kind permission of Richard Lewis)

1400-1800: Many different types of football - Rugby League's ancestors - were played throughout Britain. Unlike modern soccer, most football games allowed handling the ball. There are records of football games being played in future League strongholds such as Hull, Huddersfield, Rochdale, Whitehaven, Workington and York.

1823 - William Webb Ellis, a pupil at Rugby School, allegedly picked up the ball, ran and thereby invented rugby. There is little evidence to support this myth - even the 1895 Inquiry, which immortalised Ellis found no proof. Running with the ball became common in 1830s at Rugby School and Rugby School football became popular throughout the UK in the 1850s and 1860s.

1864 - The first rugby clubs formed in Leeds and Huddersfield, followed by Hull (1865), York (1868), followed by hundreds more in Cumbria, Lancashire and Yorkshire in the 1870s and 1880s.

1876 - Yorkshire Cup competition started for Yorkshire rugby clubs. Soon it attracted bigger crowds than the FA Cup final.

1886 - Concerned at the growing dominance of the largely working-class northern clubs, the Rugby Football Union introduced strict amateur rules.

1893 - Yorkshire clubs proposed allowing players to be paid six shillings 'broken-time' payments when they missed work due to matches. RFU voted down the proposal and widespread suspensions of northern clubs and players began.

1895 - Threatened with expulsion from the RFU if they could not prove their amateurism, 21 leading Lancashire and Yorkshire clubs met at the George Hotel, Huddersfield on 29th August 1895. They voted unanimously to form the Northern Rugby Football Union (NU) and allow broken-time payments.

1896 - Manningham of Bradford won first NU Championship.

1897 - To make the game more exciting, the NU abolished the line-out and reduced the value of all goals to two points. Tries were worth three points. Batley beat St Helens in first Challenge Cup final.

1904 - First international match: England (3) beaten by Other Nationalities (9) at Wigan.

1906 - Modern Rugby League was born when the number of players was reduced from 15 to 13-a-side. Rucks and mauls were replaced by the 'one man scrum' which became known as the play-the-ball.

1907 - Rugby League spread to Australia and New Zealand. The first New Zealand side, organised by A.H. Baskerville, toured Britain.

1908 - First Australian Kangaroo tourists visited Britain. Hunslet won 'All Four Cups' a grand slam of all available competitions.

1910 - First British tour to Australia and New Zealand.

1914 - Huddersfield's Albert Rosenfeld scored a record 80 tries in one season. British tourists defeated Australia 6-14 to win Ashes in the final Test, finishing with only 10 men in what became known as the 'Rorke's Drift' Test.

1915 - Huddersfield, known as 'The Team of all The Talents', won all four cups, led by Harold Wagstaff.

1921 - Harold Buck became the game's first £1,000 transfer when he moved from Hunslet to Leeds. Featherstone Rovers became a professional team.

1922 - Northern Union changed its name to the Rugby Football League.

APPENDIX

1926 - Castleford joined the RFL.

1927 - First radio broadcast of Challenge Cup final by the BBC.

1928 - Swinton won all four cups.

1929 - First Challenge Cup final to be played at Wembley - Wigan defeated Dewsbury 13-2 in front of 41,500.

1930 - Unprecedented fourth Test played at Rochdale after the third Test was drawn 0-0. Britain won 3-0 to take the Ashes.

1932 - First Rugby League match under floodlights: Leeds v Wigan at White City in London.

1933 - First Rugby League club in London: London Highfield.

1934 - Rugby League established in France by Jean Galia, a former Rugby Union international and champion boxer. By 1939 the French League had 225 clubs and the national side beat England and Wales to take the European championship.

1943 - A Northern Command army Rugby League side defeated a Northern Command Union side 18-11 at Headingley playing Rugby Union rules. The following year a Combined Services RL side beat a Combined Services Union side 15-10 at Bradford. These were the only cross code matches played until 1996.

1946 - Lance Todd trophy was first presented to Challenge Cup final man of the match. Wakefield's Billy Stott was the first winner. Lance Todd, killed in a car accident in 1942, was a 1907 NZ tourist who managed Salford from 1928-40.

1946 - Workington joined the League, followed by Whitehaven in 1948.

1948 - First televised RL match, Wigan versus Bradford cup final, broadcast to the Midlands.

1949 - Challenge Cup final tickets sold-out for first time. 95,050 saw Bradford beat Halifax. First Southern Amateur Rugby League formed.

1954 - 102,569 paid to see Warrington defeat Halifax 8-4 in Challenge Cup final replay at Odsal, Bradford, but thousands more got in for free.

1954 - First Rugby League World Cup staged in France. Great Britain beat France 12-16 in final at Parc des Princes, Paris.

1958 - Great Britain defeated Australia 18-25 in the second Test match at Brisbane with only eight fit players on the pitch. Captain Alan Prescott played for 77 minutes with a broken arm and the match became known as 'Prescott's Test'.

1964 - Substitutes were allowed for the first time, but only for players injured before half-time.

1966 - Four tackle rule was introduced, increased to six in 1972.

1967 - Professional Rugby League matches allowed on Sundays for the first time. Amateurs had played on Sundays since 1956.

1969 - Universities and Colleges Rugby League formed after student pioneers fought hard to get Rugby League recognised in higher education. First university game was between Leeds and Liverpool in 1968.

1970 - Great Britain won the Ashes in Australia after winning the final two Test matches.

1972 - Timekeepers and sirens were introduced for first time.

1973 - Two divisions introduced permanently into Rugby League. The British Amateur Rugby League Association was formed in Huddersfield.

1974 - Drop-goal reduced in value from two points to one point.

1980 - Australian interstate matches replaced with State of Origin.

1981 - First Oxford v Cambridge University match.

1982 - Australian tourists won all tour games for first time becoming known as 'The Invincibles'.

1983 - Try was increased in value to four points, the 'sin-bin' introduced and the 'handover' after the sixth tackle, instead of a scrum, begins.

1986 - Old Trafford hosted Rugby League for the first time when over 50,000 saw Australia overcome Great Britain 16-38.

1987 - Wigan defeated Manly 8-2 for unofficial World Club Championship.

1988 - Rugby League Hall of Fame was inaugurated. Nine players inducted in its first year.

APPENDIX

1989 - Widnes beat Canberra 30-18 in first official World Club Championship.

1990 - Russia took up Rugby League. Blood-bin was introduced.

1992 - Record crowd of 73,631 at Wembley saw Australia defeat Great Britain 10-6 in the World Cup final. Martin Offiah left Widnes for Wigan in a world record £440,000 transfer.

1993 - USA defeats Canada 54-14 in their first Rugby League international match.

1995 - Wigan won the Challenge Cup for a record eighth consecutive time. They also won the league title for a record seventh consecutive time.

1996 - First season of Super League, following the 1995 RFL decision to switch to summer and sign a lucrative contract with BSkyB. St Helens won the inaugural Super League title.

1997 - Bradford Bulls won Super League with London Broncos finishing runners-up.

1998 - Grand final and play-offs introduced into Super League. Wigan Warriors beat Leeds Rhinos 10-6 in the first grand final.

1999 - Leeds Rhinos defeated London Broncos 52-16 in the last Challenge Cup final at the original Wembley stadium.

2000 - Bradford Bulls defeated Leeds Rhinos 24-18 in the Challenge Cup final, played for the first time in Scotland at Murrayfield. St Helens won the Super League grand final 29-16 over Wigan Warriors. Australia won the World Cup final 40-12 over New Zealand at Old Trafford after a record 16 nations entered the tournament.

2001 - St Helens took the Challenge Cup final 13-6 over Bradford Bulls, the final held at Twickenham, Rugby Union HQ, for the first time ever. Over 60,000 people saw Bradford Bulls defeat Wigan Warriors 37-6 in the Super League grand final.

2002 - St Helens snatched a last-minute grand final win over the Bulls to lift the Super League trophy 19-18 before 61,138 people, the highest crowd at a championship final for 42 years. Great Britain lifted the inaugural Baskerville Trophy after the Test series against New Zealand was tied. In signposts for the future, Russia defeated the United States 54-10 in front of over 25,000 spectators in Moscow, and Lebanon beat France 36-6 in Tripoli.

2003 - First Challenge Cup final played at the Millennium Stadium, Cardiff, headquarters of the Welsh Rugby Union. Sixth grand final is the first to sell out at Old Trafford.

2004 - Wrote autobiography at age of 108!

SUBSCRIBERS

Many thanks to those kind souls who showed their support for this work in advance of publication.
Their names and favourite clubs or towns are: -

Bill Abernethy	Brisbane
Tony Ackroyd	Halifax & Keighley
Nigel Almond	Chorley Lynx RLFC
Janette & Colin Anderson	Billinge
Frederick T. Andrews	Hull FC
Lachlan Andrews	Brisbane Broncos
Derek Appleby	St Helens
Carol Ann Appleby	St Helens
Paul, Lynne, Mark & Nicola Armstrong	Wigan
Patricia Arthur	Wigan Warriors
Pat Benatmane	Hunslet
Peter Basnett	Widnes Vikings
Peter Benson	Bramley RLFC
Peter Bentham	Leigh
Toby Birchall	Wigan RLFC
Roger Birchall	Wigan RLFC
Jeffrey Black	Hull Kingston Rovers
Joseph Black	Hull Kingston Rovers
Sam & Pat Blackledge	Wigan
Eric Bolderson	Hunslet Hawks
Jack Bolderson	Hunslet Hawks
Diane Bond	Wigan Warriors
Alan Booth	Fartown
James Bridge	St Helens
T.S. Broderick	Dewsbury
Richard, Alex & James Brook	Huddersfield Giants
Mick Brown	Cleckheaton
Phil & Marian Brown	Wigan
Michael Brown	Derby
Peter Brown	Gateshead Thunder & York
W.M. Bullock	Featherstone Rovers

Stanley Butler	Shoreham by the Sea
Keith Butler	Carlisle
Chris Byron	London Broncos
Brenda Carmylie	Wigan
Lee Carson	Whitehaven
Lisa Carter	Salford
Rob Castlehouse	Dewsbury
Jeff Catley	Essex
David Cawood	Ilkley, Leeds Rhinos
Mike Clarke	York City Knights
Gary Clarkson	Batley Bulldogs
Simon Clegg	Wigan
Ilya Cobourne	Derby
Anita Cobourne	Derby
Ernest Collinson	Leeds Rhinos
Charlotte (Lottie) Collinson	Hull
Harry (Chops) Collinson	Hull
Gary & Joanne Collinson	Hull
Ian Keith Copland	Baildon
Paul Cox	Featherstone Rovers
Judith Critchley	St. Helens
David J. Crompton	Wigan Warriors
James & Emily Cross	St Helens RLFC
Michael Cross	Saints
Keith Croston	St Helens
Brian & Sandra Davies	Billinge
Ste, Lisa & Mathew Davies	Whiston
Geoff Dawber	Wigan
Jim & Margaret Diffley	Billinge
Mr AB Doughty	St Helens
Neil Dowson	Warrington Wolves
Paul Dredge	London Broncos
David Durbin	Halifax RLFC
Mick & Helen Dyer	Leicester
Darren Eccles	Sheffield
Bill Edgar	Wigan
Stuart Evans	York Historian
Mr Charlie Fairbank	Halifax RLFC
David Fairclough	Saints
John & Ali Fairhurst	Bromsgrove

Louise Fairhurst	Wigan Warriors
Joe & Karen Fairhurst	Wigan Warriors
Malcolm Ferguson	York City Knights
Graham Fialkiewicz	Hull FC
Kevin Field	Bradford
Hazel Finch	Derby City RLFC
Ray Fleming	Widnes
Mr & Mrs L & C.A Foster	Bradford Bulls
Len Garbett	*President, Life Member & Club Historian Castleford RLFC*
Dan Garbutt	Ipswich Rhinos
Paul & Nicola Gent	St Helens RLFC
Michael George Gill	Keighley Cougars
Ian Glenholme	Wigan
Helen Goldthorpe	Wigan RL
Adrian Goodrich	Bradford Bulls
Alan Gordon	St Helens
Tony Gough	Warrington Wolves
Mark Grady	Widnes
Mick, Michaela & Aiden Greasley	Bradford
Peter & Vera Gregory	Bolton
John Hague	Hoyland
Terry Hall	Workington Town
Andy Hallas	Hull FC, Switzerland
Simon Hallas	Hull FC
Simon Halling	Bradford Northern
Suzanne Hamilton	Wigan
Paul Hancock	Leeds Rhinos
Michael Hanson	Batley Bulldogs RLFC
Tim Hardcastle	Heavy Woollen Donkeys
Ken & Pauline Harding	St Helens
Rebecca Hardman	Warrington Wolves
Mr J. Hardy	Leeds Rhinos
Martin Harrison	Halifax
Mick Hartley	Wakefield
Willem & Lotte Hendriksen	St Helens RLFC
Mr Trevor & Mrs Denise Higgins	Hull FC forever
Bernard Higham	Upholland
Douglas M. Hird, BEM	Shaw Cross Sharks

Barry Hitch	Bradford Bulls RLFC
John & Phylis Holmes	St Helens
Anne & Meirion Hopkins	London Broncos
Michael, Maria & Emma Hough	St Helens
Sam & Lynn Howard	Saints
Mark Hudson	Castleford Tigers
Lisa Hudson & Family	Hull
Dr & Mrs B. Hughes	Wigan RLFC
Tim Huntley	Leeds Rhinos
Duncan Jackson	Halifax
Anthony Jenkins	Leeds Rhinos
Johnson Family	Wigan
Steve Johnson	St Helens RLFC
Sarah E. Jones	Wigan Warriors RLFC
Gavin Kaye	Wigan
Gordon & Della Kaye	Wigan
Tommy Kearns	St Helens
Gareth Kelsey	Leeds Rhinos
Matthew Kemp	Dewsbury
Johnny Kennedy	Liverpool
Hannah Kilgallon	St Helens
Tom Kirby	St Helens RLFC
Tom Kirkbride	Langworthy RLFC
Kyassor's Kompost Corner	Wakefield Trinity
Baby Lawrenson	Wigan RL
Stuart Leadley	Cottingham
Greg Lears	Warrington
Alan & Vera Lenord	Salford
Richard Lewis	*Executive Chairman, The Rugby Football League*
Graham Lockwood	Wakefield Trinity
Adrian & Pauline Lodge	Doncaster
Dave Lowe	Salford RLFC
Kevin & June Maguire	Dewsbury
Dave Makin	Leeds
Joe Marcroft	Wigan
Neil Margerison	Bradford
Alan J. Mark	Leeds
Dave Martin	Mere
Robert Martindale	Saints

Sharon McDonald	Carnlough, N. Ireland
John & Carol McEniff	St Helens
James McGrath	Keighley Cougars
Gerard McLoughlin	The Sungods
Shaun McMullen	Workington Town
Eamonn McNulty	Croydon
Dennis Meade	Bradford Bulls
Alex Mercer	Sheffield
Russell Merrikin	Beverley
Mr Jack Merry	Castleford Tigers RLFC
John & Christine Middleton	Cornwall
John A. Mitchell	Prescot
Peter A. Moir	Rickmansworth
Gerry Moore	Hull
Janinder Singh Morgan	Leeds Rhinos
Stephen Morris	St Helens RLFC
Paul Morris	Widnes
Denise Morris	Widnes
James Morris	Widnes
Graham & Shirley Morris	Billinge
Andy & Sam Mullaney	Lytham
Angela Mullen	Billinge
M. Murphy	Leigh
Wendy Neal	Upholland
Kath Neild	Wigan
Ken Neild	St Helens
K.B. Oakes	Dewsbury
Donald S. Oates	Leeds Rhinos (53 years)
Kathryn Owen	Bradford
Stephen Parker	Featherstone Rovers
Martin & Pam Phair	Standish
Colin Pheysey	Widnes
John Piercy	Bingley
Nigel Pogson	Bradford Bulls
Ste, Linda & Karen Pownall	Saints
Mr & Mrs C.D. Priestley	Bradford Bulls
Mr D. J. Priestley	Bradford Bulls
James & Barbara Read	Wigan
Alan J. Reid	Wigan
Jonathan Rhinow	Sheffield

David Richards	Preston
Steven & Karen Richardson	Bradford Bulls
Alan Roberts	Nottingham
Tim Roby	Leyland Warriors ARLFC
Carl & Ruth Rogers	Leeds Rhinos
I.A. Routledge	Whitehaven RLFC
Ben Rowlin	Hull
Cindy Russell	Hull
Wayne Russell	Hull
John Rutter	Leeds
Geoff & Sue Sarsfield	St Helens
John & Norma Scott	Wigan
Graeme Scully	617 Squadron
Rob Shaw	Lancaster
Albi & Ann Shields	Wigan
Jayana Shires	Leeds Akademiks RLFC
Dennis & Margaret Slater	Wigan
John & Lynsey Smith	Wigan
Cllr Robert Sowman	Bradford Bulls
Simon Speight	St Helens
Robbie Spencer	Dudley Hill RLFC
Ian Stafford	Bradford Bulls
Branko Stajic	Halifax RLFC
Jeffrey Stanyer	Exeter
John Stimpson	Swinton
Phil Stockton	Salford Reds
Mr Edward Davis Storry	Hull FC
Jim Stringer	Rochdale Hornets
Jack Stubbings	Warrington Wolves
Ron, Ivy & Sue Sumner	Saints
M. A. Taylor	Leeds Rhinos
Robert Edwin Taylor	Wakefield Trinity Wildcats
John & Eileen Taylor	Billinge
Nia Thomas	Keighley Cougars
Keiron & Cath Traynor	St Helens
John & Pam Turner	St Helens RLFC
Peter & Sandie Walker	Hull RLFC
Ron Walker	St Helens
Neil Warburton	Bradford Bulls
Phillip J. Watson	York City Knights

Eric Watterson	Bradford Bulls
Gavan Westwood	Barrow
Barbara & Trevor Whitaker	Wilsden
Adam and Amy Wilkinson	Otley Rhinos
Geoffrey & Brenda Wilkinson	Leeds Rhinos
Dave & Sue Wilkinson	Standish
Martin R. Williams	Ilkley
Tony & Margaret Williams	Widnes Vikings
Ronnie Williams	Widnes Vikings
Nick Wilson	Leeds Rhinos
John Wilson	Leeds Rhinos
Martin Wilson	Leeds Rhinos
George & Chris Wiswell	Garswood
G & B Wood	Huddersfield Giants
Ms J. Wood	Wigan Warriors
Tomas & Lucy Wood	Ashton-in-Makerfield
Maureen & Joe Woods	St Helens
Janine Woodward	Wigan
Mike Worthington	Wigan RLFC
Gerry Wright	
Elizabeth Wright	Salford City Reds
Terry Wynn, MEP	Wigan